DATE DUE

OCT 2 4 1988			
FAC			
MAY 1 1989			
APR 2 3 1990			
APR 2 7 1992			

D0965981

DEMCO 38-297

The Psychology of Language and
Communication

The Psychology of Language and Communication

Andrew Ellis
Department of Psychology, University of Lancaster

Geoffrey Beattie
Department of Psychology, University of Sheffield

The Guilford Press
New York   London

For Anna Ellis and Eileen Beattie

Copyright © 1986 Andrew Ellis and Geoffrey Beattie

Published in the United States of America by
The Guilford Press
A Division of Guilford Publications, Inc.
200 Park Avenue South, New York, NY 10003

All rights reserved

No part of this book may be reproduced, stored in a retrieval system, or transmitted, in any form or by any means, electronic, mechanical, photocopying, microfilming, recording, or otherwise, without written permission from the publisher

Printed in the United States of America

Library of Congress Cataloging-in-Publication Data

Ellis, Andrew W.
    The psychology of language and communication.

    Bibliography: p.
    Includes indexes.
    1. Psycholinguistics. 2. Communication. I. Beattie, Geoffrey. II. Title.
[DNLM: 1. Communication. 2. Language. BF 637.C45 E47p]
P37.E47 1986 401'.9   86-14828
ISBN 0-89862-691-1
ISBN 0-89862-911-X (pbk.)

Contents

P
37
.E47
1986

13795936

V31-820458

Preface

The psychology of language and communication is a vast topic – far wider than the scope of conventional texts on psycholinguistics. While we have made no attempt in writing the present book to be encyclopaedic, we have tried to be rather more broad-ranging than usual. The mainstream concerns of psycholinguistics – speech production, speech perception and comprehension, language acquisition, the psychological reality of linguistic theories, etc. – all receive due coverage, but they are interspersed with treatments of gestural and facial communication, conversational management, social class influences on language, animal communication, neuropsychology and other topics which we feel to be equally deserving of mention in a book like this.

If the book has a theme, it is that human language use will best be understood if viewed in its natural context as one of a set of channels available to humans to transmit and receive information. Language has the structure and properties it has because of the functions it must serve. If we are to understand those functions we must not be in awe of discipline boundaries. Various aspects of language have been appropriated for study by a wide assortment of disciplines ranging from philosophy and linguistics, through sociology, anthropology and psychology, to physiology and engineering. Even within psychology the topic is carved up rather arbitrarily into social psychology, cognitive psychology, developmental psychology, neuropsychology and other sub-disciplines. Although our selection will inevitably reflect our perspective as psychologists of particular sorts, we have at least tried to put Humpty Dumpty back together again by pursuing language into these different, often strange territories, and by trying to show how insights gained in one corner can shed light on puzzles elsewhere.

In the process of researching the material we became increasingly aware that psycholinguistics did not, as is commonly believed, originate in Massachussetts, U.S.A., in the early 1960s. Though neither of us would claim to be a historian, we have tried to provide a degree of historical perspective on present-day concerns, showing how questions debated today have been addressed with profit in other times and places, from ancient Greece (of course), via the court of Akhbar the Great, Moghul Emperor of India (1542–1605), to the laboratories and clinics of turn-of-the-century Europe and America. We hope that the reader finds these occasional historical jaunts as entertaining as we did. We also hope that by giving the book a fourth dimension we will have produced something with a deeper appeal and longer shelf-life than a review of last year's experiments and theories.

We begin our book with a brief review of communication among other animals, and between animals and people. From this background we extract a working definition of communication which serves us throughout the rest of the book. Chapter 2 surveys the range of channels of communication used by humans, then in Chapter 3 we look in depth at the kinesic channels (facial movement, eye gaze, head movements, posture, hand movements and gestures). Chapter 4 is concerned with the language channel, and in particular with the insights into the properties of language that have been gained within the discipline of linguistics.

Chapters 5 and 6 investigate two forms of language variation – variation between languages and variation within a language. Speech production as a psycholinguistic skill – the translation of ideas into articulations – is the subject matter of Chapter 7. Chapters 8, 9 and 10 are all concerned with aspects of conversation: the roles of verbal and nonverbal information, the cooperative requirements of successful conversational interaction and the structure of conversations.

In Chapter 11 we turn our attention to psychological aspects of writing – its origins in simpler forms of visual communication, the impact of literacy on culture and ways of thought, differences between speech and writing, and the processes of composing, spelling and writing. Having surveyed the production of spoken words in Chapter 7 and written words in Chapter 11, we review what is known about the recognition of spoken and written words in Chapter 12. Sentence comprehension and memory for language are the subject matter of Chapter 13, while Chapter 14 looks at the disorders of communication and language which can occur as a consequence of injury to the adult brain, and at what we can learn from those disorders about the nature of normal, intact communicative processes. Our last chapter deals with the vast topic of the development of communicative and linguistic skills in children. In that chapter, as with all the others, we are painfully aware of the fact that whole books have been devoted to what we have tried to cram into a single chapter or less. The necessary reduction can only be achieved by being highly selective: we can only hope that our decisions as to what to leave out and what to put in meet with the approval of the reader.

We owe a debt of gratitude to Alan Baddeley – first for playing a part in nominating us as potential authors, and second for reading and commenting carefully on an earlier draft. Robert Baldock waited patiently as our estimates of expected time of arrival became progressively more realistic. Gillian Hempshall, Gay Rich, Sylvia Sumner and Sheila Whalley typed various portions of the manuscript.

Finally, when we wrote this book we started at the beginning, continued through the middle, and finished at the end. We believe that the reader who follows the same course will get the most out of our work. We hope you enjoy it.

Andrew Ellis
Geoffrey Beattie

1 The nature of communication

Humpback whales, those large and, if the truth be known, none too beautiful creatures (at least when seen through our eyes) spend their summers feeding on small crustaceans and fish in the polar waters. They migrate to tropical waters for winter and spring, scarcely feeding at all. During the winter and spring they mate, give birth and sing – a long, complex, haunting song which can last for over twenty minutes before being repeated in its entirety. The song changes gradually through the season and may be quite different at the end of the spring from the beginning of winter.

Why do whales sing? Biologists are loath to conclude that they do so because they get bored just swimming around all day; instead the scientific mind looks for a function and evolutionary purpose to the song. Singing only happens in the breeding season, and most singing humpbacks are males. Female humpbacks approach singing males, apparently using the song as a means of selecting a mate, while males often avoid singers. Thus, while one might prefer to think that the whales' songs relate epic battles with whalers in days of yore, it is more likely that they function to make the whales aware of each other's location, attract females to males and keep rivals spaced apart. The song may be ornate for the same reason that the peacock's tail is ornate and the dress of disco-goers is ornate – all the better to attract a partner (Tyack, 1981).

Communication is widespread throughout the animal kingdom (see Sebeok, 1977). Though we shall be concerned in most of this book with human communication, a brief survey of a few examples of communication in other species will help establish our concern with the natural *uses* and *functions* of communication, and will allow us to make some general observations regarding the nature of communication which will inform our discussion of human communication in later chapters.

Of fish, chimps and bees: communication in the natural world

As the breeding season approaches, the male three-spined stickle-back builds a tunnel-like nest of reeds or grasses at the bottom of its pond. When the nest is completed, this small fish performs an elegant 'zig-zag dance', spiralling up and down, to attract a mate. The dance *communicates* to any nearby female that this is a male who has done the necessary preparation and is ready to become a father. If a receptive female is attracted by the dance, the two swim together with the male butting the female's abdomen to stimulate egg laying. The eggs are laid in the nest by the female and are fertilised by the male who then guards the nest, fanning the eggs to keep them aerated until the eggs hatch. The female plays no further part in rearing the young once she has laid the eggs (Tinbergen, 1951).

When a scouting honeybee discovers a new source of food some distance from the hive, it communicates the location of the new source in another much studied way – the remarkable 'waggle dance'. Von Frisch (1967) describes the dance as follows:

> In the typical tail-wagging dance the bee runs straight ahead for a short distance, returns in a semicircle to the starting point, again runs through the straight stretch, describes a semicircle in the opposite direction, and so on in regular alternation. The straight part of the run is given particular emphasis by a vigorous wagging of the body.

Research by von Frisch and others (see Holldobler, 1977) has shown that the duration of the straight run, during which the dancer waggles and emits a buzzing sound, communicates to nearby bees the distance of the food source (probably measured as the amount of energy required to fly to the source). The angle of the straight run relative to the sun (or gravity) indicates the direction of the source. A vertical dance on the honeycomb means that the food is in the direction of the sun, while an angled dance communicates the angle away from the sun that foraging bees must fly. Clearly the evolution of this dance has brought enormous benefits to the bees in terms of more efficient food gathering.

As a final example of communication in the natural world we might look briefly at communication among our nearest relatives, the monkeys and apes. Seyfarth, Cheney and Marler (1980) studied a colony of vervet monkeys, and found that they give different alarm calls to different predators. There is one call given when an eagle is spotted, another for a snake, and a third for a leopard. If recordings of these alarms are played back to the monkeys, the eagle alarm call causes the monkeys to look up, the leopard call causes them to run into the trees, and the snake call causes them to look downwards – this all in the absence of any of the three predators. Infant monkeys apparently have to learn these different calls and 'overgeneralize' initially in the way young children do, making eagle calls to many different birds, leopard calls to a variety of mammals, and snake calls to various different long, thin objects.

Chimpanzees in the wild display a wide repertoire of communicative signals, including a range of calls and facial expressions (van Lawick-Goodall, 1971; Marler and Tenazak, 1977). Each signal communicates something of the internal state of the sender. A soft, barking noise indicates annoyance or mild aggressiveness toward another individual, while a 'grin' with the mouth closed or only slightly open indicates submission or fright. Again, communication benefits the apes by regulating their social interaction and by relaying information about events in the external world to other members of the group.

A working definition of communication and some comments

What do all these examples have in common that qualifies them to be grouped together as acts involving communication? Can we capture those common features in a working definition of communication? All of these acts clearly involve the transmission of a signal from one organism to another. The signal carries information from a transmitter organism to a receiver organism. Having decoded the signal, the receiver is now in the position to make an appropriate response should one be required.

Drawing all of these threads together we can formulate a working definition of communication which asserts that *communication occurs when one organism (the transmitter) encodes information into a signal which passes to another organism (the receiver) which decodes the signal and is capable of responding appropriately.*

In terms of some of our earlier examples, a bee returning to the hive transmits information about the direction and distance of a food source by encoding that information in a signal (the waggle dance) which other bees can receive, decode and act appropriately upon. Similarly a vervet monkey can transmit information about the identity of a threatening predator by selecting the appropriate call from among its repertoire. That encoded signal can then be received and decoded by other monkeys who, again, can now take appropriate (evasive) action.

Any communicative act, whether by animal or human, can be analyzed in terms of:

1) A transmitter who encodes information into a signal;
2) The physical transmission of a signal; and
3) A receiver who decodes the signal to recover the information encoded by the transmitter.

Failures of communication may also be analyzed in these terms; that is, in terms of faulty encoding, faulty transmission or faulty decoding. Faulty encoding may occur because you make an inadvertent slip of the tongue, or cannot remember the name of someone you want to mention in the discussion. Faulty transmission may be caused by a bad telephone line or by a low flying aeroplane drowning the sound of your voice. A misreading or mishearing would be an example of faulty decoding, as in the case reported by Rolfe (1972) of the depressed first officer on a plane who, when his captain said 'cheer up' as the plane raced along the runway, misheard the signal as 'gear up' and promptly raised the under-carriage!

A final category of communication failure involves some form of mismatch between the encoding processes of the transmitter and the decoding processes of the receiver. If I talk in an accent or dialect you find hard to understand, the fault does not lie in me or in you but in the mismatch between us. Similarly, when English or American tourists give the 'thumbs up' gesture to a Sardinian or a Greek they cannot really be blamed for not knowing that in Sardinia and Greece the gesture is a sexual insult (Morris, Collett, Marsh and O'Shaughnessy, 1979). At a higher level, if a teacher talks over your head, or if a conversation breaks down because a speaker assumes certain knowledge on the part of the listener which he or she in fact does not possess, then who is to say whether the blame lies with the encoder or the decoder? In conversation we naturally assume that the listener shares much of our knowledge of the world, and that much can accordingly go unspoken. If we are talking to a child, or a foreigner, or someone who is not an ardent football fan, then we know we must be careful in what knowledge we take for granted, but it is not surprising that a performance as complex and delicate as holding a conversation should occasionally run aground through one or other of the sources of communication failure that we have just outlined.

Returning to our definition of communication, there are a number of further points and comments we wish to make. We shall take them one at a time.

Comment 1. Communication is a fuzzy concept. Few if any of the concepts humans operate with are clearly bounded such that we can always say confidently, 'This is an *x*' or 'This is not an *x*'. Take the homely concept 'item of furniture'. A chair is clearly an item of furniture, and so is a table. But how about a radio? Or an ashtray? An apple is clearly *not* an item of furniture, but it equally clearly *is* a 'fruit'. A chair is not a fruit, but is a coconut? How about an olive? What all of this apparent sophistry goes to show is that most of the concepts we work with happily in everyday life are 'fuzzy' concepts whose boundaries are blurred and indistinct. Some instances are clearly members of the category defined by the concept, and others equally clearly do not qualify, but in the middle are awkward, half-way cases we are uncertain how to treat (Rosch, 1975, 1977). The anthropologist Mary Douglas has noted how natural objects which resist assimilation to everyday categories may become objects of superstition or taboo – like the hapless bat which, neither four-legged animal nor bird, is condemned to a twilight world of witches and vampires (Douglas, 1966).

We cannot reasonably expect the concept of 'communication' to be any less fuzzy than concepts like 'fruit' or 'item of furniture', and we therefore doubt the wisdom of trying to devise a watertight definition which will hold in all the instances we wish to retain, keep out all negative instances and brook no intermediates. Communication between men and machines, or between machines and machines, is an example of a borderline case for our particular definition. Can we be said to 'communicate' with computers, and can they reasonably be said to communicate with us? If computers communicate, do 'Speak Your Weight' machines? Or telephone answering machines? We have no strong position on such matters: fortunately all the instances of communication *we* shall discuss will involve living, metabolising organisms, so our definition will suffice for our purposes.

Comment 2. A signal is an encoded message, and transmitting and receiving are acts of translation. A communicative signal, when successful, conveys information from transmitter to receiver. The information content of a signal we may call the *message*. The message is in the signal, but only in the sense that it is *recoverable from* the signal by a suitably equipped receiver. A communicative signal carries its message in code. The requirement that a signal should cross space or time means that we and other organisms must entrust our emotions, feelings and thoughts to a physical code like a sound wave if we are ever to make others aware of them.

Comment 3. The same message may be communicated in more than one way. Humans have undoubtedly developed the art of communication further than any other species if only in the number of different 'channels' of communication employed. Facial expressions, gestures, eye contact, body posture, clothing, speech and nonverbal sounds like laughter and sighs are just some of the channels which can communicate information between people. We shall see in later chapters that these channels are to some extent specialised for transmitting different sorts of information, but it is also the case that the same information may often be successfully transmitted along a variety of different channels. Thus a nod of the head conveys the same message as saying 'yes', while a shrug means 'I don't know'.

The message is independent of the channel used to communicate it. We may choose one channel on one occasion and another on a different occasion (there is no point waving goodbye on the telephone, but a gesture may be preferable to words when trying to communicate with a foreigner). A third option is to exploit the safety in redundancy and use both channels simultaneously – nodding and saying 'yes' at the same time if you are particularly anxious that your message not be lost. Finally, a complex message may be split up and its parts transmitted along different channels to be reassembled by the receiver. We shall encounter plenty of examples of this last option later in the book.

Comment 4. A potentially available response is sufficient to define a communicative act. Our working definition of communication simply required that the receiver be 'capable of responding appropriately'. Very often communication occurs without the receiver giving any overt indication that anything has happened. You, the reader, may at this moment be seated at a table, lying on the beach or curled up in an armchair in front of a blazing fire. Unless you are taking notes, nodding in agreement here and there, or maybe reading bits aloud, there will be nothing in your overt behaviour (ear scratching, leg crossing, mosquito swatting or whatever) to indicate that any communication is going on. Yet thanks to the invention of writing we (hopefully) *are* communicating information to you. Proof of that communication could be obtained by asking you questions based on what you have just read, or perhaps by presenting a sentence which you must categorize as having been in the text or not. Such techniques are the mainstay of psychologists wishing to understand the process of language comprehension, and we shall see some examples of their use in Chapter 13.

It may be unsatisfying to some to have to build into our definition the fact that the receiver need only be capable of a *potential* response which may never be realized, but it seems to us to be asking for trouble to adopt any other position. Indeed trouble arose when the school of psychology that called itself Behaviourism attempted to build a science based only on overt behaviour. This approach dominated psychology in the United States between about 1920 and 1960 before its inbuilt contradictions caught up with it and forced it to hand power over to the born-again cognitive psychology movement represented here.

Comment 5. Neither transmitter nor receiver need be consciously aware of the passage of a communicative signal. Fish communicate; snails communicate; even lowly slime moulds communicate; yet we feel that even the most ardent advocate of animal consciousness would be hard pressed to maintain that conscious awareness was involved in all of these cases. Psychologists of various persuasions have for a long time argued that communication can occur between people without one party or the other having any awareness that a coded signal has passed between them. Freud and psychoanalysts since have suggested that our gestures, pauses, slips and so on may communicate information about our unconscious thoughts and wishes; much theorizing in the field of nonverbal communication has been concerned about the possibility of unconscious 'leakage' of information; and cognitive psychologists have from time to time become excited about purported demonstrations of the 'subliminal' uptake of information from signals so weak as to be outside of awareness. We shall consider the evidence for these different claims later in the book, and also ask whether such phenomena, even if genuine, play any important part in our daily lives, but for now it is sufficient to note that nothing in our approach to communication requires that the transmitter and/or receiver be *necessarily* aware of the fact that communication has happened.

If we could talk to the animals

Dr Doolittle, in the film of the same name, enthuses about the possibility of being able to 'talk to the animals'. This enthusiasm has also infected many philosophers and psychologists, and led to reports of successful communication with parrots, dogs, dolphins, horses, chimps and gorillas among other species. These efforts have indeed taught us a great deal, though often not what we set out to discover, and usually more about ourselves than about the creatures we sought to make contact with.

Birds

Starting with the birds, Mowrer (1954), in his Presidential Address to the American Psychological Association, entertained the assembled company with a recorded excerpt from the vocalizations of a virtuoso budgerigar called 'Blueboy'. The performance included several phrases and sentences, along with the complete first stanza of 'Mary had a little lamb'. And yet, as Mowrer noted, it seems most unlikely that, for example, the sentence 'Its fleece was white as snow' meant the same to Blueboy as it does to us. At the same time Mowrer (1950, Ch. 24) reviewed evidence, much of it admittedly anecdotal, suggesting that talking birds can learn to associate certain words or phrases with particular circumstances or objects. More recently, Pepperberg (1981, 1983) has claimed success in teaching an African Grey parrot to 'name' a variety of colours, materials and objects.

Horses

The byways of history are full of the amazing feats of performing horses, especially horses credited with the ability to count and perform other acts of calculation (Sebeok, 1979). The secret of the trick was in fact revealed by one Samuel Rid in his book on *The Art of Juggling* (1612) in which he writes:

> As, for ensample, his master will throw you three dice, and will bid his horse tell you how many you or he have thrown. Then the horse paws with his foot while the master stands stone still. Then the master sees he hath pawed so many as the first dice shews itself, then he lifts up his shoulders and stirs a little. Then he bids him tell what is on the second dice, and then on the third dice, which the horse will do accordingly, still pawing with his foot until his master sees he hath pawed enough, and then stirs. . . . And note, that the horse will paw an hundred times together, until he sees his master stir. And note also that nothing can be done but his master must first know, and then his master knowing, the horse is ruled by him by signs. This if you shall mark at any time you shall plainly perceive.

Had this passage been known to the German psychologist Oskar Pfungst (1874–1932) it would have taken him and his colleagues less time than it did to discover the secret of a horse called Clever Hans. This remarkable animal was apparently able to tap out the answers to arithmetic problems set him by his owner and trainer, Herr van Osten. Once he had been 'taught' to tap a certain number of times for different letters of the alphabet, he could then 'answer' nonarithmetical questions. Clever Hans's abilities confounded one investigating committee who declared him to be possessed of mathematical and linguistic skills. A second committee, of which Pfungst was a member, finally discovered the secret when Pfungst realised that Clever Hans could only solve problems for which the setter already knew the answer. In fact, Clever Hans never understood either the question or the answer, but simply kept on tapping his hoof until some slight movement by the setter, possibly quite unconscious, indicated that he had reached the target. Unlike earlier horse trainers, Herr van Osten was apparently not deliberately signalling to Clever Hans, but the horse was still able to pick up slight shiftings or relaxations which leaked the information that it was time for the horse to stop.

It is not just horses who can respond to minute, unconscious movements. Humans can too – and magicians, who know it as 'muscle reading', may specialize in it. A magician who went under the name of Eugen de Rubini displayed apparent telepathy in being able, for instance, to correctly choose one of an array of boxes in which someone had hidden an object. Rubini was exceptional in being willing to submit his talent to long and exhaustive scientific investigation. In summarizing these investigations, Stratton (1921) concluded that:

> . . . when all visual cues from his guide's behaviour are excluded, the success at once drops to the number expected by pure chance . . . Rubini received visual aid from signs unintentionally given him by each of the persons who acted as his guide – signs which indicated whether he was approaching or was going away from the right object. These signs were extremely obscure . . . The hints seem to have come from fleeting glimpses of the guide's · changes of place and posture caught in the very margin of vision perhaps without any conscious intention by the subject to notice or use them. Yet upon these . . . his truly remarkable power seems to depend. (Stratton, 1921, pp. 313–14).

The importance of Clever Hans and the skills he displayed lies in the demonstration that people, psychologists included, can be misled into thinking that an animal is responding to one set of cues when in fact it is responding to some other signal unwittingly and unknowingly provided by the human experimenter. The ghost of Clever Hans has continued to haunt more recent researchers, for example those studying communication between men and apes, with the allegation repeatedly being made that the animals are not responding to the stimuli they are supposed to be responding to, but are instead monitoring and reacting to other cues leaked by the experimenter.

Dogs

Men have probably been communicating with dogs for as long as dogs have been domesticated. Shepherds control their dogs with whistles and calls, while pets all over the world are taught to respond to commands like 'sit' or 'stay'. This responsiveness to the spoken word was especially highly developed in a German Shepherd dog by the name of 'Fellow' who starred in many films in the 1920s and was acknowledged by all who knew him to be a dog among dogs. Fellow's prowess came to the attention of C. J. Warden and L. H. Warner of the Department of Psychology at Columbia University (Warden and Warner, 1928). These investigators were, of course, sensitized to the possibility of 'Clever Hans'-type influences, and took precautions to exclude such cues by concealing both themselves and Fellow's owner (who gave the commands) from the dog's view.

Under these testing conditions Fellow proved capable of responding correctly to 53 different commands, including 'sit', 'stand up', 'roll over', 'turn around', 'lay down', 'lie still', and 'put your foot on the chair'. To the command 'do that once more' Fellow would reliably repeat his last action. To 'speak' or 'talk' he would utter a long, guttural growl, while to 'I don't trust him' he would bark and 'attack' (he would fortunately cease attacking to the command 'he is alright').

On stage Fellow could retrieve named objects to command, but he failed to do this convincingly under Warden and Warner's controlled conditions. He seemed to know that he had to fetch *something*, but would often fetch the wrong thing. It is likely that his normal competence at this task was achieved through a combination of the verbal commands and nonverbal cues leaked by his owner, detected by Fellow in Clever Hans fashion, and used to zero in on the required object.

Despite these latter reservations Fellow still showed himself to have learned to associate actions to 53 different commands. This competence, restricted as it was to comprehension (Fellow having no output channel), still implies an impressive ability *a*) to discriminate between the 53 commands he knew, and *b*) to map each one onto the appropriate response. These are two of the capabilities required of a human language user, though the many others were lacking in Fellow for all his obvious intelligence (as Bertrand Russell once observed, 'No matter how eloquently a dog may bark, he cannot tell you that his parents were poor but honest').

Apes

Though these cases are fascinating and rewarding to study, the greatest endeavour and the most dramatic claims have been reserved for the higher apes, especially chimpanzees and gorillas. Speculation that apes might learn to 'talk' with us has a long history (Fouts and Rigby, 1977). Samuel Pepys made the following entry in his famous *Diary* in August 1661:

> By and by we are called to Sir N. Battens to see the strange creature that Captain Jones hath brought with him from Guiny; it is a great baboon, but so much like a man in most things. . . . I do believe it already understands much English; and I am of the mind it might be taught to speak or make signs.

The philosopher Julien Offray de la Mettrie (1709–1751) is famous for having been one of the first to explore in any depth the similarities between the behaviour of men and machines. In his *L'Homme machine* (1748) he wrote:

> Why should the education of monkeys be impossible? Why might not the monkey, by dint of great pains, at last imitate after the manner of deaf mutes, the motions necessary for pronunciation? . . . . it would surprise me if speech were absolutely impossible in the ape.

In the present century several attempts have been made to bring about the goals of Pepys and la Mettrie. One chimpanzee by the name of Vicky, raised as a human child would be, learned after six years to say 'mama', 'papa', 'cup' and 'up', but even these words were not well articulated and were often used incorrectly (Hayes and Hayes, 1952). For purely anatomical reasons apes do not seem capable of articulating speech sounds (la Mettrie's surprise notwithstanding), and subsequent work has concentrated on alternative channels of communication such as gestures, plastic shapes or computer keyboards. Many of the important papers in this area are gathered together in Sebeok and Umiker-Sebeok (1980; see also Seidenberg and Petito, 1979, and Terrace, 1979). Aitchison (1983) provides a readable but critical introduction.

Perhaps the best known of these recent attempts concerns a chimpanzee called Washoe reared by Allen and Beatrice Gardner. Like Vicky before her, Washoe was reared in as 'childlike' a manner as possible, except that instead of talking to her, Washoe's caretakers used a sign language based on American Sign Language as used by the deaf community in the United States. Her 'words', like the words of sign language, were gestural signs; for example, holding the fingertips of one hand together and touching the nose with them meant 'flower', while repeatedly touching the fingertips together meant 'more'. By the age of around six years Washoe was credited with some 160 signs which she would combine into communicative utterances such as 'gimme flower', 'more fruit', 'tickle Washoe', 'comb black' or 'baby mine'. Washoe's achievements stimulated Gardner and Gardner (1978) to write:

> The results of Project Washoe present the first serious challenge to the traditional doctrine that only human beings could have language . . . [Washoe] learned a natural human language and her early utterances were highly similar to, perhaps indistinguishable from, the early utterances of human children. Now, the categorical question, can a nonhuman being use a human language, must be replaced by quantitative questions; how much language, how soon, or how far can they go.

The claims of the Gardners and other ape language researchers have not, however, gone unchallenged (e.g. Seidenberg and Petito, 1979; Terrace, 1979). No-one seriously doubts that chimps can associate together meanings and arbitrary signs both in comprehension and production, but we have already seen that dogs can do this (at least in comprehension), and parrots may have a limited productive naming capacity. Producing or responding to names, whether spoken or gestured, is one skill required of a language user, but most people would want to say that there is more to language than naming.

Language orders its words into structured, rule-governed sentences. Sentence structure indicates how named concepts relate one to another. English uses word order for this purpose, so that 'The psychologist tickled the chimp' means something different from 'The chimp tickled the psychologist'. There is no strong evidence for consistent, productive use of word order or any similar grammatical device by any of the signing chimps. Terrace's (1979) chimp Nim Chimpsky had a preference for putting certain signs in certain positions (e.g. 'more' at the beginning of sign sequences, and his own name at the end), but otherwise his choice of sign order was quite random.

A feature of animal displays in the wild is their extreme repetitiveness. Wilson (1975) writes:

If a zoologist were required to select just one word that characterizes animal communication systems, he might well settle on 'redundancy'. Animal displays as they really occur in nature tend to be very repetitious, in extreme cases approaching the point of what seems like inanity to the human observer. (p. 200)

Such repetition (e.g. 'Me banana you banana me give you') was characteristic of Washoe and the other signing apes, though it is largely absent from the language of young deaf or hearing children. Ape signing is also highly imitative: close analysis of Nim's signing at the age of two years revealed that 38 per cent of his signs were imitations of signs recently used by his caretakers. Unlike the imitations of children, which are far fewer than this and decline with age, Nim's imitative signs reached 54 per cent by the age of 4 years. Further, only 12 per cent of Nim's utterances initiated interactions: the remainder were produced in response to prodding by his teachers.

Other criticisms levelled at the chimp research include an excessive reliance on a small number of oft-repeated anecdotes, somewhat generous criteria for what constituted a correct response in formalized naming experiments, the possible contribution of natural, unlearned gestures, and the lack of extensive, 'raw' transcripts of chimpanzee conversations. But perhaps the most intriguing criticism is the paradox expressed by the linguist Noam Chomsky when he wrote:

In some ill-considered popularisations of interesting current research, it is virtually argued that higher apes have the capacity for language but have never put it to use – a remarkable biological miracle, given the enormous selectional advantage of even minimal linguistic skills, rather like discovering that some animal has wings but has never thought to fly. (Chomsky, 1976)

If chimps are capable of acquiring language, why have they not done so of their own accord? The only viable counter to this argument is to propose that the natural lifestyle of chimps is one that does *not* require language. Hewes (1973a, b) and Kortlandt (1973) have suggested that only with the switch from fruit picking to hunting did language become advantageous to man, because of the group co-ordination needed. These authors have also noted that infant babbling would attract the unwanted attentions of predators and might have been a luxury that could only be afforded once weapons and fire had been developed as successful means of defence (see Beattie, 1979b).

Kortlandt (1973) claims that fruit pickers 'have less to discuss with one another than co-operative big-game hunters'. This brings us to our final question regarding communication between *Homo sapiens* and the other species: if we *could* talk to the animals, what would we talk *about*? Would we discourse with parrots upon the relative merits of peanuts and sunflower seeds, or learn from chimps how to tell when a banana is just right? Would dogs be found to have as many words for cats as the Eskimos have words for snow, and would dolphins share with us their racial memories and folk tales of how and why they returned to the sea? On reflection it seems to us that the best and most informative place to study animals communicating is in their natural habitat, displaying the range of behaviours and potentialities which they have evolved to suit that habitat. Arguably the same goes for studying humans too: one needs at least a very good reason for dragging human subjects off the streets and into the laboratory, requiring them to perform unnatural tasks upon unnatural stimuli. Sometimes this is justified by the results obtained – and we shall draw here upon some of the better work in the laboratory tradition – but we are in dangerous territory if we ever lose sight of the natural uses and functions of communication and language.

2 Channels of human communication

Human beings have evolved into refined and complex communicators. We communicate successfully in many different situations – in intimate face-to-face encounters, separated by inches; in shops, separated by feet; in lecture halls, separated by yards; in telephone conversations, separated by half the world. We communicate in conditions in which the entire body is visible and in conditions in which none of the body is visible. We communicate in conditions where the communication is pre-planned, entirely intentional, and executed with care and total control (as in a public speech) and also in conditions where the intention to communicate is entirely missing. As Watzlawick and his colleagues said in 1968:

> . . . no matter how one may try, one cannot *not* communicate.
> Activity or inactivity, words or silence all have message value:
> they influence others and these others, in turn, cannot *not*
> respond to these communications and are thus themselves
> communicating. It should be clearly understood that the mere
> absence of talking or of taking notice of each other is no exception
> to what has just been asserted. The man at the crowded lunch
> counter who looks straight ahead, or the aeroplane passenger
> who sits with his eyes closed, are both communicating that they
> do not want to speak to anybody or be spoken to, and their
> neighbours usually 'get the message' and respond appropriately
> by leaving them alone. This obviously is just as much an inter-
> change of communication as an animated discussion. (Watz-
> lawick, Beavin and Jackson, 1968, p. 48)

We communicate when we talk and we communicate by our silence when we don't. Speech may be the channel of communication *par excellence*, but speech is never naturally disembodied. In face-to-face conversations people will speak whilst maintaining a distinctive posture and at a certain distance. They may smile as they produce the sentence and gesture in the middle of it; their speech will have a distinctive tone and they may 'um' and 'ah' whilst they are saying it. They may look their partner in the eye and then, suddenly, break eye contact. They will have a distinctive appearance. When we think of communication we may naturally think of speech, but speech is just part of the stream of communicative behaviour – the behaviours which accompany speech may emphasize it, contradict it or even substitute for it. In order to understand human communication we have to understand the functional role of the separate channels which go to make up the stream of behaviour and how they interact. Some of the channels are relatively static; these have been termed 'standing features' by Argyle and Kendon (1967). These *relatively* unchanging aspects of an interaction such as inter-personal distance and the appearance of the participants can themselves be used to communicate. Others are more dynamic. Thus speech itself, the vocal accompaniments of speech – the posture, gesture and looking behaviour of the participants – are constantly in a state of flux. In a later chapter we will consider how some of these dynamic features of social behaviour interact and try to unravel some of the important connections, especially between speech and the dynamic non-verbal channels. But first let us consider some distinctions commonly made in the analysis of face to face communication – some ways of grouping various communi-cative channels.

In Table 2.1 we have set out the five primary systems of com-munication beginning with the verbal system – speech itself – through to the standing features of the interaction that we have already mentioned. There are different ways of conceptualizing these five systems, and in order to avoid confusion we wish to draw a number of important distinctions. First let us consider very briefly the main components of each system.

Verbal: The verbal system comprises speech itself. Speech is made up of words, clauses and sentences, which are themselves connected into higher-order units. The words are made up of morphemes, the smallest linguistic units that carry meaning, and phonemes, the sound units of language.

Prosodic: Prosody comprises intonation, rhythm and those

Table 2.1 Systems of human communication

words ─┐			
clauses ──── 1 Verbal	Verbal	Linguistic	(mainly) Auditory-vocal channel
sentences ─┘			
rhythm ─┐			
pausing ──── 2 Prosodic			
intonation ─┘			
3 Paralinguistic	Nonverbal		
4 Kinesic		Non-linguistic	Visual channel
5 Standing features			

pauses in speech whose position and function are linguistically determined. The positioning of pauses in speech can affect meaning. Consider the phrase 'Old men and women'. A silent (or unfilled) pause after 'men' changes the meaning (try saying it with and without a pause here). Intonation is the pitch pattern of speech. It is composed of patterns of pitch and stress with junctures marking the boundaries of the units over which pitch and stress are interacting. Intonation affects meaning – 'He died' can be either a statement or a question depending upon whether there is a drop or rise in pitch at the end of the utterance.

Paralinguistic: When we speak we do more than use the verbal and prosodic system of language. We 'um' and we 'ah', we laugh and we cry, we whine and yawn. These are all vocal behaviours which form part of what is called 'paralanguage'. In addition, we do something which surprisingly takes up as much time as the speech itself. That is we pause, or fall silent, and only seldom for any clear linguistic reason. The individual pauses may be brief but they are frequent. In studies of spontaneous speech, Frieda Goldman-Eisler (1968) found 'a wide variation from 16% to 62% of utterance time spent in silence. Most of the group, however, paused between 40% and 50% of their total speaking time. These values seem to be ample evidence that pausing is as much part of speech as vocal utterance' (p. 18).

Kinesic: The main kinesic channels of communication are movements of the face, head and body, posture and gesture. We will consider each of these components in some detail later.

Standing features of interaction: The principal standing features of interaction are interpersonal distance (and touch), orientation and appearance. Appearance is generally more static than the other two – after all, interpersonal distance and orientation do often change during the course of an interaction. They are usually referred to as standing features, however, because they are much less dynamic than the main kinesic systems which often seem to be in a constant state of flux.

Having very briefly specified the components of each of these systems, we will now consider some of the distinctions which have been made. The first distinction is between the verbal and nonverbal channels of communication. The verbal system refers to the speech itself – the words and sentences spoken. We have said that it is *mainly* transmitted via the auditory-vocal channel because we will present evidence later that lip movements (which of course are visually transmitted) play an important role in everyday speech perception. 'Nonverbal' refers to everything else – the prosody, paralanguage, kinesic and standing features of the interaction. The linguistic/non-linguistic distinction is different however. The linguistic channels of communication involve both the verbal *and* prosodic systems of communication. Prosody is part of the linguistic set of channels but is nevertheless nonverbal. As John Lyons said in 1972, 'Intonation and stress . . . are almost universally regarded as being part of language. They are nonverbal: they do not identify or form part of the words of which the utterance is composed' (p. 53). Prosody is nonverbal but is an essential part of linguistic communication, hence the distinction. A further distinction can be made between the channels of communication in terms of the sensory-motor apparatus involved in their transmission and reception. The verbal, prosodic and paralinguistic channels are all transmitted via the auditory-vocal modality (though as we have said, 'lip movements' may be important here) whereas the kinesic channels and standing features of an interaction are all transmitted, and received, via the visual modality (touch, of course, is an exception). It is important to bear these various distinctions in mind when we consider the channels of communication in more detail.

In the past, it has been argued that we can also separate the various channels on the basis of their functional role in interaction. It has been suggested that the verbal channel has primarily a cognitive function – to convey factual information, give orders and instruction etc – whereas the nonverbal channels have primarily a social function – 'to manage the immediate social relationships – as in animals' (Argyle, 1972). Indeed, referring to the verbal and nonverbal systems, Argyle and Trower (1979) said 'Humans use two quite separate languages, each with its own function'. It is only after we consider the channels of communication in some detail in Chapters 3 and 4, and study their connections in the stream of behaviour in Chapter 8 (where the verbal and nonverbal channels interact to great effect) that we will be able to express our misgivings about such a clear functional difference as this.

Standing features of interaction

Appearance: There are certain very static aspects of appearance such as age and sex and some much less static ones such as the clothes we wear, the way we adorn our bodies and the way we style our hair. The situation, of course, is made more complicated by the fact that people often attempt to change the more permanent features of appearance using these less static devices. Many people adjust their clothes, bodily adornment and hair style in an attempt to change their appearance – even their apparent sex.

Clothes: Why wear clothes at all? The obvious answer is for physical comfort. Early man almost certainly evolved in a warm climate, but modern man lives in a variety of climates, some too hot, some too cold. In addition, clothes protect us from nature – an extra layer of skin for thorns, brambles, snakes or scorpions to penetrate. But comfort and protection cannot be the whole story, otherwise we would abandon clothes in our modern, centrally-heated, air-conditioned, 'high-tech' environments. The reason we don't is that another function of clothing is concealment. As Desmond Morris (1977) pointed out, 'Ever since early man went upright and walked on his hind legs, he has been unable to approach another member of his species without giving a sexual display. For other primates this problem does not arise. They approach on all fours and are forced to adopt a special "presentation" posture if they wish to display their genitals. The "full frontal" human body can only reduce the sexuality of its approach by hiding the sexual regions in some way' (p. 215). Desmond Morris goes on to note that it is therefore not surprising that the loin cloth is culturally the most widespread of all garments.

Of course, there is a good deal of variation in the extent of concealment of the human body. The Chador, common in Iran today, conceals almost everything; modern Western swimwear may conceal very little. The rules with respect to concealment and display vary across time – over the past hundred years female swimwear has changed from bathing machine and bulky swimming costume to one piece costume to bikini to (in some locations) the bottom half of the bikini only. In the 1930s it was necessary to conceal naked female navels in Hollywood films. Today, much more can be seen, every day, in many newspapers. But clothing is not just about comfort, protection and concealment, it is also about display (as a walk along any city high street will reveal) – display of social status, display of group allegiance, even a display of aggressiveness or sexual attitude. In earlier times there were laws governing the display of social status via clothes. In the reign of Edward IV for example, there was a law which stated that 'no knight under the rank of a lord . . . shall wear any gown, jacket or cloak, that is not long enough, when he stands upright, to cover his privities and his buttocks under the penalty of twenty shillings . . . No knight under the rank of lord . . . shall wear any shoes or boots having spikes or points exceeding the length of two inches, under the forfeiture of forty pence'. Today, unwritten rules have replaced these laws – designer clothes, rather than ordinary clothes, have substituted for the lengths of the points on shoes as display signals of social status. The punk in his bondage trousers in the 1970s in Britain (or the hippy in his patched jeans and tie-dye T-shirt in the 1960s) communicated information having more to do with group allegiance than social status, and the skinhead in his Doc Martens in the 1980s communicates group allegiance and often a certain aggressive attitude towards everyone else. Bondage trousers and designer pants might be equally good for comfort, protection and concealment, but their choice is never arbitrary.

Bodily adornment: Clothes are an important aspect of the more changeable side of human appearance but they are not the whole story of course. We decorate and transform our bodies in other ways as well. We may pierce our ears, paint our nails, cut our hair or paint our faces. Many of these alterations are temporary but in some societies, throughout history, more permanent alterations have been made. The Chinook Indians carried babies in a cradle specially designed to flatten the forehead. Chinese females for centuries bound their feet to make them smaller. Natives of new Guinea wear tight bands to constrict their waists artificially. Numerous other examples could be mentioned. Tattooing, for example, is common in many very diverse cultures throughout the world, from our own to the islands of Tahiti where very elaborate facial tattooing occurs. One area of bodily adornment where some general principle might exist is in the hair, particularly with respect to length. Hallpike (1969) has argued that long hair is generally associated with being outside society and that the cutting of hair symbolizes re-entering society. Indeed, he argues that cutting the hair is a powerful symbol of social control. He points out that intellectuals and juvenile rebels are generally credited with long hair and are less under social control than the average person. Soldiers, prisoners and monks, on the other hand, tend to have cropped hair which suggests, Hallpike argues, that they are under some form of discipline. (Even Elvis Presley's hair was cropped on registering for National Service) Hallpike (1969) further claims considerable support for this hypothesis in the Bible:

'Esau, the hunter of wild beasts, was a hairy man, while his brother, Jacob, a herdsman dwelling in tents, was a smooth man . . .' In Leviticus it is prescribed that a sufferer from leprosy and therefore an outcast, when cured and thereby ready to be reincorporated in society, shall shave off all his hair. (Leviticus XIV: 8–9) . . . The description of how King Nebuchadnezzar was overthrown and made an outcast is another very clear example of the association of hairiness and the separation from society in the state of nature: '. . . and he was driven from men, and did eat grass as oxen, and his body was wet with the dew of heaven, till his hairs were grown like eagle's features' (Daniel IV: 33).

Apart from the length of hair, the colour and style can also be important for communication. In addition, wigs may be worn. Wigs date back at least 5,000 years – the ancient Egyptians commonly shaved their heads and then wore special wigs for ceremonial occasions. In Roman times wigs were also popular – the hair for the wigs was often taken from the conquered peoples. Roman prostitutes wore wigs dyed yellow. Like many forms of bodily adornment, wigs have gone through cycles of fashion. In Elizabethan times and in the 18th century wigs were very much in fashion. In Victorian times, they were out of fashion and used only to remedy hair defects. In the 1960s their popularity revived again. Today the emphasis for men is on 'natural' look wigs that will, hopefully, be mistaken for the real thing.

Appearance is an important channel of human communication. Its effect can be extremely pervasive as George Orwell noted in *Down and out in Paris and London:*

The clothes were a coat, once dark brown, a pair of black dungaree trousers, a scarf and a cloth cap; I had kept my own shirt, socks and boots, and I had a comb and razor in my pocket. It gives one a very strange feeling to be wearing such clothes. I had worn bad enough things before, but nothing at all like these; they were not merely dirty and shapeless, they had – how is one to express it? – a gracelessness, a patina of antique filth, quite different from mere shabbiness. They were the sort of clothes you see on a bootlace seller, or a tramp. An hour later, in Lambeth, I saw a hang-dog man, obviously a tramp, coming towards me, and when I looked again it was myself, reflected in a shop window. The dirt was plastering my face already. Dirt is a great respecter of persons; it lets you alone when you are well dressed, but as soon as your collar is gone it flies towards you from all directions.

I stayed in the streets till late at night, keeping on the move all the time. Dressed as I was, I was half afraid that the police might arrest me as a vagabond, and I dared not speak to anyone, imagining that they must notice a disparity between my accent and my clothes. (Later I discovered that this never happened.) My new clothes had put me instantly into a new world. Everyone's demeanour seemed to have changed abruptly. I helped a hawker pick up a barrow that he had upset. 'Thanks, mate,' he said with a grin. No one had called me mate before in my life – it was the clothes that had done it. For the first time I noticed, too, how the attitude of women varies with a man's clothes. When a badly dressed man passes them they shudder away from him with a quite frank movement of disgust, as though he were a dead cat. Clothes are powerful things. Dressed in a tramp's clothes it is very difficult, at any rate for the first day, not to feel that you are genuinely degraded. You might feel the same shame, irrational but very real, your first night in prison. (1933, p. 115).

Appearance, like most channels of communication, interacts with others. A prolonged look from a well-groomed gentleman and a prolonged look from a tattoed skinhead may be perceived very differently. Whether a look is perceived as communicating sexual intent or menace may depend upon the appearance of the sender. The parameters of such looks, of course, may vary but whatever the background parameters of the behaviour, it may still be interpreted differently in the light of the great foreground mass of sensory information which constitutes human appearance.

Interpersonal distance

Proxemics is the name given to the study of how human beings perceive, structure and use the space in which they live, breathe and interact. The term was coined by the anthropologist Edward T. Hall who argued that 'The flow and shift of distance between people as they interact with each other is part and parcel of the communicative process' (Hall, 1959, p. 180). The use and meaning of space in different cultures is the primary focus of study here and Hall developed a series of methods and techniques for identifying the elements of space perception. These techniques included natural observation, experiment, interviews (both structured and unstructured), analysis of the lexicon of languages, and the study of space as it is recreated in literature and in art. (See, for example, Hall, 1966). The natural observation technique is self-explanatory but this was often supplemented with still photography and notes on 'the unselfconscious comment people make as a result of some breach of spatial etiquette' (e.g. 'I wish he would stop breathing down my neck. I can't stand that'). Such comments can be a very useful source of information about proxemic norms within a culture. The experimental method involved asking people to arrange simple objects (for example coins or pencils) so that they were 'close', 'far apart', 'side by side' or 'next to each other'. People from various cultures arranged the objects differently. The interviews that Hall used in his research were detailed and intensive. He notes that the shortest interviews took six hours, the longest six months! Structured interviews followed a set pattern beginning with general questions about the home and household and the activities and named areas contained in the house. It then went on to topics such as privacy, boundaries, the rights of propinquity and the place of the home in its broad social context. The fixed protocol with set questions such as 'Where do you go to be alone?' proved especially interesting since such 'normal' questions (to Western ears) often appeared much less normal to people from other cultures. The question 'Where do you go to be alone?' always puzzled and sometimes angered Arabs. A common Arab reply was 'Who *wants* to be alone?'.

The analysis by Hall of the lexicons of different cultures in an attempt to learn about the use of space within these derives from the work of the anthropologists Franz Boas (1911) and Benjamin Whorf (1956). Boas emphasized the relationship between language and culture while Whorf explored how language moulds, shapes and constrains our view of the world, arguing that 'We dissect nature along lines laid down by our natural language' (1956). Hall notes, coincidentally, that 20% of the Oxford English Dictionary are words with spatial connotations and thus the lexicon may provide a useful and detailed source of information about how space is coded within a culture. The study of art and literature from different cultures provided more valuable information for Hall in his theorizing about the communicative significance of space.

Apart from his pioneering of new methods and techniques in this field Hall's major contributions were his analysis and breakdown of different distance zones between human beings, and cultural differences in the use of them. The distance zones were as follows:

Intimate distance (0–18 inches)
Close phase – (0–6 inches). 'This is the distance of love-making and wrestling, comforting and protecting. Physical contact or the high possibility of physical involvement is uppermost in the awareness of both persons' (1966, p. 110).
Far phase – (6–18 inches). 'Heads, thighs and pelvis are not easily brought into contact, but hands can reach and grasp extremities. . . . Much of the physical discomfort that Americans experience when foreigners are inappropriately inside the intimate sphere is expressed as a distortion of the visual system. . . . The use of intimate distance in public is not considered proper by adult, middle-class Americans' (1966, p. 111–112).

Personal distance (18–48 inches)
Close phase – (18–30 inches). It was obviously the close phase of the personal distance that W. H. Auden was thinking of when he wrote:

> Some thirty inches from my nose
> The frontier of my Person goes
> And all the untilled air between
> Is private pagus or demesne
> Stranger, unless with bedroom eyes
> I beckon you to fraternize
> Beware of rudely crossing it
> I have no gun, but I can spit.

> (*Prologue: The Birth of Architecture*)

Hall likened the 'personal distance' to 'a small protective sphere or bubble that an organism maintains between itself and others' (1966, p. 112) and noted that 'Where people stand in relation to each other signals their relationship or how they feel towards each other, or both. A wife can stay inside the circle of her husband's close personal zone with impunity. For another woman to do so is an entirely different story' (1966, p. 113).

Far phase – (30–48 inches). This is the 'arm's length' phase of personal distance extending from a part that is just outside easy touching distance by one person to a point where two people can touch fingers – if they each extend arms.

Social distance (4 feet–12 feet)

Close phase – (4–7 feet). Hall notes that people who work together tend to use this social distance as well as people attending a casual social gathering.

Far phase – (7–12 feet). This is, according to Hall, the social distance characterizing more formal business and social interaction.

Public distance (12 feet or more)

Close phase – (12–25 feet). According to Hall, the most significant feature of the 12 foot social distance is that an alert person can take evasive or defensive action if threatened. In Hall's terms the public distance is 'well outside the circle of involvement'.

Far phase – (25 feet or more). Hall notes that 30 feet is the distance that automatically sets around important public figures. At such distances much of the nonverbal part of the communication shifts to gestures and body stance since the details of facial expression and intonation are lost.

These are the four distance zones which Hall identified in his classic research. It should be emphasized however that he felt this four-way classification scheme was quite specific to Western culture. He was well aware that

> In other parts of the world, relationships tend to fall into other patterns, such as the family/non-family pattern common in Spain and Portugal and their former colonies or the caste and outcast system of India. Both the Arabs and the Jews also make sharp distinctions between people to whom they are related and those to whom they are not. My work with Arabs leads me to believe that they employ a system for the organisation of informal space

which is very different from what I observed in the United States. (1966, p. 121)

One of the major differences between Arab culture and Western culture is that olfaction plays a much more important role in Arab communication, and interpersonal distance in the Arab world is arranged to accommodate this. Hall says

> Arabs consistently breathe on people when they talk. However, this habit is more than a matter of different manners. To the Arab good smells are pleasing and a way of being involved with each other. To smell one's friend is not only nice but desirable, for to deny him your breath is to act ashamed. Americans, on the other hand, trained as they are not to breath in peoples' faces, automatically communicate shame in trying to be polite. (1966, p. 149)

The potential for cross-cultural misunderstandings here is, of course, enormous. Arabs approach, Americans retreat. One group seen as intrusive, the other as cold, or weak in terms of personality.

Personal Space

A good deal of the research in proxemics after Hall has concentrated on the variables that affect *personal space* – that 'small, protective sphere or bubble'. A vast literature has explored how variables like sex, age, personality, socioeconomic status, situation, degree of friendship and attitude affect it. (See Hayduk, 1983). The evidence is sometimes confusing: 27 studies (up to 1983) found sex differences in personal space, 54 studies found mixed evidence and 29 studies found no sex effects. In the case of age however it is well documented that there is a gradual increase between 3 and 20 years. Similarly, spatial preferences are sensitive to physical setting and degree of friendship – friends require less personal space than strangers. Hayduk (1983) also notes that violent and disturbed persons typically require extra personal space, as do contacts between individuals of differing social status. Some of the cultural differences originally reported by Hall (1966) have been replicated – Arabs do require less space than Americans (Watson, 1970, Watson and Graves, 1966) but Latin Americans use only slightly less space (Watson, 1970) or possibly the same amount of space as

Americans or North Europeans (Forston and Larson, 1968). Other modifications have however been necessary. Some of Hall's contact cultures, e.g. Latin American peoples, show significant variation in spacing. Shuter (1976) observed that Costa Ricans use less space than Columbians or Panamanians – hardly as homogeneous as Hall had initially envisaged.

Indeed, since Hall's time, both the concept of personal space and the techniques used to measure it have come in for a good deal of criticism. Patterson (1975) argued that

> the notion of personal space implies a minimum comfortable distance which is, to some extent, fairly stable. However, a comfortable distance between two individuals may vary between no distance at all to several feet, depending on the sex of the interactants, their cultural background, the relationship between them, and situational constraints. . . . How can we talk of that individual's personal space? To which personal space are we referring? (p. 67)

Patterson is not denying the importance of interpersonal distance in social interaction, merely disputing the usefulness of the term 'personal space'. Hayduk (1983) has disputed the use of projective measurement strategies (such as the manipulation of miniature figures, dolls, coins or pencils) pioneered by Hall in the analysis of personal space because their correlation with real-life measures (e.g. stopping an experimenter's approach at a minimum comfortable distance, unobtrusive observations of actual spacings) are unacceptably low – Hayduk reports an average correlation of just 0.39, and in some particular cases the correlation has been negative (e.g. Love and Aiello, 1980). Despite this criticism, Hall's thesis that 'The flow and shift of distance between people as they interact with each other is part and parcel of the communicative process' is now firmly established.

Touch

As Shirley Weitz (1974) has noted, touch is the logical end of proxemics; it is the zero-point of Hall's intimate distance. And as La France and Mayo (1978) have pointed out, 'Touch is a non-verbal dimension that seems to signal intensity in a special way. Someone can look at you without your looking back, but touch is necessarily connection' (p. 70). Given this essential connection, and given the inescapable intensity of this dimension, social context is crucial in the positive or negative interpretation of touch. In the interpretation of touch, the interaction of its specific parameters and the context in which it occurs appear crucial. In a recent review, Heslin and Alper (1983) suggest that the meaning of a touch is affected by at least the following nine factors:

1) What part of the body touched the other person
2) What part of the body is touched
3) How long the touch lasts
4) How much pressure is used
5) Whether there is movement after contact has been made
6) Whether anyone else is present
7) If others are present, who they are
8) The situation in which it occurs (such as a funeral or athletic contest and the mood created by that situation)
9) The relationship between the persons involved.

Touching can convey liking, power or sexuality, depending upon the combination of these nine factors. Heslin (1974) has specified five kinds of situations/relations involving touch ranging from the most distant to the most intimate. They are:

1) Functional/professional, e.g. doctor–patient – here the context determines the interpretation of the touch. As Heslin notes it is possible within this context for the doctor to touch intimate areas of a person with whom he or she is only minimally acquainted.
2) Social/polite, e.g. the handshake – this touching is culturally constrained by norms which govern how, when and whom one can touch.
3) Friendship/warmth – this is the touch relationship around which there is most unease since it is less formal than the social/polite touch and may be interpreted as signifying love and/or sexual attraction.
4) Love/intimacy – here the relationship must be appropriate if the special kind of touch is not to create discomfort or embarrassment.
5) Sexual arousal – here the touch is primarily for stimulation and loaded with sexual meaning.

A typology of situations/relations such as this which emphasizes the importance of the function of touch and the relationship between the participants does make it clear that touch must be studied in context.

Like interpersonal distance, touch is affected by a wide variety of social variables – culture, sex, status, degree of friendship, etc. In the Watson and Graves (1966) study Arabs not only sat closer together than Americans, they also touched each other more during conversation. Heslin and Boss (1980) found that males initiated touch with females more than vice versa. There is also evidence to suggest that high status people initiate more touch with low status people than vice versa (Goffman, 1967; Watson, 1975). Jourard (1966) found that college students touch, and are touched, on far more areas of their body by friends of the opposite sex than by either their parents or friends of the same sex (see also Rosenfeld, Kartus and Ray, 1976).

In summary, even touch is a more complex form of communication than might at first appear. It can carry a multitude of meanings, and only the broad social context, the relationship between the participants and the specific parameters of the touch itself allow disambiguation. Power, liking or sexuality at your fingertips, but all of course depending upon context.

Thus far we have concentrated on channels of communication which we have termed 'standing features' of interaction. Appearance, at least for the duration of an interaction, is relatively constant. Interpersonal distance (with touch as the zero point of the distance dimension) can also be fixed – as in a classroom, a waiting room, or a cinema. We turn now to channels which are never constant, never static, but dynamic and changing – constantly: first facial expression where some individual messages last less than a second) then bodily movement.

3 Kinesic channels of human communication

Facial movement

The face is perhaps the prime source of human nonverbal communication. In most forms of social interaction the face, and especially the eyes, is the region we concentrate on. It is a region with enormous 'sending capacity'. The concept of sending capacity was developed by Paul Ekman and Wallace Friesen in 1969. They suggested that the sending capacity of any part of the body can be assessed by looking at three factors: the average transmission time of any message from that part, the number of discernible stimulus patterns which can be emitted from it, and its visibility. Clearly, in terms of all of these factors, the face is an excellent source of communication. The average transmission time of even a 'micro' facial expression is very brief – even those expressions that can be easily identified and labelled in terms of emotion often last only for half a second or less. Some 'micro' facial expressions are even briefer. The complex musculature of the human face allows for a great number of discernible stimulus patterns. Ray Birdwhistell (1970), for example, has suggested that over 20,000 different facial expressions are possible. And the face of course also has maximum visibility. In some cultures there are socially-prescribed rules about the covering of the face (as in some Arab cultures), but in Western cultures the best we can do to make it less visible is to wear spectacles or sunglasses. As Ekman and Friesen point out:

It is difficult to hide the face without being obvious about concealment, there are no inhibition manoeuvres for the face equivalent to putting the hands in the pocket or sitting upon them. A frozen, immobile poker face is more noticeable than are interlocked fingers or tensely-held feet. (1969a)

Because it is such an excellent source of communication, and because our fellow human beings do tend to concentrate on it, it is a form of communication which most people learn to control to some extent. There are two sorts of messages that can be emitted through the face, first spontaneous messages – facial expressions which are emitted unintentionally and occur even when people do not know they are in a communicative situation – and secondly, intentional facial expressions which occur when people are consciously trying to communicate particular messages via the face. Buck, Savin, Miller and Caul (1972) investigated the spontaneous display of emotion in a rather ingenious paradigm. They told subjects that they were interested in galvanic skin responses to certain types of stimuli and subjects were wired up appropriately for measurement. But what Buck et al were really interested in was the spontaneous display of emotion via facial expression; the emotion being manipulated by the types of stimuli presented to the subjects. Buck video-recorded the facial expressions of his subjects as they watched the stimuli and then showed the video recordings to a second set of subjects who had to attempt to identify what class of stimuli the transmitters were being exposed to. Buck discovered that when men were used in this experiment (as encoders and decoders), they could not identify the emotional state of the encoder at more than chance level. Women, in contrast, were well above chance, being twice as accurate as the men. There are two possible explanations for this – either women are more expressive than men and therefore easier to 'read' correctly (perhaps because in Western cultures men are socialised to control their emotional expression) or perhaps women are better at interpreting facial expression than men.

In the original study males only acted as decoders for male encoders, and females for female encoders, so there was no way of deciding between these two alternatives. In a follow-up study which employed a similar procedure but had men viewing women's faces and vice versa, Buck, Miller and Caul (1974) obtained support for the first interpretation, namely that women are more expressive, than men. No sex difference in decoding ability was observed. It does, nevertheless, seem that intentional communcation via facial expression is more accurate than is spontaneous facial expression. This was demonstrated in a study by Zuckerman and his colleagues (1979). The superiority of deliberate over spontaneous expression in the encoding of emotion was most pronounced for pleasant emotions, and less pronounced for intense emotions.

Over the years there has been a good deal of speculation about whether facial expressions are learnt or inherited. Charles Darwin in his 1872 book *The Expression of the Emotions in Man and Animals* said 'Many of our most important expressions have not been learnt', but went on to qualify this by saying 'but it is remarkable that some which are certainly innate, require practice in the individual before they are performed in a full and perfect manner: for instance weeping and laughing' (p. 350). Darwin believed strongly in the innate basis of human facial expression, arguing that:

> The inheritance of most of our expressive actions explains the fact that those born blind display them, as I hear from the Rev. R. H. Blair, equally well with those gifted with eyesight. We can thus also understand the fact that the young and the old of widely different races, both with man and animals, express the same state of mind by the same movements. (1872, p. 35)

Darwin's conclusions do however need to be modified in the light of the psychological research of the past century. Ekman, Friesen and Ellsworth (1972) tested Darwin's hypothesis a century later, on a pre-literate culture in the South-East highlands of New Guinea. Their subjects, who had little contact with Western culture, were shown three photographs of Caucasian faces each expressing a different emotion and were presented with three different emotional stories (e.g. 'A person's mother died'). Their task was to match the photograph of the facial expression with the emotion conveyed in the story. Both children and adults matched the expressions and the emotions correctly except in the case of 'fear' which the New Guineans often confused with surprise. Ekman et al. also demonstrated cross-cultural similarities in the encoding of emotions. The New Guinean subjects were asked to show the emotional expression their face would have if they were the person described in the story. These videotapes were accurately decoded by American students – at least for happiness, anger and sadness. But again the Americans, like the New Guineans, had difficulty recognizing fear or surprise. Ekman's research does suggest that a number of basic emotions are conveyed by the same facial expressions, but other research has indicated important cultural differences in emotional *display*. Klineberg (1935), for example, made the following points:

It is quite possible, however, that a smile or a laugh may have a different meaning for groups other than our own. Lafcadio Hearn has remarked that the Japanese smile is not necessarily a spontaneous expression of amusement, but a law of etiquette, elaborated and cultivated from early times. It is a silent language, often seemingly inexplicable to Europeans, and it may arouse violent anger in them as a consequence. The Japanese child is taught to smile as a social duty, just as he is taught to bow or prostrate himself; he must always show an appearance of happiness to avoid inflicting his sorrow upon his friends. The story is told of a woman servant who smilingly asked her mistress if she might go to her husband's funeral. Later she returned with his ashes in a vase and said, actually laughing, 'Here is my husband'. Her white mistress regarded her as a cynical creature. Hearn suggests that this may have been pure heroism (Hearn, 1894).

Ekman (1978) concludes that Darwin was essentially correct – there *are* universal facial expressions of emotion – but in addition:

Facial expressions do vary across cultures in at least two respects. What elicits or calls forth an emotion usually differs . . . Also, cultures differ in the conventions people follow about attempting to control or manage the appearance of their face in given social situations. People in two different cultures may feel sadness at the death of a loved one, but one culture may prescribe that the chief mourners must mask their facial expression with a mildly happy countenance. (p. 106)

Hearn's Japanese widow is a perfect example of this.

Eye-gaze and eye contact

Eye-gaze, where one person looks at another, and eye contact, where their gazes meet, are a particularly complex form of communication. Eye-gaze can act both as a visual signal in social interaction and as a channel for receiving information. It can do both simultaneously of course. Eye-gaze has been shown to be affected by a number of social variables, its association with these causing it to act as a communicative signal of the underlying state. Let us consider some of the variables that affect eye-gaze in social interaction. (A useful review is to be found in Argyle and Cook, 1976). Firstly eye-gaze is affected by the degree of liking between two or more people. Exline and Winters (1965) found that subjects in an experimental situation looked less at experimenters they disliked. (They disliked the experimenter, by the way, because he had just informed them that their performance on an experimental task was very poor). At the extreme positive end of the liking dimension, that is between people who are in love, the level of eye contact is very high indeed (see Rubin, 1970). Eye-gaze is associated with liking and becomes a powerful signal of sexual interest. Margaret Mead (1928) reported that courtship in Bali proceeded entirely by the exchange of glances, and even in modern western society the role of this form of behaviour as a social signal has not diminished. But eye-gaze does not necessarily reflect liking. It can express the opposite – aggression and hostility, and staring at someone, whether it be intentional or not, may also evoke aggression. Argyle reports the example of the 'hate stare' of white people of the Southern States of America, directed at Negroes, as one example of eye-gaze reflecting hostility. Argyle points out that the 'hate stare' is a deliberate breaking of the usual norm of what Erving Goffman (1963) calls 'civil inattention' to strangers in public places: 'It is insulting, partly because it implies the person stared at doesn't really count as a person at all.' (Argyle and Cook, 1976, p. 74.) Eye-gaze can also reflect dominance. Generally speaking, people of lower status look more at people of higher status than vice versa. On some occasions gaze can reflect shame or embarrassment. In an experiment carried out by Modigliani (1971), subjects were caused to succeed or fail in an anagram task. In the failure condition, subjects reported more embarrassment and reduced the level of eye-contact with a confederate individual.

The amount of eye-gaze in social interaction is clearly affected by a number of variables, and comes to be viewed as an important signal. Generally speaking, people who look more and with longer glances create a more favourable impression and are liked more, than those who do not. For example, Kleck and Nuessle (1968) found that people who looked at their interlocutor only a small percentage of the time were described as 'defensive' or 'evasive', whereas those who looked a lot of the time were described as 'friendly', 'mature' and 'sincere'. Scherwitz and Helmreich (1973) found that male subjects preferred girls who showed higher levels of gaze in a videotaped simulation of a video-phone encounter (as well as preferring the attractive girls).

So far, we have tended to concentrate on the social functions of eye-gaze as transmitters of visual signals, but clearly the eyes are also an important channel for receiving information. In social interaction speakers monitor listeners for signals of attention and interest (shown through eye-contact as well as through other means) and listeners monitor the faces of speakers because, after all, a good deal of information in conversation is passed on visually. Hence eye-gaze is an important channel for receiving information and it is a channel which is affected by cognitive factors as well as by social factors of the kind we have just considered. Generally speaking, people avert eye-gaze in talking when the intellectual demands of the situation are high, possibly, to reduce potential interference between the cognitive planning of speech and the processing of incoming visual information (see Beattie, 1983, p. 39). Neilsen (1962) observed that subjects averted gaze when preparing arguments in conversation, and Kendon (1967) and Beattie (1978a) found gaze aversion was more likely during slow hesitant speech, when the planning of speech is being carried out, than during fluent speech. Exline and Winters (1965) found that the overall amount of gaze in conversation was inversely related to the cognitive difficulty of the topic of conversation.

Just as with facial expression, there are cultural differences in the display of eye gaze. Some societies have explicit, socially prescribed rules about gaze in social interaction. Hall (1963) makes the following points:

> How the eye is used as a function of one's culture is regulated formally, informally and technically (Hall, 1959). That is, the culture specifies at what, when and how one looks as well as the amount of communication that takes place via the eye . . . For example, a Navaho is taught to avoid gazing directly at others during conversation . . . the Greeks, on the other hand, emphasise the use of the eyes and look for answers in each other's eyes (their intent gaze can be disturbing to the American). Americans often convey the impression to the Arabs that they are ashamed. The way Americans look at the other person during conversations is the principal reason given by the Arabs for this impression. (Hall, 1963).

In Japan, the prime focus of regard in social interaction is not the eyes, as in our culture; instead children are taught to focus on the neck (Morsbach, 1973). In Nigeria an older or higher-status person must not be looked directly in the eye during conversation (Watson, 1970). Apart from striking cultural differences, there are also very strong individual differences within members of a culture in amounts of gaze. Females generally look much more than males in social interaction (see Argyle and Dean, 1965). There are a number of possible explanations for this. It has been reported that girls attend more to faces than boys do, even at the age of six months, and Argyle and Cook (1976) suggest that there may be an innate sex difference in the form of behaviour. An alternative hypothesis, also entertained by Argyle and Cook, is that there may be a greater affiliative need in females, and that gaze is being used merely as a signal of affiliation in conversation. There are also differences between people related to personality variables. It has been found, for example, that extroverts gaze more frequently, especially while talking, than introverts. In depression, levels of gaze are significantly reduced; indeed, one classic symptom of depression is withdrawal from social interaction (see Argyle and Cook, 1976, chapter 6).

Head movements

With head movements, we get a distinct subclass of nonverbal behaviour which has been called 'emblems', a term introduced by Efron in 1941. According to Ekman and Friesen (1969b):

Emblems are those nonverbal acts which have a direct verbal translation or dictionary definition, usually consisting of a word or two, or perhaps a phrase. This verbal definition or translation of the emblem is well known by all the members of a group, class or culture . . . An emblem may repeat, substitute or contradict some part of the verbal behaviour; a crucial question in detecting an emblem is whether it could be replaced with a word or two without changing the information conveyed. People are almost always aware of their use of emblems. That is, they know when they are using an emblem, can repeat it if asked to do so, and will take communicational responsibility for it. Similarly, the use of

an emblem is usually an intentional deliberate effort to communicate; but there are exceptions.

Clearly, some categories of head movement fit into this category of
emblems described by Ekman and Friesen. A head nod meaning
'yes' in our culture and head shaking meaning 'no' are two obvious
emblems – they have a direct verbal translation and could be
replaced in each case by a simple word without changing the
information conveyed. However, not all forms of head nods or head
shakes are emblems.

A different type of head movement has been described in detail
by Ray Birdwhistell (1970) who has proposed that different forms of
'head nod' can perform different functions in controlling interaction. The functions fall into the category of 'regulators' described
by Ekman and Friesen:

These are acts which maintain and regulate the back and forth
nature of speaking and listening between two or more interactants. They tell the speaker to continue, repeat, elaborate,
hurry up, become more interesting, less salacious, give the other
a chance to talk, etc. They can tell the listener to pay special
attention, to wait just a minute more to talk, etc. . . . Most
regulators . . . carry no message content in themselves but
convey information necessary to the pacing of conversation . . .
regulators seem to be on the periphery of awareness; a person can
perform a regulative act without knowing that he does so but if
asked, can easily recall and repeat it. Similarly, the other
interactant seems quite sensitive to regulators if they are
removed, but is rarely aware of them if they are present.

Birdwhistell (1970) attempted to analyze the specific regulative
function of different types of head nod differentiated in terms of the
number and timing of their repetition. He found, for example, that
brief single head nods by listeners which occured repeatedly during
the speaker's utterance acted as simple attentional signals 'to
sustain the interaction without significant change in the level or
content of the communication' (p. 161). Longer lasting single nods
on the other hand could result in a disruption of the flow of speech
and an elaboration of an earlier point. Birdwhistell reports that
after one such long single nod, a patient interrupted his flow of
speech, shifted his stance and said 'I was only joking'. Double head

nods, Birdwhistell claimed, either modified the speech rate of the speaker or resulted in the elaboration of a previously established point. Triple head nods were said to sometimes result in a termination of the speaker's turn. Birdwhistell's detailed observations of this form of micro behaviour do need, however, to be checked in more controlled conditions with larger samples.

Other forms of head movements are intimately connected with the flow of speech and with general bodily posture, but consideration of these will be left to later chapters.

Posture

Posture – the way you stand or sit or generally position your body – is one of the most obvious and visible channels of human communication. There appear to be both important cultural and sex differences in the display of this particular form of behaviour, but there may also be some general principles involving the sharing of posture and the connection between posture and psychological states which may transcend culture and sex. Gordon Hewes (1955) has estimated that the number of different bodily postures which human beings can display is in the region of one thousand. He has suggested that certain postures may occur in all cultures and 'may form a part of our basic hominid heritage – the upright stance with arms at the sides, or with hands clasped in the midline over the lower abdomen, certainly belongs in this category. A quarter of mankind habitually squats in a fashion very similar to the squatting position of the chimpanzee, and the rest of us might squat this way too if we were not trained to use other postures beyond infancy'.

Whilst recognizing the universality of some postures and the anatomical limitations on human posture, Hewes also recognizes the broad influence of cultural factors and male/female differences. Posture is learned and passed on from person to person and even from culture to culture. With respect to this latter process Hewes cites the work of Quain (1948) on the cultural diffusion of posture in Fiji. Quain reported that older inland natives of Vanua Levu could recall when the fashion of the cross-legged sitting position was introduced from Tonga. When first introduced it was a chiefly prerogative and only later came to be used by commoners. Clearly contact between cultures can lead to a certain amount of diffusion of postural habits. One suspects that the influence of American popular culture of the 1960s produced changes in the postural habits of certain sections of British society, as it did with their speech. The 'laid-back' Californian style produced changes in the speech (e.g. the use of the term 'man' as an address term) and probably postural habits as well. The 'formal British' probably became less formal posturally as a function of the influence of American pop culture. But clearly, there are limits to this process of diffusion. Some forms of behaviour, some forms of posture, might simply be too alien ever to be comfortably adopted.

Status relationships in Western and other societies are often realized through posture, but in some cultures this is more extreme than in others. Gordon Hewes suggested that there are three general dimensions of posture – distance, verticality and orientation. Firth (1970) reported that the combination of these dimensions has an additive effect on the communication of social status among the inhabitants of Ticopia in the Pacific Ocean. Firth pointed out that 'somebody who is crouching far off facing the chief is in a highly approved position; somebody who is standing far off likewise is showing respect, but not extremely so; someone who is standing far away but turning his back is on the borderline of respect, whereas someone who is close at hand standing with his back turned is definitely disrespectful, i.e. not acknowledging the status of the other person'. In Ticopia verticality or relative height is also varied – Firth observed how senior men, but not women, sometimes used coconut-grating stools or other objects as seats which raised them off the ground, but on other occasions such objects are reserved exclusively for chiefs.

In Britain, physical analogies of body inclination and body lowering are still present if in somewhat different form. Bowing (inclining the body and/or head in salutation, acknowledgement or respect), kneeling and curtseying (a female equivalent of the bow, but a more extreme movement) all find some role in contemporary British society. Bowing is clearly the most widespread today and both men and women bow. Kneeling is confined to ceremonial and religious contexts (e.g. receiving a knighthood or praying), and curtseying is nowadays restricted to women being formally presented to royalty. In non-Western societies the dimension of verticality is taken to much greater extremes. In some Oriental cultures, one posture involves touching the feet of a person of superior status in salutation, but this is not a practice which ever found favour in Britain, despite the fact that the British Empire stretched to cultures where such behaviour was commonplace. In China, the practice is known as 'K 'o – t 'ou', literally meaning 'knock the head'. (in English it is known as 'kow-tow'). This was an expression of respect in China and apparently the insistence by the Chinese Imperial Court that Western ambassadors observe this practice was the cause of considerable difficulty in the early period of European contact. Lord McCartney, on a mission to China in 1793, refused to kow-tow, as did the English Ambassador, Lord Amherst, in 1816. Kow-towing was clearly one posture which was definitely not going to be diffused through English society. Firth (1970) makes the point that the more elaborate postures of submission or respect involving lowering the body have all been reduced considerably in scope in modern western societies. In many cases, any form of the postures are limited to formal occasions (church, the presence of royalty, etc.), though Erving Goffman (1979) has shown that when men and women are depicted together in advertisement photographs, the verticality dimension of posture relevant to status is one which often does differentiate men and women. Look at some adverts and see how often the man stands higher than the woman, who is often seated or lying down. Goffman argues that in advertisements involving still photographs of men and women, the advertisements are hyper-ritualising certain non-verbal features including posture, which may differentiate men and women. This may now be changing – Dudley Moore did become a sex symbol after all – but a look at the lengths Prince Charles and Princess Diana go to in order to disguise their true height relationship shows that it is far from having disappeared completely.

Sex differences in posture

A number of authors have suggested that there are sex differences in the habitual postures of men and women (apart from Goffman's ritualized differences). There are a number of possible reasons for such differences. Some may be due to biological factors, others may be culturally determined and culturally enforced. Among the biological factors which might affect posture is pregnancy which, Hewes points out, renders certain sitting positions more comfortable, and therefore perhaps more frequent than others among adult females. The clothing and footwear of men and women may also affect posture. Tight-fitting skirts will restrict posture more than loose-fitting trousers (and vice versa). But clearly, many of the postural differences observed cannot be explained in terms of biological differences or the simple effects of clothing. For example, Mehrabian (1972) has shown that women take up less space than men in terms of position. They tend to sit with their arms close to their sides and their legs crossed at small angles, whereas men often sprawl, draping their arms over the backs of chairs and either stretching their legs out or crossing them at larger angles. In addition, men often sit with their legs wide apart. A similar phenomenon has even been reported for book-carrying in male and female students. Women were found to wrap one or both arms around the books whereas men were more likely to support their books with one hand and arm at the side of the body (Jenni and Jenni, 1976). La France and Mayo (1978) point out that the female carrying method results in postures that are more compact while the male method is more expansive.

One of the authors carried out a study into postural differences between men and women sitting, standing or lying on a beach in Southern France (Beattie and Beattie, 1981). It was observed that males displayed more different postures than females (19 as opposed to 14) but that females changed posture more often than males – once every 78.9 seconds compared with once every 96.7 seconds for males. But what was also interesting was that several postures which were very common in males were not displayed at all in females. These were, firstly, one in which the man was lying on his back, hands crossed behind his head, left leg outstretched, right leg bent at the knee; and secondly, one in which the man was lying on his back, legs apart, hands across chest. It should be noted that this posture is very close to the burial position which Gordon Hewes (1955) suggested is probably taboo because of this association. Clearly it was not taboo on the beach (at least among men!). It is also interesting that three other postures were displayed by men, but not by women on the beach. Two of these postures involved *one* leg bent at the knee, the other leg outstretched. It would be interesting to see if this, like the legs apart seated posture, is regarded as a particularly masculine form of behaviour. Sex differences in posture of course can be culturally enforced by verbal scolding ('ladies don't sit like that'), ridicule or worse. For example, Beatrice Blackwood (1953) reports that in the Buka Passage area of the North Solomons, any woman who sits with legs stretched out is perceived to be openly inviting sexual intercourse.

Posture and interpersonal attitudes

There is a long tradition of investigating the relationship between posture and interpersonal attitudes in human social interaction. Since the overt verbal expression of attitudes is culturally discouraged in many situations, nonverbal means of communicating attitudes may become extremely important. Much of the early research on this topic was carried out by psychoanalysts interested in inferring from the posture of patients their attitudes towards the analyst and others (e.g. Deutsch, 1947; 1952). Fromm-Reichmann (1950) studied the changing postures of her clients in an attempt to infer their true feelings. But as Mehrabian (1969) points out, the observations of the psychoanalysts of posture were fairly informal and never rigorously tested.

It was psychologists who attempted to advance the study of the relationship between posture and interpersonal attitudes. James (1932) used a 'decoding' methodology to investigate the relationship between posture and interpersonal attitudes. He asked subjects to identify the attitude expressed by each posture of a masked male model and to pinpoint those aspects of the posture which were most significant in the communication. James employed 347 photgraphs in which the positions of the head, trunk, feet, knees and arms were systematically varied, and identified four main postural categories:

a) approach: an attentive posture communicated by a forward lean of the body,
b) withdrawal: a negative, refusing or repulsed posture communicated by drawing back or turning away,
c) expansion: a proud, conceited, arrogant or disdainful posture communicated by an expanded chest, erect or backward-leaning trunk, erect head, and raised shoulders,
d) contraction: a depressed, downcast or dejected posture communicated by a forward leaning trunk and bowed head, drooping shoulders and a sunken chest.

James found that head and trunk positions were the most important determinants of the type of communication. Machotka (1965) also used a 'decoding' methodology. His subjects used line drawings displaying different degrees of the openness of the arms of nude figures. Machotka found that the figures with closed arm positions were judged as being more cold, rejecting, unyielding, shy and passive than those with open arm position. Mehrabian (1968) employed an '*encoding*' methodology to investigate the relationship between posture and one person's liking for another person. Subjects were asked to display 'typical postures' for a series of liked and disliked hypothetical addressees of different sexes. Mehrabian found that the degree of backward lean of the torso significantly decreased for liked addressess but the openness and the degree of relaxation of arms and legs were not found to be significant indices of attitude in this study. It should be noted however that it was not spontaneous posture that was investigated here but deliberately encoded posture to a hypothetical other person.

Peter Bull (1978a, b) employed a different methodology to investigate natural, spontaneous postural display. Bull posed the question: does a student's interest in a given topic affect the posture he or she displays? Many, including La Barre (1947), believe the answer is 'yes'. He had said in a well-known essay: 'I believe that it is by no means entirely an illusion that an experienced teacher can come into a classroom of new students and predict with some accuracy the probable quality of individual scholastic accomplishment . . . by distinguishing the unreachable, unteachable *Apperceptions masse*–less sprawl of one student, from the edge-of-the-seat starved avidity and intentness of another'. Bull obtained experimental evidence to corroborate La Barre's intuitions. He asked subjects to listen to recorded talks and then rate them. Whilst they listened they were videotaped without their knowledge. Bull found that British male and female students leaned forward during items judged to be interesting, and leaned forward and drew back their legs when talking to the experimenter after about this extract. When subjects listened to boring talks, they lowered the head, turned to one side and turned the head away from the television monitor, supported the head on one hand, leaned back and stretched out the legs. When Bull subsequently employed a decoding methodology to investigate the communicative salience of these postures, he found that these postures were accurately perceived as communicating interest or boredom. La Barre's intuitions seem correct.

Postural congruence

Another major source of influence on posture in any social context is the respective postures of the interactants. For example, Albert Scheflen (1964, 1965) described how, in group psychotherapy sessions, members of the group not only took up similar postures, but also shifted posture after one of them had changed position so that the group maintained identical postures through a series of changes in bodily position. Scheflen (1964) gives the following example:

> Two or more of the people in a small group may sit with their legs crossed at the knee, their arms folded over their chests, and their heads cocked to the right. Their body positionings, therefore, are direct carbon copies of each other. It is also possible, however, that they will hold their extremities and heads in homologous rather than identical positions, so that they sit or stand in mirror-imaged postural relationship. (p. 328)

Scheflen called these phenomena 'direct' and 'mirror-image' postural congruence. Scheflen also suggested that old friends who have long-term ties 'sometimes shift into postural congruence at times, whenever they are temporarily arguing or taking opposite sides, as if to indicate the ultimate continuity of their relationship' (Scheflen, 1964, p. 328). When friends argue verbally, they compensate nonverbally by adopting similar postures, so Scheflen says. Unfortunately, Scheflen's work did not involve quantitative analysis of the phenomenon. Detailed quantitative analysis of the role of postural congruence was left to others. Charny (1966), for example, studied postural congruence in an interaction between a therapist and his patient. He found that the interactants spent about one quarter of the total time (555.8 seconds) in mirror-image congruence, most of the rest of the time in a non-congruent configuration (1442.8 seconds), and very little time in direct or identical postural congruence. Somewhat contrary to Scheflen, Charny observed that congruence between a therapist and patient was much more likely when the verbal channel *also* indicated rapport. Charny based his conclusion on a detailed comparison of the linguistic and nonverbal channels. Marianne La France has investigated the relationship between postural congruence and students' self-reports of rapport in the context of college seminars. She found that the higher the degree of direct and mirror-image congruence displayed by the students with respect to the teacher, the higher the ratings of involvement in the seminar (La France and

Broadbent, 1976). In a subsequent study (La France, 1979) she suggested that postural congruence may be influential in establishing rapport.

Beattie and Beattie (1981) set out to determine the levels of postural congruence in male-female pairs and male-male pairs on a beach, where posture is not restricted by items of furniture (23 different postures were in fact observed). The study found that both male-female and male-male pairs showed much higher levels of direct postural congruence than would be expected by chance alone, but that the male-female pairs spent, much more time in postural congruence than the male pairs (53% of the time, compared with 28% of the time for the all-male pairs). One possible explanation of these observations was that postural congruence on a crowded beach acts as a social signal of the bonds between individuals. Other clues to identity and group membership are minimal – proxemic norms may be violated on a crowded beach (you may find yourself seated very close to a complete stranger) and clothing signals are also reduced to a minimum. This might explain the very high levels of postural congruence observed in this context and the fact that male-female pairs showed much higher levels than all-male pairs. Posture and postural congruence is a very obvious, if largely unconscious, signal in social interaction. The pioneers of its study, the psychoanalysts who thought that it might somehow be relevant to the processes of psychotherapy, have in many ways been proven correct. Postural display may be culturally determined, and determined to some extent by sex, but it clearly does display some general principles. Some psychological states and some relationships influence posture in mysterious and largely unconscious, but now perhaps recognisable, ways.

Hand movement and gesture

Human beings seem programmed to display hand movements of various types as they talk. Watch someone making a telephone call and watch how they often display quite elaborate gestures with their free hand. One of the authors has a video-recording of a student talking about spatial arrangements in which both the student's hands were firmly placed below a table and well out of sight of her interlocutor, but nevertheless, elaborate hand gestures were displayed.

There are a number of different classificatory schemes for describing hand movements and gesture. Ekman and Friesen (1969b) distinguished between 'emblems', 'illustrators', 'regulators' and 'adaptors' in the case of hand movement. We have already come across emblems and regulators in the context of head movements. Emblems, you will remember, are those nonverbal acts which have a direct verbal translation, and which may replace or be replaced by a word of spoken dialogue without changing the information conveyed. Generally speaking, emblems are used with full awareness. An example of a gestural emblem would be, for example, the fingertip kiss – 'The tips of the fingers and thumb of the right hand are pressed together and pointed towards the gesturer's own lips. At the same time, the hand is raised towards the lips and the fingertips are lightly kissed. As soon as the kissing movement of the mouth has been made, the hand is tossed lightly forward into the air, the fingers opening out away from one another as this second movement is executed' (Morris, Collett, Marsh and O'Shaughnessy, 1979, p. 2). This is a gestural emblem used in praise most commonly, or in salutation. When it is used as praise, the specific verbal messages reported were 'excellent', 'fantastic', 'fine', 'good', 'great', 'magnificent' etc. When used as salutation, the specific verbal messages were 'greetings', 'hello', 'welcome' etc. This gestural emblem is more than 2,000 years old, having been common in ancient Greece and Rome – the Greeks and Romans threw a kiss towards the image of the deity when entering and leaving temples. The palm-back V-sign (sometimes called the 'Harvey Smith' in England) is another widespread gestural emblem. In England it is commonly used as an insult (its strict verbal translation being 'up yours'), but its predominant meaning in Europe is 'victory' – in England the hand position is reversed to signify this, and great care is taken to distinguish the two. Interestingly, in Europe, the meaning 'two' for the palm-back V-sign is more prevalent than the sexual insult interpretation.

Emblems are just one small subset of the general class of hand movements. Much more common are *illustrators* – hand movements that are directly tied to speech and which illustrate the message content and rhythmically accent or trace ideas. Unlike emblems, illustrators cannot be replaced by a word or phrase. Another difference between emblems and illustrators is that emblems usually fall within the domain of a speaker's awareness while illustrators do not. Morris et al. (1979) put it rather well:

A man is talking excitedly and, as he does so, his arms gesticulate vigorously, beating time to his words and emphasising the points he is making. These illustrators are not performed consciously or deliberately, are largely unidentified and unnamed and are difficult to recall. Ask a man who has just been gesticulating wildly, what movements his hands were making and he will be unable to tell you. He will remember that they *were* moving, but their postures and the shape of their movements will be beyond his power of description.

A second example, this time of an emblematic gesture, differs markedly: a woman crosses a road watched by two young men. One man turns to the other and winks at him; the latter replies by shaking his fingers as if they have been burned by something hot. No word is spoken between them. Here the gestures have replaced speech and, if the young men were asked precisely what gestures they had used, they would be able to recall them and, in the case of the wink, actually name one of them. (p. xvii)

There are many different types of illustrators which we will consider later when we discuss Efron's (1941) classic study of the subject.

Two other types of hand movement distinguished by Ekman and Friesen (1969b) are *regulators* and *adaptors*. We have discussed regulators before in the section on head movements. In the case of hand movements, regulators are particular hand movements which maintain and regulate the back and forth nature of speaking and listening between the interactants. Two specific regulatory functions of hand movements are as an 'attempt-suppression signal' and as a 'turn-yielding signal' (Duncan, 1972, Beattie, 1983). The continuation of hand movement – regardless of form – acts to hold the floor for the current speaker. This is why it is called an 'attempt-suppression signal' – it suppresses listener turn-taking attempts. The termination of a hand movement – regardless of form – acts to hand over the floor to the listener. This is why it is called a 'turn-yielding signal'. Regulators are usually on the very periphery of awareness – a person can perform a regulative act without knowing that he does so, but, if asked, can sometimes recall and repeat it.

The last category of nonverbal behaviour which applies to hand movements is the *adaptor*. There are three types: self-adaptors, alter-adaptors and object-adaptors. An example of a self-adaptor would be the wiping of the corner of the eye with the hands; nose picking, nose rubbing and head scratching. Alter-adaptors are, according to Ekman and Friesen, 'movements necessary to giving to or taking from another person, movements relevant to attacking or protecting oneself from attack, movements necessary to establishing affection and intimacy, or withdrawal and flight' etc. Finally, object-adaptors are movements 'originally learned in the performance of some instrumental task, driving a car, smoking, wielding a tool, etc. This movement will be repeated again only in part during conversations if the emotional or attitudinal component associated with the adaptor is triggered'. People are typically not aware of adaptors and they are rarely intended to communicate.

As with most other classes of nonverbal behaviour, we can ask the question whether the different forms of hand movement are innate or socially learned. In the case of emblems, the answer is clear. Emblems are learned culturally and the meaning may vary from one location to the next, one culture to the next. Anyone who has tried hitch-hiking on the continent using the 'thumb-up' sign will know that there is a widespread possibility of misinterpretation, especially in Greece, where it is a sexual insult symbol rather than a hitch-hiking sign.

In the case of illustrators, the answer is not perhaps so intuitive and straightforward. Illustrators are, after all, generally outside awareness and Cohen (1980) has shown that speakers continue to use illustrators when communicating via an intercom, and even when they are alone talking into a microphone. In other words, illustrators occur even when no decoding function is possible. Emblems obviously would never be used in this way. The classic study of cultural differences in the display of illustrators was carried out by David Efron in 1941. Efron produced a detailed classification of different types of illustrator, the two main types of which were:

1) batons 'representing a sort of "timing-out" with the hand the successive stages of the referential activity', and the

2) ideographic illustrator, a movement that 'traces or sketches out in the air the paths and direction of the thought pattern.'

Efron points out that his distinctions have a noble heritage: some of them date back to Cicero, the Roman writer on the art of oratory: 'For Cicero the real gesture is that kind of movement which expresses the internal *workings* of the mind; an external, natural sign of the "*affectionum animi*", in contrast to the pictorial one which expresses merely the *objects* of thought; the latter he calls "*gestus scenicus*", proper of an actor but unfitting to an orator.'

Efron studied the gestural communication of Jewish and Italian immigrants living in New York City. These included traditional Jews (from the Lower East Side), traditional Italians (from Little Italy), assimilated Jews (from the Saratoga Racetrack and Columbia University), and assimilated Italians (from Columbia University). He summarizes his results as follows:

> Both from the standpoint of number of people gesturing and of frequency and manner of gesticulation in those people who do gesture, the assimilated Eastern Jews and the assimilated Southern Italians in New York City (a) appear to differ greatly from their respective traditional groups and (b) appear to resemble each other.

In other words, there are clear cultural influences in the use of illustrators in conversation.

Eastern Jews and Southern Italians were interesting groups to compare and contrast because of the wide cultural variation between them in the first place. In terms of Efron's classification scheme:

> The 'traditional' Eastern Jew very seldom displays physiographic or symbolic gestures. In contrast to the 'traditional' Southern Italian who . . . is inclined to illustrate gesturally the 'objects' of his thinking activity (the 'referents'), the ghetto Jew is more likely to give a *gestural notation* of the 'process' of that activity, a gestural description of the 'physiognomy', so to say, of his discourse (the 'reference'). To use an analogy, the 'traditional' Jew very rarely employs his arm in the guise of a pencil, to depict the 'things' he is referring to, but uses it often as a pointer, to link one proposition to another, or to trace the itinerary of a logical journey; or else as a baton, to beat the tempo of his mental locomotion. One might say that his gestural movements are related more to the 'how' than to the 'what' of the ideas they re-enact. . . . In contrast to the gestural movements of the 'traditional' Eastern Jew . . . those of the 'traditional' southern Italian contain a rather fair number of *physiographic* forms, and betray, on the other hand, a relatively marked scarcity in ideographic ones. The gestures of the Italian appear to be related more to the objective content of discourse than to its logical trajectory.

Efron points out that some of the specific illustrators found among the traditional Southern Italians date back to ancient Rome; they can be found in Quintilian's descriptions of Roman oratorical gestures. Nevertheless, the process of cultural assimilation, as found in Efron's sample of assimilated Jews and Italians, can radically change the frequency and nature of the illustrators displayed.

Regulators and adaptors are also probably culturally learned. There is also wide individual variation in the use of hand movements as regulators (see Beattie, 1983 p. 104). In Italy, listeners may actually take hold of a speaker's arm in order to attempt to gain control of the floor. Such behaviour is not common in England. Similarly, self-adaptors and object-adaptors may be more extreme and more common in some cultures than others.

Hand movement and gesture is a class of nonverbal behaviour closely tied with speech, but as we have seen, it is a very heterogeneous group of behaviours whose specific connection with verbal language varies from category to category. Some hand movements we use with full awareness and we can even name them, some are beyond awareness and we could not even begin to describe them (or at least this is true of the lay person). Interest in hand movement is not new, but it has taken 2,000 years to untangle this complex form of behaviour. In later chapters we will see how the advent of film and video-recording and of slow motion analysis made it possible to finally uncover some aspects of its true nature.

4 The language channel

One of the central themes of this book is that language is best understood as one of a set of human channels of communication. Its natural context is the give-and-take of information between two or more individuals in conversation, and in that context it interacts in subtle and sophisticated ways with those other channels. But the language channel is in some ways special – it is the most highly developed channel of human communication, and the one whose possession makes the largest difference between human beings and other animals.

'Language' is a vast subject matter. It can be studied from many different perspectives and for many different purposes. The student of literature may value language as an aesthetic object and study its deployment by great poets, playwrights and novelists. The engineer, on the other hand, may be interested in the properties of the speech signal from the point of view of optimizing its transmission down a wire or as a radio wave. The philosopher's concern may be with how language helps or hinders the expression of true or false statements, while the sociologist may want to know how language distinguishes social groups one from another, and maintains group identity. The list could go on. In this book we must focus only on certain aspects of language and ignore many perfectly legitimate perspectives. We shall have little to say about the aesthetic properties of language, the physics of the speech wave or the discrimination of true from false statements. The more social aspects of language are dealt with at length in other chapters. This chapter will limit itself to the study of the properties and features of language itself.

The linguist Noam Chomsky, whose influential ideas on language we shall encounter later in this chapter and elsewhere in the book, has argued that academic disciplines like 'linguistics', 'sociology', 'psychology' or 'philosophy' may be convenient fictions for some purposes (e.g., administering universities or organising libraries), but are a positive hindrance when it comes to understanding language (Chomsky, 1972a). We wholeheartedly agree that attempts to fissure language along discipline lines has done as much harm as good. If we are to understand language and communication we must be prepared to garner insights from any source and cross freely across discipline frontiers. In the case of language, much of the important work has been done within the discipline of linguistics. We shall accordingly spend some time now examining the view from linguistics, seeing how ideas about language have changed down the years, and noting how those ideas have percolated out of linguistics to influence the way psychologists have thought about what language is, what we do with it, and what it does to us. We shall include in our survey a look at questions of language origins and evolution, and at the impact of Chomsky's ideas and those of earlier theorists (Edward Sapir and Benjamin Lee Whorf) who held that the language you speak exerts a powerful influence on the way you conceive of the physical world of objects and events.

Language: the view from linguistics

Early days

Language has always been an object of central concern within the Western intellectual tradition. We owe the categories of 'noun', 'verb', 'adjective' and so on, along with concepts like gender, tense, number and case, to ancient Greek scholars including Plato (c.429–347 BC) and Aristotle (384–322 BC). The great Christian scholar Erasmus published a grammar of Latin in 1513. Seventeenth-century French grammarians produced 'rational' grammars designed to emphasize similarities between different languages, and argued that languages are simply varieties of a universal logic and rationality – an idea which has been revived in recent times by Chomsky and others (see Chomsky, 1966).

But linguistics really came of age in the 19th century in the hands of scholars whose principle concern was with the *history* of language. From old books and manuscripts they were able to see how languages have changed down the years. They also noted how languages could be classified into groups based, for example, on the extent to which they shared the same or similar words for the same thing. They then argued that all languages in a group had in fact evolved from a common ancestor which they attempted to recreate by extrapolation from known changes and what were thought to be universal 'laws' of language change (see Chapter 5). Incidentally, this group of scholars included among its number one Jacob Grimm (1785–1863), better known today as the co-collector with his brother Wilhelm of traditional German folk stories – 'Grimm's fairy-tales'.

In the course of their work the German historical linguists articulated and debated rival views of language which still echo among us today. When developing their laws of language change earlier linguists argued that language could be studied as an external object with an existence of its own that is independent of the community of language users. Later radical 'neogrammarians' opposed this view. Osthoff and Brugman (1878) maintained that:

> Language is not a thing, standing outside and above men and leading its own life, but has its true existence only in the individual, and that therefore all changes in the life of a language can originate only with individual speakers.

Herman Paul in his much-used textbook, *Prinzipien der Sprach- geschichte* (1880), held the same view, writing:

> All psychic processes are executed in individual minds and nowhere else. Neither race-mind nor elements of race-mind such as art, religion etc. have a concrete existence, and consequently nothing can occur in them or between them. So away with these abstractions.

This debate is very much alive today. Some linguists, such as Katz (1981), wish to treat language as an abstract object to be studied as a body of words and possible sentences entirely divorced from the mental processes which go to create them in the first place. Other linguists, and all psycholinguists, are interested in precisely those mental processes. Like the neogrammarians they see language as the product of human cognitive operations which it is their job to uncover and describe (e.g., Clark and Clark, 1977; Foss and Hakes, 1978; Moulton and Robinson, 1981). For our part we consider both approaches legitimate, but are only interested in the second one.

Mathematicians (rightly) believe that they can study properties of the number system without concerning themselves with what happens inside a person's head when they reckon up the cost of the week's shopping. Similarly, linguists can, if they wish, treat every language as an abstract system, as if its speakers were the lost race of a dead planet, but their theories will then only be constrained by notions like simplicity or elegance, and their eventual descriptions of language may have little to teach the more psychologically-minded; we *do* want to know what happens inside people's heads when they talk, listen, write or read, so we are on the side of the neogrammarians.

Not surprisingly, the doctrine of evolution put forward by Charles Darwin in his *Origin of Species* (1859) had a major influence on 19th-century linguistics. No longer content with recreating the proto-language from which a particular family of languages had evolved, linguists now applied their minds to issues concerning the ultimate origins of language in human prehistory. Then, as now, this enterprise was perforce largely speculative – language leaves no fossil record – but that did not prevent the proliferation of imaginative and often fanciful theories concerning language origins.

One of the more interesting lines of speculation concerned the possibility that gestural sign language may have evolved before a switch occurred to the vocal channel of communication. Wilhelm Wundt, founder of the first ever psychological laboratory, con-sidered this a serious possibility, and noted in the course of an extensive study of gestural communication the use of gestures by pre-verbal infants. This, he felt, could be taken as an indicator of gesture's more primitive nature (Wundt, 1921/1973). The switch to an auditory signal (speech) as opposed to a visual signal (gesture), if it occurred, could be quite plausibly 'explained' by noting the difficulty of communicating by sign in dark caves or signing whilst holding tools or weapons. Although there can be no archaeology of speech, Philip Lieberman (e.g., 1979, 1981) has gone close in first of all attempting to reconstruct details of the vocal tracts of our prehistoric ancestors, and then trying to determine what range of sounds their possessors would have been capable of producing. According to Lieberman, Cro-Magnon Man, who died out some 35,000 years ago, could have managed only a very limited repertoire of sounds. In contrast, his contemporary, Neanderthal Man, probably had the potential to produce a much wider range. Did

Neanderthal Man negotiate the transition from gestural to vocal communication? Is this why he prospered while Cro-Magnon Man died out? Or was the Paris Société de Linguistique right in 1866 to ban any discussion of language evolution as inescapably speculative, and was Whitney (1870) on target when he wrote of the subject: 'No theme in linguistic science has been more often and more voluminously treated than this, and by scholars of every grade and tendency; nor any, it may be added, with less profitable result in proportion to the labour expended.'? We shall return to the relation between speech and gesture in later chapters, but our brief flirtation with the ultimate origins of language will rest here.

Ferdinand de Saussure

Linguistics' next major step forward occurred at the hands of Ferdinand de Saussure (1857–1913). After working for much of his life in the historical tradition, he developed a new framework in a succession of courses taught at the University of Geneva between 1906 and 1911. He died in 1913 without having published any of his new ideas, but fortunately two of his colleagues, Charles Bally and Albert Sechehaye, gathered together Saussure's own notes and those taken by students during his lectures and were able to reconstruct and publish the *Cours de linguistique générale* in 1916, so preserving Saussure's ideas for posterity.

In opposition to all that had gone before, Saussure argued that we must make a clear and firm distinction between the historical development of language, and language as it exists at any moment in historical time. Although individual speakers play a part in language change they do not carry the history of language around in their heads – they know only the language they presently speak. Saussure argued that there must exist two separate forms of linguistics: *diachronic linguistics*, concerned with language history and language change, and *synchronic linguistics*, concerned with language as it exists at any moment in time, including the present. This distinction liberated linguists from an obsessive dwelling on the past, and paved the way for the sort of linguistics (and psycholinguistics) that is dominant today.

Another of Saussure's distinctions is important and of continuing relevance. 'Language', he argued, 'is not complete in any speaker; it exists perfectly only within a collectivity.' Sampson (1980) draws an analogy with the legal system to explain this assertion. In a society like ours everyone knows some of the laws, but no-one knows all of them. Yet it makes sense to talk of a 'legal system' as an abstract thing which is but imperfectly reflected in the mind and behaviour of any one person. Saussure used the term *langue* to denote the analogous abstract 'language system', echoing in the process the views of those German linguists whom the 'neo-grammarians' had opposed. What any one of us speaks is *parole* – talk in which *langue* is but reflected.

There is, of course, much else in Saussure's *Cours*, but the two distinctions we have briefly alluded to – synchronic/diachronic and *langue/parole* – are the ones whose influence is still felt most strongly today.

Language moulds thought: descriptive linguistics and the 'linguistic relativity hypothesis'

Franz Boas (1858–1942) was an almost exact contemporary of Saussure. His training and his influence on linguistics were, however, very different, because Boas was trained not as a linguist but as an anthropologist. Born in Westphalia (now part of West Germany), Boas moved to the USA in the late 1880s. There he began to work on the cultures, and the languages, of North American Indians. This was an urgent task. Indian numbers had been reduced by wars, maltreatment and the introduction of European diseases to which they had no immunity. Additionally, many Indians were moving off the reservations into towns and cities, and their children were growing up native speakers of English rather than of their ancestral tongue. A major research programme, with Boas as its figurehead, was launched in an attempt to capture and describe these strange unwritten languages before many of them disappeared forever (Boas, 1911).

And they *were* strange languages – to Western ears. What could be more natural to speakers of English and other European languages than to distinguish between past tense ('I read the book'), present tense ('I am reading the book'), and future tense ('I shall read the book')? Past, present, future – surely all languages would make such a distinction? Well, the language of the Hopi Indians of Arizona turned out not to. Hopi listeners must use the context of what is being said to infer the time of occurrence. Although Hopi has no grammatical device for marking past, present and future it does make an obligatory three-fold distinction between 1) statements of general timeless truths ('Mountains are high'), 2) reports of known or presumably known happenings ('I came here yesterday'), and 3) events still in the realm of uncertainty, including, but not only, future events ('I shall be leaving tomorrow'). The language of the Kwakiutl Indians also does not mark time of action, but it is obligatory to indicate by word endings (inflections) whether or not the speaker personally witnessed the reported action. (Boas observed how excellent it would be if newspaper reporters were forced to use the same system!).

Such striking differences between languages in how they treat apparently fundamental notions such as time impressed linguists, causing some of them to ask whether these patterns did not induce radically different conceptualisations of the world – of objects, time, and space – in their speakers. Edward Sapir wrote:

> It is quite an illusion to imagine that one adjusts to reality essentially without the use of language and that language is merely an incidental means of solving specific problems of communication or reflection. The fact of the matter is that the 'real world' is to a large extent unconsciously built up on the language habits of the group . . . The worlds in which different societies live are distinct worlds, not merely the same world with different labels attached. (Sapir, 1929, p. 209)

Benjamin Lee Whorf, who was originally a fire insurance inspector, but a student of language and culture in his spare time, endorsed and developed Sapir's ideas. Whorf later devoted himself to the full-time study of different cultures, and tried to connect aspects of the way members of a culture think to their language. He took many of his examples from the Hopi Indians, comparing them with speakers of what he called 'Standard Average European' (e.g. English, French or German). It was through his professional work for the fire insurance company that he first came across instances of language affecting behaviour. Whorf discovered that many fires were attributable to careless behaviour by people in the vicinity of 'empty' petrol drums. The problem was that the drums were not empty (i.e. null and void; negative; inert) but rather were full of invisible but dangerous explosive vapour. Whorf points out that we use the term 'empty' in two different ways in English: (1) as a virtual synonym of 'null and void; negative; inert;' and (2) in certain physical situations, without regard to trivial remaining fragments, vapour, etc. A drum may be described as 'empty' despite a few droplets lingering in the bottom or clinging to the sides. Whorf reasoned that the careless behaviour of otherwise intelligent people around petrol drums occurred because they reacted to the drums as if they were 'empty' in the first sense as well as in the second. A costly mistake for them – and for Whorf's company! Thus Whorfianism was born.

In English, words connected with time (of day or year) are nouns, e.g. summer, winter, September, morning, noon. In Hopi they are not. According to Whorf the nearest 'Standard Average European' (S.A.E.) equivalent for the Hopi words is a kind of adverb. In English temporal terms are treated like other nouns – they can be subjects or objects of sentences; they can be pluralized and numerated. Whorf argued that because of this, 'Our thoughts about the referents of such words hence became objectified. Without objectification it would be a subjective experience of real time, i.e. of the consciousness of "becoming later and later" – simply a cyclic phase similar to an earlier phase in that ever-later-becoming duration' (Whorf, 1941). In the case of Hopi, Whorf argued that because temporal terms are not nouns this (illusory) objectification does not occur and 'Nothing is suggested about time except the perpetual "getting late" of it'.

Whorf then attempted to link this linguistic difference to differences in the habitual behaviours of the two cultures. The behavioural difference he focussed on was the emphasis on *preparation* prevalent in Hopi culture and much less important in our own. Preparation in Hopi culture included announcing and getting ready for events well beforehand, taking elaborate precautions to ensure the persistence of desired conditions, and emphasizing the importance of goodwill for the achievement of the right results. In their preparation there is according to Whorf 'an emphasis on persistence and constant insistent repetition'. Whorf reasoned that 'To the Hopi, for whom time is not a motion but a "getting later" of everything that has ever been done, unvarying repetition is not wasted but accumulated. It is storing up an invisible change that holds over into later events' (Whorf, 1941).

Whorf attempted to connect language and behaviour in order to show the important influence language has on the way we perceive and conceptualize the world we inhabit. The hypothesis that the language we speak strongly influences the way we think came to be known as the 'linguistic relativity hypothesis' (or the 'Sapir-Whorf hypothesis'), and the general perspective as 'Whorfianism'. The main point to be noted here is the extremely hazardous nature of the whole enterprise. How can we know that Hopi language influences Hopi thought rather than the other way round? Or perhaps features of the culture independently affect both. Would a Hopi linguist conclude that because all nouns in French are either masculine or feminine, all French speakers believe that objects are themselves imbued with masculinity or femininity? How can we gain evidence that will allow us to assess the linguistic relativity hypothesis?

Various attempts have been made to put the linguistic relativity hypothesis to scientific test. One tradition expertly and amusingly reviewed by Brown (1979) looked to see whether people's perception and/or memory for colours varied according to how many colour terms their language has, and how those terms divide up the spectrum. Despite early results which looked promising to the linguistic relativity hypothesis, the final conclusion seems negative. Speakers of languages with only two basic colour terms apparently perceive and conceptualize colours in just the same way as speakers of languages with ten or eleven basic colour terms. In Heider's (1972) assessment, '. . . far from being a domain well suited to the study of the effects of language on thought, the colour space would seem to be prime examples of the influence of underlying perceptual-cognitive factors on the formation and reference of linguistic categories'.

More promising to the hypothesis is Bloom's (1981) work on language and thinking in China and the West. Bloom notes that in English 'a dog' refers to any dog, while 'the dog' can refer either to a particular dog mentioned earlier or to the *general class* of dogs ('The dog is man's best friend'). Similarly when an English speaker moves from talking about 'his success' or 'her success' to talking about 'success' in general ('Success breeds arrogance') there is again a switch from particular instances to the general, abstract concept. According to Bloom the traditional Chinese language lacks these sorts of devices for moving from specific exemplars to general concepts, and he claims that this difference is mirrored in the characteristic Western and Chinese modes of thought. Thus he quotes a Chinese professor from Taiwan National University as commenting: 'You know, English has a whole complex of ways of talking, and hence thinking, on an abstract, theoretical level, which Chinese doesn't have. We speak and think more directly.' Bloom holds these differences in ways of thinking responsible for differences in the general style of Western and Chinese philosophy, religion, mathematics and science, and demonstrates experimentally differences between Chinese and English speakers in their approach to, and success with, abstract logical problems.

But as Bloom notes, there is an issue of causality here. Sapir and Whorf would presumably have wanted to say that the properties of the Chinese language have shaped the Chinese way of thinking. The reverse, however, is also possible – the Chinese way of thinking may have shaped the Chinese language. This, in fact, is the alternative Bloom prefers, remarking that, 'From a historical point of view, languages are much more the products of their cultures than the determiners of them.' In support of this claim he notes how, under the impact of Western ways of thinking, the Chinese language is beginning to develop grammatical devices for distinguishing abstract concepts from particular instances. In support of a conclusion similar to Bloom's, Sampson (1980) quotes the German philosopher J. G. Hamann as having written in 1760, 'a mind which thinks at its own expense will always interfere with language'.

Though many descriptive linguists stopped short of the sweeping claims of Sapir and Whorf, they were all deeply impressed with the sheer variety of languages they discovered. They became understandably suspicious of assertions regarding 'language universals' or 'innate propensities'. This tendency was accentuated when Leonard Bloomfield, a leader of the school, declared himself a born-again Behaviourist. Behaviourism was an approach to psychology which dominated the discipline in the United States from the 1920s to the early 1960s and which forbad any mention whatsoever of inner mental processes, including linguistic intuitions, and insisted on dealing only with externally observable facts. As the slogan of the day quoted by Sampson (1980) ran, 'Accept everything a native speaker says in his language, and nothing he says about it.'

But to every such dogmatism there comes in time an equal and opposite reaction. And the reaction when it came was dramatic.

Chomsky and modern linguistics

In the winter of 1969–1970 the Institute of Contemporary Arts in London organised a series of lectures on 'Linguistics at Large'. Fairly recondite, one would have thought: alright for dedicated scholars and the odd member of the public at a loose end and wanting to get out of the cold for an hour or two. But no. Tickets were sold out way in advance. Extra seats had to be placed on the rostrum, and lecturers found themselves addressing packed audiences. That would not have happened ten years earlier. The reason for that sudden upsurge of interest in linguistics was one man.

Avram Noam Chomsky was born in 1928 into a Jewish family of Russian origins and politically radical views. Politics has remained an enduring interest of Chomsky's – he was, for example, influential in the anti-Vietnam war movement. Chomsky's prolific output on political themes would more than satisfy many academics (e.g., Chomsky, 1969, 1973); yet for him it is almost a second string – a committed hobby. For Chomsky is also Professor of Linguistics at the Massachusetts Institute of Technology, where he has worked since 1955, and it is his linguistic thought that concerns us here.

It is important to note from the outset that Chomsky is not a scholar like Saussure whose ideas are all encapsulated in one volume to which one can turn to discover what he thought about X. Chomsky's ideas are, and always have been, in continuous evolution. The details of his theories have changed considerably from his first and highly influential book *Syntactic Structures* (1957) to more recent works like *Reflections on Language* (1976) or *Rules and Representations* (1980). This creates problems for the expositor. What we shall try to do here is give the reader some feel for the general flavour of Chomsky's theories, avoiding technicalities as much as possible, and highlighting those aspects which have been most influential in psycholinguistics.

Creativity rules: Chomsky first came to the notice of psychologists when he published a highly critical review of a book on language by the Behaviourist B. F. Skinner (*Verbal Behaviour*, 1957). Skinner had argued that utterances should be viewed as learned responses to specific situations. In reply Chomsky (1959) claimed – and no-one has seriously disputed since – that the majority of utterances we produce are ones we have never spoken in precisely that form before, and that the majority of utterances we hear and comprehend without difficulty are ones we have never heard before. We do not need to haggle over the absolute proportions of new to old sentences spoken in order to establish the basic point that assembling and decoding novel sentences creates no problems for the language user. We do not even need to invent bizarre sentences like *My aunt's hippo adores missionaries* to prove this point. We bet you cannot find precisely this sentence in any book you have ever read, and we also bet you have never heard it spoken before, yet it is perfectly intelligible (isn't it?).

Chomsky lays great emphasis on the *creativity* of language; and creativity, he argues, can only be explained if we credit speakers not with a repertoire of learned responses but with a repertoire of linguistic *rules* used to generate or interpret sentences. The body of rules constitutes the *grammar* of the language – their job is to assemble or describe grammatical sentences, and only grammatical sentences. Because the rules generate rather than simply describe sentences, this type of grammar is known as a *generative grammar*.

Many people, influenced perhaps by dim memories of studying 'grammar' at school, may think that a linguist's rules will be rules that tell you how you *ought* to speak. In fact, linguists take a different view. They are not interested in enshrining and preserving 'the language' as some sacred (abstract) object to be protected from defilement by mere speakers. If the intuitions of a speaker of Black English tell him or her that 'Ain't you is a hag' is an acceptable, well-structured sentence, then the grammar proposed by a linguist for speakers of that dialect must be able to generate such sentences. They may be ungrammatical in the linguist's particular dialect, but that is unimportant. The job of linguistics is to describe how people speak, not prescribe how they ought to speak. This attitude of 'descriptive not prescriptive' is not new in linguistics: Fromkin and Rodman (1974) quote the English grammarian John Fell as having written back in 1784, 'It is certainly the business of a grammarian to find out, and not to make, the laws of language'.

Competence, performance and intuition: How should one set about establishing the 'laws of language' as it is actually used? Well you could set off down the street with your portable cassette recorder under your arm and record some real, down-to-earth, as-it-happens talk. But when you came back to the quiet of your room and began searching for laws you would find that your newly-acquired material presented many problems. Speech as it happens is replete with false starts, hesitations, errors which the speaker freely acknowledges as errors, interruptions, and so on – all in all, pretty unpromising stuff for the would-be diviner of laws. To circumvent this problem Chomsky argues that beneath the corrupt *performance* of language there lurks a purer, undefiled language *competence* (note the echoes of Saussure's distinction between *parole* and *langue*). Competence is tapped, not by getting speakers to speak, but by asking them to *judge whether strings of words are grammatical or not*. (Actually Chomskyan linguists usually short-circuit this process by making the grammaticality judgements themselves – a practice which has not gone uncriticized).

For Chomsky, then, the laws of language are to be erected upon the body of sentences native speakers are (supposedly) willing to accept as grammatical. Note that you can be persuaded to accept as grammatical a sentence you would never dream of actually saying, either because of all its grammaticality it is nonsensical (e.g. 'Opaque purple linguists theorize damply') or because it is too complex for the human mind to unravel (e.g. 'The sociologist the linguist the psychologist hated tickled laughed' which, if we've got it right, is a grammatical but hyper-complex way of saying 'The psychologist hated the linguist who tickled the sociologist who laughed.').

Deep and surface structures: So according to Chomsky a linguist tries to explain competence as assessed through judgements of grammaticality without making value judgements about the 'correctness' of a speaker's intuitions. The laws when formulated constitute a grammar which is a set of rules capable of generating grammatical sentences and only grammatical sentences. However, Chomsky makes a further demand of a grammar. He argues that it must additionally explain why speakers feel some sentences to be 'related' and others 'unrelated'. The following four sentences are all rather different in form yet speakers accept them as closely related:

1 'Charles proposed to Diana.'
2 'Did Charles propose to Diana?'
3 'Diana was proposed to by Charles.'
4 'Was Diana proposed to by Charles?'

In contrast, two sentences may be identical in form yet feel very different, for example:

5 'Henry is difficult to wash'.
6 'Henry is reluctant to wash.'

In (5) Henry is on the receiving end of the wash whereas in (6) he is the one doing the washing. Similarly, to adapt one of Chomsky's oft-quoted examples, 'William is easy to please' and 'William is eager to please', have similar surface structures but do not feel closely related because in the former William is the one being pleased whereas in the latter he is the one doing the pleasing.

Chomsky's solution to this dilemma is to propose that every sentence must be given *two* grammatical descriptions. The *surface structure* of a sentence is its description as produced, but underlying that is a separate *deep structure*. Sentences (1) to (4) concerning Charles and Diana have different surface structures but the same deep structure, and that, Chomsky argues, is why they are felt to be closely related. In contrast, sentences (5) and (6) about Henry's attitude to washing have the same surface structure but different deep structures and are therefore felt to be but distantly related (like the two sentences about pleasing William).

Distinguishing deep and surface structure carried another advantage for Chomsky. Suppose you read in a newspaper that 'Charles likes polo more than Diana.' What do you conclude? Well, you could conclude that Charles likes polo more than he likes Diana. But there is another possible interpretation – that Charles likes polo more than Diana does. The original sentence is *ambiguous* – it lends itself to more than one interpretation. Another example might be 'Striking miners can be dangerous' which can be interpreted in at least three ways – as 'Miners who are on strike can be dangerous' or 'It can be dangerous to strike miners' or 'Miners who are striking (in appearance) can be dangerous'. (N.B. As spoken this is ambiguous six ways, since 'miners' is a homophone of 'minors'. One can probably think of yet more construals based on the analogy with 'Striking matches can be dangerous', but we prefer to stop here.) For Chomsky ambiguous sentences are ambiguous because they permit two or more different deep structures, one related to each interpretation. Readers should be clear, however, that a deep structure is not a representation of the meaning of a sentence, but rather a description of a sentence's underlying grammatical (syntactic) structure.

Transformational grammar in action: In a book like this we can do no more than to give the reader a flavour of Chomskyan transformational grammar. The form of grammar we shall illustrate is the form which most influenced psycholinguistic research, namely an amalgam of the ideas presented in *Syntactic Structures* (1957) and *Aspects of the Theory of Syntax* (1965). Greene (1972) and

Aitchison (1983) provide more detailed, but still accessible, accounts of the influence of TG on psycholinguistic research, and Smith (1979) and Smith and Wilson (1979) review more recent developments in linguistic theory with an eye to their possible psychological implications.

Consider the sentence 'Henry was washed by Charles.' What sort of a derivation would be given for that sentence? First of all we must build a deep structure. The deep structure, remember, must express the felt relatedness of 'Henry was washed by Charles' to 'Charles washed Henry', 'Did Charles wash Henry?', 'Henry was not washed by Charles,' and so on. In fact the deep structure is closest to the simplest of this family of sentences – 'Charles washed Henry'. To build the required deep structure we begin, as we always must, with the symbol S for Sentence. We expand that into NP for Noun Phrase and VP for Verb Phrase:

$S \rightarrow NP + VP$.

The Noun Phrase is a single Noun in this instance ('Charles') though in other sentences it could be more expansive (e.g. 'The dashing young Prince of Wales'):

$NP \rightarrow N$

$N \rightarrow$ 'Charles'.

The Verb Phrase of the original NP + VP expands into verb (V) plus another Noun Phrase:

$VP \rightarrow V + NP$.

The Verb is 'wash' in the Past Tense, which is represented in the deep structure as Auxilliary (PAST) + Verb 'wash':

$V \rightarrow Aux + V$

$Aux \rightarrow PAST$

$V \rightarrow$ 'wash'

The final Noun Phrase is again but a single noun 'Henry', though it too could be more expansive (e.g. 'his wriggly second son'):

$NP \rightarrow N$

$N \rightarrow$ 'Henry'

The rules which generate deep structures are called 'base' or 'phrase-structure' rules. The term 'rewrite rules' describes the sort of rules they are – rules which take a symbol and expand, or rewrite it. As an alternative format to a list of such rules we can express the growth of a deep structure as a 'tree' which neatly captures the relatedness of the elements in the deep structure. The tree 'grows' from top to bottom in the order specified by the phrase-structure rules, for example:

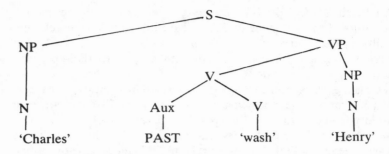

To get beyond the deep structure and generate a speakable sentence, *transformational rules* must be applied. The sentence which could be created by the fewest rules is 'Charles washed Henry', but that is not our goal. Our goal is the passive sentence 'Henry was washed by Charles'. To generate it we apply a set of optional transformational rules. These operate upon the deep structure tree to create the desired surface structure. Different optional transformations would turn our deep structure into the surface structures of other related sentences ('Did Charles wash Henry?', 'Was Henry not washed by Charles?' and so on).

According to which version of TG you subscribe to the *semantic component* which interprets the meaning of the sentence interacts with either the deep structure alone or the deep structure and the surface structure. The phonological component includes a word store (the lexicon) and knowledge of the sound system of your language. It plugs the desired words, represented as strings of phonemes (individual consonants and vowels), into the surface structure, creating a description of the sentence which could serve as input to articulatory processes.

That, in brief and with much fudging and simplification, is a generative, transformational grammar. When first proposed by Chomsky this description of language took linguistics by storm and fired the public imagination. Deep and surface structures were everywhere – in sociology, in theology, in music and art and architecture. Psychologists looking for relief from the suffocating strictures of Behaviourism fell upon Chomsky's ideas. In no time at all TG was being put forward as a model of how we speak and comprehend sentences. Many illustrious figures in psycholinguistics made their names by exploring the consequences of imputing psychological reality to TG. There is much to be learned from charting the territory covered in the course of that exploration.

The psychological reality of transformational grammar: Did Chomsky intend TG to be taken as a literal model of what happens inside a speaker's head when a sentence is produced or comprehended? That is a moot point. On page 9 of *Aspects of the Theory of Syntax* (1965) Chomsky writes: 'When we say that a sentence has a certain derivation with respect to a particular generative grammar, we say nothing about how the speaker or hearer might proceed, in some practical or efficient way, to construct such a derivation.' This seems to deny any necessary psychological reality to his grammar, but further down the very same page Chomsky describes the aim of a generative grammar as being:

> to characterise in the most neutral possible terms the knowledge of the language that provides the basis for actual language use by a speaker-hearer . . . No doubt, a reasonable model of language use will incorporate, as a basic component, the generative grammar that expresses the speaker-hearer's knowledge of the language.

Statements by Chomsky in this latter vein inspired psycholinguists who sought to prove that 'the sequence of rules used in the grammatical derivation of a sentence . . . corresponds step by step to the sequence of psychological processes that are executed when a person processes the sentence' (Hayes, 1970, p. 5). Much of this research was founded upon the so-called 'derivational theory of complexity'. This theory held that transforming deep structures into surface structures or vice-versa takes time and effort, and that a sentence which requires several transformational operations to recover its deep structure will take longer to comprehend, and/or be harder to memorize, than a less transformationally complex sentence. As so often happens, early results looked promising. The time necessary to convert one type of sentence into another seemed proportional to the number of transformations that had to be applied (Miller and McKean, 1964). Complex sentences seemed harder to recall than simpler ones (Savin and Perchonock, 1965) with errors tending towards transformational simplicity (Mehler, 1963). Complex sentences took longer than simple ones to judge as true or false in relation to a picture (Gough, 1965, 1966; Slobin, 1966), and so on.

But later research, combined with some deeper thought about what was actually being assumed by the derivational theory of complexity, served to dispel the early optimism. Wason (1965) showed that despite its greater complexity a negative sentence could be responded to faster than a positive one if it was being used in a natural way, to correct a false assertion. Johnson-Laird and Stevenson (1970) found that subjects were likely to confuse in memory pairs of sentences whose meanings were similar, but whose deep and surface structures were quite different (e.g. 'John liked the painting and bought it from the duchess' versus 'The painting pleased John and the duchess sold it to him'. Fodor and Garrett (1966) pointed out that the derivational theory of complexity was founded upon the highly implausible (and demonstrably false) assumption that listeners do not begin to process a sentence until it is finished. Similarly, when a generative grammar seeks to assemble a sentence, it begins with a single abstract S symbol, unpacks it into a sentence frame, and only then slots in particular words corresponding to particular meanings. As a psychological theory that is nonsensical. Speakers do not first assemble a sentence frame then decide what to say with it; rather they begin with a message that they wish to communicate. That message is itself structured, and the structure of the initial conceptual representation shapes and determines the structure of the final sentence which, in acoustic form, is to act as the communicative signal.

Once structured conceptual (message) representations are admitted into your theory, much of the original motivation for separating deep and surface syntactic structures disappears. Sentences which are 'felt to be related' will have similar or identical conceptual descriptions, rather than similar or identical deep structures. Sentences similar in surface form but not intuitively related will have distinct conceptual descriptions. Ambiguous sentences will be interpretable in terms of two distinct messages, and so on.

Gradually psycholinguists stopped trying to attribute transformational grammars to listeners, but they had learned much in the course of their flirtation with generative grammar. They came to realize that while it may be valid for a linguist to embrace competence and eschew performance, a psycholinguist *must* be interested in performance. A generative grammar can run amok producing infinitely long, infinitely complex and entirely nonsensical sentences. Real speakers would, like as not, be confined indefinitely for producing such jargon (unless perhaps they were contract lawyers or Pentagon spokesmen).

Psycholinguists need grammars that will generate only sensible, comprehensible, contextually relevant utterances. In pursuing such goals they have discovered that the very aspect of performance shunned by theoretical linguists – such things as hesitations and involuntary slips of the tongue – in fact provide key insights into language processes (see Chapter 7).

Domains and units of language

For all its changes of fashion and approach linguistics has contributed much to our understanding of language. In particular it has provided us with a *vocabulary* for talking about language. If you are learning about how cars work there is a vocabulary of terms you must master. The same applies if you are learning about cookery, or wines, or biology, or astronomy. Detailed, scientific analysis of an area often requires one to create terms with technical meanings not required in everyday discourse, though such terms can, in the wrong hands, become a device for surrounding a subject with a pseudo-scientific aura. We shall try hard to avoid mere jargon, but a few linguistic terms really are essential and we shall find ourselves using them time and again.

The terms we should like the reader to grow accustomed to, and eventually feel at home with, are terms relating to *domains* and *units* of language. The domains issue relates to different *types* of knowledge necessary for effective language use. We have encountered most of these already, but will pause now to draw together what we have learned.

Syntax is concerned with sentence structure and how that structure is expressed in sentence form. It traditionally pays no attention to the meanings of words or sentences, but seeks to capture the rules a sentence must obey for a speaker to accept it as grammatically correct, even though it may be nonsensical. Syntax is as at home with Jabberwocky ('Twas brillig and the slithy toves did gyre and gimble in the wabe . . .') as it is with natural utterances. So the devices for indicating what is the subject of a sentence and what the object (e.g. word order and inflection) belong in syntax, as do rules for assembling different types of sentence, for embedding or conjoining clauses, for expressing agreement of number, or tense, or gender etc. – are all aspects of syntax.

Semantics deals with the meanings of words and of sentences. A semantic theory must explain how we identify two sentences as having the same meaning though they may employ different words, different syntax, and even be in different languages. It must explain why some sentences are perceived as self-contradictory ('That bachelor is happily married') and why a sentence like 'Colourless green ideas sleep furiously', for all its grammaticality, is anomalous nonsense. Semantics must explain why one sentence logically entails another – why 'Charles washed Henry' entails 'Charles washed somebody'. Issues of meaning, entailment, reference and sense make up the domain of semantics. It is a domain which has received renewed attention following a period of comparative neglect in the heyday of transformational grammar.

Pragmatics is another domain that linguists rescued from neglect when they began to ask *why* we utter one sentence rather than another in a particular situation. For a generative grammarian 'John hit the ball' and 'The ball was hit by John' are merely two different surface manifestations of the same deep structure. But the circumstances under which we would utter the one or the other are different. Specifically, passive sentences are normally used to contradict a prior statement or belief:

'Sam, you hit this ball through the window, didn't you?'

'No, sir. The ball was hit by John.'

Gazdar (1980) lists several other pragmatic aspects of language use. For example, in a bilingual situation, social or even political considerations may affect the choice of language. Word choice may similarly be under pragmatic influence: Moroccan Arabic has two words for 'needle' – one for use in the morning and the other for use in the afternoon (Gazdar, 1983). Conversational rules which instruct a speaker to be relevant, concise and truthful may also be viewed as pragmatic influences (see Chapter 9). The list could be extended almost indefinitely. Linguists of some schools may wish to deny that pragmatic issues are the proper concern of linguistics, but they are clearly important to anyone seeking to explain normal, natural language use.

Discourse. Syntax stops at the sentence level, but there are things to be said about how sentences combine into text. These are the concern of *discourse analysis*. For example, the formality of a text will affect the words and sentence types people use, as will the function of the text (whether it is journalism, literature, conversation, etc.). Devices for cross-referencing between sentences and for structuring them into coherent 'paragraph' units create cohesion and continuity in a text. They are all aspects of discourse to which one's attention is drawn when one looks above the sentence at the creation of text, either by one speaker or writer in a monologue, or by two participants in a conversation.

Morphology, phonology and phonetics. Discourse analysis deals with paragraphs and texts. Syntax deals with sentences, clauses, phrases and words defined in terms of classes such as noun, verb or adjective. To get inside the words themselves we must delve into the domains of morphology, phonology and phonetics.

'Cat', we hope you will agree, is a word. But so is 'cats'. 'Purr' is a word, but so are 'purrs', 'purring' and 'purred'. 'Loud' is a word, but so are 'louder' and 'loudest'. Contemplating these words is enough to make us appreciate the need to recognize meaningful units of language that are larger than the phoneme but smaller than the word. Linguists call these units *morphemes*. The word 'cats' divides into the morphemes *cat* + −s; 'purrs' divides into *purr* + −*s*, 'purring' into *purr* + −*ing*, 'purred' into *purr* + −*ed*, 'louder' into *loud* + −*er*, and 'loudest' into *loud* + −*est*.

Linguists call morphemes like 'purr', 'cat' and 'loud' 'free morphemes' because they are free to occur in isolation. The other morphemes like −s, −ing, −er, and −est can have no free life of their own, but can only occur bound to other morphemes. That is why linguists call them 'bound morphemes'. Two classes of bound morpheme are recognized. All those we have mentioned so far are *inflectional* bound morphemes. These have entirely predictable effects on the interpretation of the free morpheme to which they attach, turning it from singular to plural, for example, or from present to past. They do not affect a word's grammatical class – an inflected noun remains a noun, and an inflected verb remains a verb. The function of inflections is largely to indicate the roles of words in sentences and their relations one to another. Some languages, like Latin, rely heavily on inflections (see Chapter 5). In English they act in concert with words like 'of', 'the', 'by' or 'and' as indicators of sentence structure.

The second class of bound morphemes are the *derivational* morphemes which in English include both suffixes (e.g. -ish, -ous, -er, -ly, -ate and -able) and prefixes (e.g. un-, im-, re-, ex-). Derivational morphemes *can* change the grammatical class of a word: -ish changes 'boy' from a noun to an adjective ('boyish'); -ize changes 'moral' from a noun to a verb ('moralize'). What is more, derivational bound morphemes have rather unpredictable effects on the subsequent interpretation of the bound morpheme to which they attach themselves. Take -er. In words like 'runner', 'walker', 'baker' and 'sinner' it denotes one who performs the action of the verb to which it is attached. But a 'butcher' does not 'butch', while a 'cooker' is an appliance used by a 'cook' to 'cook' (see Henderson, 1985, for further elaboration).

A word is minimally made up of one free morpheme (e.g. 'man', 'snow', 'sport', or 'ball'). A compound noun is made up of more than one potentially free morpheme (e.g. 'snowman', 'snowball', 'sportsman'). A word may also grow by taking on extra morphemes; thus:

> sportsman
> sportsmanlike
> unsportsmanlike

Or again:

> man
> gentleman
> gentlemanly
> ungentlemanly
> ungentlemanliness

One of the most popular words of the schoolyard, 'antidisestablishmentarianism', manages according to Fromkin and Rodman (1974) to combine no fewer than nine morphemes:

anti + dis + e + stabl(e) + ish + ment + ari + an + ism

Morphemes, in turn, are built up from *phonemes*. These are the individual, indivisible sounds of the language. English has about 40 (the precise number varying according to a speaker's accent). The newcomer to linguistics often confuses phonemes with letters, but phonemes are elements of the spoken language while letters belong to the written language. We have 40 phonemes but only 26 letters, so while some phonemes can regularly correspond to one letter ($l =$ /l/, $m =$ /m/, $f =$ /f/ etc.), other phonemes have to be represented by two or more letters (e.g. *ch*, *th*, *sh*, *oo*, *ee*, and *ou*). 'Teeth' has five letters but only three phonemes (/ti θ/).

To say that phonemes are individual sounds is an oversimplification, since the pronunciation a phoneme receives will vary from context to context. The phoneme /p/, for example, is pronounced slightly differently in 'pill' and 'spill'. If you place your fingers in front of your lips and say 'pill', you will feel a slight puff of air accompanying the /p/ (linguists say the phoneme is 'aspirated' in that context). The aspiration is lacking from the /p/ in 'spill'. What matters is that English does not use the difference between the two forms of /p/ to distinguish between pairs of words with different meanings. The Thai language *does* use aspiration to distinguish between words, so for a Thai speaker each of our two p's is a separate phoneme. Similarly, /r/ and /l/ are two different phonemes for us, but two forms of the same phoneme for Japanese speakers. Adult Japanese speakers, well entrenched in the habits of their native tongue, find it hard to perceive and produce our distinction between /r/ and /l/, just as we would have difficulty perceiving and producing the aspirated and unaspirated phonemes of the Thai language. The study of the phonemic domain is called *phonology*.

Finally, the physical realization of speech as a sound wave is the concern of *phonetics*, which has two branches. Articulatory phonetics, as its name suggests, studies the process of articulation – the way that the structures of the oral cavity (tongue, teeth etc.) mould the basic vibrations produced by the vocal cords, and the intricate muscular co-ordination this requires. Acoustic phonetics takes the sound wave as its starting point. It studies how different phonemes are realized in the speech wave; what acoustic cues enable us to distinguish phonemes one from another, and so on.

The hierarchy of language units: We have encountered several different language units identified by linguists as relevant to understanding the properties of different domains. If we step back and view these units from a distance, an important fact emerges. They form a *hierarchy*. Texts are made up of paragraphs. Paragraphs are made up of sentences, which are made up of clauses, which are made up of phrases, which are made up of words, which are made up of morphemes, which are made up of phonemes. What is more, a boundary at any one level will also be a boundary at every lower level. Thus the boundary between two sentences will also be a boundary between two clauses, two phrases, two words, two morphemes, and two phonemes. This hierarchical organization cannot be purely fortuitous: it must exist for a reason. We shall argue later that these units are all active in speech planning as it unfolds from ideas to articulations, and active again in the recreation of the speaker's message in the listener's mind.

Prosody: The exception to the hierarchical principle is that cluster of nonsegmentable phenomena known as *prosody*. The term 'prosody' covers such things as intonation (the rise and fall of voice pitch), rhythm, variations in speech rate or amplitude (which combine with intonation to impart greater emphasis to some words or syllables), pausing and so on. Now the interesting thing about prosody is that its use is affected by virtually all of the language domains we have identified earlier. We shall have cause to look at these influences at various points in the book, so a brief set of illustrative examples will suffice for now (Brown, 1977, and Cutler and Isard, 1980, provide further examples and discussion).

At the discourse level, Butterworth (1975) has shown that when speakers are producing a sustained monologue, boundaries of paragraph-like 'idea units' are often marked by changes in speech fluency. Rees and Urquhart (1976) found that when speakers are reading aloud the overall pitch setting of their voice tends to start high at the beginning of a paragraph, drift downwards during it, then rise again at the beginning of the next. Other prosodic cues to paragraph or 'idea' boundaries are discussed in Chapters 7 and 13.

Turning to pragmatic and semantic influences, a speaker's *attitude* to what he or she is saying can be clearly marked by intonation and tone of voice. Consider the sentence, 'The defendant claimed that the valuables he was carrying in the sack slung over his back were a gift from his grandmother'. By altering the way you say that sentence you can switch from expressing an attitude of honest, sincere acceptance of the statement, to one of disbelief, to one of astonishment, to one of thinly-disguised hilarity.

Pragmatic factors can influence which words receive maximum emphasis or 'stress' in a sentence. To adapt an example from Cutler and Isard (1980), imagine the various ways you could say:
'They don't grow pineapples in Pudsey'
There are contexts in which it would be appropriate to emphasize any one of those words. Thus,
'*They* don't grow pineapples in Pudsey' (but someone else does)
or
'They don't grow *pineapples* in Pudsey' (they grow cricketers instead)
or
'They don't grow pineapples *in* Pudsey' (but they grow them nearby).
You can fill out the rest for yourself. Note also that you can use intonation to change a sentence from a statement into a question:

'They don't grow pineapples in Pudsey?'

For a generative grammarian, changing a sentence from a statement to a question is the responsibility of transformational rules, and they are an aspect of syntax. Yet prosody can achieve at least some of the same effects. Syntax and prosody also interact in the way speakers mark grammatical units such as clauses and sentences in their speech by intonation, pausing or changes in speech rate. We shall discuss this marking further in Chapter 7 and the use listeners make of it in Chapter 13.

Finally, although we drew a distinction in the previous chapter between prosody and paralanguage, it is in reality hard to make a hard and fast division. Paralinguistic features include things like tone of voice, loudness, tempo and articulatory precision. All of these can be used communicatively to convey aspects of a message (as can visual features like gestures or facial expression). Thus 'Come up and see me sometime' conveys a very different message and invites the drawing of very different implications when said in an everyday, matter-of-fact tone of voice than when said in the husky tone of a Mae West. To some extent the various domains of language we have discussed seem to have psychological reality as separate aspects of language processing, but as with prosody and paralanguage, or syntax and semantics, the boundaries are far from clear. There is probably a degree to which they are, like academic discipline boundaries, convenient fictions. We must certainly be prepared to leapfrog over them at will if we are to fully understand human language and communication.

5 Linguistic diversity: Babel and beyond

Thus far in the book we have talked a little about how nonverbal behaviour may vary across cultures, but we have said virtually nothing about how language may vary across cultures and peoples. In this chapter and the next, we will attempt to remedy this. Here we consider the languages of the world, their obvious differences and their much less obvious similarities. But a consideration of linguistic diversity means much more than a consideration of the differences between different languages – French and Chinese, for example. There may be considerable linguistic diversity even within a group supposedly using the same language. As Oscar Wilde remarked 'We have really everything in common with America nowadays except, of course, language'. Such differences may be every bit as important to human communication and human misunderstanding, and they may not be so obvious as one set of people calling something 'petrol' while another calls it 'gasoline'. Let us begin by considering the extent of linguistic diversity generally.

Fromkin and Rodman (1978) posed the following question:

How many people of the world can be brought together so that no one person understands the language spoken by any other person? Considering that there are billions of people in the world, the number of mutually unintelligible languages is rather small – 'only' about 3,000 according to one suggestion, and as many as 8,000 according to another. Despite the seemingly large number of languages spoken in the world today, three-fourths of the world's population (2,5000,000,000 people) speak but thirteen languages. Therefore, if you spoke Chinese (or the eight major 'dialects' of Chinese), English, Hindi and Russian, you could speak with approximately 1,600,000,000. Of the 400,000,000 English speakers, 280,000,000 speak English as a first language and another 120,000,000 speak it as a second language. In addition, about 60 per cent of the world's radio stations broadcast in English and more than half the periodicals of the world are published in English. (Fromkin and Rodman 1978, p. 329)

These may be comforting thoughts for the English speaker and even more so for the English speaker fluent, in addition, in Chinese, Hindi and Russian. A choice of 1,599,999,999 possible co-conversationalists (or just 399,999,999 for the monolingual English speaker). But things may not be this simple (they rarely are!). Some degree of intelligibility is one thing – real comprehension without a substantial degree of mis-understanding is something else. Most of us live in modern multi-cultural societies with additional divisions due to class, sex, age, occupation and geographical location. These divisions generally affect language and mean that perfect intelligibility, even within a single language group, is often not achieved. This is an important aspect of linguistic diversity. Let us consider one apparently trivial linguistic example reported by Gumperz (1982). Gumperz found that the Indian and Pakistani women working in the staff canteen at Heathrow Airport in England were perceived as very surly and uncooperative by their customers. Why? Gumperz studied the situation and found that the problem centred on language and specifically the intonation patterns of the Indian workers:

When a cargo handler who had chosen meat was asked whether he wanted gravy, a British assistant would say 'Gravy?' using rising intonation. The Indian assistants, on the other hand, would say the word using falling intonation: 'Gravy'. We taped relevant sequences including interchanges like these, and asked the employees to paraphrase what was meant in each case. At first the Indian workers saw no difference. However, the English teacher and the cafeteria supervisor could point out that 'Gravy' said with a falling intonation is likely to be interpreted as 'This is gravy', i.e. not interpreted as an offer, but rather, as a statement, which in the context seems redundant and, consequently, rude. When the Indian women heard this, they began to understand the reactions they had been getting all along, which had until then seemed incomprehensible. They then spontaneously recalled intonation patterns which had seemed strange to them when spoken by native English speakers. At the same time, supervisors learned that the Indian women's falling intonation was their normal way of asking questions in that situation, and that no rudeness or indifference was intended. (Gumperz, 1982, p. 173)

The possibility for such misunderstandings originating through language are, of course, enormous; and the importance of such misunderstanding in cultural disharmony cannot be under-estimated. Problems may arise in terms of the interpretation of the prosody, paralanguage or nonverbal behaviour which accompany language, or in terms of the basic syntax, semantics or lexicon of the language itself. One interesting example of the latter, with poten-tially fatal consequences, was found by Boyle (1975), who investigated what a sample of doctors and patients (all native English speakers) understood by a number of basic medical terms such as 'arthritis', 'heartburn', 'diarrhoea', 'constipation', 'a good appetite' etc. For mutual intelligibility and sound medical practice, it is of course important that doctors and patients should agree on the meanings of such basic terms. Boyle's results were quite alarming. While 100% of the doctors agreed that 'heartburn' was 'a burning sensation behind the breast bone', 8% of the patients thought that it meant 'passage of wind through the mouth', while 4.5% thought it meant 'excess saliva'. The majority of doctors agreed that 'diarrhoea' meant 'passing loose bowel motions' , while 3.7% of patients thought it meant 'straining to pass bowel motions' and one thought it meant 'passing a lot of wind by the back passage'. Such differences in the understanding of basic terms for common symptoms could have drastic consequences for doctor-patient communication, and, ultimately, the whole medical endeavour. 399,999,999 co-conversationalists maybe, perfect intelligibility very seldom.

In the next chapter, we will consider how variables like geo-graphical location, class, sex and ethnic background affect language and speech within a single language group; but first let us consider some of the major features of the principal languages of the world.

Languages of the world

As Jean Aitchison (1981, p. 16) has noted: 'In a world where humans grow old, tadpoles change into frogs, and milk turns into cheese, it would be strange if language alone remained unaltered.' And as the Swiss linguist Ferdinand de Saussure (1915) noted: 'Time changes all things: there is no reason why language should escape this universal law. Languages constantly change, they grow, they have daughters, they die.' The English spoken in the heart of England one millennium ago is scarcely recognisable as English today. Consider the following sentence from the 10th-century epic *Beowulf*: 'Wolde guman findan pone pe him on sweofote sare geteode' (p is pronounced like the 'th' in 'think'). This sentence can be translated as 'He wanted to find the man who harmed him while he slept' (see Fromkin and Rodman, 1978).

The language of Beowulf is now called Old English. Almost four hundred years later Chaucer wrote *The Canterbury Tales* – here the English (now called Middle English) is recognizable and even understandable today. Thus

> 'Whan that Aprille with his shoures sote
> The droghte of March hath perced to the roote . . .'

means:
> 'When April with its sweet showers
> The drought of March has pierced to the root . . .'

Nearly two centuries after Chaucer, Shakespeare had Hamlet say: 'A man may fish with the worm that hath eat of a king, and eat of the fish that hath fed of the worm.' Certainly recognizable and intelligible.

The English of the 16th century such as the English of Shakespeare is seen as forming the beginnings of Modern English. But English has of course changed since then. In the couplet below from Macbeth:

> 'Where's the place? Upon the heath
> There to meet with Macbeth.'

'heath' orginally rhymed with 'Macbeth'. Since it was written the pronunciation of 'heath' has changed.

Tha branch of linguistics which deals with how languages change, what kinds of changes occur and why these occur is called 'historical and comparative linguistics'. We mentioned briefly in Chapter 4 how in the 19th century Darwin's theory of biological evolution had a profound influence on linguistics and led to the development of 'geneological trees' for languages in which each language is traced back to common or non-common ancestors. The method for this ancestral mapping involved the examination of the similarities and differences between certain languages. Such a method was not new. In 1786 Sir William Jones pointed out the strong relation among Sanskrit, Greek and Latin: 'No philologer could examine them all three, without believing them to have sprung from some common source, which perhaps no longer exists'. (This argument was however disputed by a Scottish philosopher, Dugall Stewart, who suggested the alternative hypothesis that Sanskit and Sanskrit literature were inventions of Brahmans, who used Greek and Latin as models to deceive Europeans.) But Jones was proven correct by the German linguist, Franz Bopp, in 1816. In 1822, Jakob Grimm (also encountered in Chapter 4) collected regular sound corres-pondences between Sanskrit, Greek, Latin and the Germanic languages and identified the systematic sound shifts from Greek, Latin and Sanskrit to the Germanic languages. On the basis of the examination of the existing daughter language it does seem possible to deduce facts about the parent language which may or may not still be alive. Consider, for example, the following three words in four Romance languages (from Lehmann, 1973):

French	*Italian*	*Spanish*	*Portuguese*	
cher	caro	caro	caro	'dear'
champ	campo	campo	campo	'field'
chandelle	candela	candela	candeia	'candle'

The first thing to note is the similarity in the words between the four languages, and the difference from English. But what is also important is the differences between the four. In French we find [Š] whereas we find ['k'] in the three other languages. The general regular sound correspondences support the view that French, Italian, Spanish and Portuguese are descended from a common language with a [k] in 'dear', 'field' and 'candle' of the parent language. Three of the 'daughters' retained the original [k] sound. *One* did not. Using such a comparative method the entire sound system of the parent can be reconstructed. Parents can be re-constructed from 'daughters', 'grandparents' in turn from 'parents'. Using this technique the common ancestor of the Celtic languages, the Germanic languages, the Italic languages, the Hellenic languages, the Balto-Slavic languages and the Indo-Iranian languages (among others) has been identified. This has been called 'Proto-Indo-European' and is believed to have flourished about 6,000 years ago. (Knowing that Proto-Indo-European had no terms for silver, gold and iron, it can be inferred that they were pre-Iron-Age people, placing them in time before 4,000 BC.) Figure 5.1 shows the Indo-European family in more detail – a formidable family tree indeed! One distant ancestor spawned languages now spoken by over half the world's population.

Table 5.1 shows the number of people who speak some of the languages of this great family and the areas in which they are spoken.

Table 5.2 details some other major languages which are not part of the Indo-European family.

How languages differ

The differences between languages are both extensive and immediately obvious. For example, the number and kind of speech sounds and the ways they are combined vary in different languages. English has 40 different phonemes (speech sounds), while Hawaiian has only 11 or 12. Abkhaz (spoken in the Caucasas) has 70. The German and Scottish [kh] as in 'loch' is not found in English or in many other languages. Languages also differ in their methods for combining speech sounds. For example, no consonant clusters such as 'strike' occur at the beginnings of words in the Ural-Altaic Language Family (such as Korean or Japanese). Vowel-to-consonant ratios can vary in different languages. Hawaiian has about an equal number of vowels and consonants, while Abkhaz has only 2 vowels and 68 consonants. Languages like Japanese and Korean do not use stress patterns either for signalling different aspects of meaning or for rhythmic effects.

The languages of the world also differ greatly in the variation of word forms found. The Indo-European language family, for example, is heavily inflected. The forms of nouns, pronouns and sometimes adjectives and articles vary according to gender (masculine, feminine or neuter – as in 'he', 'she', 'it'), number (singular, plural – 'he', 'they'), and case (nominative, genitive, etc. – 'he', 'his'). Verbs vary according to person and number ('he goes',

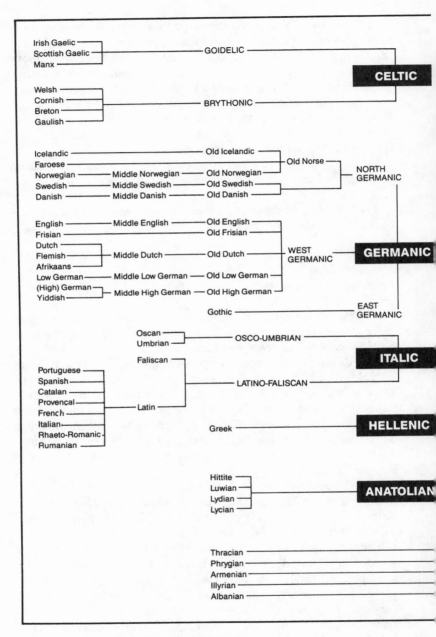

Figure 5.1: The Indo-European Family

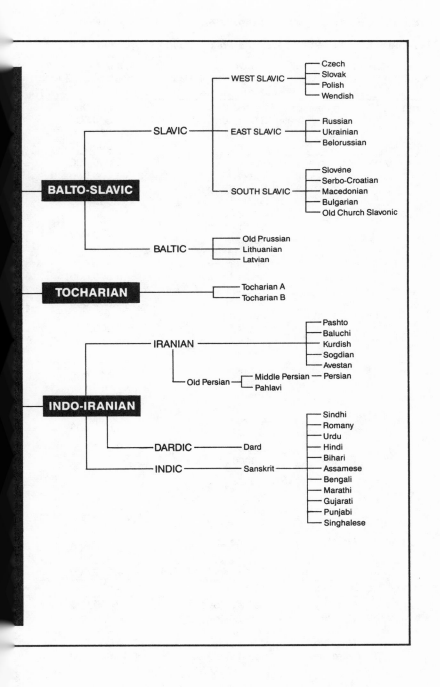

Table 5.1: Some languages of the world. The Indo-European Family

Language subfamily	Language	Principal geographical areas where spoken	number of speakers	Rank (up to 20th)
CELTIC	Irish Gaelic	Ireland	500,000	
	Scottish Gaelic	Scotland	500,000	
	Welsh	Wales	750,000	
	Breton	Brittany	1,000,000	
GERMANIC	Icelandic	Iceland	200,000	
	Norwegian	Norway	4,300,000	
	Swedish	Sweden	8,000,000	
	Danish	Denmark	5,000,000	
	English	Great Britain North America Australia New Zealand	280,000,000	2
	Frisian	Northern Holland	400,000	
	Dutch	Netherlands Indonesia	13,000,000	
	Flemish	Belgium	5,000,000	
	German	Germany Austria Switzerland	100,000,000	7
	Yiddish	(Diffuse)		
ITALIC	Portugese	Portugal Brazil	100,000,000	7
	Spanish	Spain Latin America	200,000,000	3
	Catalan	Andorra Spain	5,000,000	
	Provencal	Southern France	9,000,000	
	French	France Belgium Switzerland Canada	75,000,000	11
	Italian	Italy Switzerland	60,000,000	12
HELLENIC	Greek	Greece Cyprus	10,000,000	
ARMENIAN	Armenian	South West U.S.S.R.	4,000,000	
ALBANIAN	Albanian	Albania	4,000,000	
BALTO-SLAVIC	Czech	Czechoslovakia	10,000,000	
	Slovak	Czechoslovakia	4,000,000	
	Polish	Poland	35,000,000	
	Russian	U.S.S.R.	200,000,000	3
	Ukrainian	South West U.S.S.R.	40,000,000	20

	Serbo-Croatian	Yugoslavia	15,000,000	
	Macedonian	Southern Yugoslavia	1,000,000	
	Bulgarian	Bulgaria	8,000,000	
	Lithuanian	Lithuania (U.S.S.R.)	3,000,000	
	Latvian	Latvia (U.S.S.R.)	2,000,000	
INDO-IRANIAN	Persian	Iran	25,000,000	
	Urdu	Pakistan	40,000,000	20
	Hindi	Northern India	180,000,000	5
	Bengali	Bangladesh	110,000,000	6
	Marathi	Western India	45,000,000	17
	Punjabi	Northern India	50,000,000	13

Table 5.2: Major languages of the world not part of the Indo-European Family

Language family	Language	Principal geographical areas where spoken	Number of speakers	Rank (up to 20th)
AFRO-ASIATIC	Arabic	North Africa Middle East	100,000,000	7
ALTAIC	Japanese	Japan	100,000,000	7
	Korean	Korea	34,000,000	
ASIATIC	Vietnamese	Vietnam	28,000,000	
AUSTRO-TAI	Indonesian	Indonesia	50,000,000	13
	Javanese	Java	45,000,000	17
	Thai	Thailand	30,000,000	
DRAVIDIAN	Tamil	South East India Sri Lanka	45,000,000	17
	Telugu	South East India	50,000,000	13
SINO-TIBETAN	Hakka	South East China	30,000,000	
	Mandarin	North China	387,000,000	1
	Wu	East Central China	46,000,000	16

'they go') and tense ('he goes', 'he went'). The only invariant parts of speech are prepositions (in, to) and adverbs (always, never). The Sino-Tibetan family (Burmese, Cantonese, Mandarin, Tibetan, etc.) lacks inflections.

Sentence structure also varies across different languages. In languages which are heavily inflected, for example Latin, word order can be very flexible. In Latin, '*Julius videt Augustum*' and '*Julius Augustum videt*' mean the same – the endings designate actor and recipient. In English, which is less inflected than Latin, word **order plays** a crucial role. In every language sentences contain a noun-phrase subject (S), a verb or predicate (V), and possibly a noun-phrase object (O). In some languages the basic or 'preferred' order of these elements is subject-verb-object (SVO) (e.g. English, French, Spanish). Other languages such as Japanese and Korean have the preferred order subject-object-verb (SOV). Others, such as classical Hebrew and Welsh, are VSO languages; very rarely one finds a language like Malagasy (from Madagascar) which is VOS, or Dyirbal (from Australia), which is OSV. No language has been discovered which has the preferred word order OVS.

Some languages have honorifics (polite manners of speech) which are quite alien to speakers of Indo-European languages. In Japanese honorifics are so pervasive that the choice of vocabulary as well as the conjugation of every verb and copula (the verb 'to be') is affected. In fact not a single sentence can be uttered without indicating the level of politeness; the level depending upon the sex, occupation, age and status of both the speaker and the listener. There are over ten different words referring to 'I', for example – '*boku*' (male, informal), '*watashi*' (female, informal), '*ware*' (male addressing an inferior person), all reflecting degrees of politeness.

Of course the relations between strings of sounds and particular meanings (lexical differences) are the most obvious differences between language. 'Water' in English is '*wasser*' in German, '*agua*' in Spanish, '*uisce*' in Irish, '*maji*' in Swahili, '*pani*' in Hindu, '*naam*' in Thai and '*oyu*' in Japanese. Within a single language family, however, the similarities may be just as striking as the differences. Consider the word 'three' in English within the Indo-European family – within the Germanic sub-family it is '*thrjá*' in Icelandic, '*drie*' in Dutch, '*drei*' in German, '*tre*' in Swedish, Danish and Norwegian. Within the Italic sub-family it is '*tres*' in Portuguese, '*tres*' in Spanish, '*trois*' in French, '*tre*' in Italian, '*tri*' in Rumanian. Within the Balto-Slavic sub-family it is '*tri*' in Russian, '*tris*' in Lithuanian. Within the Indo-Iranian sub-family it is '*trayas*' in Sanskrit. Within the Celtic sub-family it is '*tri*' in Irish. Close family resemblances indeed.

Of course different languages can also appear similar because individual words may be imported into a language from its neighbours. In English today, we have words imported from French in hairdressing (e.g. costume, coiffure), architecture (e.g. terrace), and many other areas (e.g. café, garage). From Dutch, the language of England's greatest rival at sea for centuries, we have 'dock', 'boom', 'skipper' and 'yacht'. From Italian we have many words in music: 'forte', 'pianissimo'. From German we have 'zeppelin', 'straf' and 'blitz' reflecting a certain type of contact between these two nations over the past centuries. Wars generally can speed up this process of borrowing. Soldiers returning from India in the last century brought back native words like 'thug' and 'pyjamas' (see Wright, 1974). More recently Russian has supplied English with many words for the new technology – for example 'sputnik' (which originally meant fellow-traveller in Russian) and 'robot' (from the Russian noun 'work'). This process of borrowing never stops. From America and the hippy culture of the 1960s, we have 'vibes', not yet in English dictionaries but getting there.

Linguistic universals

In the last section we considered how the languages of the world may differ. Here we will consider some suggested invariant properties of human language. Invariant properties of language which some have suggested (e.g. Chomsky, 1976) may reflect important properties, constraints and details of the human mind.

The recognition that different human languages may share common, or universal, features is not new. In 1788 James Beattie wrote:

Languages, therefore, resemble men in this respect, that though each has peculiarities, whereby it is distinguished from every other, yet all have certain qualities in common. The peculiarities of individual tongues are explained in their respective grammars and dictionaries. These things that all languages have in common, or that are necessary to every language, are treated of in a science, which some have called *Universal* or *Philosophical* grammar (Beattie, 1788, cited in Chomsky, 1965, p. 5).

The common or universal features of language have been sought at almost every lingustic level and evidence has now accumulated that there do exist phonological, syntactic and even semantic universals, (indeed Chomsky, 1979, has even suggested the possibility that we may have a sort of 'universal grammar' of possible forms of social interaction 'and it is these systems which helps us to organise intuitively our imperfect perceptions of social reality' although he does not really elaborate this point in any great detail).

An example of a lingustic universal at the phonological level is Jakobson's theory of distinctive features in which each output of the phonological component of language can be characterized in terms of a small number of fixed universal phonetic features (perhaps in the order of fifteen or twenty). Each of these fixed phonetic features has a substantive acoustic – articulatory characterization independent of any particular language. An example of a linguistic universal at the syntactic level is that all languages have fixed syntactic categories (noun, verb, etc.) which provide the general underlying syntactic structure of the language. An example of a linguistic universal at the semantic level is that all languages will contain certain terms that designate persons, specific kinds of objects, feelings and behaviour etc. (see Chomsky, 1965, p. 25). Of course, the specific mapping relationships between word and objects will vary considerably from culture to culture. We would expect most human languages to have a word for something so central and so basic as the human eye, but whereas in English the word 'eye' can refer either to the thing that opens and closes in the upper part of the face or to the eyeball, the Japanese word refers only to the facial feature, not to the eyeball. The Mongolian word for eye, in contrast, refers only to the eyeball, not to the facial feature (see Miller, 1981, p. 101).

Chomsky has called the universals listed above 'substantive linguistic universals' and he says that: 'A theory of substantive univerals claims that items of a particular kind in any language must be drawn from a fixed class of items' (1965, p. 28). He does suggest, however, that it is possible to locate universal properties of language of a more abstract sort – these he calls formal linguistic universals. Again he suggests that these may exist at different levels. At the semantic level, for example, he proposes that the following features would qualify: The assumption that proper names, in any language, must designate objects meeting a condition of spatiotemporal contiguity, and that the same is true of other items designating objects; or the conditions that the colour words of any language must subdivide the colour spectrum into continuous segments; or the condition that artifacts are defined in terms of certain human goals, needs and functions instead of solely in terms of physical qualities' (1965, p. 29). At the syntactic level he proposes a whole series of abstract syntactic operations. Let us consider the argument here in some detail with respect to one such operation:

Consider, for example, the way in which questions are formed in English. Consider the sentence 'The dog in the corner is hungry'. From this we can form the question 'Is the dog in the corner hungry?' by a simple formal operation: moving the element 'is' to the front of the sentence. Given a variety of examples of question formation, a linguist studying English might propose several possible rules of question formation. Imagine two such proposals. The first states that to form a question, we first identify the subject noun phrase of the sentence, and we then move the occurrence of 'is' following this noun phrase to the beginning of the sentence. Thus in the example in question, the subject noun phrase is 'the dog in the corner'; we form the question by moving the occurrence of 'is' that follows it to the front of the sentence. Let us call this operation a *structure-dependent operation*, meaning by this that the operation considers not merely the sequence of elements that constitute the sentence, but also their structure; in this case, the fact that the sequence 'the dog in the corner' is a phrase, furthermore a noun phrase. For the case in question, we might also have proposed a *structure-independent operation*: namely, take the left most occurrence of 'is' and move it to the front of the sentence. We can easily determine that the correct rule is the structure-dependent operation. Thus if we have the sentence 'the dog that is in the corner is hungry, we do not apply the proposed structure-independent operation, forming the question 'is the dog that – in the corner is hungry?' rather, we apply the structure-dependent operation, first locating the noun-phrase subject 'the dog that is in the corner', then inverting the occurrence of 'is' that follows it, forming: 'is the dog that is in the corner – hungry?' (Chomsky, 1972, p. 29–30)

Chomsky goes on to argue that although children make certain kinds of errors in the course of language learning, they do not make the mistake of applying the structure-independent rule despite its evident simplicity and the 'slim evidence of experience' for the child to learn one rule rather than the other. He goes on to say that all known formal operations in the grammar of English and any other languages are structure-dependent and these are examples of *formal* linguistic universals or principles of universal grammar. In *Reflections on Language* (1976), Chomsky considers two arguments that might be adduced against this conclusion. First, that we know of no genetic mechanisms adequate to account for the innate structures postulated. Secondly, that it is improper to assign such complexity to the mind as an innate property. His counter arguments are blunt and to the point. The first, he says, is 'correct but irrelevant', 'The genetic mechanisms are unknown, just like the mechanisms responsible for such learning as takes place or for the development of physical organs' (p. 91). The second argument, Chomsky says, 'merely reiterates empiricist prejudice'.

The crucial feature of the argument of structure-dependence is that there is no *functional* explanation for the observed effect. Chomsky calls this feature consequently a *strong* linguistic universal. In the case of other relatively invariant properties of different languages functional explanations can be advanced. For example, the fact that sentences are not likely to exceed a certain length (see Chomsky, 1972, p. 42), or the fact that in different languages turn-taking occurs which means that for the majority of time one person alone holds the floor. Such features can be explained in functional terms, for example in terms of human beings' limited processing capacity. The fact that transformations in language are structure-dependent cannot however be explained in functional terms (see Comrie, 1983). Chomsky's conclusions are striking:

> Such principles . . . are a priori for the species – they provide the framework for the interpretation of experience and the construction of specific forms of knowledge on the basis of experience – but are not necessary or even natural properties of all imaginable systems that might serve the functions of human language. It is for this reason that these principles are of interest for the study of the nature of the human mind. (Chomsky, 1972, p. 42)

The languages of the world may differ but they show curious and remarkable similarities at more abstract levels. Different tongues maybe, but one *uniquely* human mind.

6 Variation within a language

In the last chapter we considered the diversity of different languages. Now we wish to consider possible diversity within a single language. Diversity within a language may be due to geographical location, class, sex or ethnic background.

Geographical location is perhaps the most obvious – the English spoken in Surrey is different from the English spoken in Belfast or Glasgow, or New York or South Carolina. Sometimes accent makes the speech mutually unintelligible. Geographical location principally affects pronunciation but clearly there are other differences as well, for example in word usage or grammar. A variety of language which is *grammatically* different from any other (as well, perhaps, as having a different vocabulary or pronunciation) is called a *dialect*. Dialects are defined in terms of grammar, which means that speakers can employ colloquial styles of speech including slang or swear-words (for example in a very informal context) and still be using standard English. As Peter Trudgill points out:

' "I'm bloody knackered" may be part of a conversation in standard English (in an informal style, of course) while, "I be very tired" cannot be considered as an example of the standard English dialect' (1975, p. 19).

Standard English is itself a dialect and like all other dialects is subject to regional variation. Consider the following grammatical contrasts between American, Scottish and English Standard English:

American standard English: 'He'd gotten it'
English standard English: 'He'd got it'
Scottish standard English: 'You had a good time, hadn't you'
English standard English: 'You had a good time, didn't you'
(from Trudgill, 1975, p. 18).

Certain grammatical features are very characteristic of specific regional dialects. Thus:

'I wants it' is characteristic of the West Country;

'He want it' is characteristic of East Anglia.

Words common in one regional dialect may never have been heard of in another. For example, in the South of England they make a pot of tea; in the North, in many dialects, they may 'mash' a pot of tea. (In the South they may mash potatoes but definitely not tea).

Sometimes the regional variation in word usage can be historically explained. In the North and East of England, where the Vikings raided and settled, certain words used today can be traced to this Viking ancestry, e.g. 'claggy' (sticky) or 'addle' (to earn).

Differences in pronunciation within a language make for differences of *accent*. The lower down the social scale one goes the wider is the range of dialects and accents one finds. As Trudgill (1975) points out, 'School-teachers from Newcastle and Bristol will not speak English alike, but they will sound more similar than, say, most factory workers from the same two places' (p. 21). Geographical locality might be the most obvious influence on language but there are important theories that linguistic usage depends critically upon social class, sex and ethnic background and it is these variables which we will concentrate on in the rest of this chapter.

Social class and language

There is a good deal of evidence to suggest that social class affects language at a number of different levels. Over twenty years ago in the United States, the sociolinguist William Labov investigated the effects of social stratification on a number of phonological variables in speech. At approximately the same time in England a sociologist, Basil Bernstein, was investigating the effects of social class on a host of linguistic variables which went far beyond specific phonological features. Bernstein's claims and aspirations were much grander than those of Labov, but unfortunately his methodology was not as sophisticated. Labov's observations still stand; Bernstein's, on the other hand, at least within the linguistic field, have come in for a good deal of criticism (indeed Chomsky, 1979, said, 'The work of Bernstein may very well be . . . hardly worth discussing as a specimen of the rational study of language', p. 56). Nevertheless, Bernstein's theory influenced a whole generation of educationalists and is therefore worth considering in some detail. But first, Labov.

William Labov

Labov began his investigation by confronting a classic problem in communication research –

> The means used to gather the data interfere with the data to be gathered. The primary means of obtaining a large body of reliable data on the speech of one person is the individual tape-recorded interview. Interview speech is formal speech – not by any absolute measure, but by comparison with the vernacular of everyday life. On the whole, the interview is public speech – monitored and controlled in response to the presence of an outside observer. But even within that definition, the investigator may wonder if the responses in a tape-recorded interview are not a special product of the interaction between the interviewer and the subject. (Labov, 1972, p. 43)

This, of course, is an enduring dilemma which many researchers have sought to ignore rather than confront. Labov's particular solution to the problem was to see how people use language in a natural context where there is no explicit observation going on – he approached the informant in the role of a customer asking for directions to a particular department in three department stores (Saks Fifth Avenue, a high prestige store, Macy's, a middle-ranking store, and S. Klein, a low prestige store) in New York. The interviewer's standard question was, 'Excuse me, where are the women's shoes?'. The usual answer would be, 'Fourth floor' (with the /r/ pronounced or not). The interviewer would then lean forward and say, 'Excuse me?'. The informant would then usually repeat, 'Fourth floor', in a careful style with emphatic stress. The independent variables in this study were the store's variation in social prestige and the sex, age, occupation and race of the informant. The dependent variable was the use of '(r)' in four possible occurrences:

casual: fou*r*th floo*r*
emphatic: fou*r*th floo*r*

Labov interviewed 264 subjects in all. As predicted, he found r-pronunciation to be highest among Saks's employees and lowest among Klein's employees (with Macy's somewhere in between). Labov points out that the New York community has a basically 'r-less' vernacular, but that after the end of World War Two r-pronunciation became the prestige norm. Labov also found an interesting difference between the casual and emphatic speech – in emphatic pronunciation Macy's employees came very close to the level of Saks's employees. 'It would seem that r pronunciation is the norm at which a majority of Macy employees aim, yet not the one they use most often' (Labov, 1972, p. 52). In the case of the Saks employees there was a much less marked difference between casual and emphatic pronunciation. Labov termed this phenomenon *hyper-correction* – 'The lower-middle class speakers go beyond the high status group in their tendency to use the forms considered correct and appropriate for formal styles' (Labov, 1972, p. 126). Labov has demonstrated quite clearly that some linguistic variables are affected by social stratification and has explored these connections with some subtlety (interested readers are referred to Labov, 1972, for a collection of some of his empirical investigations).

However, the person who suggested the most radical effects of class and language is not a linguist at all but a sociologist – Basil Bernstein. Unlike Labov, Bernstein largely ignored questions of methodology but nevertheless developed an influential theory linking language and cognition in different social classes. This theory has had a major social impact (see Labov, 1969). We will consider now whether that impact was justified.

Basil Bernstein

Bernstein's investigations also began in the early 1960s; he proposed that working-class and middle-class people used distinctly different linguistic codes.

> It is suggested that the typical, dominant speech mode of the middle-class is one where speech becomes an object of special perceptual activity and a 'theoretical attitude' is developed towards the structural possibilities of sentence organisation. This speech mode facilitates the verbal elaboration of subjective intent, sensitivity to the implications of separateness and difference, and points to the possibilities inherent in a complex conceptual hierarchy for the organisation of experience. It is further suggested that this is not the case for members of the lower working-class. The latter are *limited* to a form of language use, which although allowing for a vast range of possibilities, provides a speech form which discourages the speaker from

verbally elaborating subjective intent and progressively orients the user to descriptive, rather than abstract, concepts. (Bernstein, 1974, p. 62)

The speech mode of the middle-class which facilitates the verbal elaboration of subjective intent is termed an *elaborated code*; the speech mode of the working-class, which discourages the speaker from verbally elaborating subjective intent is termed a *restricted code*. (Note the echoes here of the Sapir-Whorf 'linguistic relativity' hypothesis we discussed in Chapter 4. Bernstein acknowledges Sapir and Whorf as influences on his own thinking.)

Consider for example the following (invented) examples from Hawkins (1969):

Three boys are playing football and one kicks the ball – and it goes through the window – the ball breaks the window – and the boys are looking at it – and a man comes out and shouts at them – because they've broken the window – so they run away – and then that lady looks out of her window – and she tells the boys off.

This is, according to Hawkins, typical of the way five-year-old middle-class children tell stories when presented with four pictures showing in turn three boys playing with a football next to a house; the football going through a window, a man gesturing wildly, and the children running away while a woman looks out of the window. Hawkins claims however that working-class children of the same age typically provide a very different verbal description with respect to these picture cards, e.g. 'They're playing football and he kicks it and it goes through there – it breaks the window and they're looking at it – and he comes out and shouts at them – because they've broken it – so they run away – and then she looks out and she tells them off' (Hawkins, 1969, p. 127).

Bernstein says that the first story is *universalistic* in meaning – 'meanings are freed from the context and so are understandable by all' (Bernstein, 1974, p. 179). He says that the second story is *particularistic* in meaning – 'meanings are closely tied to the context and would be fully understood by others only if they had access to the context which originally generated the speech' (Bernstein, 1974, p. 179).

One important measure that Bernstein's associates have used to measure how context bound the speech is, is the number (or ratio) of exophoric and endophoric references. Exophoric references are deictics (such as 'it' and 'they') which refer back to something beyond the verbal context.

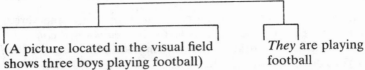

(A picture located in the visual field shows three boys playing football)   *They* are playing football

'They' here is an exophoric reference. In the examples Hawkins provided, the child began the description with an exophoric reference; this reference of course would not be clear to anyone who did not have the pictures in front of them. Endophoric reference, on the other hand, refers back to something already identified in the verbal context, e.g.

one kicks the ball and it goes through the window (see Hill and Varenne, 1981).

According to Bernstein, one important aspect of the particularistic meanings of the restricted code is the heavy usage of exophoric as opposed to endophoric pronouns. Exophoric pronouns tie the message to nonverbal context; endophoric pronouns do not.

Bernstein (1974) outlined the typical characteristics of a restricted code:

1) A lexicon drawn from a narrow range.
2) Condensed meaning (because, according to Bernstein, 'The speech is played out against a background of communal, self-consciously held interests which removes the need to verbalise subjective intent and make it explicit' (1974, p. 77).
3) Reduced verbal planning and therefore more fluent utterances (see Goldman-Eisler, 1968).
4) An increased reliance on the nonverbal accompaniments of language. These according to Bernstein 'will be a major source for indicating changes in meaning'.
5) *Impersonal* utterances 'in that the speech is not specially prepared to fit a particular referent'.
6) The content of the speech 'is likely to be concrete, descriptive and narrative rather than analytical and abstract'.

The major function of the restricted code, according to Bernstein, 'is to reinforce the *form* of the social relationship (a warm and

inclusive relationship) by restricting the verbal signalling of indi-
viduated responses' (1974, p. 78).

Bernstein originally tested his hypothesis of class-related linguistic differences by investigating the speech of two social groups
differing considerably in class background: one group of post-office
messenger boys and one group of boys at a private boarding school.
Bernstein tape-recorded different groups discussing the topic of the
abolition of capital punishment (consider Labov's qualms about
such a method). Bernstein felt that his major predictions were
confirmed. His principal finding was: 'The working-class subjects
used a longer mean phrase length, spent less time pausing and used
a shorter word length. Holding non-verbal intelligence constant,
social-class differences were found in the same direction' (p. 92).
Since Bernstein hypothesized that 'Fluency and hesitation would
seem to discriminate between two kinds of speech and differentiate
levels of verbal planning' (p. 89) these observations would at first
sight seem to support Bernstein's theory of verbal planning
differences in the two codes.

Bernstein subsequently analyzed the differences between the
speech of the groups at the lexical level and in terms of simple
grammatical features. Bernstein found that the middle-class groups
used a higher proportion of the following features: subordinations,
complex verbal stems, passives, total adjectives, uncommon adjectives, uncommon adverbs, uncommon conjunctions, egocentric
sequences. The working-class groups on the other hand used a
higher proportion of personal pronouns (p. 116). But how sound
was Bernstein's basic methodology? It is worth noting (and not
many of Bernstein's critics have noted this) that Bernstein's
middle-class and working-class subjects were treated differently.
This difference may have been critical. 'It was thought that the
working-class group would find the test situation threatening and
that this would interfere with the speech, and consequently all
working-class groups had two practice discussions (one a week)
before the test discussion. This was not the case for the middle-class
groups as such trials were impracticable' (p. 84). One group were
practised in the task, one group were not! Goldman-Eisler (1961)
had demonstrated that practice reduces pausing in speech and, it
should be noted, Bernstein found that the practised group spent less
time pausing than the non-practised group. Any attempt to draw
inferences about levels of verbal planning on the basis of amount of
pausing, given this procedural inequality, is not justified. There is
one other important difference between the two groups: some of

the working-class subjects knew each other, the middle-class almost certainly did not (p. 84). Since Bernstein had suggested that in the restricted code meanings are condensed because 'the speech is played out against a background of communal, self-consciously held interests' it seems especially unfortunate to use acquaintances or friends in the working-class (restricted code) group. Friends may indeed have communal interests and may condense their meanings (see Vygotsky, 1965). The problem here is that Bernstein has confounded class and relationship of subjects, a confusion which may indeed be critical. In other words Bernstein's original empirical investigation was very poorly executed and controlled. His principal discovery concerning pause differences between the two groups is, because of this poor methodology, theoretically un-interpretable. His discovery of statistical differences in the use of certain lexical and grammatical features is perhaps less suspect but also less interesting. 'Trivial' grammatical features are unfortu-nately not what Bernstein's grand theory was about.

Subsequent attempts to test the theory have also failed to produce conclusive results. Let us concentrate on the notion that the elaborated code is characterized by a higher level of verbal planning, and the operational measure that Bernstein focused upon – amount of pausing. Hawkins (1973) analysed the speech of young (6½ to 7 years old) working-and middle-class boys and girls as they made up a bedtime story for a teddy bear. Hawkins focused upon the speech of 48 subjects and analysed all unfilled pauses longer than 300 milliseconds. The prediction of course was that the working-class subjects should be most fluent in terms of speech rate per minute. But this was not what he found. He found that the working-class girls were the most fluent and the working-class boys were the least fluent, and the middle-class groups fell somewhere in between. The working-class boys paused longest and the working-class girls for the shortest amount of time overall. The results were not in line with the prediction. But worse was to come. When the 48 stories were submitted to experienced teachers to be graded, the stories of the working-class girls were judged to be best (despite the fact that this group paused for the least amount of time and yet amount of pausing was meant to reflect amount of verbal planning). This led Hawkins to the inevitable conclusion: 'Perhaps we need to question, then, our original assumption that greater fluency in-evitably means less planning and hence inferior quality.' In other words not only did Hawkins not produce confirmatory evidence for

Bernstein's hypothesis linking codes and verbal planning, his empirical evidence in fact leads one to doubt the very validity of the operational measure Bernstein proposed.

But perhaps it was naîve in the first place to assume that different social classes could be compared in terms of pause rates in order to draw conclusions about levels of verbal planning; naîve for a very important reason – it ignores social context and its influence on pausing in speech. Goldman-Eisler (1968) demonstrated that some delay in output of speech was necessary for novel encoding (see also Beattie and Bradbury, 1979) but that is very different from saying that all delays in output (all unfilled pauses in speech) regardless of context are connected with verbal planning. We may pause for other reasons, for example, to segment speech for the listener to facilitate decoding. Beattie (1979a) found that pauses at clause junctures in fluent phases of speech tended to be accompanied by the speaker looking directly at the listener. Since speakers tend to avert eye-gaze when engaged in cognitive planning, this ob-servation suggested that juncture pauses in fluent phases do not have a cognitive function, but presumably a more social function. Therefore it seems that even in conversation not all pauses in speech are used for cognitive planning (Beattie, 1979a, considered con-versational-type speech).

In monologues the situation gets much worse because there is not the same pressure to keep up a steady flow of speech. In conversation, if you remain silent for too long someone may interrupt, in monologues there is no-one to interrupt. Hawkins had his subjects tell stories to teddy bears – they presumably never interrupted. Hawkin's subjects had special privileges (rarely found in natural contexts). They could get bored with the task and then resume after a pause. It should be noted that the longest pause recorded in the Hawkins study was 67.1 seconds. This contrasts with the kinds of pauses studied by Goldman-Eisler (1968). In samples of discussions involving adults she found no pauses exceeding three seconds. Whatever Hawkins's subjects were doing during that one minute plus pause it was probably not verbal planning. Of course it is interesting and pertinent that Bernstein himself had originally analyzed speech taken from discussions and he had obtained (in his view) confirmatory evidence for his theory, although as we have already said, because of the methodological pitfalls of the study, the results are not readily interpretable.

The important point is that Bernstein should have recognized that social context, as well as the cognitive operations involved in language, will exert a powerful influence on the temporal structure of language. This however was never done. Bernstein's claims do not evidently generalize across social context and he never specified in which contexts differences should obtain. Contexts have been almost randomly sampled. The ensuing results seem almost equally random (for discussion of other conceptual problems with Bernstein's theory see Coulthard, 1969; Gazdar, 1979; Hill and Varenne, 1981).

Bernstein's theory was a powerful one linking cognition and social processes. It sought to explain the underachievement of working-class children in schools. One of its major problems however is its failure to recognize that speech is a medium adapted for use in the context of natural conversation. In certain types of conversation, pressures to keep the floor may mean that temporal structure becomes well used for cognitive operations and that pauses in speech may be a useful index of verbal planning. In other contexts the flexibility of speech asserts itself. It may change its whole shape and the temporal structure may reflect a good deal more than the operations connected with the encoding of speech. Hawkins found this to his cost.

Do working-class and middle-class people speak differently? The answer seems to be yes. Certain phonological, lexical and even grammatical features do seem to be affected by social class, but these features appear to be part of a continuum rather than arranged neatly into discrete codes, as Bernstein had suggested. Do working-class and middle-class people have differential access to different speech codes which either facilitate or discourage the 'verbal elaboration of subjective intent'? This is the heart of Bernstein's theory. As we have said, the evidence is weak – it is sometimes contradictory and often theoretically uninterpretable. Bernstein did observe some class-related speech differences but they do not support his general claims. Perhaps the last word here should be left to Labov. He is referring specifically to the work of Bernstein:

There is little connection between the general statements made and the quantitative data offered on the use of language. It is said that middle-class speakers show more verbal planning, more abstract arguments, more objective viewpoints, show more logical connections, and so on. But one does not uncover the logical complexity of a body of speech by counting the number of subordinate clauses. The cognitive style of a speaker has no fixed relation to the number of unusual adjectives or conjunctions that he uses. . . . The relation of argument and discourse to language is much more abstract than this, and such superficial indices can be quite deceptive. (1972, p. 258)

Unfortunately the deceptiveness fooled many.

Sex differences in language

It has been suggested for some time that the speech used by men and women may differ considerably. Traditionally (and somewhat embarrassingly today), women's speech was viewed as 'deficient' or 'abnormal'. The Danish scholar Otto Jesperssen (1949) spoke of 'feminine weaknesses' in speech. The linguist Edward Sapir whom we encountered in Chapter 4 included women's speech in his study of 'abnormal' types of speech. Priebsch and Collinson (1934), in discussing the German language, said that: 'Women naturally have certain peculiarities in their German as in other languages.' Such statements, so starkly put, seem remarkable today, and yet there have been claims in the last decade about women's speech which are every bit as extreme as those made half a century ago.

Let us begin by considering the influential views of Robin Lakoff (1975). Her thesis is very straightforward: 'Women prejudice the case against themselves by their use of language' (p. 19). She has attempted to show the ways in which women do this in order that women may overcome these barriers – to remove the linguistic chains that bind them, so to speak. She argues that 'women's language' shows up in all levels of the grammar of English.' We find differences in the choice and frequency of lexical items; in the situations in which certain syntactic rules are performed. In intonational and other super segmental patterns' (p. 8). Lakoff gives three examples of lexical differences between male and female speech. The first example is to do with colour names, the second with intensifiers and the third with particles (like 'oh dear' and 'shit'). In terms of colour names she suggests that women make more precise discriminations in naming colours than do men. She says a woman might say 'the wall is mauve' and she argues that if a man said this 'one might well conclude he was imitating a woman sarcastically or was a homosexual or an interior decorator' (p. 8). Men, she argues, find such discriminations 'trivial, irrelevant to the real world' (p. 9).

Lakoff also says that women use more intensifiers than men, e.g. 'so' in 'That sunset is so beautiful' (1975, p. 15). Intensifiers, she argues, occur in women's speech instead of absolute superlatives. Lakoff also says that women tend to use mild expressions like 'oh dear' where men tend to use the more direct 'shit'. What all these lexical differences have in common according to Lakoff is that they are 'devised to prevent the expression of strong statements' (p. 19). Lakoff says that exactly the same things happen in the case of the syntax and intonation of women's speech. In the case of syntax she says that women use more tag questions than men, e.g. 'John is here, isn't he?' which suggests, she says, uncertainty and 'lack of confidence'. (Not all tag questions may act like this however. In her linguistic investigation of a working-class, teenage subculture in Reading, Jenny Cheshire (1982) found that many tag questions were used to provoke fights, e.g. 'You're a fucking hard nut, in't you?' These tag questions were said with a falling rather than rising intonation). In the case of intonation, Lakoff suggests that women sometimes produce declarative answers with a rising intonation to certain questions. The rising intonation being typical of yes/no questions, e.g. 'When will dinner be ready?'. 'Oh . . . around six o'clock . . .?' Lakoff says that it is as though the second person was saying 'six o'clock if that's OK with you', and claims that men do not use this intonation pattern on such declaratives.

In her influential book, Lakoff has argued the case for 'feminine peculiarities', every bit as striking as the linguists in the first half of the century (even if she is pointing out these 'peculiarities' so that women can become aware of them). But what is very striking about her arguments is that when they were formulated they were based almost exclusively on intuition and stereotype rather than firm empirical evidence. Like Bernstein, she presents her arguments in terms of examples and assertion with little hard data to be seen.

Dale Spender has certainly got it right when she says:

> While it is perfectly possible that most English speakers believe that men use 'shit' and women use 'oh dear' this does not constitute evidence that males and females use these terms. All it proves is that the speakers are familiar with sexist stereotypes and, given their pervasive nature, it would be amazing if they did

not know what vocabulary was 'appropriate' for a woman and what was 'appropriate' for a man. (1982a, p. 34)

Spender's point cuts through many of Lakoff's arguments, and even if Lakoff could muster empirical evidence for the claims she is making there is still the problem of interpretation. Consider for example the case of the colour terms. Lakoff says that men may find such fine discriminations trivial but as Spender points out they may be anything but trivial to people engaged in interior decorating, and in our society women may be more frequently engaged in such an activity than men. Spender (1982a) concludes, 'It requires a patriarchal frame of values to interpret this as evidence of the triviality of women's vocabulary' (p. 35).

Having noted these criticisms, it is interesting to see how since Lakoff published her views some empirical evidence has accumulated for some of the features of women's speech she suggested. McMillan, Clifton, McGrath and Gale (1977) analyzed the speech of men and women in same-sex and mixed-sex problem-solving groups. A total of 98 subjects (61 women, 37 men) were studied. These researchers produced some confirmatory evidence for Lakoff's views. The women used intensifiers six times more often than men, and tag questions twice as often (Jenny Cheshire, whose work we have already mentioned, found tag questions to be particularly common in boy's speech and these were of the provoking as well as the conformation-seeking kind). McMillan et al. also found that women used modal constructions (constructions which express doubtfulness about an event e.g. 'can', 'could', 'shall', 'should', 'may', 'might', etc.) about twice as often, and imperative constructions, in question form, about three times as often as men. McMillan et al. also found that men use more of these same four linguistic constructions when women are present than when in all-male company. This presents problems with the interpretation – does men's self-confidence diminish in the presence of the opposite sex? This is presumably the interpretation one would favour if one accepted Lakoff's views on the meaning of these syntactic constructions. Yet this seems unlikely. McMillan et al. favoured the interpretation that these features signal 'interpersonal sensitivity' – women are more sensitive than men, and men have more sensitivity in the presence of women. This interpretation is, however, equally speculative. If we now know that some linguistic differences between the speech of men and women do exist, we still don't know what these differences mean.

There is also now empirical evidence showing other linguistic differences between the speech of men and women, and not just in English. In some other languages, males and females pronounce certain sounds in particular words differently. Amongst speakers of Cham in Vietnam in women's speech 'r' becomes 'y' in some contexts (see Blood, 1962, Key, 1975). In Bengali there is a tendency to substitute 'n' for 'l' in initial positions (the women share this tendency with children and the uneducated classes, see Chatterji, 1921; Key, 1975). One other linguistic difference between men and women that has been consistently replicated is that women use higher prestige pronunciation than men, especially in careful speech (see Labov, 1966, p. 288; Labov, 1972, p. 243, Trudgill, 1974). Similarly, black females are more likely to use standard forms of language than black men (see Wolfram, 1969). In English there is evidence that the topic of conversation varies between men and women – Moore (1922) recorded 174 conversations in New York City and reported that man-to-man topics included money and business (48%), amusements or sports (14%) and other men (13%). Woman-to-woman topics on the other hand were men (44%), clothing or decoration (23%) and other women (16%). These observations were replicated by M. Landis and Burtt in 1924 in Columbus, Ohio and by C. Landis in 1927 in London. It would be interesting to see what differences in topic exist today between men and women, if any.

Men, women and interruption

Traditional wisdom has it that women talk a good deal: '*Si femme il y a, silence il n' y a*', or Washington Irving's 'A woman's tongue is the only weapon that sharpens with use'. But such views have recently been challenged. For example, Dale Spender (1982b) asks: 'Women are the talkative sex. Right?'. 'Wrong', she replies.

The new evidence she cites comes from linguistics. The classic study which she mentions (like everyone else), is the one that Zimmerman and West (1975) carried out at the Santa Barbara campus of the University of California in the early 1970s. In conversation between men and women, men, it seems, were responsible for 96% of all interruptions. West and Zimmerman (1977) were in no doubt as to what this means. Interruptions, they interject, are 'a display of dominance or control to the female (and

to any witnesses) and . . . a control device since the incursion
(particularly if repeated) disorganises the local construction of a
topic', (p. 527). Dale Spender puts it more simply:
'Those with power and status talk more and interrupt more.'

But how sound were the observations in Zimmerman and West's
classic study? We wish to propose that the observations may not be
as sound as its frequent citation might suggest. We will argue that
the sample in the study was small and unrepresentative, the figures
potentially misleading and the interpretation provided probably too
narrow. First, the sample: 31 conversational segments consisting of
everyday chit-chat. We are not however told anything about the
length of these segments. All of the people recorded were middle-
class, under 35 and white. Moreover in the results section, we are
simply told that in 11 conversations between men and women, men
used 46 interruptions but women only 2. The problem with this is
that you may simply have one very voluble man in the study which
may have a disproportionate effect on the total. Indeed, one man
did contribute 11 interruptions (nearly one quarter of the total).
This means that the other 10 men contributed on average just 3.5
each. If the segments are sufficiently long such frequencies may be
hardly ₁oticeable. If there was another particularly voluble man in
the sample, these figures would again drop dramatically.

Zimmerman and West also studied only conversation between
two people where it may not be necessary to interrupt to gain the
floor. In a series of studies of televised political interviews one of the
authors (see Beattie, 1982) found that Margaret Thatcher is
typically interrupted more often by her interviewer than she herself
interrupts, although of course she speaks for much longer periods of
time than her interviewer. In other words, we cannot draw any
conclusions about the amount of talk allowed on the basis of
frequency of interruption in conversations involving just two
people. One of the authors analyzed rates of interruption in larger
conversational groups (see Beattie, 1981c). The study was based on
natural university tutorials which were videorecorded. In such
groups it may be necessary to interrupt to gain the floor since there
are more people to whom any current speaker can hand over the
floor. The study involved approximately 10 hours of tutorial
discussion and some 557 interruptions (compared with 55 in the
Zimmerman and West study). The results were that women
interrupted men in 33.8% of floor exchanges, and men interrupted
women in 34.1% of floor switches. No difference! In other words

the effects may be culturally or situationally specific.

The point to be made here is that the results concerning male-female differences in interruption rate are not nearly as clear cut as a perusal of many contemporary books (academic or otherwise) would suggest. Zimmerman and West's results have been replicated by Esposito (1979) in children and by Natale, Entin and Jaffe (1979) and McMillan et al. (1977) in adults; Beattie (1981c), Roger and Schumacher (1983) and Stephens (1983) however failed to replicate the effects. We have however tried to make the additional point that the original classic study in this field by Zimmerman and West may have had some shortcomings. But even if we obtain a consistent effect here, we are still left with the problem of interpretation. Does interruption necessarily reflect dominance as Zimmerman and West and Spender (1982 a, b) suggest? The answer is probably not. Gallois and Markel (1975) have provided evidence to suggest that interruptions may have different psychological relevance during different phases of a conversation. They suggest that on occasion it may signal heightened involvement rather than dominance. Natale et al. (1979) found that a person who has a high need for social approval tends to interrupt more often, and that at least some interruptions may serve to express 'joint enthusiasm' (p. 875). Ferguson (1977) did not find any significant relationship between overall measures of interrupting and self-ratings of dominance by interactants. Beattie, Cutler and Pearson (1982) demonstrated that many interruptions in Mrs Thatcher's political interviews occurred because of the misapplication of turn-yielding cues (see Chapter 10) rather than by attempts by either participant to dominate the conversation.

In other words, the question of male and female dominance in conversation through the medium of interruption is far from conclusively answered. The data are still somewhat contradictory, and the interpretation of the data still not certain. Zimmerman and West (1975) never claimed that male-female conversations would invariably exhibit the asymmetric patterns they observed and suggested that 'A challenging task for further research is the specification of conditions under which . . . sex roles become relevant to the conduct of conversationalists'. Their challenge has still not been fully met.

'*Si femme il y a, silence il n'y a*'? – *peut-être, peut-être.*

Language and ethnic background

Most of us today live in multicultural societies and it is probably true
to say that the majority of multicultural societies are not trouble
free. The trouble often derives from problems in communication
between the different ethnic, racial or national groups. At the
beginning of Chapter 5 we considered a seemingly trivial example
noted by Gumperz (1982). The problem centred on intonation in
certain words; the intonation pattern of one group was incorrectly
interpreted by another. But of course the problem did not stop at
the level of interpretation – people make strong inferences about
the personality and character of others on the basis of their habitual
behaviours. The Indian and Pakistani women working in the staff
canteen at Heathrow were perceived as uncooperative and surly by
their native English customers. Such inferences, on the basis of
fairly 'trivial' linguistic differences between groups, do little to assist
the processes of cultural harmony.

John Gumperz has outlined many possible sources of cultural
misunderstanding in communication, including some of the more
obscure and less obvious ones. The basis for some misunderstandings, however, may be quite obvious. For example, in the
vocabulary of many black English speakers in Britain today there
are words which are simply not familiar to mainstream English
speakers. For example, in British Black English 'lickhead' means to
meet or to meet up with, 'mashmouth' means the shape of mouth
associated with whites, 'red eye' means jealous, 'scrape head'
means bald-headed or short-haired, 'tracing match' means quarrel.
In addition, the grammar may be unfamiliar, for example: 'Ain't
you is a hag?' ('You're a witch, aren't you?') or 'Di biebi niem
Rabat' ('The baby is named Robert'). (see Sutcliffe, 1982).

These examples of British Black English not only seem somewhat
unfamiliar in terms of syntax to speakers of other dialects but
distinctly ungrammatical as well. Indeed, the last example looks
like a poor attempt at the standard English sentence but with pieces
missing. And this is one of the major problems of the languages of
different ethnic groups – when they do resemble English there is a
tendency to view them as a failed attempt at 'proper speech' rather
than as sentences of a language with its own special rules and
linguistic constraints. In the above example, 'niem' in Black English
is the equivalent of the French 's'appeler' (to be called), in other
words it is reflexive in meaning. Thus, the example above, 'di biebi

niem Rabat' is a proper grammatical sentence, with 'di' as the definitive article ('the') and a distinct phonology on all the words.

If there are differences between ethnic groups in the terms of vocabulary or grammar, problems in communication may be troublesome and irritating, but they should be fairly obvious. But in communication there is considerable potential for much more subtle misunderstandings to take place, and this is where the work of John Gumperz has been so revealing. In Chapter 9 we will argue that conversation was essentially a cooperative activity rooted in a huge fund of background knowledge and assumptions. Gumperz has traced how cooperation in conversation may break down as a function of different background knowledge and assumptions about the nature of the conversation which occur as a consequence of the participant's social or ethnic background. Consider the following example:

> When a housepainter arrived at the home of a middle-class couple in California, he was taken around the house to survey the job he was about to perform. When he entered a spacious living room area with numerous framed original paintings on the walls, he asked in a friendly way, 'Who's the *artist*?'. The wife, who was British, replied, 'The painter's not too well known. He's a modern London painter named ——'. The house painter hesitated and then, looking puzzled, said, 'I was wondering if someone in the family was an artist', (Gumperz, 1982, p. 144).

As Gumperz notes, this exchange is part of a casual encounter between strangers who were aware of the dissimilarity of their background because of the difference in their accents yet they were not prepared for the interpretation problems encountered in the conversation. 'Who's the artist?' is a *formulaic* comment often used by Americans when shown around a house. They act as conventionalized complimentary comments. This formulaic compliment is designed to initiate a routine in which the addressee indirectly acknowledges the compliment by making, for example, some self-deprecatory remark. However, the British wife in the above example was not familiar with this and she took the house painter's question to reflect an objective interest in the paintings. The questioner's puzzled look after her response indicated his question had not been understood as intended. Gumperz suggests that there are three linguistic signals present in this one question to indicate to the addressee the possibility of a formulaic usage and these are: firstly the semantic content, secondly the specific syntax, and thirdly the prosody (e.g. the stress and high pitch on the first syllable of artist). In the example, Gumperz also suggests that there are extra linguistic signals acting as well here, particularly the setting and the participants' knowledge of what preceded the interaction. Despite these linguistic and extra-linguistic signals, misinterpretation is what occurred. Gumperz summed up ominously:

> Formulaic use of language is always a problem for non-native speakers. It is perhaps even more of a danger, however, between people who ostensibly speak the same language but come from different social or regional backgrounds. Since they assume that they understand each other, they are less likely to question interpretations. (Gumperz, 1982, p. 145)

Of course problems in interpretation can transcend the use of formulaic expressions. Consider, for example, the following exchange: 'In a taped elementary school classroom session, the teacher told a student to read. The student responded, "I don't wanna read". The teacher got annoyed and said, "All right, then, sit down".' (Gumperz, 1982, p. 147). Now it just so happens that one of the participants in this brief exchange – the teacher – was white. The child on the other hand was black. Here the teacher may easily perceive the child as rude and uncooperative. The child it appears refused to read, despite the teacher's direct request. What's problematic about this? The answer is that whites and blacks seem to differ systematically in their interpretation of what the black child's reply means. Whites tend to interpret the response as a direct refusal, blacks on the other hand tend to say that what it really means is 'Push me a little and I'll read. I can do it, but I need to know that you really want me to'. Blacks who choose the second interpretation also tend to agree that it was the child's rising intonation at the end of his sentence that leads to their conclusion, and many of them also say that if the child had meant it as a direct refusal, he would have stressed 'want'. Thus the two different intonation contours seem to operate here to change meaning for blacks but not for whites.

The possibility of serious misunderstanding in inter-ethnic communication is enormous and the problems may be a good deal more subtle than simple lexical or grammatical differences between styles of speaking. Gumperz has attempted to navigate the maze of communicational misunderstanding so that real cross-cultural communication becomes possible. An important construct he has developed in his explorations is that of a *contextualization cue* that is 'Constellations of surface features of message forms . . . by which speakers signal and listeners interpret what the activity is, how semantic content is to be understood and *how* each sentence relates to what precedes or follows' (Gumperz, 1982, p. 131). In the last example from the elementary school classroom it was the intonation contour which acted as a contextualization cue telling listeners how the sentence was to be interpreted – not as a direct refusal but as an 'encourage me' request. Identification of different 'contextualization cues' has become a prime focus of study in inter-ethnic communication. Only when these features 'habitually used and perceived but rarely consciously noted and almost never talked about directly' (Gumperz, 1982, p. 131) have been identified and described will some of the real problems of inter-ethnic communication be cleared up.

One last point perhaps needs to be made about the study of the language of different ethnic or racial groups. As we said in our brief discussion of some grammatical features of British Black English, some sentences in this speech mode may resemble the standard form very closely and there may be a tendency to view such sentences as both different and necessarily deficient. Indeed much serious academic effort both in Britain and the United States has been devoted to training different ethnic groups, such as blacks, to speak a form of standard English on the basis that they must have a language with which they can learn, and that their own language is deficient for that purpose (e.g. Bereiter and Engelmann, 1966). The rationale behind such training programmes has however been contested by Labov (1969) in a now classic article. His case is very simple: Negro-English despite its 'strange' syntax (with negative inversion, 'Don't nobody know . . .', optional copula deletion, 'If you good . . . If you bad, etc.) nevertheless allows for a complex set of interdependent propositions to build to a convincing argument. Consider one subject – Larry's answer to the question 'What happens to you after you die?':

JL: What happens to you after you die? Do you know?
Larry: Yeah, I know.
JL: What?

Larry: After they put you in the ground, your body turns into –
ah – bones, an' shit.
JL: What happens to your spirit?
Larry: Your spirit – soon as you die, your spirit leaves you.
JL: And where does the spirit go?
Larry: Well, it all depends . . .
JL: On what?
Larry: You know, like some people say if you're good an' shit,
your spirit goin' t'heaven . . . 'n' if you bad, your spirit goin'
to hell. Well, bullshit! Your spirit goin' to hell anyway, good
or bad.
JL: Why?
Larry: Why? I'll tell you why. 'Cause, you see, doesn' nobody
really know that it's a God, y'know, 'cause I mean I have seen
black gods, pink gods, white gods, all color gods, and don't
nobody know it's really a God. An' when they be saying if you
good, you goin' t'heaven, tha's bullshit, 'cause you ain't
going' to no heaven, 'cause it ain't no heaven for you to go to.
(Labov, 1969)

Labov unravels the logical form of the answer and sets out the
Standard English equivalents in linear order:

The basic argument is to deny the twin propositions

(A) If you are good, (B) then your spirit will go to heaven.
(−A) If you are bad, (C) then your spirit will go to hell.

Larry denies (B), and asserts that *if* (A) *or* (−A), then (C).
His argument may be outlined as follows:

(1) Everyone has a different idea of what God is like.
(2) Therefore nobody really knows that God exists.
(3) If there is a heaven, it was made by God.
(4) If God doesn't exist, he couldn't have made heaven.
(5) Therefore heaven does not exist.
(6) You can't go somewhere that doesn't exist.
(−B) Therefore you can't go to heaven.
(C) Therefore you are going to hell.

The argument is presented in the order: (C), because (2) because
(1), therefore (2), therefore (−B) because (5) and (6). Part of the
argument is implicit: the connection (2) therefore (−B) leaves

unstated the connecting links (3) and (4), and in this interval Larry strengthens the propositions from the form (2) *Nobody knows if there is . . .* to (5) *There is no . . .* Otherwise, the case is presented explicitly as well as economically. The complex argument is summed up in Larry's last sentence, which shows formally the dependence of (−B) on (5) and (6):

An' when they be sayin' if you good, you goin' t'heaven,
(The proposition, if A, then B)
Tha's bullshit,
(is absurd)
'cause you ain't goin' to no heaven
(because −B)
'cause it ain't no heaven for you to go to.
(because (5) and (6))."
(Labov, 1969)

Larry is an excellent reminder that linguistic difference need not necessarily imply linguistic deficit. A point constantly worth bearing in mind.

7 The psycholinguistics of speaking

Speech, as we have seen, is just one of a number of channels through which humans can communicate. In this chapter we shall look at the internal cognitive processes which make speech encoding possible. Concepts and ideas cannot be directly communicated, and speech is perhaps the most highly developed channel for the transmission of ideational as opposed to emotional or other sorts of interpersonal messages. To understand speech production we will ultimately need to understand both how conceptual messages are represented in the mind, and how those messages are translated into sounds which can pass from speaker to listener. In the words of Pillsbury and Meader (1928):

> . . . man thinks first and then expresses his thought in words by some sort of translation. To understand this it is necessary to know how the words present themselves in the consciousness of the individual, how they are related to ideas of another type than the verbal, how the ideas originate and how they arouse the words as images, how the movements of speech are evoked by these ideas, and finally how the listener or reader translates the words that he hears or the word that he sees into thoughts of his own. Speech has its origin in the mind of the speaker or writer and the process of communication is completed only when the word uttered or spoken arouses an idea in the listener or reader. (pp. 92–93)

Imagine you are talking on the telephone (a speech-only channel) while, at the same time, gazing out of the window. Suddenly you see a truck smash into your brand new car parked outside. Now you actually *see* much more than that – you see the clouds in the sky, the fact that the pavements are still wet after last night's rain, a group of children playing in the park across the road, and so on, but those are not the things you want to tell your listener about. You want to tell her about the sudden demise of your car. Your first task must be to select, from all of the information you *could* talk about, those elements you actually wish to communicate, and your second task must be to formulate those elements into a message. That message will not yet be represented in language, as can be seen from the fact that the same message (or information, or 'gist') can be encoded numerous ways in the same language, or even in different languages (a surprisingly high proportion of the world's population is fluent in more than one language).

Psychologists have not yet progressed very far in unravelling the 'language of thought' in which conceptual messages are represented, but we can at least list some of the things those representations must contain. First there must be representations of *objects* and *actions* – the pre-linguistic conceptual counterparts of 'car', 'truck' and 'smash' in our example. These objects and actions may have *qualities* we wish to comment on: the car might be 'new', the truck 'large', and the smash 'sickening'. In addition to communicating that the event we have just witnessed involved a car, a lorry and a smash, we must also communicate who did the smashing and who got smashed. In other words, we must convey the *relations* between elements in the conceptual representation.

Elements and *relations* then, are two of the basic components of conceptual representations. Elements include objects, actions and attributes. Simplifying somewhat, we might say that elements are translated into the 'content words' of sentences; objects into nouns ('car', 'lorry', 'house', 'chair' etc.), actions into verbs ('smash', 'drive', 'decorate', 'sit' etc.), attributes of objects into adjectives ('new', 'enormous', 'rambling', 'uncomfortable' etc.), and attributes of actions into adverbs ('sickeningly', 'recklessly', 'lovingly', 'carefully' etc.). There is not always a one-to-one mapping of conceptual entities into words – 'hot water bottle' or 'man in the moon' are single concepts expressed in multi-word phrases.

Expressing relations is part of the function of what linguists call the *syntax* of a language. The principal syntactic device that English exploits to express relations between elements is *word order*. Thus, 'A truck has just smashed into my car' expresses one relationship between the truck, the car, and the action, while 'My car has just smashed into a truck' expresses a very different relationship between the protagonists through a simple change in word order. Other languages have other means for expressing relationships, for example putting different suffixes on the ends of words to indicate their roles in sentences. In such languages (e.g. Latin) word order is then freer. English makes some grammatical use of such inflections (-*ing*, plural -*s*, past tense -*ed* and so on); and 'function words' like 'the', 'is', 'and', 'but', 'should', 'which' and 'although' may also be more closely tied to syntax (expressing relations in sentence structure) than to communicating element information.

The approach to speech production that we have just outlined which views speaking as translating thoughts into sentences, words and sounds is not new. It was espoused by Wilhelm Wundt, the man commonly credited with founding psychology as an independent discipline, in his work *Die Sprache* (1900). The German neurologist Arnold Pick developed in his *Aphasia* (1931) quite a detailed 'expressionist' or 'functionalist' theory based on his experience of language disorders caused by brain injury. Wundt's theory is presented and discussed by Blumenthal (1970), and Pick's by Butterworth (1980a). This approach has gained a fresh acceptance in the last 15 or 20 years with the reawakening of psycholinguistics and cognitive psychology (e.g. Moulton and Robinson, 1981; Bock, 1982; Garrett, 1982).

Conceptual planning for speech

Speech production is not an easy skill to study. Presented with a speaker holding forth fluently on some topic or other, how can we get a handle on explaining the way that speaker is formulating messages, translating them into language, and articulating the chosen words and sentences?

Deese (1978, 1980) studied the speech of people talking in committees, academic seminars, business meetings and similar contexts where, unlike normal conversational speech, extensive monologues from single speakers are not uncommon. First of all, Deese found that his speakers spoke in sentences. Ninety-eight per cent of sentences were grammatically correct. Most sentences were fairly short (over 90% lasted less than 10 seconds), though some were dramatically longer. One syntactic *tour de force* ran 59 seconds without an error.

Some of the speech Deese analyzed involved people giving talks whose content they had thought out in advance, while other samples were of a much more impromptu and spontaneous nature. The preplanned speech was found, not unsurprisingly perhaps, to be much more fluent than the impromptu speech, containing fewer hesitations, false starts, sentence fragments and internal corrections. This observation accords well with the more experimental work of Goldman-Eisler (1961, 1968) and Butterworth (1975). Goldman-Eisler gave speakers a cartoon strip to talk about. Some speakers were asked to describe the events in the strip, while others had to interpret the meaning of the cartoon (i.e. the 'point' of the joke). This second conceptually more complex task produced much more hesitant speech than the simpler descriptive task. Goldman-Eisler also showed that asking speakers to talk for a second or third time on a particular topic produced more fluent, less hesitant speech, even though the actual words used may be quite different in the successive attempts. This reduction in hesitancy reflects the reduction in high-level planning required once the gist of the monologue has been worked out.

Butterworth (1975) obtained speech samples by asking speakers 'to make out the best case they could' in support of some social or political proposition. Transcripts of the speech obtained were typed out and given to fresh subjects whose job was to read through the transcripts and mark boundaries between one 'idea' and the next. The instructions to subjects deliberately did not specify what was to be taken as an 'idea', Butterworth preferring that the subjects should use their own intuitions. The majority of idea boundaries that subjects identified were also clause boundaries, an observation consistent with the hierarchical nature of language units discussed in Chapter 4. In addition, Butterworth found that idea boundaries tended to coincide with changes from fluent to hesitant speech. What is apparently happening here is that subjects asked to talk on, say, why capital punishment should be abolished, think of one argument and express it in reasonably fluent speech. Because of the requirement to continue talking, they now formulate a new justification, identified by the later subjects as a new 'idea'. That formulation is initially a complex process, slowing down the speech rate, though once formulated its completed expression may be fluent. When the idea has run its course, speech becomes hesitant again until the next idea is formulated.

The work of Deese, Goldman-Eisler and Butterworth highlights the *planning* aspects of speech. Much of our cognitive life requires planning – what sequence of jobs to do today and how to do them, what sequence of points to make and how to make them. In both cases planning occurs at several different levels of detail. You may decide at one level to tidy the room, make a cake, then write a letter. Each of these acts must then be planned out in more detail and each sub-goal executed. Sometimes you can plan what to do next while carrying out the present task, particularly if it is not too demanding, but on other occasions your current task may so occupy your attention that you are unable simultaneously to plan the next one. In this latter case, when you have finished your present task (making the cake) you may need to *pause* while you plan your next task (writing the letter). Within the letter-writing task, you may need to pause after finishing one topic while you plan the next (just as the speakers in Butterworth's 1975 study did).

Pausing, then, is time to think – time to plan. This is as true of speech as of any other sphere of cognition, though in speech we must also acknowledge that some pauses are for effect, or are required by the syntax of what we are saying. Speakers will sometimes pause, not to plan, but to allow a point to sink in, or even to stimulate laughter or applause (comedians and politicians are especially prone to this). Alternatively, to borrow an example from Butterworth (1980b), if I say 'John, the older boy, is away at school', then pauses are more or less obligatory at the points marked by commas in the written version, because of the syntax of what I am saying. Finally, pauses in conversation may cue a switch from one speaker to another (see Chapter 10). That said, investigators seem agreed that most pauses in speech are for planning. The planning units revealed in the work of Butterworth and others are very high level, conceptual units. One 'idea' may span several sentences. Ideas are probably best conceived of as conceptual rather than linguistic things. They are plans which are not *in* language but can be *translated* into language. Evidence from pauses and errors in speech provides clues as to what the units of translation of thought into language – the units of encoding – might be.

Encoding into language

Evidence from two sources, pauses and slips of the tongue, converges on the conclusion that the *clause* is an important unit of speech encoding. For our purposes a clause may be regarded as a verb along with the nouns and other words that are in close association with it. 'I worked 'til eight' is a one-clause sentence, whereas 'I worked 'til eight then went out for a meal' is still one sentence but has two clauses, one centred on 'worked' and the other on 'went out'. Thus the clause can stand on its own as a sentence or may combine with other clauses in a multi-clause sentence. Work by Boomer (1965), Barik (1968) and Butterworth (1980b) has shown that pauses tend to cluster at or near the beginnings of clauses in spontaneous speech. Getting at least one word of a clause out indicates to the listener that more is to come (e.g. 'Well, first I'll tidy the room then I'll – er – make a cake').

Evidence from slips of the tongue also points to the significance of clauses in language encoding. A slip of the tongue is defined by Boomer and Laver (1968) as 'an involuntary deviation in performance from the speaker's current phonological, grammatical or lexical intention'. Because we shall make extensive use of data from speech errors, a brief diversion to introduce them is in order. Garrett (1982) estimates that one in every thousand words spoken is distorted by some sort of tongue slip. Slips come in a wide variety of different types. Whole words may exchange places between the intended utterance and the error (examples 1 and 2 below), or the exchange may be between smaller parts of words (examples 3 and 4). Alternatively, words or parts of words may be replaced by elements not present anywhere in the intended utterance, as in examples 5 and 6. In examples 1 to 6, and all future examples, I denotes the Intended utterance (what the speaker meant to say) and E denotes the Error (what the speaker actually said).

1) I: One SPOON of SUGAR
 E: One SUGAR of SPOON

2) I: I put the BOOK on the BED
 E: I put the BED on the BOOK

3) I: The HILLs are SNOWy
 E: The SNOWs are HILLy

4) I: The Sun is SHining
 E: The SHun is Sining

5) I: You'll find the ice-cream in the FRIDGE
 E: You'll find the ice-cream in the OVEN

6) I: The CONDENSATION   on the bathroom walls
   E: The CONDESCENTION on the bathroom walls

These examples from our own corpus illustrate just some of the different sorts of speech error that occur. Though such slips may seem at first glance to be a remarkably obscure facet of communicative behaviour, they have proved surprisingly informative and valuable in understanding speech production. There have been basically two 'waves' of speech error research, one stimulated by the work of the German linguist Rudolf Meringer (Meringer and Mayer, 1895; Meringer, 1908) and including the work in America of Bawden (1900), Wells (1906) and Jastrow (1906). Later in this chapter we shall consider the contribution of the best known member of this early band, Sigmund Freud. The work of the new wave of speech error researchers can be accessed through the chapters in Fromkin (1973, 1980), Butterworth (1980c) and Cutler (1982b).

The relevance of slips of the tongue to the clausal planning hypothesis can be seen if we consider word exchange errors like examples 1 and 2 earlier, and examples 7, 8 and 9 below.

7) I: you've SEEN me EAT that
   E: you've EAT me SEEN that

8) I: the BLOOD supply to the BRAIN
   E: the BRAIN supply to the BLOOD

9) I: I'll need to get this KETTLE on to get the HOT WATER BOTTLE for the bed
   E: I'll need to get this HOT WATER BOTTLE on to get the KETTLE for the bed

In example 8, at the point in time when the speaker intended to say 'blood' he inadvertently produced the word 'brain' which was due to be spoken four words later. This implies that at the moment 'blood' was due, the utterance up to and including the word 'brain' had been planned. By looking at the distances spanned by anticipated elements, and at the higher-level linguistic units within which they occur, we can infer something about the units of language planning. Garrett (1975, 1976) found that in around 85% of word exchanges the two words involved occur in the same clause. This confirms the conclusion drawn from the study of pause distributions, that while language encoding may sometimes extend over more than one clause, the clause is nevertheless an important unit of speech planning.

If we accept the psychological reality of the clause we still have to specify the *level* in the translation of ideas into articulation at which the clause is important. Example 9 may help in that regard. 'Kettle', a single word, was exchanged with 'hot water bottle', three words but one concept or meaning. We wrote earlier of a stage in language planning at which the elements that will be expressed in content words are identified and their relations coded in a way that can be communicated by syntactic devices such as word order. At this early pre-verbal stage, which Garrett (1982) calls the *functional level*, 'kettle' and 'hot water bottle' will both be single elements though the latter is eventually realized as three words. The clause appears to be the linguistic unit in which elements are selected, related, and mapped out as grammatical structures. It is an abstract level at which words are coded as meanings and have not yet been spelled out as strings of sounds (phonemes). The question of how the spoken forms of words are selected to match meanings the speaker wishes to communicate is the question we must tackle next.

Speakers caught in a 'tip of the tongue' state know full well what concept they wish to articulate but cannot recall the word which names that concept. Tip of the tongue states provide a clear intuitive demonstration of the distinction between concepts as non-linguistic message elements and words as their encodings in a particular form of communicative signal. In order to explain such observations, psycholinguists have found it necessary to introduce the notion of one or more internal word-stores, or 'lexicons', from which the spoken (and written) forms of words are retrieved in language production, and which are also involved in recognizing spoken and written words. We shall discuss evidence in Chapters 11 and 12 which points to the possible existence of more than one of these internal lexicons. The spoken forms of words are almost certainly retrieved from a different lexicon from the one in which the written forms of words are stored, and the lexicons used in output may also be separate from those used to recognize words. For safety's sake we will use the term *speech output lexicon* here and in later chapters to refer to the hypothetical internal word-store from which spoken word forms are retrieved in speech production. On this analysis we can now characterize a tip of the tongue state as one in which the speaker has in mind the conceptual (message or functional level) representation of a word but is temporarily unable to access its spoken word form in the speech output lexicon.

Word-finding for speech

Everyone is familiar with the experience of temporarily forgetting a word you nevertheless know you know. Sometimes the difficulty lasts for only a moment; sometimes it may be several days or even weeks before the word is recalled.

The mental experience which accompanies the search for a lost word is a peculiar and tantalizing one, well captured by William James in this oft-quoted passage from his 1890 classic, *The Principles of Psychology*:

> Suppose we try to recall a forgotten name. The state of our consciousness is peculiar. There is a gap therein; but no mere gap. It is a gap that is intensively active. A sort of wraith of the name is in it, beckoning us in a given direction, making us at moments tingle with the sense of our closeness, and then letting us sink back without the longed-for term. If wrong names are proposed to us, this singularly definite gap acts immediately so as to negate them. They do not fit into its mould. . . . The rhythm of a lost word may be there without a sound to clothe it; or the evanescent sense of something which is the initial vowel or consonant may mock us fitfully, without growing more distinct. (James, 1890, p. 251)

Words which catch us in this 'tip of the tongue' stage are typically words we use fairly infrequently. You will not often block on a common word like 'table' or 'door', but might on a rarer one such as 'bureau' or 'vestibule'.

Now, a tip of the tongue state is effectively just a very long pause. Shorter pauses in speech which do not fall at clause boundaries often seem to reflect less dramatic, more quickly resolved, word finding problems. Within-clause pauses usually occur before words which the speaker uses relatively infrequently, or which are unpredictable in the particular context in which they occur, or both (e.g. Beattie and Butterworth, 1979). These brief hesitations seem to occur because speakers sometimes embark on a clause with the meaning and grammatical form of what they want to say worked out, but without having retrieved the spoken form of all the necessary words from their speech output lexicon.

Occasionally, rather than blocking on a word, the word-finding processes throw up the wrong word in error. Slip number 5 (p. 120) was an example of a similar-meaning substitution, as are the following:

10) I: Have you tried Jeremy on BIKKY PEGS?
    E: Have you tried Jeremy on BONIOS?

11) I: Can you wriggle your ANKLES?
    E: Can you wriggle your ELBOWS?

Similar-sound errors also occur as word substitutions in slips of the tongue; see example 6 (p. 121) and the following:

12) I: palace of ANTIQUITIES
    E: palace of INIQUITIES

13) I/E: oh, and I love to watch otters – they're such fantastic APRICOTS – my god, what did I say – ACRO-BATS!

Similar-meaning errors may occur because the wrong semantic representation is activated, or perhaps because the right semantic representation activates the wrong entry in the speech output lexicon. Sometimes two words with very similar meanings are activated simultaneously and combine together in a 'blend' (examples 14 and 15).

14) I: Think about it in all SINCERITY/SERIOUSNESS
    E: Think about it in all SINCERIOUSNESS

15) I: Have we PERSUADED/CONVINCED you?
    E: Have we CONSUADED you?

Similar-sound errors are harder to explain. Perhaps, as Fay and Cutler (1977) suggest, these errors reflect the internal structure of the lexicon, with adjacent storage of similar sounding words. Alternatively, interactions between the phoneme level and the speech output lexicon may sometimes result in the erroneous activation of a word similar in sound to the intended target but different in meaning (Stemberger, 1985).

Slip number 4 on p. 120, and examples 16 to 18 below, illustrate yet another type of speech error, this time one in which the root morphemes of content words exchange leaving their inflectional endings stranded:

16) I: a HOUSEful of CATs
    E: a CATful of HOUSEs

17) I: the PRONGs of a FORK
    E: the FORKs of a PRONG

There are three points worth making about these errors. First, like the word exchanges, they occur predominantly within rather than between clauses, so provide yet more support for the psychological reality of the clause as a unit of language encoding (Garrett, 1975). Second, because they separate root morphemes from their inflections, they provide evidence that roots and inflections may be separately represented in, and retrieved from, the speech output lexicon (in Chapter 14 we shall present evidence from language disorders occurring after brain injury which supports this claim). The third point can be appreciated if one compares the precise pronunciation of the plural /s/ in the intended and error versions of slip 17. In 'prongs' the plural is actually pronounced /z/ – 'prongz' – whereas in the slip, after fork and prong had reversed, the stranded plural was pronounced /s/ as befits its new root – 'forks'. The fact that the form of the inflection changes to suit its new root suggests that inflections are fitted to roots after the point in the planning process at which the exchange occurs (Garrett, 1975, 1982).

The phoneme level

We suggested earlier that a word which has been retrieved from the speech output lexicon ready to be spoken is held prior to articulation as a string of individual speech sounds or *phonemes*. This is not a necessary truth – words could be retrieved as a pattern of continuous muscular commands for articulation – but slips of the tongue like example 4 (p. 120) and examples 18 to 21 below, taken from the Appendix to Fromkin (1973), show that individual phonemes may be misordered just as words and morphemes may be misordered.

18) I: you Better stop for Gas
    E: you Getter stop for Bas

19) I: bRake fLuid
    E: bLake fRuid

20) I: bEd bUgs
    E: bUd bEgs

21) I: an ice Cream cone
    E: a Kice ream cone

Errors like these provide several insights into the sound level of speech planning. First, like the word and morpheme exchanges they show that planning occurs in units larger than the word. In example 18, for instance, the fact that the /g/ of 'gas' replaced the /b/ of 'better' shows that, at the moment when the speaker wanted to say 'better', the phonemic form of 'gas' had already been retrieved from the speech output lexicon ready for articulation. In Lashley's (1951) words, these phonemic errors are 'indications that prior to the internal or overt enunciation of the sentence, an aggregate of word units is partially activated or readied'. Readers will not by now be surprised to learn that phoneme exchanges occur predominantly within rather than between clauses (Garrett, 1975).

Error 21 is especially noteworthy. The intended utterance referred to 'an ice-cream cone', whereas after misplacing /k/ of 'cream' to the front of 'ice' to produce 'kice', the speaker then spoke of 'a kice ream cone'. This indicates that the choice between 'a' and 'an' is made after the stage in speech planning at which phoneme exchanges occur (Fromkin, 1971; Garrett, 1982).

The fact that consonants and vowels will migrate away from their home words to take up residence in other words, sometimes breaking up well-established clusters in the process (e.g. example 19), suggests that at the stage in planning where these errors occur the individual phonemes of a word are separate and ordered like beads on a string. However, by the time they come to be articulated this separateness is often lost. Listen carefully to everyday, casual speech and you will realize how much words can be reduced and simplified in production. A phrase like 'last year' will lose its /t/ and come out as 'lasyear', 'stands still ' will lose its /d/ and the distinctiveness of its two /s/'s producing 'stanstill'. The word 'similar' may be reduced to 'simla', 'prisoner' to 'prizna', 'perhaps' to 'paps', and 'will have been' to 'wilabin' (Brown, 1977). These simplifications are to some extent rule-governed, though the degree of reduction will depend on such factors as the predictability of a word and the formality of the speech (formal speech being more carefully enunciated than casual speech).

Formality and predictability are not the only factors that can affect *how* something is said as opposed to *what* is said. If we hark back to the example of the speaker on the telephone relating the fate of his car, then while the words will convey the event that has occurred, the mixture of surprise, anger and dismay are likely to be communicated in the speaker's tone of voice. Simple emotions are not all that can be conveyed in one's tone of voice. Disbelief, for instance, represents one's attitude to the content of one's message, as do incredulity, cynicism and sarcasm. All of these are as often communicated in the way something is said as in what is said.

Unformulated speech

Most of the utterances we produce in our daily speech are formulated to convey messages about thoughts or events. There are one or two exceptions to this generalization, however. A speaker who says 'How are you?' is rarely asking a genuine question. Phrases like 'How are you?', 'Hello', 'Good morning', even 'Have a nice day' do not so much communicate information as help oil the wheels of social intercourse. The anthropologist Malinowski coined the term 'phatic communion' for these exchanges which Desmond Morris in *The Naked Ape* likened to the social grooming of monkeys.

Phatic speech is unformulated in that the phrases come 'ready made' for use. Verbal 'fillers' in speech such as 'er', 'well', 'you know', 'kind of' and 'like', along with the less printable interjections which litter some speakers' utterances, are other ready-mades. Unformulated speech reaches its pinnacle, however, in the recitation of poems, lyrics or prose. It is no use an actor uttering the gist of Hamlet's famous soliloquy; he must utter the right words and the exact words. We shall see in Chapter 14 that unformulated, nonpropositional speech like this may be retained when brain injury has robbed a speaker of the capacity to assemble information-bearing, grammatically formulated speech.

Consciousness and speaking

Lashley (1958) drew attention to how, 'When we think in words, the thoughts come in grammatical form with subject, verb, object and modifying clauses falling into place without our having the slightest perception of how the sentence structure is produced'. In somewhat provocative mood, Lashley coined the dictum *No activity of the mind is ever conscious* to encapsulate his contention that we are conscious only of the *products* of cognitive operations, not of the operations themselves. We have no conscious access to the mechanics of language encoding: if we had, psycholinguists would not need to resort to time-consuming analyses of pauses, slips and other minutiae of language in their struggle to understand how their own minds work.

Where Lashley merely pointed out the inaccessibility to consciousness of language formulation processes, Sigmund Freud went further in arguing that slips of the tongue may reveal a parallel and unconscious message competing for expression with the conscious, intentional plan. In his *Psychopathology of Everyday Life* (1901, trans. 1975) and in the *Introductory Lectures on Psychoanalysis* (1916–17, trans. 1974) Freud proposed that speech errors 'arise from the concurrent action – or perhaps rather, the mutually opposing action – of two different intentions'. Of these two intentions, one is the message of which the speaker is consciously aware, while the other is often an entirely unconscious message. Thus Freud states: 'My interpretation carries with it the hypothesis that intentions can find expression in a speaker of which he himself knows nothing, but which I am able to infer from circumstantial evidence.' An example will help illustrate the mode of reasoning. On one occasion a President of the Lower House of Parliament who intended to open the sitting said: 'Gentlemen, I take notice that a full quorum of members is present and herewith declare the sitting *closed*.' Freud comments: 'It is clear that he wanted to open the sitting [the conscious intention], but it is equally clear that he also wanted to close it [the disturbing intention]. That is so obvious that it leaves us nothing to interpret' (Freud, 1974, pp. 73–74).

There is no doubt that speech errors can on occasion produce embarrassing results as the following pearls from Simonini (1956) demonstrate:

I: At the ringside I see several ladies in STRAPless evening GOWNs

E: . . . in GOWNless evening STRAPs

I: Ladies and gentlemen, the INKSPOTS

E: Ladies and gentlemen, the STINKPOTS

I: Are you a man or a mouse? Come on, SPEAK up!

E: . . . Come on, SQUEAK up!

I: Remember, it's Wonderbread for the best in bread

E: Remember, it's Wonderbread for the breast in bed

The question that is hard to answer is whether these embarrassing outcomes reveal anything about the speakers' unconscious wishes or are the chance products of mundane mechanical breakdowns (Ellis, 1980a). In Freud's own words, 'Was it . . . merely a deceptive illusion or a poetic exaltation of parapraxes [slips] when we thought we recognised an intention in them?' Many psychologists have thought so, but some evidence favouring Freudian proposals has recently been presented by Baars (1980) and Motley (1980; Motley, Camden and Baars, 1983). In a typical Baars/Motley experiment speakers are asked to say aloud as rapidly as possible a pair of words or non-words such as 'darn bore', or 'gad boof'. Sometimes they reverse phonemes in the attempt (saying 'barn door', or 'bad goof' in these examples). To induce 'Freudian' slips word pairs like 'goxi furl' or 'bine foddy' are used (target errors 'foxy girl' and 'fine body' respectively). Finally, the whole experiment is run on male speakers either by a male experimenter or by an 'attractive, personable, very provocatively attired and seductive' female experimenter(!) Slips with 'Freudian' outcomes apparently occur more often with the female experimenter than the male. This is not a general arousal or nervousness effect since errors with neutral outcomes occur equally often with experimenters of either sex.

In a compromise formulation we might propose that context of the sort induced by Baars and Motley might produce a bias towards a general class of error outcomes without there being any formulated but repressed message competing with the intended message for expression. The bias in question might be due to increased activation in the speech output lexicon for context-related words. For this suggestion to work we must regard the speech output lexicon and the phoneme level not as two stages in a linear sequence, but as two components each interacting with and influencing the other. Stemberger (1985) maintains that we should move away from entirely linear stage models of speech production towards more interactive models, and Ellis (1985b) has argued that such models give a better account of various disorders which can afflict speech production following brain injury (see Chapter 14).

8 The stream of behaviour: co-ordinating verbal and nonverbal channels

In this chapter we turn our attention to how some of the main channels of communication interact. Explorations of the interconnections of the channels of human communication is a fairly recent endeavour.

> Language, in its natural occurrence as speech, is never disembodied but is always manifested through behavior. For example: what does the lowering of the voice, 'while' the eyes widen, 'while' the brows raise, 'while' an arm and fingers move, 'while' the head lowers, 'while' a leg and foot shift, 'while' the face flushes, have to do with what was said or left unsaid? How is this modified by the equally complex configurations of change which immediately precede and follow? And how are all of the above changes, in turn, related to the similarly involved behavior of the other person or persons in the interaction?
>
> We are quite often very clear about what a person said and meant but cannot tell precisely how he accomplished it or how we are able to accomplish our understanding of it.
>
> The search for the units of behavior, their organisation and their empirical validation thus constitutes *the* central problem of behavioral analysis. (Condon and Ogston, 1967, p. 221)

This is how Condon and Ogston posed the central question of the organization of the behaviour of people engaged in conversation nearly two decades ago. *The* central problem of behavioural analysis has still not been fully solved but we now know a great deal more about the 'complex configurations' and the organizational ties than we did two decades ago.

The empirical work of Condon and Ogston themselves was concentrated at the syllabic level of speech and the lowest level of nonverbal behaviour. Their technique involved micro-analysis of sound movie films of interaction (filmed usually at 48 frames per second). They transcribed all of the phonemes of speech and the behaviour of extensive parts of the body such as the head, eyes, brows, upper lip, lower lip, trunk, right shoulder, right elbow, right wrist, first, second and third finger on right hand and right thumb on to complex and detailed charts.

For example, in one film (taken at the standard rate of 24 frames per second) of a three-person interaction (involving a mother, father and their four-year-old son at dinner), Condon and Ogston (1967) found the following pattern of nonverbal behaviour of the mother to accompany the tripartite segmentation of the word 'around' as she articulated it. Their detailed, exhaustive search proved fruitful:

Table 8.1: Non-verbal behaviour accompanying the word 'around'

	a	rou	nd
Head	Up slight	Back & up slight	Down
Eyes	Left slight	Widen	Right slight
Mouth	Forward & purse	Open and widen	Close & back & narrow
Trunk	Forward	Bend & back slight	Back
Right shoulder	Lock	Forward slight	Forward
Right elbow	Extend slight	Extend	Extend slight
Left shoulder	Forward slight	Abduct slight	Back slight

During the intensive microanalysis of the three-person inter-action . . . a startling discovery was made. The father and son were found to share patterns of bodily changes in a precise harmony with the mother as she spoke. These changes occurred in both in relationship to the mother at exactly the same frame (1/24 of a second). All three sustained directions of change across syllable and word length segments of speech and changed together at the same 1/24 of a second that these segments ended, to again sustain directions of movement together across the next ensuing segment. This occurred throughout the two utterances examined and in all other films of 'normal' interaction subsequently studied. (Condon and Ogston, 1967, p. 229)

This phenomenon was dubbed 'interactional synchrony' by Condon and Ogston and was, they argued, a basic organizational principle linking people in social interaction. An even more primitive principle was also observed, that of self-synchrony – 'The organisation of change of a speaker's body motion occurs synchronously with the articulated, segmental organisation of his speech. The body dances in time with speech' (Condon and Ogston, 1967, p. 225). The example provided earlier of the behaviours accompanying the articulation of 'around' is, according to Condon and Ogston, an example of 'self-synchrony'.

In another investigation, involving a therapist and a schizophrenic patient, Condon and Ogston found that interactional synchrony still occurred between the patient and his therapist but that self-synchrony partially broke down in that certain parts of the body were out of synchrony with certain other parts (Condon and Ogston, 1966). The painstaking analyses of Condon and Ogston suggested that there are close organizational ties binding speech and nonverbal behaviour together at the most microscopic of levels. Organizational ties founded in the syllabic structure of speech are, they suggest, probably essential for successful communication.

The connections between language and nonverbal behaviour at more macro levels were explored by Albert Scheflen and Adam Kendon. Scheflen was principally interested in the analysis of psychotherapy sessions. His goal was to describe the hierarchical structure of nonverbal behaviour, and he took his lead from linguists and linguistic studies of the structure of language.

> Observed through time, the behaviors that make up communicative programs appear to be a continuous stream of events, but actually they are grouped into standard units of structure. These units are not arbitrary divisions made up spontaneously by an interactant or imposed presumptively by an investigator; they are specific constellations of behavior built into a culture, learned and perceived in communication as Gestalten. (Scheflen, 1964, p. 319)

Scheflen attempted to describe the hierarchical structure of nonverbal behaviour corresponding to the hierarchical structure of language – the 'point' (a fixed head posture corresponding crudely to a point in discussion); a 'position' (a gross postural shift involving at least half the body and lasting from about half a minute to 5 or 6 minutes and corresponding to a point of view that an interactant may take in a given interaction); and a 'presentation' ('the totality of one person's positions in a given interaction'). Through his investigations of psychotherapy sessions Scheflen discovered a phenomenon related to interactional synchrony which he termed postural congruence – where two or more individuals adopt identical or mirror-image postures. Scheflen also noted how in group psychotherapy sessions members of the group not only took up similar postures but also shifted posture after one of them had changed position so that the group maintained postural congruence through a series of changes in body position. As we have said earlier Scheflen also suggested that old friends may shift into postural congruence during an argument 'to indicate the ultimate continuity of their relationship'. Again we have hints of strong inter-connections between speech and nonverbal behaviour as well as *speculation* about the duality of functioning of the two systems. When friends argue verbally they compensate nonverbally by adopting identical postures, so Scheflen says. Once again, Scheflen's work attempts to come to grips with the complexity of conversation by dealing with the interaction between the main systems of communication.

Very much in the Scheflen mould is some of the work of Adam Kendon (1972), who also described the relationship between speech and nonverbal behaviour at a fairly high level. Unfortu-nately, Kendon introduces a new terminology again. For dividing up language he used the terms: 'discourse' (the highest level unit), 'the locution cluster' (corresponding to a paragraph in written language), 'the locution group' (a group of locutions or complete sentences) and 'the locution' (a complete sentence separated by a 'distinct pause' from any immediately preceding locution). Kendon, like Scheflen, studied the relationship between the hierarchical structure of language and the hierarchical structure of behaviour. He found that

The larger the speech unit, the greater the difference in the form of movement and the body parts involved. For example, the locution groups were distinguished by the limb or limbs involved in gesticulation. Each locution was distinguished by a different pattern of movement within the same limb. . . . Prior to each speech unit there is a change in position of one or more body parts. This was termed 'speech preparatory' movement. The larger the speech unit, the more body parts there are that are involved in this movement. . . . Our analyses confirmed Condon and Ogston's finding that changes in the patterning of movement which occurs as the subject is speaking are coordinated with changes in the pattern of sound. (Kendon, 1972, p. 205)

However, it is important at the outset to mention that there are a number of methodological problems with the research just described. McDowall, in an investigation reported in 1978, called the whole phenomenon of interactional synchrony into question on methodological grounds. He had two principal objections. The first one concerned reliability of measurement – the extent to which two independent observers of the same interactional sequence would produce the same observations and measurements. He argued that reliability was low for the very fine-grain measurements of the boundaries of movements necessary for the kind of work that Condon and Ogston carried out. His second objection was that chance probability was not taken into account. If several people are engaged in a conversation, one would expect that some of their boundaries of movement would coincide by chance alone. In a study of a six-person discussion group, McDowall did not find any real evidence of interactional synchrony at an above chance level. This led him to doubt the existence of interactional synchrony. (The existence of postural congruence is not however in doubt, see Beattie and Beattie, 1981, Chapter 3). Of course, it could be argued that six first-year students in the laboratory (some unacquainted) might not be relaxed enough or intimate enough to show interactional synchrony, especially since they knew that filming was taking place. Nevertheless, the McDowall study must plant the seeds of doubt in our minds, especially since Condon and Ogston seemed to ignore certain basic methodological principles (such as computing inter-observer reliabilities, or percentage agreement between observers; or computing chance probabilities for the co-occurrences of actions). Similarly, Scheflen and Kendon fail to report inter-observer reliabilities in their studies; instead we just get the reports of these expert observers on behaviour.

Furthermore, Scheflen tells us that people show postural congruence when arguing whereas Charny (1966) found that congruence between a therapist and patient was much more likely when the verbal channel also indicated rapport (see Chapter 3, p. 46).

Charny's findings seem to go directly against Scheflen's observations and it is difficult to decide between them because of the methodological inadequacies. Kendon in his study used a single subject and failed to show that any effects generalized across subjects. In addition he used a somewhat vague and idiosyncratic system for the analysis of language (e.g. is a complete sentence not separated by a pause from any preceding locution *not* a locution, and if not, what is it? What does he mean by a 'distinct pause'? The perceptual thresholds of pauses in speech depend critically upon their linguistic location (see Martin, 1970). Is this to be taken into account in the definition?). One of the present authors' own research has been concerned with a description of the organization of speech and nonverbal behaviour in conversation in certain social settings, and it has attempted to deal with some of these methodological problems (for detailed consideration of the methodological aspects of the investigation, the reader is referred to the original papers – Beattie, 1978a; Beattie and Bogle, 1982; Butterworth and Beattie, 1978).

Here we consider the organization of two central components of nonverbal behaviour in conversation. The two components under investigation are speaker eye-gaze and speaker hand movement and gesture, and how they relate to speech.

Gaze – that is looking at another person – is of central importance in social behaviour (see Chapter 3). We both send and receive signals with our eyes. As Erving Goffman said in an interview in the *New York Times* (12 February 1969), 'Eyes, you know, are the great intruders'. They intrude into every aspect of social interaction. Michael Argyle and Mark Cook, in their book *Gaze and Mutual Gaze*, outlined some of the ways in which gaze and speech are connected. They say:

Gaze is intricately connected with language, in the following ways:
1) *As a visible signal*
a) Long glances are used by speakers as full-stop signals, and for other grammatical breaks.
b) Glances are used by speakers to emphasise particular words or phrases, or to make the whole utterance more persuasive. Other kinds of commentary on the utterance can be given by varying facial expression.
c) The line of regard is used to point at persons or things, e.g. to

suggest who should speak next.

d) Glances are used by listeners to indicate continued attention and willingness to listen. Aversion of gaze means lack of interest or disapproval.

e) Glances made by listeners after particular points of an utterance act as reinforcers, and encourage the speaker to produce more of the same.

f) Glances made by listeners vary in meaning with facial expression, including that in the region of the eyes; raised eyebrows indicate surprise, fully raised eyebrows disbelief; lowered eyebrows puzzlement, fully lowered eyebrows anger.

g) Gaze is one signal among others for the communication of interpersonal attitudes; however, there is no linkage with speech here, glances are simply longer or shorter and accompanied by different facial expression.

2 *As a channel*

a) Speakers look up at grammatical pauses to obtain feedback on how utterances are being received, and to see if others are willing for them to carry on speaking.

b Listeners look at speakers a lot of the time, in order to study their facial expressions, and their direction of gaze.

3) *Aversion of gaze*

Gaze is used intermittently, so that when it is used it gives a signal. The reason that people do not look all the time is probably to avoid overload of information. (1976, p. 121)

Patterns of speaker eye-gaze

A number of the functions listed above depend critically upon the speech context in which the gaze occurs. A detailed description of the interconnections between gaze and speech in conversation would thus be of the highest priority. The majority of studies on speaker gaze in conversation have, however, tended to confine themselves to attempting to measure the amount rather than the precise patterning of this form of behaviour. The studies which have explored the patterning of gaze with speech have often employed rather ubiquitous and sometimes vague categories of language such as 'remark' or 'question'. As a result, the patternings of gaze which have been reported have shown considerable variation.

Libby (1970), for example, observed that in an interview in which the interviewer gazed steadily at subjects who were replying to questions, nearly 85% broke gaze during their reply, although less than 10% broke gaze before the end of the question. Here, 'embarrassing' and 'unembarrassing', 'personal' and 'impersonal' questions, demanding long and short answers, were combined in the analysis of gaze patterning. Nielsen (1962) observed that subjects broke gaze at the beginning of a 'remark' in conversation in almost 45% of all cases, and they looked at their interviewer at the end of a 'remark' in about 50% of all cases. But in these studies we end up with various gross averages. The nature of the 'remarks' presumably varied and presumably also affected subjects' gaze, but this was not really analyzed.

The most intensive early investigation of the patterning of gaze in conversation, and the only early study to consider the psychological planning processes behind speech, was the seminal study by Adam Kendon (1967). One of his principal observations was that speakers tended to look at listeners more during fluent speech than during hesitant speech (50% of the time spent speaking fluently as compared to only 20% of the time speaking hesitantly). Kendon hypothesized that speaker-gaze frequently performs a monitoring function (as we discussed earlier) and that such monitoring may interfere with the planning of spontaneous speech. Such inter-ference was subsequently demonstrated – Beattie (1981a) showed that in an interview situation, if you asked speakers to look at their interlocutor all the time whilst answering questions their speech showed a marked increase in the proportion of false starts. Speakers may therefore avert gaze during the hesitant periods in spontaneous speech to reduce potential interference. This is of course what Kendon found.

Kendon also described the patterning of gaze with respect to 'phrases' and 'phrase boundary pauses' (some of the principal units of analysis in his corpus), and found that the speaker tended to look at the listener as he approached the end of a phrase and continued to look during the phrase boundary pause, but averted his gaze as the next phrase began. It was also observed that 'utterances' terminated with prolonged gaze (one problem with this study, however, was that the linguistic units around which the analyses were based – 'phrase', 'utterance', etc. were not defined). Kendon hypothesized that gaze had a signalling function at the ends of utterances, specifically concerned with the transmission of information to the listener about the appropriateness of a response at these points (but see Beattie, 1978b).

The aim of one of the author's own investigation was to analyze the distribution of gaze with respect to the units of planning of spontaneous speech, specifically the 'temporal cycles' identified by Henderson et al. (1966), Goldman-Eisler (1967), Butterworth (1975), and Beattie (1979) and discussed by us in Chapter 7. The experimental evidence suggests that cognitive processing is asymmetrically distributed throughout these cycles. More cognitive planning seems to occur in the hesitant phase of the cycle than in the fluent phase, since both short-term clausal planning and more long-term semantic planning occur in the hesitant phase, whereas the evidence suggests that only immediate lexical decisions are made in the fluent phase (Beattie, 1979a). Thus, if we assume that speaker gaze has a monitoring function (and therefore makes demands on the speaker's processing capacity) then we would predict an approximately inverse relationship between the relative hesitancy of speech and the amount of speaker gaze at the listener.

Previous research has also suggested that these cycles represent semantic units in speech; cycles have been found to correspond to 'ideas' in the speech text (Butterworth, 1975, see also Chapter 7). Thus, these cycles will probably function as important units in conversation and speakers may seek to avoid any interruption of ideas by inhibiting (where possible) cues such as eye-gaze which might elicit listener responses during the cycles, and by employing such cues more forcefully and more frequently at the boundaries of the units. Thus, it can be predicted that speaker eye-gaze at the boundaries of these units will be very common in conversation. The experimental method used by Beattie (1979a) owed a lot to Condon and Ogston – frame-by-frame analysis of video-recordings of natural dyadic verbal interactions (tutorials).

Gaze and 'temporal cycles'

Four conversations were video-recorded; three were university tutorials just involving two people (typical of Cambridge), one was part of a seminar involving just two participants. All speakers analyzed were male. The recording was done through a one-way mirror and a split screen technique was employed – a technique which allows high reliability and validity of measurement (see Beattie and Bogle, 1982).

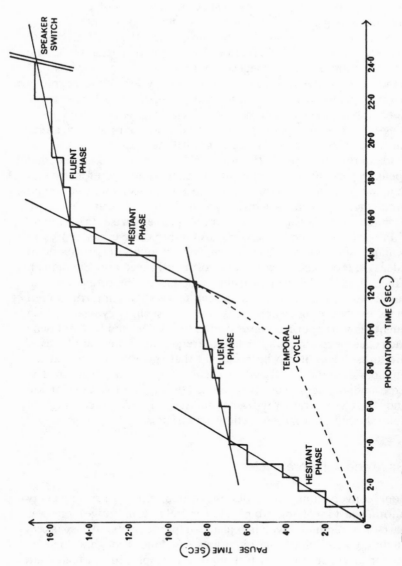

Figure 8.1 Sequential temporal patterns within one sample of spontaneous speech

The analysis focussed on long turns; pauses (≥200 milliseconds) were identified and measured using an Ediswan pen oscillograph and pause detector (see Goldman-Eisler, 1968). Then every individual pause and period of phonation was measured and plotted on a graph (with phonation on the x axis and pausing on the y axis) and lines fitted to represent changes in the pause/phonation ratio across time, in such a way as to attempt to minimize local changes in these two variables from the lines (see Henderson et al., 1966, p. 205) – see Fig. 8.1. The time of initiation of each period gaze and gaze aversion by the speaker at his interlocutor was judged from the videoscreen (a timer was mixed onto the videotape to assist in this process) and plotted on to the graphs, thus building up a complex and fine-grain record of speech and looking in conversation.

When pause/phonation plots were made, a cyclic pattern did tend to emerge as predicted by Henderson et al. (1966) (but see Power 1983, 1984 and Beattie, 1984 for some recent discussion of this topic). The mean cycle time was 22 seconds and the average cycle length 8.8 clauses (the hesitant phases were on average 3.6 clauses long; the fluent phases on average 5.2 clauses long). These cycles are thus substantially longer than individual sentences.

The number of hesitant and fluent phases in the temporal cycles dominated by gaze or gaze aversion (i.e. with more than or less than 50% gaze, respectively) were then noted, as was the slope of each phase measured in degrees; a 45° slope of course would indicate an equal proportion of pausing and phonation, a 0° slope indicates uninterrupted phonation, a 90° slope indicates extended pausing.

A difference in the relative number of hesitant and fluent phases dominated by gaze did emerge: 41% of hesitant phases were dominated by gaze aversion compared with 17% of fluent phases but this difference failed to reach significance because of the small numbers involved. There was a tendency for both types of phase to be accompanied by more gaze than gaze aversion, indicating a high level of speaker gaze generally in this type of academic situation. In regular tutorials, speakers do of course tend to know each other and this is one reason why the level might be high.

The slopes (reflecting the mean percentage of pausing per phase) of the various hesitant and fluent phases were then compared. In the case of fluent phases, those phases dominated by gaze aversion tended to be significantly more hesitant than the phases dominated by gaze (mean slopes 13.7° and 6.3° respectively). In the case of hesitant phases there was no significant difference in the slopes of those phases dominated by gaze or gaze aversion (mean slopes 47.1° and 47.6° respectively).

It should be noted that the dominance of a phase by gaze or gaze aversion is not simply attributable to there being more phonation or hesitation in the phase, since 6 of the 13 hesitant phases dominated by gaze had slopes which were greater than 45° (i.e. there was more pausing than phonation), and none of the fluent phases had slopes greater than 45°, although four of these phases were dominated by gaze aversion. In a number of cases, the distribution of gaze can be clearly seen not to be optimal for cognitive purposes. For example, two hesitant phases had slopes of 90°, i.e. they consisted of prolonged pausing, but these were accompanied by uninterrupted gaze, and not gaze aversion.

Gaze and syntactic clauses

Gaze across the first 12 boundary locations of surface structure clauses between 2 and 12 words in length was analyzed, and the percentage of each boundary location occupied by gaze was calculated. (Interested readers are referred to Beattie, 1983, p. 62.)

Very briefly when all clauses were considered, the distribution of gaze was found to be quite random: similarly with clauses falling within hesitant phases. However, in the case of clauses in fluent phases, the distribution was not random. The percentage of successive boundary locations occupied by gaze in fluent phases tended to increase in a fairly systematic fashion – the mean percentage increase from boundary location 1 to boundary location 12 was 25.1%. The mean percentage of gaze at clause junctures throughout the speech was found to be 60.5%.

Table 8.2: Incidence of gaze at clause junctures nearest termination of temporal cycle compared with the incidence at all other clause junctures

	Gaze	Gaze aversion
Clause junctures nearest termination of cycle	18	4
Other clause junctures	100	71

Gaze, temporal cycles and clause junctures

The incidence of gaze at clause junctures nearest the terminal points of temporal cycles was compared with the incidence of gaze at all other clause junctures (see Table 8.2).

Gaze was found to occur significantly more frequently at clause junctures nearest the terminal points of temporal cycles than at other clause junctures. The mean percentage gaze at clause junctures nearest the terminal points of temporal cycles was approximately 82%.

The gaze which coincided with the ends of temporal cycles was not however, in any sense, a discrete cueing signal. This terminal gaze was initiated a mean of 1.83 syntactic clauses before the end of a cycle (a mean of 12.0 words earlier), and it continued into the subsequent cycle for a mean of 1.44 clauses (mean of 5.7 words). These figures suggest that such a gaze does not function solely as a signal that an appropriate listener response point has been reached. They perhaps suggest instead that such a gaze performs a dual function – firstly, that of signalling, and conversational regulation, and secondly that of monitoring the reception of the semantic unit by the listener. Speakers look before the end of the unit to see, presumably, how it's going down.

Filled hesitation and temporal cycles

The analyses just described revealed that the patterning of gaze and proportion of gaze within individual hesitant and fluent phases was not simply a function of a basic cognitive variable plus a compatible, reciprocal, social signalling function. There did seem to be considerable divergence from the patterns which would be optimal on speech planning grounds. An analysis was thus performed to determine if this divergence had any significant effects on the speech produced. The amount of filled hesitation (consisting of filled pauses, repetitions, false starts and parenthetic remarks) occurring in each cycle was analyzed. This measure should prove sensitive to deficits in forward planning because it had been demonstrated that in an artificially controlled situation, where you ask interviewees to look at their interviewer all the time when they answer questions, frequency of filled hesitation did increase (see Beattie, 1981a). In this natural test, a similar result was obtained.

False starts were approximately five times as common, (per unit word spoken) in cycles where the speaker was looking at his interlocutor during the planning phase. [There was also an increase in rate of repetition and parenthetic remarks (per unit word) in such cycles, although these differences failed to reach significance].

In cycles where speakers tended to look at their interlocutor for the majority of the time in the planning phase a false start occurred approximately every 10 words, compared with every 50 words in speech where the speaker tended to avert gaze during the planning phase.

In summary, this investigation revealed that speaker eye-gaze is connected in an intricate pattern with the flow of spontaneous speech. Speakers tend to look most at listeners during the most fluent phases of speech. If they fail to avert their eyes during the planning periods of spontaneous speech, there is a marked increase in speech disturbances, particularly false starts. The temporal cycles which seem to reflect some of the basic planning processes of spontaneous speech have a great influence on the patterning of speaker eye-gaze. But some divergence from what might be expected on purely cogitive grounds was observed. This is almost certainly to do with social processes. Speakers have to plan what they are going to say, but in addition they often want to make a good impression – they wish to appear 'competent', 'believable', 'knowledgeable'. This may be achieved in part by looking directly at the listener. Anyone who refused to look at their interlocutor at all would probably not be perceived as very 'competent', 'believable', or 'knowledgeable', regardless of topic. Unfortunately, these competing demands can sometimes lead to problems in speech where the frequency of various types of speech 'disturbance' increases dramatically. Clearly conversations are sometimes difficult to handle.

Speaker-movement and gesture

An obvious characteristic of conversation is that speakers seldom remain perfectly still during it. The hands of most speakers rarely stop moving. There appear to be two fundamentally different kinds of speaker hand activity: one class of movement, which is not speech-related, involves self-stimulation (e.g. finger-rubbing, scratching, nose-picking, etc.). These have been termed body-focussed movements (Freedman and Hoffman, 1967) or self-adaptors (Ekman and Friesen, 1969b). The second class of movement does appear to be related to speech and furthermore a subject of these movements does seem to reflect the meaning of what is said. These related to speech movements can be termed speech-focussed movements. In terms of the categories discussed in Chapter 3, the class of speech-focussed movements would include 'emblems', 'illustrators' and 'regulators' mainly.

There have been two principal theoretical orientations concerning the significance of speaker hand movement (it should be noted that many early studies did not differentiate speech-focussed and body-focussed movements). One view, based in the psychoanalytic tradition, holds that such movements can reveal speakers' emotional or affective state (Freud, 1905; Deutsch, 1947, 1952; Feldman, 1959). A second view holds that such movements constitute an alternative channel of communication, either augmenting the verbal component (Baxter, Winters and Hammer, 1968) or substituting for it (Mahl, Danet and Norton, 1959). It should be noted that no demonstrable benefit from these nonverbal behaviours generally has been found to accrue to the listener (emblems, of course, would be an exception), except in the case of the communication of shape information in an experimental situation requiring subjects to describe two-dimensional drawings (Graham and Argyle, 1975). However, Dobrogaev (cited by Schlauch, 1936) found that the elimination of gesture resulted in marked changes in speech performance, with decreased fluency and a reduced vocabulary size. Graham and Heywood (1975) also found that the elimination of gesture (subjects were instructed to keep their arms folded) produced some changes in speech content (for example, an increase in expressions denoting spatial relationships, and a reduction in the use of demonstratives), as well as increase in the proportion of time spent pausing. Graham and Heywood concluded that this pattern of results suggested that gestures normally facilitate language production, at least on certain topics (e.g. those involving spatial descriptions).

There have been other attempts to relate various types of bodily movement to structural units of language, most notably Condon and Ogston (1966, 1967), Scheflen (1964, 1965) and Kendon (1972), but as was discussed earlier, all suffered from methodological pitfalls and in some cases limited data bases.

Other studies have attempted to relate movement to the psychological processes underlying speech. Dittmann (1972) investigated the relationship between an undifferentiated class of 'nervous' movements of the head, hands and feet (detected by an 'accelerometer') and phonemic clauses or tone groups – phonologically marked segments containing only one primary stress. He discovered that these movements clustered towards the beginnings of *hesitant* phonemic clauses and thus concluded, following Boomer (1965), that these nervous movements were motor manifestations of the speech encoding process. McNeill (1975) presented a theory of the relationship between gesture and speech (this unfortunately preceded detailed naturalistic description of their inter-relations). McNeill's theory was based on the assumption that speech is integrated in terms of the 'syntagma' which is, according to Kozhevnikov and Chistovich (1965, p. 74), 'one meaning unit, which is pronounced as a single output'. (Syntagmas have similar dimensions to phonemic clauses, but considerably more emphasis is laid on semantics in their definition.)

McNeill argued that throughout development, speech remains directly adapted to the sensory-motor and representational levels of cognitive functioning but with time there occurs a 'semiotic extension' of the basic speech mechanism to cover more abstract levels of operational thought. Gestures, according to McNeill, have their origin in this semiotic extension, but they correspond to the sensory-motor schemas underlying speech. The evidence for the theory (based on observations of individuals simultaneously performing tasks, such as mental paper folding, and describing their actions) revealed that iconic gestures were initiated with the onset of speech associated with the basic action schemas, and were prolonged for the duration of these schemas. This theory, however, can be challenged on a number of accounts. First, the assumption that the *fundamental* unit of encoding is of the same dimension as a clause can be questioned. Other larger units after all do seem to be involved (see Butterworth, 1975; Beattie, 1979a and Chapter 7). Second, the relevance of such restricted data for natural movement and speech may be doubted.

Thus, in an investigation reported in 1978 one of the authors with Brian Butterworth analyzed the relationship between the temporal structure of spontaneous speech and a number of types of speaker hand movements (see Butterworth and Beattie, 1978). They distinguished:

1) Speech-focussed movements: all movements of the arm or hand except self-adaptors (e.g. finger-rubbing, scratching, etc.).

2) Gestures: more complex movements (most frequently illustrators, with the very occasional emblem) which appear to bear some semantic relation to the verbal component of the message.

3) Changes in the basic equilibrium position of the arms and hands, that is, changes in the position the hands return to after making a movement.

The speech was analyzed into its pause/phonation components as described earlier. The analysis of the hand movement (again using the slow motion facility of the video and again taking advantage of the fact that a timer to one-hundredth of a second was mixed onto the tape) revealed that speech-focussed movements occurred most frequently per unit time during the fluent phases of temporal cycles. The highest incidence of the onset of this class of behaviours was in pauses in the fluent phases. These movements were approximately three times more frequently initiated during such pauses than during pauses in the hesitant phases (per unit time).

Gestures yielded an essentially similar distribution, but in the case of gestures the trends were much more pronounced. Gestures were approximately five times as frequently initiated per unit time during pauses in the fluent phases than during pauses in the hesitant phases. Gestures were also almost three times as frequent during pauses in the fluent phase as during periods of phonation in the fluent phase. The start of the gesture tended to precede the start of the word it was associated with (the mean delay between the start of the gesture and the start of the word being around 800 milliseconds).

The residual class of hand movements displayed a very different distribution. This time there was no overall difference in the number occurring per unit time during pauses in the hesitant and fluent phases and these behaviours were most common during periods of phonation, particularly in hesitant phases.

This distributional difference between gestures and other speech-focussed movements suggests a functional difference. Speech focussed movements other than gestures consist mainly of simple batonic movements, and their close relation to periods of actual phonation in both hesitant and fluent phases indicates that a common-sense interpretation of them as emphasis markers is well-founded. The asymmetry in the distribution of gestures, on the other hand, shows that these are not mere emphatic markers, but are functionally related to planning. This is compatible with Cohen's (1980) observation that speakers use illustrators even when alone in a room talking into a microphone. They are intimately connected with the planning of speech rather than being purely 'social' in origin. Since gestures are relatively infrequent in the hesitant phase itself, it seems they are not connected with the ideational planning process but rather with the lexical planning process. This hypothesis is supported by their close association with pauses in the fluent phase.

Further evidence of the functional distinction between gestures and other speech-focussed movements is to be found by comparing their distributions in respect of the form-class of the words they are associated with. Gestures are heavily concentrated on nouns (41.3%), verbs (23.8%), and adjectives (15.9%) – classes which contain most of the infrequent and high-information lexical items. Other movements, however, are much more evenly spaced over form-classes.

The relationship between changes in the basic equilibrium position of the arm and hands, phasal transition points and clause junctures was analyzed (see Table 8.3). A significant tendency for changes in the basic equilibrium position to correspond to both the terminal points of hesitant phases and to the terminal points of fluent phases was observed. (Changes in equilibrium position were

Table 8.3: Position in speech of changes in the basic equilibrium position of the arm and hand

	Number of changes in equilibrium position corresponding to each category	Number of occurrences of each phenomenon not accompanied by change in equilibrium position
End of hesitant phase	5	20
End of fluent phase	8	20
Clause juncture	24	180
Other	14	1620

also found to coincide generally with junctures between clauses). These results provide further evidence that the hesitant and fluent phases, identified from changes in the gross temporal patterning of the speech, have probably some underlying psychological significance.

A number of conclusions may be tentatively advanced. Firstly, there are two fundamentally distinct kinds of speech-focussed movement – gestures (mainly illustrators) and other speech-focussed movements. Secondly, the suggested distinction between the hesitant and the fluent phase discussed in Chapter 7 receives further support from the distribution of equilibrium changes, and from the relative distribution of gestures observed. Thirdly, gestures appear to be by-products of lexical preplanning processes, and seem to indicate that the speaker knows in advance the semantic specification of the words he will utter; in some cases he has to delay to search for a relatively unavailable item. Some crude semantic specification of lexical items might therefore be part of the ideational planning process. Finally, lexical planning is a necessary, though not a sufficient, condition for the occurrence of gestures.

One hypothesis that can be offered to account for the fact that gestures precede lexical items (rather than occur simultaneously with them) is that there is a greater repertoire of lexical items than of gestures to choose from. Lexical items have to be drawn from a large corpus – the mental lexicon probably consists of 20,000–30,000 items. Not all will be candidates at each choice point – some items will necessarily be excluded by the preceding linguistic context – but in some cases the number of lexical items which satisfy the semantic and syntactic constraints will be large (these of course will be words of low transitional probability; that is to say, words unpredictable in context). On the other hand, the repertoire of gestures typically employed in conversation is comparatively small. Word choice will, therefore, generally take longer.

Conclusions

This chapter reported some research into the inter-connections in time between some aspects of nonverbal behaviour and spontaneous speech in conversation. It focussed on speaker eye-gaze and hand movement and gesture. It suggested that there are strong inter-connections between the planning units underlying spontaneous speech, as reflected in the patterns of hesitations, and the organization of these nonverbal forms of behaviour. Speaker eye-gaze is most common during the most fluent phases of spontaneous speech; and the most complex speaker hand gestures also tend to occur in these phases, although they often arise during the short pauses which punctuate these otherwise fluent episodes. Blaise Pascal, the French philosopher of the 17th century, said: 'Our nature consists in motion; complete rest is death.' Our nature does consist in motion, and what is interesting is that this motion is based around complex speech rhythms. Not rhythms of sound, interestingly – and here we differ from Condon and Ogston (1966, 1967) – but rhythms of mental processing: operations which result in, and are necessary for, the originality and the very spontaneity of spontaneous speech, operations which seem to guide and direct many other aspects of speaker activity.

The central problem of behavioural analysis – the search for the units of nonverbal behaviour – may not yet have been solved, but we have gone a fair way towards understanding some of the links and connections to be found in the stream of behaviour.

9 Conversation as cooperative interaction

People sometimes speak in monologues – alone in a room or on a mountain top. But the vast majority of speech takes place in the context of conversation. Perhaps one of the most obvious things to say about conversation is that it is an extremely cooperative form of interaction. As George Miller says, 'participants must agree on a topic, they must take turns developing it, and their contributions must be intelligible, relevant and truthful' (1981, p. 121). Whilst having some doubts about the 'truthfulness of contributions' as an important condition of successful conversation (after all, some of the best conversations of salesmen, at least in terms of their outcome, involve contributions less than entirely truthful), the general point remains. Consider, for example, the following extract of conversation in which John, Carol and Jane discuss the question of a United Ireland:

John: 'So you agree in principle with a United Ireland?'
Carol: 'Yes I think I do.'
Jane: 'Well they don't want one.'
Carol: 'Who doesn't?'
Jane: 'Southern Ireland doesn't want the – they don't want the unity.'
Carol: 'I am – I am not saying that I can come up with a *solution* to the problems, 'cause I don't think there is one immediately. . . .'

Here the conversationalists possess very different views on the topic under discussion, but nevertheless they cooperate to produce an orderly exchange of turns. Three people have their say and the speaker role is exchanged without any perceptible delay and no evidence of overlapping talk or interruption. This is indeed a cooperative form of interaction involving a good deal of precision and skill (more will be said on this in the next chapter).

For another example, consider the degree of cooperation involved in closing an ordinary conversation. It is not sufficient for one participant simply to say 'good bye' and remain silent or leave, because the other participant(s) may not wish to terminate the conversation at that point. Schegloff and Sacks (1973) proposed that the minimum requirement for closing a convsation is a 'terminal exchange' composed of conventional parts, e.g. an exchange of 'good byes'. The advantage of such an exchange is that the second person is able to indicate that he or she understood what the first person intended, and also whether he or she is willing to go along with it.

Thus participants cooperate to close conversations in a distinctive fashion. The cooperation of course extends beyond the very final utterances in that conversationalists must somehow signal the closing section using what Schegloff and Sacks called a 'pre-closing', e.g. ('We-ell . . .', 'O.K. . . .', 'So . .oo' etc. with downward intonation contours). Such pre-closings signal the imminent arrival of a closing section but also allow the other participant to introduce a new topic if he or she so desires. (E.g. 'Oh, yeah I wanted to mention . . .'). If no new topic is introduced, the conversation closes:

A: 'O.K.'
B: 'O.K.'
A: 'Bye Bye.'
B: 'Bye.'

Schegloff and Sacks (1973) also include the following 'modest' example of the closing of a different conversation:

B: 'Well that's why I *said* I'm not gonna say anything, I'm not making any comments // about anybody.'
C: 'Hmh.'
C: 'Ehyeah.'
B: 'Yeah.'
C: 'Yeah.'
B: 'Alrighty. Well I'll give you a call before we decide to come down. O.K.?'

C: 'O.K.'
B: 'Alrighty.'
C: 'O.K.'
B: 'We'll see you then.'
C: 'O.K.'
B: 'Bye bye.'
C: 'Bye.'
(// indicates point at which following line interrupts)

Utterances in conversation must also be intelligible and relevant. If they are not, those involved in the conversation may attempt to remedy the problem (e.g. 'What do you mean by that' or 'Why do you bring that up?'). Samuel Vuchinich (1977) investigated the way participants in a conversation react to irrelevant utterances introduced into conversation. For example, consider the following exchange between a naive subject (S) and a confederate (C) who introduced an irrelevant utterance in her fourth turn (C(4)):

S(1): 'I really worked hard my second semester and finals came and I freaked out, the guy I like couldn't believe it, my girlfriend and my room mate and I would stay up all night and then we'd just go out on the roof of Stockwell and just go AUUGGHHH eee – it was really bad and I'm still a little tense and hyper from it.'
C(1): 'Yeah.'
S(2): 'It hasn't worn off.'
C(2): 'Uh huh.'
S(3): 'God it was really icky.'
C(3): 'Yeah I know, well, the University is really – they want your money . . . you know.'
S(4): 'They sure do.'
C(4): 'They sure do.'
C(4): 'Monopoly is a really fun game.'
                         (2.2. sec)
S(5): 'Why do you bring that up?'
             (from Vuchinich, 1977, p. 235).

Here the irrelevant turn 'Monopoly is a really fun game' is followed by a long gap before the next turn (2.2. seconds) and what Vuchinich calls a 'remedy sequence' – 'a mechanism of the conversational system which functions to repair misunderstandings and offences which occur during conversation' (1977, p. 236). This was the way participants generally reacted. However, irrelevant utterance need not produce a dramatic end to the conversation. Consider the following exchange:

C(1): '. . . what countries in South America are you planning on going to?'

S(1): 'Well, the last time we went through Central America, we drove in a van and we just flew over to Columbia and now this time I don't know, if we go for two months or something jus have no real plans jus (1 sec) Columbia, Ecuador, Peru, Bolivia, Paraguay, Uruguay.'

(2.0 sec)

C(2): 'Yeah my room mate went to New York last summer.'

(2.0 sec)

S(2): 'I went to New York ah New York.'

C(3): 'Yeah.'

(from Vuchinich, 1977, p. 247).

Here following the irrelevant turn 'Yeah my room mate went to New York last summer' (introduced after a pause) there is a gap before the next turn, and an effective change in topic. The subject starts to talk about New York, which appears totally unconnected with the topic of conversation up to that point – countries visited in South America.

Grice (1975) attempted to describe some of the ways in which participants in a conversation may adhere to a basic principle of cooperation. He begins by formulating a general cooperative principle. Thus:

Our talk exchanges do not normally consist of a succession of disconnected remarks, and would not be rational if they did. They are characteristically, to some degree at least, cooperative efforts and each participant recognises in them, to some extent, a common purpose or set of purposes, or at least a mutually accepted direction. This purpose or direction may be fixed from the start (e.g. by an initial proposal of a question for discussion), or it may evolve during the exchange; it may be fairly definite, or it may be so indefinite as to leave very considerable latitude to the participants (as in a casual conversation). But at each stage, SOME possible conversational moves would be excluded as conversationally unsuitable. We might then formulate a rough general principle which participants will be expected (ceteris paribus) to observe, namely: make your conversational contribution such as is required at the stage at which it occurs, by the accepted purpose or direction of the talk exchange in which you are engaged. One might label this the COOPERATIVE PRINCIPLE. (Grice, 1975, p. 45)

He then outlines the four subcategories of this principle which are: Quantity, Quality, Relation, Manner. Quantity relates to the amount of information to be provided. Under this subcategory fall the following maxims:

1) Make your contribution as informative as is required (for the current purposes of the exchange).
2) Do not make your contribution more informative than is required.

Under Quality, we have:

1) Do not say what you believe to be false.
2) Do not say that for which you lack adequate evidence.
In the case of Relation, the maxim is rather terse:
1) Be relevant.
In the case of Manner, there is a supermaxim:
1) Be perspicuous.

Grice acknowledges that in conversation a participant may fail to fulfil a maxim in a variety of ways – they may quietly and unostentatiously violate a maxim. Or they may be faced by a clash – unable for example to fulfil the first maxim of Quantity (be as informative as required) without violating the second maxim of Quality (have adequate evidence for what you say). They may also flout a maxim – that is, blatantly fail to fulfil it.

   Let us consider the following examples provided by Grice in which the maxims can be seen to be at work. Thus:

A is standing by an obviously immobilized car and is approached by B.
A: 'I am out of petrol.'
B: 'There is a garage round the corner.'

Now Grice says here that no maxim is violated. 'B would, however, be infringing the maxim "Be relevant" unless he thinks, or thinks it possible, that the garage is open and has petrol to sell or he implicates that the garage is, or at least may be, open etc.' (Grice, 1975, p. 5).

But consider the following example:

A is planning with B an itinerary for a holiday in France. Both know that A wants to see his friend C, if to do so would not involve too great a prolongation of the journey.
A: 'Where does C live?'
B: 'Somewhere in the South of France.'

Here according to Grice, one of his maxims is violated (the first maxim of Quantity – 'Make your contribution as informative as is required') but its violation is to be explained by the supposition of a clash with another maxim ('Do not say that for which you lack adequate evidence').

Grice has provided some form of analysis of how participants in a conversation may adhere to a basic cooperative principle. Presumably, Vuchinich's subjects recognized this principle (at some level) as well as the importance of the maxim 'Be relevant' and this is why the deliberate introduction of irrelevant utterances in their conversations generally led to such confusion, (some subjects however simply developed a new topic around the irrelevant turn which, perhaps, points to the considerable flexibility of human beings in conversation).

But cooperation in conversation may even extend beyond the willingness of participants to take turns and the constraints we have discussed on intelligibility, quantity, quality, relevance and manner of contribution. The way we understand and discuss things must also mesh. In everyday speech, many concepts are understood and interpreted in terms of other concepts – this is the essence of metaphor. Consider, for example, the kinds of things we say about 'arguments' in everyday life. We say things like:

'Your claims are indefensible.'
'He attacked every weak point in my argument.'
'His criticisms were right on target.'
'I demolished his argument.'

'If you use that strategy, he'll wipe you out.'
'He shot down all of my arguments.' (see Lakoff and Johnson, 1980)

In these cases 'argument' is understood in terms of concepts related to 'war'. According to Lakoff and Johnson, these are examples of an 'Argument is war' metaphorical frame. A rather old example of this very metaphor comes from Sir Thomas Browne's *Religio Medici* (1642): 'Yea, even amongst wiser militants, how many wounds have been given, and credits slain, for the poor victory of an opinion, or beggarly conquest of a distinction.' Lakoff and Johnson (1980, p. 5) go on to make the point:

> Imagine a culture where an argument is viewed as a dance, the participants are seen as performers, and the goal is to perform in a balanced and aesthetically pleasing way. In such a culture, people would view arguments differently, experience them differently, carry them out differently and talk about them differently.

Now imagine a conversation in which participants have settled on a topic of conversation but have not settled on the metaphorical frame in terms of which to discuss it. This is not as strange as it might seem – for some concepts there are alternative frames available. Consider for example politicians discussing the 'economy' and the related issues of 'unemployment' and 'inflation'. From a series of analyses of political interviews, one of the authors discovered a number of alternative frames for discussing these concepts. (G. Beattie and L. Speakman, *The Guardian*, March 7, 1983). There is first a metaphorical frame based around illness and health as in:

> 'There's been a world recession, not our fault – Germany, France, Europe, *suffering* as well – some *suffering* even worse.' (Mrs Thatcher)
> '. . . a new bout of inflation' (Mrs Thatcher)
> 'I still have to say to people who talk and talk and talk about unemployment but say nothing about how in practical terms to cure it.' (Mrs Thatcher)

However, there is an alternative war/violence metaphorical frame for understanding the 'economy', 'unemployment' and 'inflation' as in:

'Now, er, they eh, the idea that to *fight* inflation and to fight unemployment are alternatives in the longer run just isn't true.' (Mrs Thatcher)

'There are some other countries that have even worse unemployment than we have, some less, all *struck* by world recession.' (Mrs Thatcher)

'But unemployment is our worst problem and of course we've had to try to spend more than we planned in order to *cushion* people from its worst effects.' (Mrs Thatcher)

There is also a prevalent gardening metaphor which talks of 'pruning', 'dead wood', 'clearing the way', 'hedges against inflation', 'cultivating new growth', 'sowing the seeds of a recovery' etc. These different metaphorical frames will significantly affect how we understand the concepts and will have implications for what we aim to do about them.

'Fighting' inflation and unemployment and 'cushioning' people from its effects suggest a different strategy to attempting to 'cure' it. And if people do settle on different metaphorical frames in conversation, an explicit challenge may be necessary, as in the following example from an interview between Llew Gardner and Mrs Thatcher ('TV Eye', 1982):

LG: 'Prime Minister, you're now completing your third year in office, the third year of what's almost become your personal fight to get Britain back on its feet. Are we winning the battle of the economy?'

MT: 'I think we're winning. I think I could perhaps best describe it by saying I think we've laid the foundations for a competitive industry that can expand the moment we get improvement in world trade and that's quite some achievement because we weren't competitive before.'

LG: 'In em sort of historical terms where are we? Have we just had the battle of Dunkirk or the defeat at Dunkirk or have we got as far as Alamein?'

MT: 'Oh I don't think those analogies hold at all. We have to fight our battles every day. They're never won. You've got to sell your goods every day. You've got to be efficient every day. You've constantly got to think of the morrow. It's a daily battle for each and every day.'

Thus, in conversation, participants must not only agree on a topic but, on occasion, on the very metaphorical frame in terms of which to interpret and discuss the topic. They must stay intelligible and relevant. They must be informative but not too informative. And in addition, they must adhere to a structure and set of rules which allow each participant to hold the floor uniquely for a limited period. All in all, a good deal of cooperation and skill in the multitude of common everyday conversations which make up a unique part of our social life.

Conversation and background knowledge

Having begun by acknowledging the essentially cooperative nature of conversation, the next obvious feature is that conversations are more than collections of words arranged into grammatical strings and juxtaposed in time. Any description or analysis of conversations couched solely in terms of the literal meanings of the words or sentences which comprise them will fail to capture much of the real significance of conversation.

Consider, for example, the following brief conversation, recorded in a small office:

A: 'Are you gonna be here for ten minutes?'
B: 'Go ahead and take your break. Take longer if you want to.'
A: 'I'll just be outside on the porch. Call me if you need me.'
B: 'O.K., don't worry.' (from Gumperz, 1982)

In this exchange, A begins with a question which requires a yes or no answer, but B does not answer it in this fashion. Rather B makes a suggestion which doesn't even acknowledge the prior existence of the question in any direct way. As Gumperz points out, since there are no overt linguistic cues 'it seems reasonable to assume that both A and B rely on a shared understanding that the interaction takes place in an office and on their expectations of what normally goes on in offices. That is, it is taken for granted that both participants are office workers, that it is customary to take brief breaks in the course of a working day, and that staff members should cooperate in seeing that someone is present at all times.' Such background assumptions then enable B to hypothesize that A is most probably asking her questions because she wants to take her break and is checking to make sure that her absence will not inconvenience B. A's reply in the third utterance which implies that she does indeed intend to go out for a while confirms this interpretation. B's final 'O.K., don't worry' can then be understood as a reassurance that A's absence will not cause any problem. 'Conversationalists thus rely on indirect inferences which build on background assumptions about context, interactive goals and interpersonal relations to derive frames in terms of which they can interpret what is going on' (Gumperz, 1982, p. 2).

As conversationalists we rely on our background knowledge about social context, about the goals of our interlocutors and about interpersonal relations to interpret and understand each sentence as it is produced. The general study of how context influences the way we interpret sentences is called *pragmatics* (see p. 172). Our background assumptions and knowledge about language and context tell us that at the dinner table the question 'Can you pass the salt?' is a request for an act to be performed, rather than a request for information (cf. 'Can you play the game?'). Our background knowledge about language also allows us to perceive the humour in the following exchange from *Hamlet*:

Hamlet:	'Whose grave's this, sir?'
First Clown (gravedigger):	'Mine, sir . . .'
Hamlet:	'What man dost thou dig it for?'
First Clown:	'For no man, sir.'
Hamlet:	'What woman then?'
First Clown:	'For none, neither.'
Hamlet:	'Who is to be buried in't?'
First Clown:	'One that was a woman, sir; but, rest her soul, she's dead.'
Hamlet:	'How absolute the knave is! We must speak by the card, or equivocation will undo us.'

(Hamlet, V, i)

The Clown insists on a literal interpretation of each of Hamlet's questions rather than making background assumptions about his goals in the conversation.

Background knowledge underpins everyday conversation. Harold Garfinkel (1967) has explored the relationship between what participants in a conversation actually say and what is understood by them. The following is an exchange between one of Garfinkel's students and his wife:

What was said	*What was understood*
Husband: 'Dana succeeded in putting a penny in a parking meter today without being picked up.'	'This afternoon as I was bringing Dana, our four-year-old son, home from the nursery school, he succeeded in reaching high enough to put a penny in a parking meter when we parked in a meter zone, whereas before he had always had to be picked up to reach that high.'
Wife: 'Did you take him to the record store'	'Since he put a penny in a meter that means that you stopped while he was with you. I know that you stopped at the record store either on the way to get him or on the way back. Was it on the way back, so that he was with you or did you stop there on the way to get him and somewhere else on the way back?
Husband: 'No, to the shoe repair shop.'	'No, I stopped at the record store on the way to get him and stopped at the shoe repair shop on the way home when he was with me.'
Wife: 'What for?'	'I know of one reason why you might have stopped at the shoe repair shop. Why did you in fact?'

Husband:	'I got some new shoe laces for my shoes.'	'As you will remember, I broke a shoe lace on one of my brown oxfords the other day so I stopped to get some new laces.'
Wife:	'Your loafers need new heels badly.'	'Something else you could have gotten that I was thinking of. You could have taken in your black loafers which need heels badly. You'd better get them taken care of pretty soon.'

(Garfinkel, 1967, p. 34)

It is clear from this example that:

a) many things that the participants understood they were talking about were not specifically mentioned (e.g. that their four-year-old son was being brought back from nursery school);

b) many things were understood on the basis not only of what was actually said, but what was left unsaid;

c) references were made to the biography and prospects of the present interaction which each used and attributed to the other as a common scheme of interpretation and expression;

d) both participants waited for something more to be said in order to interpret what had previously been talked about, and each seemed willing to wait.

Of course, it need hardly be pointed out that, generally speaking, the closer the interpersonal relationship between two people, the larger the fund of background knowledge they will share and the more abbreviated and condensed the speech between them may become. In the conversation involving Garfinkel's student and his wife, it was not necessary for either participant to mention that Dana was their son. Neither was it necessary for either participant to mention or query which shoes the laces were being bought for. They knew their son; they knew which shoes had broken laces. With less familiar interactions some of the speech and some of the conversation would have been different. The late Russian psychologist L. S. Vygotsky suggested that 'A simplified syntax, condensation and a greatly reduced number of words characterise the tendency to predication which appears in external speech when the partners know what is going on' (1965, p. 141). He points to the Russian author Tolstoy as someone who understood that abbreviated speech is the rule rather than the exception when shared understanding and knowledge is high:

> Now Levin was used to expressing his thought fully without troubling to put it into exact words. He knew that his wife, in such moments filled with love, as this one, would understand what he wanted to say from a mere hint, and she did. (*Anna Karenina*, Ch. 3)

But in everyday conversation, people continually understand what we mean from the merest hint. Consider the following exchange:
Car driver to stranger: 'Is there a car park about?'
Stranger (pointing): 'Over there mate.' The stranger may never have set eyes on the driver before, but he nevertheless answers entirely appropriately. The driver did not have to inform the stranger that he wanted directions to the car park, neither did he have to inform him that he wished to know the location of the nearest car park and one suitable for the motor vehicle he was currently driving. Neither did he have to inform him that he wanted directions to the nearest public car park. A lot was left unsaid. Interactants actively construct an interpretation even of mere linguistic fragments in the light of the social context and the enormous fund of background knowledge which underpins all conversations. Again, this suggests a strong degree of active cooperation between the participants in a conversation.

Language and nonverbal behaviour in conversation

But conversation is more than a cooperative form of verbal interaction rooted in a huge reservoir of background knowledge and assumptions, it is also the context in which the multifarious channels of human communication operate and interact. The verbal, prosodic, paralinguistic and kinesic channels all play distinctive and interacting roles. Verbal utterances are continually interpreted in the light of background knowledge and in the light of the accompanying prosodic, paralinguistic and kinesic channels. 'Well done' may be said as a compliment but it may be said sarcastically – in which case some of the accompanying behaviour will probably differ. 'Move over, you twit' may be not only a request but an insult. It may, however, act as a joking request in which case the accompanying behaviours will certainly differ. The behaviours accompanying verbal utterances can affect their interpretation. Individual channels accompanying verbal utterances can also offset interpretation. Consider, for example,

> 'My sister who lives in New York / is very nice.//'
> (i.e. I have more than one sister, and the one who lives in New York is very nice.)
> vs
> 'My sister / who lives in New York / is very nice.'
> (i.e. I have one sister who both lives in New York and is very nice.)
> (/ : minor, nonfinal phrase boundary marker;
> //: major, final phrase boundary marker.) (from Gumperz, 1982)

Here intonation can be used to distinguish the different interpretations of a syntactically ambiguous utterance. Crystal (1975) has suggested that intonation may in addition convey affective meaning as in:

> 'I said sit down'
> vs
> 'I said / sit / down'
> (i.e. I am very annoyed, or I think maybe you didn't hear me, or it is very important to me that you sit down, etc).

Nonverbal behaviours, like a stern facial expression, could, of course, perform a similar function in this case.

A major theoretical issue here is the functional role of language and nonverbal communication (NVC). Both are clearly important aspects of conversation but they have often been kept quite separate, on apparently conceptual and functional grounds, in the psychological literature. Indeed, as we said earlier, Argyle and Trower have maintained that we use two quite separate languages, each with its own function. This is a rather extreme version of the more familiar claim that 'In human social behaviour it looks as if the NV (nonverbal) channel is used for negotiating interpersonal attitudes while the verbal channel is used primarily for conveying information' (Trower, Bryant and Argyle, 1978, p. 42). Here it is suggested that the nonverbal channel – the silent channel of eye contact, head nods, gestures, posture, interpersonal distance, winks, fidgetings and eyebrow raisings (as well, of course, as prosody and paralanguage) – carries out essentially social functions such as the communication of interpersonal attitudes while the verbal channel of words and sentences primarily conveys semantic information. It has been suggested by Argyle, Alkema and Gilmour (1971) that there may be an innate pattern of communication and recognition of cues for interpersonal attitudes and that one advantage of interpersonal matters being dealt with nonverbally is that attitudes can be kept vague and flexible – 'People need not reveal clearly nor commit themselves to what they think about each other' (p. 400).

But perhaps the time has come to pause and examine the accuracy of this important claim. Intuitively it may seem fine. The verbal channel is very good at conveying semantic information; the nonverbal channel is much less useful in this respect. Of course, there are special nonverbal languages specifically designed to convey semantic information such as the sign languages of the deaf. And in noisy environments, where speech becomes problematic, nonverbal signals can substitute efficiently for speech if only in a limited domain (head nods, shrugs, two fingers for two or victory, etc.). But of course, these accomplishments are dwarfed by the enormous range and flexibility of verbal language, a system with an incredibly complex rule system governing possible utterances, a rule system involving a series of universal principles which are thought by some to be innate to all human beings (see Chomsky, 1976 and chapter 5). Therefore the part of the quotation from Trower et al. about the role of the verbal channel in conveying semantic information is probably beyond question. The first part of the quotation, though, is perhaps not. This is one of those areas of psychology which makes some intuitive sense – it may seem reasonable that we communicate our attitudes to another person by means of nonverbal signals (eye contact, degree of smiling, interpersonal distance etc.). But in addition, here a psychologist has carried out a seemingly compelling experiment which seems to sew the issue up. In this particular case the experiments in question were carried out by Michael Argyle and his co-workers (Argyle, Salter, Nicholson, Williams and Burgess, 1970; Argyle, et al., 1971). They purported to show a marked difference in the power of NVC and language in the communication of interpersonal attitudes.

The methodology of these experiments is fairly straightforward. Very briefly, three verbal messages (hostile, neutral or friendly in one experiment; superior, neutral or inferior in another) are delivered in each of three different nonverbal styles, care being taken at the outset to ensure that the verbal message and the nonverbal style of each kind have approximately the same effects on listener evaluation on certain specific dimensions. An example of a hostile verbal message is included below:

'I don't much enjoy meeting the subjects who take part in these experiments. I often find them rather boring and difficult to deal with. Please don't hang around too long afterwards and talk about the experiment. Some people who come as subjects are really rather disagreeable.'

The combined communications are then rated on the same scales. The results apparently demonstrate quite clearly that the nonverbal channel greatly outweighs the verbal channel in the combined communication. Friendly verbal messages delivered in a hostile manner are perceived as very hostile, etc. In the case of the friendly-hostile dimension, Argyle et al. estimate that the non-verbal cues accounted for 12.5 times as much variance as verbal cues. In the case of the superior-inferior dimension the accompanying ratio was 10.3, again in the same direction.

Let us, however, consider some possible limitations of these studies:

1) Firstly, in order to attempt to measure the relative importance of language and NVC, the strength of the two channels had to be controlled at the outset. They had to be equal in strength when measured independently. These studies therefore tell us about people's perceptions of a certain class of communication with the range of the strength of the components artificially set. The studies of course do not tell us anything about the range of effects produced by language and NVC in the world at large. Perhaps in the real world people do not use such obvious friendly or unfriendly or superior or inferior verbal messages, e.g. the inferior verbal

message in the Argyle et al. (1970) study was: 'These experiments must seem rather silly to you and I'm afraid they are not really concerned with anything very interesting and important. We'd be very glad if you could spare us a few moments afterwards to tell us how we could improve the experiment. We feel that we are not making a very good job of it, and feel rather guilty about wasting the time of busy people like yourself.' And perhaps therefore the study overestimated the importance of language. Is such a verbal statement ever likely to be encountered in everyday life, except as a joke? Alternatively, perhaps the study was forced to employ exaggerated styles of NVC in order to balance with the language; styles totally outside the range we find in the real world. The hostile nonverbal message was 'harsh voice, frown with teeth showing, tense posture'. Common? realistic? plausible? Of course, people may not use such direct verbal expressions of friendliness anyway – would more indirect styles (e.g. 'Would you like a coffee?') produce the same effect or would they be judged to be more powerful? A demonstration that the types of language and NVC used in these studies approximate to, and indeed are representative of, those found outside the laboratory world, make the studies much more compelling.

2) One striking feature of both studies is that only one encoder was used – 'an *attractive, female* student aged 23'. In other words, encoders are treated as 'fixed effects' (see Clark, 1973). This means that we do not know if the results can be generalized to encoders generally. What about male encoders? Does sex of encoder affect the outcome? We now know that there are important sex differences in the ability to use NVC and we certainly know that women are more expressive than men (see Buck et al., 1974, and p. 33). How would this affect the outcome of this study?

One of the authors attempted to replicate the Argyle et al. (1971) study following the original procedure very closely but using both a female and male encoder, only one of each (see Beattie, 1981b). Ten students rated separately the original Argyle et al. friendly, neutral and hostile messages which were typed out, and the three nonverbal styles (the two encoders reading numbers in a friendly, neutral or hostile manner) on six 7-point scales. This was to ensure approximately equal strengths (see point 1 above). In the actual experiment 16 female and 14 male students rated the 18 combined communications (nine from each encoder) presented on videotape. The results were striking. Here we will only consider the results on the hostile-friendly dimension. For the female encoders the results came out as expected – the nonverbal style outweighed verbal content, but for the male encoder this 'typical' pattern did not emerge. (See Table 9.1 which includes Argyle et al.'s (1971) results for comparison).

In the case of the female encoder the hostile verbal message delivered in a friendly nonverbal style was perceived as significantly more friendly than a friendly verbal message in a hostile nonverbal style for both male and female decoders. In the case of male encoders there was no significant difference for either male or female decoders. In other words, in the case of male encoders not only does the nonverbal component not greatly outweigh verbal content, it does not even appear reliably stronger across decoders.

Clearly, this study has all the faults of the original – encoders for example are again treated as fixed effects, there having been only

Table 9.1: Mean ratings of messages on hostile-friendly dimensions for male and female encoders

Female encoder

Verbal	Nonverbal: Friendly	Neutral	Hostile
Friendly	6.1	5.2	2.1
Neutral	5.2	4.4	1.8
Hostile	5.2	3.3	1.7

Female encoder (Argyle et al., 1971)

Verbal	Nonverbal: Friendly	Neutral	Hostile
Friendly	6.03	4.27	1.60
Neutral	6.03	4.10	1.37
Hostile	5.17	2.83	1.80

Male encoder

Verbal	Nonverbal: Friendly	Neutral	Hostile
Friendly	4.9	5.1	3.9
Neutral	5.1	4.6	2.6
Hostile	4.7	2.9	2.4

one of each sex. It is introduced here to highlight concern about the use of only one female in the original much-quoted study. (Perhaps we also attend more to the nonverbal behaviour of attractive people than to unattractive people. It would be interesting to see if the effects also generalized to the old or the not so attractive).

3) A third reservation about the Argyle studies concerns the fact that decoders in such experiments are compelled to attend to the communication. In real life people are not usually compelled to attend to behaviour to such an extent. We can put our fingers in our ears to shut out what people are saying (rather extreme) or we can simply not attend. It is perhaps easier, however, to shut out visible NVC than language by simply averting eye gaze. Ralph Exline (1971) demonstrated that people are more likely to avert eye gaze when someone has just said something negative to them. How do people behave in terms of attention when others are being friendly or hostile towards them? And how do patterns of attention change with various combinations of language and NVC? If most facial expressions are fairly fleeting (see Ekman and Friesen, 1969) are we likely to miss many of the nonverbal expressions of hostility but find it impossible to avoid the explicit verbal message of hostility being hammered into consciousness? In these experiments, attentional shifts which may be important in decoding communication in the real world are not tapped. Furthermore, what about memory of events? Presumably we can remember the details of explicit verbal communication better than nonverbal style which will presumably just leave you with a vague 'feeling'. Perhaps after some time has elapsed we may re-assess the communication. 'I thought she was being very unfriendly but she did say she liked me', etc. This kind of thing does seem to happen. NVC may have more immediate effect than language but if we assume that communication is important in the development of human relationships then memory for com-munication (and perhaps even the mental reliving of important episodes) may also be significant. Language, it may be supposed, is likely to have a profound effect on our memory of events and may with time become more significant generally.

We must be extremely cautious in drawing general conclusions from somewhat limited laboratory experiments. Language is a subtle medium and its subtlety was not tapped in these experiments. The verbal channel may be the prime channel for conveying semantic information, but that is a far cry from concluding that it is a channel used primarily for conveying semantic information. Argyle et al. (1971) suggest that the advantage of interpersonal matters being dealt with nonverbally is that attitudes can be kept 'vague' and 'flexible'. But does this advantage not also accrue to verbal language when it is used in a more subtle and indirect fashion than in these experiments? Consider the following (hypothetical) verbal exchange:

Scene: *train moving through the English countryside: in the compartment sit one man and one woman, both young.*
Man: 'Beautiful weather isn't it?'
Woman: 'Yes, not bad for this time of year.'
Man: 'Are you going far?'
Woman: 'To Edinburgh.'
Man: 'Oh, my brother lives there.'
Woman: 'Oh, whereabouts?'
Man: 'Castle Street.'
Woman: 'Oh, I know it well. I used to have a boyfriend who lived there. But we don't go out any more. Small world isn't it.'
Man: 'You've got a nice Scottish accent.'
Woman: 'Thank you.'
Man: 'What's your name?'
Woman: 'Zoe – Zoe Purvis.'
Man: 'Hello Zoe, mine's Ben.'

Now, we would wish to suggest that this invented (but we hope plausible) verbal exchange involves a good deal of signalling of interpersonal attitudes, without any reliance on accompanying nonverbal behaviour. Of course, in the real world, the accompanying behaviours would be both present and appropriate, but even written down on the page, some expression of interpersonal attitudes does occur, the main attitude being one of friendliness. Let us consider the conversation in more detail.

'Beautiful weather isn't it?' is an example of what Malinowski (1923) called 'phatic communion' – 'a type of speech in which ties of union are created by a mere exchange of words'. Such an utterance is not really a statement about the weather at all – it would be quite inappropriate for the listener to challenge the accuracy of the statement – rather it is an attempt to open a conversation, successful in this particular case. The woman signals her attitude by responding not just with a 'yes' or 'no' but with some verbal extension. The man follows this with a request for information: on receiving an answer he then discloses some information about his family 'Oh, my brother lives there'. Participants in a conversation often match the intimacy levels of their self-disclosure and indeed intimacy of topics in self-disclosure typically increases as brief encounters progress (Davis, 1976). And this is exactly what happens here – the woman asks for some further information and then self-discloses in return. The intimacy of her self-disclosure shows an increase over what went before. The man replies with a compliment. The compliment, like most compliments, isn't very original – Manes and Wolfson (1981) found that compliments are formulaic in nature – in a corpus of 686 compliments they found that 'nice' appeared in 22.9%. Second person pronouns appeared in 75% and 53.6% of compliments were made up of a single syntactic pattern – as in the example. According to Manes and Wolfson, the function of compliments is to 'express a commonality of taste or interest with the addressee, thus reinforcing, or in the case of strangers, creating at least a minimal amount of solidarity' (1981, p. 124). The woman accepts the compliment; the man asks her name. She tells him. The man then uses her first name (rather than title plus last name – Miss Purvis) to address her. First names, of course, are used in more intimate conversations (Brown and Ford, 1961). The conversation is now ready to progress – both have signalled a friendly attitude at least through verbal means – and both now know something about the background of the other. The conversation can now be played out against this fund of background knowledge. The accompanying nonverbal behaviour undoubtedly supported, augmented and emphasized the communication of interpersonal attitudes in the linguistic channel. But the language itself proved to be effective.

In summary, in this chapter we have considered some of the central aspects of conversation – that it is an essentially cooperative activity and that it is a type of activity which relies on a huge fund of background knowledge. It is also a type of activity in which the multifarious channels of human communication come into play. In the past it has been suggested that verbal language transmits semantic information while nonverbal communication is responsible for the social aspects of conversation. But this is too simplistic a view. Language is a subtle medium and it can transmit information of both a semantic and social nature, often simultaneously. It is, of course, aided by the multifarious nonverbal channels – the tone, the paralanguage, the posture, the gesture, the eye-gaze. That is what makes conversation so fascinating and so complex.

10 Conversational structure

In conversation people may disagree, they may squabble, they may argue, they may even shout, and yet for the most part, their conversations will display a remarkably orderly structure. The structure is founded on the principle (or principles) of turn-taking; that is:

1) Speaker-change recurs.
2) Overwhelmingly, one party talks at a time.
3) Occurrences of simultaneous talk are usually very brief.
4) Transitions (from one turn to the next) with no gap and no overlapping talk are common. Together with transitions characterized by slight gap or slight overlap, they make up the vast majority of transitions (see Sacks, Schegloff and Jefferson, 1974).

These features become all the more suprising when it is remembered that turn length, turn order and turn content are not arranged in advance in ordinary conversation, nor is the relative distribution nor length of the turns.

When the role of speaker has been exchanged at an apparently appropriate point – that is where the first speaker's turn appears complete – and when this occurs without simultaneous speech, we call such an exchange a smooth speaker-switch. The turn is usually exchanged in conversation via smooth speaker-switches:
(Interview between Margaret Thatcher (MT) and Denis Tuohy (DT) broadcast in 1979):

(Symbols used in transcription are as follows: (adapted from Schegloff and Sacks, 1973): / indicates unfilled pause ≥200 milliseconds; ( ) indicates switching pause of x milliseconds)

MT: 'I hope it will succeed / We can put the ball at / peoples'
     feet / Some of them will kick it.'
                        (0)
DT: 'What about the people below the top rate tax payers. The
     people who you feel might come back to the country.'

In the above example, Mrs Thatcher and her interviewer are
disagreeing over a point and yet the floor is handed over without
interruption, without simultaneous speech, and with no perceptible
gap between turns.

Or consider the following example taken from a university
tutorial involving one male lecturer and three students (two male,
one female)

Tutor: 'But i-i-i- its important within / within the confines of
          the figure.'
                        (300)
Student: 'Within the confines of the figure yes, but not / in the
          general visual field . . .'

Again, there is no interruption, or simultaneous speech, and there
is only a slight delay of 300 milliseconds (measured by machine) – a
delay which is hardly perceptible at all – and yet the student replies
in an entirely appropriate fashion right in the middle of a
demanding tutorial.

How is this accomplished? In the last chapter we suggested that it
is indicative of the very cooperative nature of conversation, but how
specifically do speakers and listeners cooperate to produce such an
orderly exchange of turns? The simplest account might be based on
the notion of a between-speaker pause threshold. When the silence
following the first speaker's utterance exceeds some temporal
threshold, the listener may infer that the speaker has finished his
turn and that he, the listener, might now safely begin his own turn.
The problem here, however, is that within-turn pauses are
frequently longer than between turn pauses. In a corpus of natural
tutorials, one of the authors found that the mean length of pauses at
the end of clauses within turns was 807 milliseconds (see Beattie,
1983, p. 45) and the mean length of pauses between turns in the
same types of conversation was 764 milliseconds. Moreover,
approximately 31% of speaker-switches occurred with a latency of
200 milliseconds (or less), which is below any perceptual threshold

for pauses (see Beattie, 1978b, p. 11). In the example from the interview with Mrs Thatcher included earlier, there were three within-turn pauses which exceeded 200 milliseconds and yet the interviewer was able to respond with a latency below this level. Any mechanism based on the notion of a temporal threshold will simply not account for the data.

Two broad types of model have been proposed to account for turn-taking in conversation. One type is a rule-based model. This was developed by the ethnomethodologists Sacks et al. (1974). A different type of model is one based around the concept of specific signals in conversation. This was originally developed by Kendon (1967) and later modified by Duncan (1972) and Beattie (1983).

A simplest systematics for the organization of turn-taking for conversation

This was, in fact, the title of the original paper by Sacks et al. In their account, turn-taking is described in terms of two 'components' and a set of rules, as follows:

Turn-constructional component

Sacks et al. suggest that there are various 'unit-types' with which a speaker may set out to construct a turn – these may include sentential, clausal, phrasal and lexical constructions. Instances of different unit types allow a *projection* of the unit-type under way. This concept of projectability is central to their account – it allows participants to predict and recognize *possible completion points*.

Sacks et al. provide the following examples of:

a) single-word turns
   Desk: 'What is your last name   { Lorraine'
   Caller: { Dinnis'
   Desk: 'What?'
   Caller: 'Dinnis'
            [{indicates simultaneous speech]
b) single-phrase turns
   Anna: 'Was last night the first time you met Missiz Kelly?'
                          (1.0)
   Bea: 'Met whom?'

Anna: 'Missiz Kelly?'
Bea: 'Yes'
c) single-clause turns
A: 'Uh you been down here before { havenche'
B: { Yeh'
A: 'Where the sidewalk is?'
B: 'Yeah.'

Sacks et al. argue that a speaker is initially entitled, in having a turn, to one 'unit-type'. 'The first possible completion of a first such unit constitutes an initial transition-relevance place. Transfer of speakership is coordinated by reference to such transition-relevance places, which any unit-type instance will reach' (p. 703).

The second component of the turn-taking process, according to Sacks et al., is the *turn-allocation component*; that is, the selection of the next speaker. Turn-allocational techniques fall into two groups:

a) those in which the current speaker selects the next speaker, e.g.:
   Sara: 'Bill you want some?'
   Bill: 'No.'
b) those in which the next speaker self-selects, e.g.:
   Jim: 'Any a' you guys read that story about Walter Mitty?'
   Ken: 'I did.'

In conversation, according to Sacks et al., the basic rules for turn-taking are that if the current speaker has selected the next speaker then the selected participant 'has the right and is obliged to take the next turn to speak' (p. 704). If the current speaker has not selected the next speaker, then self-selection may, *but need not* occur – the 'first starter acquires rights to a turn, and transfer occurs at that place' (p. 704).

The 'current speaker selects next' techniques may be carried out at the very beginning of a turn but any turn-transfer does not happen until the first possible transition-relevance place. If the current speaker has selected the next speaker, he or she may, but need not, continue until someone self-selects.

According to Sacks et al. this system allows for efficient turn-taking, with minimal gap and overlap because the system is organized around transition-relevance places which, they say, can be projected and are therefore predictable. Some overlap, of course, would be expected from this model because of this feature of projectability, e.g.:

A: 'Sixty-two feet is pretty good si ⎰ ze'
B: ⎱ Oh boy'

Self-selection also encourages participants to make the earliest possible start and again predicts some degree of overlap:

Lil: 'Bertha's lost, on our scale, about fourteen pounds.'
Damara: 'Oh ⎰ no'
Jean: ⎱ 'Twelve pounds I think wasn't it?'

Sacks et al. describe a number of techniques by which a current speaker may select the next speaker:

a) addressed question, e.g.:
    Sara: 'Ben you want some?'
    Ben: 'Well alright I'll have a'
b) complaint/denial, e.g.:
    Ken: 'Hey yuh took my chair by the way an I don't think that was very nice.'
    Al: 'I didn't take your chair, it's my chair.'
c) complaint/rejection, e.g.:
    A: 'I'm glad I have you for a friend.'
    B: 'That's because you don't have any others.'
d) challenge/rejection, e.g.:
    A: 'It's not break time yet.'
    B: 'I finished my box, so shut up.'
e) request/grant, e.g.:
    A: 'Mommie, I don't want this other piece of toast.'
    B: 'You don't? Well, O.K., I guess you don't have to eat it.'
f) tag questions, e.g.:
    A: '. . . don't you agree?'
    B: 'Yes I do.'

This indeed, is a comprehensive model but it has one major short-coming, which Sacks et al. do recognize (p. 721): that is the vagueness in the description of the features which define a transition-relevance place. Consider, for example, the following extract of another political interview involving Mrs Thatcher (this time being interviewed by Brian Walden for 'Weekend World' in 1981). Brian Walden begins with a question about the future course of inflation. Now we would wish to suggest that in Mrs Thatcher's reply there are *at least five* possible transition-relevance places *before* she gets to the end of her turn. These are marked with oblique strokes:

> BW: 'But let's start with the things that you think are going well – the reduction in inflation. Now would you care to give a prediction of how you think inflation is going to go from now on?'
>
> MT: 'Oh – we're always asked about predictions and as I look back on the history of predictions, it doesn't encourage me to give any / but in the next few months the rate of inflation will fall / er One can't predict more than a few months ahead. / There are two things that would affect further fall. One is the course of the exchange rate. You know full well that if an exchange rate fell rapidly it would have an effect – all the raw material we import would cost more, all the prefabricated goods, all the finished goods. If the exchange rate fell rapidly then inflation would rise. I hope it will not fall rapidly. It may fall a little, but a really serious fall in the exchange rate would have a very adverse effect on many people in this country although it's a little bit high at the moment for a number of industries. And the second thing is this. It is that company profits have been squeezed and squeezed until they're almost non existent. What happend last year, and we warned about it. Nevertheless, it happened – people took out so much in pay that companies sacrificed all their profits to pay. That's going to make it very much more difficult for them to invest in the future and they will have to restore their profits. / Now I hope they're going to do it and indeed they are doing it by increasing efficiency. You can see signs of that all around. They're cutting costs *er* their workforces and management are working together with a will but I'm very, very conscious, you've got to restore profitability if you've got good prospects for the future and good investment. / But they can do it by increased efficiency and are.'

'Oh – we're always asked about predictions and as I look back on the history of predictions, it doesn't encourage me to give any' would be a perfectly adequate answer to the question – a sentential unit-type appropriate and relevant to the question. And yet it does not constitute the end of the turn. And Brian Walden did not attempt to self-select at that point and take the floor. Neither did he attempt to take the floor at any of the other possible 'transition-relevance places' marked. But at the end of the turn he took the floor with no gap and no overlap. Why? And how? The answer presumably is that there are some specific behavioural features possibly intonational, possibly paralinguistic, possibly even kinesic which act as signals to the listener that some possible completion points are really locations where a change in speaker is possible and that others are locations where a change in speaker is neither possible nor desired. Sacks et al. have not elucidated what these signals might be. In their favour, they do recognize this short-coming: 'Discriminations between "what" as a one-word question and as the start of a sentential (or clausal or phrasal) construction are made not syntactically, but intonationally. When it is further realised that any word can be made into a "one-word" unit-type, via intonation, then we can appreciate the partial character of the unit-types description in syntactic terms' (pp. 721–722). Sacks et al. omit to mention here the possible additional role of paralinguistic or kinesic phenomena. This is the major problem with their model and it has been left to others (most notably, psychologists, such as Duncan, 1972) to attempt to uncover the specific signals which operate in conversations with respect to the turn-taking process.

One other point should perhaps be made. Sacks et al. identify a number of techniques by which the current speaker may select the next speaker, such as the addressed question (or any question in a two-party or dyadic conversation). In this model the onus is on these techniques to be highly effective. 'Question' is one instance of the first part of a sequential unit termed an 'adjacency pair'. Question should lead to answers, but in real life conversations they sometimes do not. Mishler (1975) has found that in conversation, a question can often be followed by another question. This is called 'arching'. This apparently is particularly common when children ask questions of adults:

Child: '. . . where's my little thing?'
Adult: 'What little thing? The thing you cut up?'

In a study carried out on university tutorials, one of the authors found the following sequential organization of questions:

Tutor: 'What on his digit span?'
Student: 'Was there a test ⎱ of that?'
Tutor: ⎰'On H.M.?'
            'Oh yes'
Student: 'Before the'
Tutor: 'Four digits'
Student: 'Before the operation?'
Tutor: 'Before the operation?'

Moreover, a considerable proportion of questions in the tutorial samples (especially asked by tutors) were never answered. The tutor merely continued, sometimes after a pause, e.g.:

a) Tutor: 'Yeah um, I mean suppose the / interpretation of the cries is inaccurate / and how how does one know that the interpretations / are accurate? (1.5 second pause). I mean we assume that crying means certain things / and / some of the assumptions / are probably right . . .'

b) Tutor: '. . . Um what sort of account of language development would you give them? How would you / orient it? (2.4 second pause). 'I mean what sort of issues would you consider if you were asked / to / talk about / how children learn to speak?'

Student: 'Um / um / difficult / ah'

Tutor: 'Well, I mean, up to a point that's what you've / tried to do in your essay I guess. What sort of account did you give them then? (400 millisecond pause). I mean you said that you considered some of the diary studies.'

Student: 'And um / the interactions.'

In summary in the Sacks et al. model, the turn-constructional component is problematic because in extended turns we come across a number of possible transitional-relevance places and we need some mechanism, some set of signals for indicating the appropriateness of a change in speaker at these different points.

This set of signals has been ignored in the model. The turn-allocation component, moreover, is also problematic – even some of the apparently straightforward allocation techniques such as addressed questions (or any form of question in a dyadic conversation) do not behave in a straightforward fashion in real conversations. The Sacks et al. model is a comprehensive model but one with some important gaps.

Turn-taking and nonverbal signals in conversation

The search for those specific signals which may operate in conversation to regulate turn-taking has tended to occur within Psychology. The first study to analyse systematically the role of any form of nonverbal behaviour on turn-taking was that carried out by Kendon (1967). He concentrated on *speaker gaze* at the listener and compared the listener's (q's) responses to the speaker (p) when p ended his utterance with or without gaze. Listener responses were categorized as 'q fails to respond or pauses before responding' and 'q responds without a pause'. Kendon found that if the utterance terminated with speaker gaze, 70.6% of listener responses followed without a pause, as compared with 29.3% of utterances terminating without speaker gaze (it is not clear from the study how many of the remaining 70.6% of utterances were responded to after a pause, as opposed to not being responded to at all). Kendon thus demonstrated a form of association between the presence of one form of speaker behaviour at the ends of 'utterances' and the listener's subsequent behaviour. However, there are problems with this study. The first problem is that the linguistic content of the conversation was completely ignored, to the extent that the central concept of 'utterance' was not even defined (it was defined by Kendon, in 1978, as a speech segment complete in form and content). The second problem with the study is that only two dyads were considered in the analysis of turn-taking (seven dyads were considered in the main part of the study). Such a restricted data base obviously limits the conclusions one can draw. This study, however, proved to be seminal in its influence in the field, and many other researchers sought to seek associations between speaker nonverbal signal and listener attempts to take the floor.

One of the authors has suggested that this study by Kendon, and much subsequent research, is based on a 'traffic signal' meta-

phorical frame (see Beattie, 1983) in that the signals thought to
regulate turn-taking in conversation were kinesic and therefore
visual in nature, obligatory in their operation and possessing
universal significance (like the onset of the ubiquitous green light at
traffic signals). Thus 'floor apportionment is also requested by eye
movements which act as signals of a speaker's intention' (Argyle,
1974, p. 202). Of course, gaze was not as efficient a signal as a traffic
signal in that there were a number of instances in the Kendon study
when the signal did not come on and when the listener set off
immediately (29.3% of all immediate listener responses followed
utterances terminating without speaker gaze). Moreover, in some
cases, when the light 'turned green' the listener failed to move off.
This 'traffic light' approach has found its way into the clinical
psychology literature. Thus, one treatment which Trower, Bryant
and Argyle (1978) suggests for people with poor turn-taking skills in
conversation is 'ask the other a question and continue looking at
him, this may include leaning forward'.

Other observational studies have suggested that different kinesic
behaviours may perform a similar floor-apportionment function.
De Long (1974, 1975) found an increase in certain types of kinesic
activity towards the ends of utterances, in the case of nursery school
children, although Wiemann, cited by Wiemann & Knapp (1975)
did not find an increase in any form of behaviour, except speaker
gaze, towards the ends of utterances in the case of adults. These
studies are, however, less direct than that of Kendon, because they
did not consider the relationship between the occurrence of any of
these behaviours and the efficiency (or speed) of the turn-taking
process. Subsequent attempts to test the main line of evidence for
the hypothesis that speaker gaze acts as a regulatory signal in
conversation have produced conflicting results. One of the authors
investigated the relationship between the presence of speaker gaze
at the ends of utterances and the durations of the succeeding
switching pauses in samples of dyadic university tutorials (Beattie,
1978b). The hypothesis under test was that if gaze does perform a
regulatory function, as Kendon suggested, speaker gaze at the ends
of syntactically and intonationally complete utterances should
reduce the speaker switch latency. (It is of course necessary to
consider only complete utterances in a test of this hypothesis, in
order to exclude interruptions; that is to say, speaker switches
where the current speaker had not intended to relinquish the floor,
and where his or her utterance is not intonationally complete.) The

results obtained in this study revealed that speaker gaze did *not* significantly reduce the length of the succeeding switching pause, at the ends of complete utterances. Elzinga (1978) obtained confirmatory evidence for a floor-apportionment function for gaze for English-speakers, but not for Japanese-speakers. Rutter, Stephenson, Ayling and White (1978) produced partially confirmatory evidence in the case of conversations between strangers but not in the case of conversations between friends. Clearly there are a number of highly complex social variables which seem to interfere with the effectiveness of this particular set of 'traffic lights'. One may, in fact, harbour doubts on the basis of these studies about whether this green light is as universal a signal as was once claimed.

The alternative methodology to these observational studies is an experimental one and involves the removal of visual signals. In a sense, this is analogous to attempting to determine the effectiveness of traffic lights simply by turning them off and observing the inevitable chaos. Thus, a number of studies have looked at the temporal structure of conversations in sound-only conditions, in which interactants were either separated by some physical barrier (Jaffe and Feldstein, 1970; Cook and Lalljee, 1972; Butterworth, Hine and Brady, 1977; Rutter and Stephenson, 1977) or were conversing by (simulated) telephone (Kasl and Mahl, 1965; Butterworth et al., 1977). The general conclusion of these studies is that conversation is in no way disrupted in sound-only conditions.

In a parallel approach to this problem, one study attempted to determine whether telephone conversations are disrupted, not by looking at normal town driving where the traffic lights have been switched off (as all other studies have done), but by looking at the ability of drivers to cross intersections where traffic signals are never available, i.e. in natural telephone calls. In this study (Beattie and Barnard, 1979) switching pauses (the gap between speaker turns) and interruption rate (defined as simultaneous turn-claimings) were analyzed in a corpus of natural directory enquiry calls. Some of these calls display a somewhat unpredictable structure. For example:

Op 1:   'Directory Enquiries, for which town please?'
          (400)
Sub 1:   'Woburn Sands.'
          (800)
Op 2:   'Woburn Sands, yes.'
          (1067)

Sub 2:   'And the name is Anyname.'
         (1067)
Op 3:   'The name of the person is Anyname?'
         (0)
Sub 3:   'Anyname, yes.'
         (8400)
Op 4:   'What initials please?'
         (800)
Sub 4   'A.B.'
         (2800)
Op 5:   'A.B. / is it Wood Place? // Apsley Guise?'
Sub 5:   'Er'
         (1000)
Sub 6:   'Apsley Guise, that's right // Wood Place.'
Op 6:   'Yes.'
         (467)
Op 7:   'It's Woburn Sands 9999.'
         (800)
Sub 7:   '9999 er now / um is, there's not been any change of coding or anything like that about that number?'
         (1000)
Op 8:   'Just checking for you. / I've got a list of changed numbers but I don't think that's one of them. / No that's not on the changed numbers list. / It should be alright.'
         (400)
Sub 8:   'Well, I can't get it. I've just tried it.'
         (467)
Op 9:   'Have you? // Well I should dial 100 and ask the operator to help you.'
Sub 9:   'Yeah.'
         (1000)
Sub 10: 'Err well / I see. Who will know if there is any change of / ah exchange um and all the rest of it?'
         (0)
Op 10:   'Well you know I've got the changed number list for Woburn Sands so it / um'
         (2733)
Sub 11: 'And it's definitely not one of them?'
         (400)
Op 11:   'No it isn't. / No.'
         (1067)

Sub 12: 'Ah the thing is this. Bit of a mystery. I've been trying this number for two days. / // Um yesterday somebody told me to put 58 in front of it / which got me a very unusual dialling / situation. / I haven't been able to get through and I'm you know. I have a letter from a large company saying he's there waiting for me to phone, and I can't get through.'

Op 12: 'Yes.'
(1867)

Op 13: 'Yes, well, 58 should be put in front of some numbers but these these um / let me just read this / You've tried it with 58 in front?'
(0)

Sub 13: 'Yes.'
(6000)

Op 14: 'Oh, I should dial 100 and ask the operator to help you then because um / you know if you dial it with 58 in front it should certainly be alright.'
(667)

Sub 14: 'But I should be able to dial it without the 58 in front?'
(10667)

Op 15: 'Just a moment let me read this list here properly. No, you should have the 58 in front of it.'
(400)

Sub 15: 'I should have a ⎰ 58 in front.'
　　　　　　　　　　⎱ 'Yes yes and'

Op 16: 'I'll just check the code for you while you're on the line. Perhaps it's the code you see. / Your code should be 0908.'
(800)

Sub 16: 'Yes, that's what I've been dialling.'
(1000)

Op 17: 'And / then 58 and then the number. / That should definitely be alright.'
(0)

Sub 17: 'Yes, I I've got a feeling there's something going on, on the exchange there, because it gives a very funny, very sort of, you know, it dials, then it stops.'
(1667)

Op 18: 'Oh ⎰ that sounds like'
Sub 18:   ⎱ And then it'
              'goes on again'
              (800)
Op 19: 'That sounds like a fault on the phone itself / not on, not
       on an dialling. If you're actually getting a ringing tone it
       should be alright. It's a ⎱ faul-'
                                 ⎰ 'who do'
Sub 19: 'I get on to about fault enquiries anyway?'
        (1067)
Op 20: 'Fault / enquiries, or or / eh dial 100 and ask the
       operator to help you and she'll report it.'
       (1667)
Sub 20: 'Yes, O.K., then.'
        (200)
Op 21: 'One or the other. 191 is faults if you would prefer to go
       through them.'
       (933)
Sub 21: 'Alright, thank you very much indeed.'
        (0)
Op 22: 'Goodbye.'
Sub 22: 'Bye bye.'

Symbols used in transcription are as follows (adapted from
Schegloff and Sacks, 1973):
   /   indicates unfilled pause ⩾200 milliseconds
   //   indicates point at which following utterance interrupts
   (x) indicates switching pause of X milliseconds
   {   indicates simultaneous speech

In a telephone conversation such as this one, turn-taking is not
entirely straightforward. Turns may be longer than individual
sentences.

When the telephone conversations were analysed and compared
with a sample of face-to-face conversations it was discovered that

   a) there was no significant differences in the 'switching pauses'
      (pauses between turns) of the two samples.
      Mean switching pause (subscriber → operator)
                                              507 milliseconds
      Mean switching pause (operator → subscriber)
                                              474 milliseconds
      Mean switching pause (face-to-face conversation)

575 milliseconds
(excluding question-answer delays)
b) there was no significant difference in the proportion of speaker-switches which were immediate (i.e. ≤200 milliseconds in duration) in the two samples; in both cases the proportion was 34.2%.
c) face-to-face conversations were characterized by a higher proportion of turn-exchanges involving simultaneous claimings of the turn – 10.6% for face-to-face conversations, 6.3% for telephone conversations.

In other words this study did not produce any evidence that conversations, which occur without visual information, are noticeably disrupted – quite the reverse in fact. If anything the telephone conversations were smoother. It was noticed however that speakers made more use of filled pauses ('um', 'ah', 'er' etc.) on the telephone to hold onto the floor (see Ball, 1975; Beattie, 1977), e.g.: Subscriber: '9999 er now / um is, there's not been any change of coding or anything like that about that number?'

In fact filled pauses were nearly four times as common in telephone conversations than in face-to-face conversations (controlling for the number of unfilled pauses in speech).

Thus, this study produced some evidence of speakers adjusting their behaviour on the telephone to compensate for the loss of visual information. But the general efficiency of turn-taking on the telephone suggests that kinesic signals cannot be absolutely crucial to the turn-taking process.

Turn-taking and nonverbal signals: the transition-readiness hypothesis

Starkey Duncan (1972, 1973, 1974, 1975; Duncan and Fiske, 1977) has proposed a different model of how participants in a conversation exchange the speaking turn with minimum gap and minimum overlap. This is similar to Kendon's (1967) hypothesis in that it focuses attention principally on the role of nonverbal signals in conversation but it differs in that it does not focus exclusively on one possible signal – rather it focuses upon a set of possible signals occurring in the verbal, intonational and kinesic channels of communication. Duncan (1972) identified the following behaviours as being implicated in the turn-taking process – the following are *'turn-yielding signals'* (or 'cues'):

1) Intonation: The use of any rising or falling intonation contour.
2) Drawl on the final syllable, or on the stressed syllable of terminal clause.
3) Sociocentric sequences: the use of one of several stereotyped expressions, typically following a substantive statement, e.g. 'or something', 'you know' etc.
4) Pitch/loudness: a drop in pitch and/or loudness in conjunction with a sociocentric sequence.
5) Syntax: The completion of a syntactic clause involving a subject-predicate combination.
6) Gesture: The termination of any hand gesticulation or the relaxation of a tensed hand position, but excluding self- and object-adaptors (Ekman and Friesen, 1969b).
     According to Duncan, these signals are used by speakers in combination to hand over the floor. Duncan also described an *'attempt-suppressing signal'* – a signal to prevent turn-taking from occurring.
7) One or both the speakers' hands being engaged in gesticulation, again excluding both self- and object-adaptors.

In his original study involving just two two-person conversations (but only three different speakers), Duncan correlated the number of turn-yielding signals conjointly displayed at certain locations with the probability of the listener attempting to take the floor. The locations were defined as being at the ends of phonemic clauses, which additionally were marked by the display of one or more of the turn-yielding signals, and/or by the display of one of the following phenomena:

1) Unfilled pauses,
2) turning of the speaker's head towards the listener,
3) a drop in pitch and/or loudness, either across an entire phonemic clause or across its final syllables, or
4) body-motion – in one subject only – a relaxation of the foot from a marked clausal flexion.

Duncan discovered that in the absence of speaker gesticulation 'the correlation between number of turn-yielding cues displayed and percentage of listener turn-taking attempts was 0.96' (1972, p. 259). The display of one or more turn-yielding signals also led to a significant reduction in the probability of both participants attempting to claim the speaker turn. On the other hand, when the speaker was gesticulating, the incidence of listeners' turn-taking attempts fell virtually to zero.

The theoretical model proposed by Duncan is as follows:

> We may begin by assuming that one participant is in the speaker state and the other participant is in the auditor state. Let us say that the transition readiness for each participant is represented by an ordinal scale readable by that participant. On this scale a high reading represents high transition readiness, and vice versa. Through periodic signal activation, the speaker can represent his current status on transition readiness. Specifically, through activating or not activating turn cues the speaker can indicate a point on the scale from zero to six (or whatever the maximum number of turn cues proves to be). Moreover, by activating the gesticulation signal, it appears that the speaker can indicate a zero value for transition readiness (regardless of concurrent turn-cue activation), or perhaps a negative one. (Duncan and Fiske, 1977, p. 197)

This is a good summary of Duncan's 'transition-readiness' model. When we considered Kendon's (1967) model we suggested that the signal he identified could be thought of as akin to the operation of a 'traffic signal': a kinesic-visual signal, obligatory in its operation, universal in its significance. If we keep the same traffic metaphor here, then Duncan's model is perhaps more like a driver trying to get onto a main road from a side road. There is no one signal which tells him when to move forward (there are no traffic lights at the intersection). A driver on the main road may slow down, may leave a gap between himself and the car in front, may even flash his headlights to invite in a driver, waiting in the side road. But none of these 'cues' are obligatory, and the driver on the side road's decision will almost certainly be affected by the combination of 'cues' offered. He's more likely to move forward if the driver on the main road slows down *and* flashes his headlights. The driver on the side road's response is optional. Similarly, Duncan says, the listener 'is not obliged to take a speaking turn in response to a regular turn-yielding signal by the speaker. The listener may alternatively communicate in the back channel (that is say something such as "yeah", without claiming the floor (Yngve, 1970), or remain silent' (Duncan 1972, p. 286).

But unfortunately, Duncan's model has a number of shortcomings:

1) The model depends critically upon the correlation between 'number of turn-yielding cues displayed' and 'percentage of auditor turn-taking attempts'. This was computed by dividing the 'number of listener turn-taking attempts' by the 'frequency of display' of the relative number of turn-yielding cues. The correlation was found to be very high (0.96). However, only two instances of the simultaneous display of six turn-yielding cues were recorded. Thus the percentage of listener turn-taking attempts following the simultaneous display of six turn-yielding cues was calculated on the basis of a total of two instances. Duncan observed that in one case out of two, a turn-taking attempt occurred; thus the percentage of such junctures accompanied by a turn-taking attempt was calculated to be 50%. If this one response had not occurred, the percentage of such junctures accompanied by a turn-taking attempt would have fallen from 50% to 0%! *This would have resulted in the correlation between percentage of listener turn-taking attempts and number of turn-yielding cues conjointly displayed falling from 0.96 to a non-significant 0.21.* Thus, the overall conclusions seem to depend critically upon the occurrence of one response by the listener and so the effect cannot be considered statistically reliable. When Duncan himself attempted to replicate this finding, he failed – the comparable correlation was 0.42 in the replication study (see Duncan and Fiske, 1977, p. 194).

2) Duncan's model depends upon the ability of judges to score pitch and the other intonational features he discusses using a system devised by Trager and Smith (1957). Unfortunately, this system does not seem to be reliable. Lieberman (1965, p. 52) used the same basic system for scoring intonation and found that 'when two competent linguists independently transcribe a set of sentences, 60 per cent of the pitch levels and junctures of the two Trager-Smith transcriptions vary'.

3) One may raise doubts as to whether combinations of five or six turn-yielding cues are theoretically possible anyway. For example, so-called sociocentric sequences (e.g. 'you know') cannot complete a syntactic clause, they can just appear in the juncture between clauses.

4) There is a problem in identifying each individual cue as a 'turn-yielding signal'. After all, only a small proportion of completed clauses occur at the ends of conversational turns. Listeners do not react to every instance of clause completion as a signal but, of course, they may react to combinations of such cues as a clustered social signal.

One of the authors attempted to replicate Duncan's observation in a corpus of six natural academic conversations (see Beattie, 1983). Inter-observer reliability in scoring the various verbal, intonational and nonverbal cues was high.

The following conclusions were drawn:

1) Verbal, intonational and kinesic features do mark the ends of turns in conversation. Nearly 50% of smooth speaker-switches occurred where three of these cues were present at the same time. Furthermore, only 1.8% of attempted speaker-switches, at points where three cues were present, resulted in simultaneous turn-claimings. On the other hand, only 13.6% of smooth speaker-switches occurred at points where none of these six cues were present, and when the listener did try to take the floor at such points nearly 30% of the attempts resulted in simultaneous turn-claimings. The specific features most frequently associated with turn-endings were syntactic clause completion with a falling intonation pattern and drawl on the final or stressed syllable. The kinesic feature – gesture termination – was implicated in only 8.7% of speaker-switches overall but in the case of one dyad it was involved in 22.9% of all turn-exchanges (in the case of two dyads it was not involved at all). Thus:

2) There are probably important individual differences in the cues used to hand over the floor in conversation.

3) The 'transition-readiness' model proposed by Duncan (1972) and Duncan and Fiske (1977) was not supported, in that there was not a linear relationship between the number of 'turn-yielding cues' conjointly displayed and the probability of a listener turn-taking attempt. Most turn-taking attempts occurred where three cues were present rather than where more cues were present.

4) Special cue combinations – clause completion accompanied by falling intonation with drawl on the stressed syllable (plus optionally the termination of a hand gesture) seem effectively to mark the end of a speaker turn and probably communicate to the

listener when to take the floor (see Beattie, 1983).

Duncan's research has also come in for some criticism from another quarter. Cutler and Pearson (in press) have argued that a fall in pitch, a decrease in amplitude and some segmental lengthening (or drawl) is characteristic of the ends of all utterances in speech, not just the ends of turn. Oller (1973), for example, found that a given word will be uttered with longer duration in phrase-final than in non-phrase-final position. Cutler and Pearson point out that Duncan does not provide any metric for the (non-defined) drawl feature to determine the relationship between the expected and the observed phrase-final lengthening. They also argue that because the speech was transcribed with full reference to the discourse context there exists the possibility that the scoring of the prosodic features of any utterance would be affected by the syntax and content of the utterance as well as by its position in the discussion (see also Lieberman, 1965, discussed earlier).

Cutler and Pearson pioneered an experimental technique to establish whether perceptually effective prosodic turn signals do indeed exist. They had speakers read aloud short dialogues – the dialogues having been written in such a way that the same utterances occurred in either turn-medial (in the middle of a turn) or turn-final position (at the end of a turn) in different versions of the texts, e.g.:

Speaker 1: 'Foster was pretty upset that you rejected his design
            – any particular reason?'
Speaker 2: 'It's simply not good enough, and *that's all I have to
            say on the subject! I don't see why I have to justify my
            decisions.*'
Speaker 1: 'O.K. – sorry I asked!'
       The second version of this dialogue was identical except that
Speaker 2's turn read:
Speaker 2: '*I don't see why I have to justify my decision.* It's
            simply not good enough, and *that's all I have to say
            on the subject.*'

Both versions of each of five dialogues of this kind were read onto tape by ten native speakers of British English. Then the critical extracts (in italics in the sample dialogue) were presented singly in random order to subjects who had to judge whether it sounded turn-medial or turn-final. The results were that overall judges could not do this above chance level *but* the range of turn final judgements per utterance ranged from 0% to 100%. Cutler and Pearson did a prosodic transcription of those utterances consistently judged to be turn-final or turn-medial and found that turn-final judgements were associated with down-stepped contours (i.e. a tonic syllable starting significantly lower than the previous syllable) whilst turn-medial judgements were associated with upstepped contours (i.e. a tonic syllable starting on a higher pitch than the previous syllable).

In other words this study did produce some confirmatory evidence for Duncan's model. Listeners overall did not differentiate consistently between turn-medial and turn-final utterances *but* importantly, they had learned to associate certain cues with the ends of turns (e.g. down-stepped contours). As Cutler and Pearson note, 'If listeners have learned to use cues to turn structure, they surely must have learned this by being exposed to cues produced by speakers'. Moreover the fact that the listeners did not differentiate consistently between turn-medial and turn-final utterances does not tell us that in real conversation they are not differentiated prosodically. The speech in this experiment was not spontaneous and professional actors, who might have been able to reproduce a full range of natural prosodic turn signals when reading a written test aloud, were not used. The positive evidence that the study did obtain, however, suggests that Duncan's hypothesis – that any terminal contour other than a sustained mid-level pitch functions as a turn-yielding signal – might have to be modified. Cutler and Pearson found a down-step in pitch to be a good turn-yielding cue, with a pitch upstep being a good turn-holding cue.

In conclusion, in order to understand how participants in conversation manage to produce such orderly exchanges of talk, we must attempt to amalgamate the comprehensive model of Sacks et al. (1974) outlining a basic turn-constructional component and a turn-allocation component with the identification of specific cues marking the ends of turns in conversation. The turn-constructional component described by Sacks et al. is relevant and necessary to turn-taking in conversation. The ends of some turns are projectable and this alone can account for the fact that a proportion of turn-exchanges occur without any delay at all. But projectability cannot be the whole story. In some turns we come across any number of possible 'transition-relevance places' – loci at which the turn so far is appropriate and potentially complete (consider the Margaret

Thatcher–Brian Walden interview discussed earlier). In conversation there must be some way of marking the ends of turns to distinguish possible 'transition relevance places'. The distinguishing features it seems comprise verbal, prosodic and kinesic elements. Slugoski (1984) has recently queried the role of prosody in the process – he compared the relative efficiency of semantic and prosodic elements by asking subjects to indicate as quickly as possible when they judged a series of turns to be complete. He used a similar methodology to Cutler and Pearson by having people read sample dialogues which were then re-edited to yield turns which were semantically complete (S+) or incomplete (S−) and intonationally complete (I+) or incomplete (I−), e.g.:

> A: 'Whatever became of that old painting you once had over the mantelpiece? It looked so beautiful hanging there.'
> B: 'Oh, didn't you know, it was stolen a little over two months ago. John and I were terribly upset.'
> plus
> S+ I+ A: 'Was it insured?'
>   B: 'Unfortunately, no'
> or
> S+ I− A: 'Was it insured?'
>   B: 'Unfortunately no . . .' (edited out)
> S− I+ A: 'What was it worth?'
>   B: 'Unfortunately no'
> or
> S− I− A: 'What was it worth?'
>   B: 'Unfortunately, no . . .' (edited out)

Slugoski found, not surprisingly, that the fastest response times by subjects were to the semantically complete utterance. But what was perhaps surprising (at least at first glance) was that a complete intonation pattern did not significantly reduce response time. However, the problem with this study is that it focuses exclusively on either *extremely* predictable turns (e.g. A: 'Was it insured?', B: 'Unfortunately, no') or turns which are *entirely inappropriate* (A: 'What was it worth', B: 'Unfortunately, no'). It did not investigate the role of intonation in relationship to turns somewhere in between these extremes – turns which are appropriate and relevant, but which can be extended beyond phrasal, clausal and sentential boundaries. That is, the kinds of turns found in real life, natural conversation.

But Slugoski's main point stands: the content of turns is relevant to conversational structure. This is hardly new, but other channels of communication are also implicated in the process. Prosody and kinesic behaviour operate around the main channel of speech to demarcate suitable response junctures. This much is now clear. They highlight suitable response locations. Listeners, it seems, do get the message.

11 Writing

The evolution and consequences of writing

Humans have been smiling, gesturing and talking to one another for millions of years, but writing as a channel of communication is only about 5,000 years old (Gelb, 1963). Though of recent origin, it is hard to underestimate the impact of writing on those societies which have acquired it, and hard to imagine such societies continuing to function without it.

No-one knows for sure just how many times writing has been invented, but in each case it seems to have evolved out of earlier, nonlinguistic systems of pictorial or object communication. 'Picture writing' in one form or another has been observed in many nonliterate cultures and in some cases achieved quite a high degree of formality and sophistication, as for example among some North American Indian tribes. Figure 11.1 shows a picture writing 'letter'

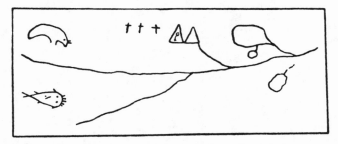

Figure 11.1: Letter from an Ojibwa girl to her lover. (From G. Mallery, *Pictographs of the North American Indians.* Fourth Annual Report of the Bureau of Ethnology, Smithsonian Institute, Washington, 1893.)

sent by an Ojibwa girl to her boyfriend. The boy is represented by his totemic symbol, the mud puppy, and the girl by her bear totem. In the upper centre of the picture are two tents. The girl's arm protrudes from one, beckoning the boy to her. The circles to the right are lakes, and the lines are paths by which the boy might reach her. The three crosses show that three Christian girls are encamped nearby.

In Jonathan Swift's celebrated (i.e. little read) political satire *Gulliver's Travels* (1726) one of Gulliver's many ports of call is Lagado, the capital of Balnibarbi. In the School of Languages at the Academy of Lagado three professors have devized a scheme for abolishing speech because 'it is plain that every word we speak is, in some degree, a diminution of our lungs by corrosion, and consequently contributes to the shortening of our lives.' The alternative devized is to converse with objects. Inside the house this is a reasonable procedure since 'the room where company meet who practice this art is full of all things, ready at hand, requisite to furnish matter for this kind of artificial converse'. Further, 'for short conversations, a man may carry implements in his pockets, and under his arms, enough to supply him'. The wise man or man of business is obliged, however, 'to carry a greater bundle of things upon his back . . . almost sinking under the weight'. When such men met in the street they 'would lay down their loads, open their sacks, and hold conversation . . . then put up their implements, help each other to resume their burdens, and take their leave'.

Though Swift's tale points up the obvious limitations of object-mediated communication, some real-life examples have been reported from time to time. Gollmer (1885) recounts the tale of a Yoruba tribesman of Africa who was taken into captivity when his city was attacked by a king of Dahomey. Wishing to inform his wife of his predicament he sent her a stone, coal, pepper, corn and a rag. We are told that the stone denoted health and meant 'as the stone is hard, so my body is hardy, strong'. The coal expressed gloom, meaning 'as the coal is black, so my prospects are dark and gloomy'. The pepper indicated heat ('as the pepper is hot, so my mind is heated'), the corn leanness ('as the corn is dried up by parching, so my body is dried and become lean through the heat of my affliction and suffering'), and the rag wornness ('as the rag is, so is my cloth cover worn and torn to a rag'). Not the most cheerful of letters home, but probably true to the feelings of its sender which were, apparently, communicated effectively. Gelb (1963) provides several more examples of object-mediated communication.

What distinguishes these sorts of pictorial and object-based communications from written texts? In object and picture communications the elements stand directly for concepts or ideas – the boy being represented by his totem, the mud puppy; the corn representing leanness; and so on. The content of the message could be expressed many ways in speech. Two members of the Ojibwa tribe would relate Figure 11.1 in words using different phrases and sentences, and we can express its message equally well several ways in English. If it were a written text, however, the two Ojibwa speakers would read it aloud in identical phrases and sentences (if they didn't, one would be called a paraphrase), and our English version would be a translation. The source of this difference is that picture writing symbolizes conceptual messages more or less directly, often iconically. True writing, in contrast, symbolizes *units of language* – sentences, words, syllables or phonemes – and is therefore one step removed from concepts, being a code of a code.

All the earliest known writing systems operate on the principle of one symbol for each *word*. Their symbols are 'logographs' in which little or nothing of the sounds of words is encoded into the symbols. Some modern writing systems have persisted with this principle, notably Chinese. Although this makes printing in Chinese laborious, and typewriters impossible, logographic writing is actually rather well suited to the Chinese language as it is a language containing many homophones – words which sound the same but have different meanings, like 'bank' (where money is kept) and 'bank' (of a river) in English. The Chinese word 'i', for example, has 69 different meanings including 'one', 'dress', 'rely on', 'cure' and 'city'. At present each meaning is represented by a different logographic symbol, whereas if an alphabetic writing system were introduced into China all 69 meanings could collapse onto a single spelling.

Other cultures have carried their writing systems further in developing separate symbols for each syllable or phoneme (distinctive speech sound) in the language. An alphabetic writing system is one in which there is a regular and predictable mapping between phonemes (sounds) and letters. All modern alphabets are descendants of that perfected by the Greeks some three thousand years ago. Modern Finnish, Latvian and Italian are among those which have maintained a high degree of regularity and predictability, while

English has slipped considerably and contains many irregular words like *two, was, knight* or *yacht* (though as we shall see later, these imperfections may have their advantages).

Picture writing systems, the precursors of true writing, served a number of social functions apart from transmitting love letters. They provided a permanent record of transactions and exchanges of goods between individuals. They also recorded details of a society's history, its escapades in war, the reprisals it extracted and the treaties it made. These functions were inherited by true writing when it developed. Thus many of the earliest known documents are dull but invaluable lists, ledgers and accounts. Because of the permanence of writing people no longer had to rely on their memories to remember who had sold what to whom and for how much. This function is still with us: modern governments and multinationals are built on mountains of paper and ink. Also, because written text permits only one reading it is more explicit and less ambiguous than picture writing. It is therefore better suited to encoding the treaties, laws and contracts so essential to a complex society.

As the Chinese proverb says, 'The palest ink is worth more than the most retentive memory'. In nonliterate cultures certain individuals seek to memorize the important history of their culture, but inevitably details become lost or distorted with time. Once writing has been developed noteworthy events can be committed to print, thereby building up a written archive of the society's history. This can be invaluable in maintaining a group's sense of identity and continuity: it is hard, for example, to imagine how the Jewish people could have sustained their separate identity for so long without the written chronicle provided by the Old Testament.

With writing comes a quite new attitude to language, for writing is a permanent record of *words*, not just of events. When a storyteller in a nonliterate culture insists that the tale he has just told is exactly the same as the last time he told it, what he means is that the people, places and events were related exactly as before. Hunter (1985) debunks the myth of extensive word-for-word ('verbatim') recall in nonliterate cultures and amasses evidence to show that 'lengthy verbatim recall', as illustrated in an actor's delivery of all 1,422 lines of Hamlet's role, is unique to cultures possessing written languages (see Chapter 13).

The nonliterate storyteller is judged on his fluency, his wit, the excitement of his tales and the like. The precise wording is soon forgotten and is regarded as relatively unimportant. To an extent we could argue that the same is true of, say, a newspaper article skimmed for its gist, or a paperback thriller that grips you with its ripping yarn but which, once put down, will never be picked up again. But because written language has permanence that speech (at least until the invention of recording techniques) never had, it encourages a different perspective of language. That perspective focusses on form rather than content, on text rather than on gist. The novelist, playwright or poet will deliberate long and hard over the choice between one of two words. Both convey the gist equally well, that is not the issue; what matters is what *sounds* (or perhaps *looks*) best. Some abstract poetry and prose has gone so far as to dispense with content altogether, preferring to be appreciated for its form alone.

The emphasis on form and on text appears to accompany the development of literacy and to hinge upon the immutability of written language. It is that same immutability which allows the student of literature to scrutinize and criticize the language of a play or poem. The concentration on text that accompanies literacy also means that, unlike the nonliterate storyteller, the Shakespearean actor cannot be content merely to get the gist right each time. His livelihood depends on his capacity for lengthy verbatim recall, and his art dwells in his pausing, intonation, posture, expression, and gestures – aspects of communication that writing captures poorly, if at all.

Like literature, science could hardly have developed without writing. Once a theory is written down it is laid open to criticism just like a poem or play. Science depends upon the criticism, improvement or rejection of theories and their ultimate replacement with better ones. A theory committed to print takes on a life of its own distinct from that of its own creator. For this reason the scholars of the Italian Renaissance (around 1300 to 1500 AD) were able to discover the lost scientific and mathematical theories of the Greeks and Romans in addition to rediscovering their literature, philosophy and art. Writing objectifies knowledge, and objectification is crucial to the accumulation of facts and the refinement of theories that is the scientific enterprise (see Popper, 1972).

Spoken and written language

If we compare the language of natural conversation with that of formal writing as found, say, in an essay or a newspaper article, then a number of differences are evident (see Table 11.1). The language of writing characteristically contains longer and grammatically more complex sentences than the language of speech. It also contains a higher proportion of uncommon and abstract words, and the repetitions, rewordings and false starts that litter conversation are, of course, edited out of writing (Akinasso, 1982). It would be misleading, however, to think of these differences as necessarily tied to speech and writing as communicative channels; rather the differences are due to the functions that speech and writing typically have, and the conditions under which they are produced.

Table 11.1: Some characteristic differences between speech and writing

Speech	Writing
Normally occurs in the context of shared social activity	Normally occurs in isolation
Immediate feedback from individuals to whom message is directed	Social feedback is delayed or nonexistent
Development of text is negotiated between co-conversants	Development of text is determined by writer alone
Little revising and editing	Often extensive revising and editing
Syntactically and lexically simple	Syntactically and lexically complex
Message complemented by other communicative channels	Single channel only
Brief, temporary signal	Potentially permanent signal

We have already seen in Chapter 9 how in conversational speech much goes unsaid. You often know your fellow conversant well, so you can assume a good deal of knowledge on their behalf. They are also free to indicate by expression or interruption when something you have said is unclear. When you are writing, in contrast, you are often addressing without feedback an unknown audience whose background and knowledge you cannot be sure of. This forces you to be much more explicit and detailed than you are in casual conversation. Also, if you are writing an essay, the informational content may be more complex and more abstruse than what you usually chat about, so you may be obliged to use less common and more abstract words, and more complex sentence structures (N.B., matters may be complicated by the desire to give the impression of cleverness by using a long word where a short one would do, and a convoluted sentence in the place of two simpler ones. Alas, this is all too often a successful ploy having been copied from one's teachers in the first place).

Such cynicism apart, it remains true that the different functions of speech and writing often call for different styles of language. In fact, a complex society will have within it numerous different roles calling for different styles of language. Some individuals will master many of these styles, others only a few. Some styles will usually be conveyed through speech and other styles through writing. In general, more casual styles are expressed in speech and more formal ones in writing, but we can find plenty of exceptions to this generalization: the spoken language of a job interview, a speech or a lecture may be more 'literate' than the written language of a casual letter to a close friend (Leech, Deuchar and Hoogenraad, 1982).

Composing text

Teachers often evince surprise at the difficulty pupils have expressing themselves in writing. A little reflection on the difference between talk and writing should, however, soon dissipate that surprise. As we have seen, talk usually occurs in short, conversational bursts with much assumed and left unsaid. Composing text calls for very different skills and for a style of language that might be quite alien to the pupil (or, at least, the pupil may have heard or read that style but had little or no practice in using it, and we should no more assume for language than for hang-gliding or football that you can learn purely by observing).

The difficulty that people perfectly competent in other spheres of life can have in composing text has interested a number of psycholinguists and has spawned a fair amount of research. Some researchers have focussed on the problems of the 'poor' or novice writer (e.g. Shaughnessy, 1977; Martlew, 1983), while others have studied skilled writers in the hope that learning how they do it will provide clearer guidelines for teaching others (e.g. Gregg and Steinberg, 1980; Hartley, 1980; Nystrand, 1982).

The processes involved in composing texts have come in for particularly detailed study, and the model developed by Hayes and Flower (1980) has been influential. Hayes and Flower divide writing into three processes – *planning*, *translating*, and *reviewing*. Planning is the 'pre-write' phase, involving the retrieval from memory of the information to be conveyed, the organizing of that retrieved information and the setting of goals to be achieved in the writing process. Translating is the 'write' phase where the conceptual material is converted into paragraphs, sentences and words and written down. Reviewing is the 're-write' phase of editing and revising successive drafts of a piece of work.

Difficulties can occur at any of these stages. Writing an essay (or a novel or a scientific paper) calls for the production of a sustained, coherent narrative quite unlike anything a person may ever have produced in speech. It may be very hard to distil what you have read and memorized into relevant, expressible thoughts, and hard too to decide what is the best sequence in which to make your points. Lack of practice in the style of formal writing may limit your capacity to express your ideas clearly and without mistakes. Daiute (1981) studied the syntactic writing errors of college students. These errors included such things as producing, as a sentence, something which is only a sentence fragment (e.g. 'Because the type of training the child gets is nothing compared to playing.' or 'More and more people saying they want freedom', failures of agreement between verbs and preceding nouns (e.g. 'The recent outbreak of riots *are* upsetting and disturbing to the peace efforts'), and omissions of necessary words (e.g. 'Mechanical devices have tendency to lose student's attention'). Of note is the fact that the students were an average of 11 words into a sentence before the grammatical hiccup occurred. That is, they were trying to construct elongated sentences of greater length than they might typically use in conversational speech and which sometimes overstrained their syntactic abilities. Finally, unfamiliarity with the formal written language style is likely to limit the degree to which you can effectively evaluate and edit what you have written.

A point that emerges very clearly from the work by Hayes and Flower is that planning, translating and reviewing do not occur in a linear order as discrete stages, but are closely intertwined in the writing process. Phases of planning and translating would often interleave closely, with reviewing and editing being a more or less continuous procedure ranging from changing a single word just written to recasting whole paragraphs. Another point to emerge is the wide range of individual differences between writers of acknowledged skill in the way they compose texts. Some writers assiduously plan out their compositions in detail before they begin to write, while others jump in and hope that the momentum will carry them through to the end. Jumping in is often recommended to those who find it hard ever to start writing: so aware are they of the complexities and nuances of all the issues that they freeze up entirely. For such people it can help to be told to forget the plan, start writing *something*, and don't stop to correct or alter any of it until you have got to the end and produced some sort of draft which you can then begin to hone and polish.

The act of writing can often cause new thoughts and new ideas to occur to the writer – thoughts and ideas that were not in the original plan. When Wason (1980) elicited the comments of skilled writers on how they perceive the act of writing, the unanticipated discovery of new thoughts was given as one of the commonest sources of enjoyment and motivation in writing. A mathematician quoted by Wason says: 'Writing is part of the research; in striving to make the work more intelligible, results improve and arguments get simpler and more elegant.' A historian comments: '. . . only in the course of working out exactly how I wish to present the findings in my subject do I finally arrive at the discovery of what I have found out.' As Wason observes, 'those who enjoy writing do so in large measure because it helps them to think'.

English spelling

Rightly or wrongly, our society places great store on the ability to spell correctly. An essay may be good conceptually, but if it is poorly spelled it will probably be marked down. Similarly, a job application that is replete with misspellings is unlikely to be successful. English spelling is another obstacle that must be surmounted by the apprentice writer. Why is English spelling so difficult? Put another way, why are there so many words in English whose spellings conceal rather than reveal their pronunciations?

We mentioned earlier that the English alphabet is a descendant of the regular and transparent Greek alphabet. Five hundred years or so ago, English spellings were also regular and transparent. Words were spelled as they sounded, spellings would vary from region to region to reflect local differences in pronunciation, and a spelling was acceptable as long as it sounded right (Stubbs, 1980). Why then do we now have a spelling system littered with opaque irregularities like 'yacht', 'debt', 'scissors', 'knife' and 'light'? In fact these five words illustrate three different sources of irregularity in modern English spelling. 'Yacht' was once spelled 'yott'; we owe its present spelling to Dutch printers who came to England following the establishment by William Caxton (c. 1421–1491) of the first printing press in England. These Dutch printers pronounced 'yacht' with an 'a' vowel and a consonant like the 'ch' in the Scottish pronunciation of 'loch'. Unfortunately they seem not to have taken the trouble to find out how the locals pronounced the word before setting it up in their presses.

'Debt' and 'scissors' were once spelled 'dette' and 'sisoures', respectively. Their spellings were 'reformed' by a back-to-roots movement influential in the 16th and 17th centuries which held that spellings should mirror the classical origins of words in Greek and Latin. The *b* entered in 'debt' to reflect its origin in the Latin word '*debitum*'. The *c* in 'scissors' was put there because the reformers thought it derived from the Latin word '*scindere*' (to cleave). As it happens they were wrong – 'scissors' descends from medieval Latin *cisoria*, meaning a large pair of shears.

'Knife' and 'light' illustrate the third, and commonest, source of irregularity. Five hundred years ago the /k/ was pronounced at the front of 'knife', 'knee', 'knave' and similar words so their spellings then were regular. What has happened in the intervening years is that the /k/ has been dropped from the pronunciation which has consequently diverged from the spelling. The same is true of 'light'. The *gh* originally reflected the presence in the word of the 'lo*ch*' sound, which also occurred in 'bright', 'bought', 'fight' and so on. That sound lingered on until recently in some Scottish dialects, but has now almost entirely disappeared. 'Knight' has changed twice over since the days when its *k* and its *gh* were both pronounced.

Dictionaries have effectively fossilized the spellings of words, but pronunciations continue to change. Given the resistance to spelling reform, the spellings and pronunciations of words are likely to continue drifting further and further apart. This in turn means that knowledge of a word's pronunciation is going to be of ever diminishing value to you when you are trying to spell a word. The 15th-century writer of English could do what the modern Italian writer can still do, namely assemble the spelling of a word from its sound in accordance with the alphabetic rules for translating phonemes into letters, and be confident that the resultant spelling would be at least very close to the correct spelling. Not so the modern writer of English. Assemble spellings from sound nowadays and many of your words will be 'phonetic misspellings', efforts like 'chare', 'taybul', or 'hows' which sound right but are very wrong. In fact, they look childish for reasons we shall shortly explain.

The vagaries of 20th-century English spelling mean that the only successful way to spell is to store the spellings of words in your memory and retrieve them on demand. Even many supposedly regular words are unpredictable in the sound-to-spelling direction, so must be memorized. 'Street', 'heat', 'thief' and 'complete' are all 'regular' words whose pronunciations follow reliably from their spellings, but if all you knew about the word 'seat' was what it means and the way it sounds, then you wouldn't know whether to spell it 'seat', 'seet', 'siet' or 'sete'.

A model for spelling

Most cognitive psychologists who have sought to explain spelling ability in recent years have converged upon the view that English writers retrieve the spellings of familiar, known words as wholes from a word store broadly analogous to the speech output lexicon that we introduced in Chapter 7 (e.g. Seymour, 1979; Morton, 1980; Ellis, 1984a). We shall call this store the *graphemic output lexicon*. The idea is that learning the spelling of a word involves establishing an entry for it in a corner of one's memory – the graphemic output lexicon – so that each time you wish to write the word in future the letter string which constitutes the word's accepted spelling is retrieved in its entirety from that lexicon.

Having postulated a graphemic output lexicon we can now ask how spellings are actually retrieved from it. From which other language components does the activation necessary to retrieve a word's spelling come? Morton (1980) proposed that there are two inputs to the graphemic output lexicon. One input comes from the semantic system so that the word's meaning is intimately involved in activating its spelling. The second input comes from the speech output lexicon. Morton introduced this second input to explain a common variety of unintentional slip of the pen that anyone who has done any substantial amount of writing will be aware of having made on several occasions. The slip in question involves involuntarily writing one version of a homophone for another – writing 'their' when you meant to write 'there', writing 'one' instead of 'won', or 'piece' instead of 'peace'. These slips undoubtedly come from the graphemic output lexicon because writers do not produce nonwords as homophone slips; you do not, for example, involuntarily write 'chare' when you meant 'chair' or 'taybul' when you meant 'table' as you might if homophone slips indicated an involvement of low-level alphabetic spelling rules in the writing of familiar words. Homophone slips do, however, indicate that the phonemic (spoken) forms of words play some part in activating their spellings, hence Morton's (1980) suggestion that one input to the graphemic output lexicon (but not the only input) comes from the speech output lexicon.

Although we have argued that the spellings of familiar words are retrieved from memory as wholes, at the same time there is no denying that writers of English also have a capacity for assembling spellings piecemeal from the spoken forms of words. This is easily demonstrated by devising a new word (i.e. a nonword) and asking someone to invent a plausible spelling for it. Alternatively yoo kann asque peepul tu kreeate olturnativ butt plorzibul spelingz forr fammiliyer wurdz. Such skills reveal an ability to take the spoken form of a word, segment it down into its component phonemes, and translate those phonemes into graphemes (letters).

If the word a writer is trying to spell through the strategy of phoneme-grapheme conversion is a regular one, then the spelling that is assembled piecemeal will have a chance of being correct. We have seen, however, that this is not guaranteed even for regular words, and phoneme-grapheme conversion will often produce 'phonetic' misspellings. We noted earlier how childish such spellings look. The reason for this is clear: young children will only have memorized a few spellings, and so will only have a few words stored in their graphemic output lexicons. They will be obliged therefore to use knowledge of English sound-spelling correspondences to assemble spellings for the words they have yet to learn. In adulthood phoneme-grapheme rules may only be used when you cannot be bothered to look a word up in your dictionary, or when asked by a cognitive psychologist to dream up plausible spellings for invented nonwords.

A spelling does not have to come *either* from the graphemic output lexicon *or* from phoneme-grapheme conversion. It is quite possible for the two routes to combine in producing a candidate spelling. Adult 'phonetic' misspellings typically resemble their targets more closely than do children's misspellings. This may be because an adult writer has often encountered the word he or she is having difficulty with and knows at least something about how it is spelled. Phoneme-grapheme conversion is called upon to flesh out the skeletal information retrieved from memory. The fact that it is possible for part but not all of a word's spelling to be stored in the graphemic output lexicon can be seen from spelling errors which, though incorrect, include irregular portions of words which could not be predicted by phoneme-grapheme conversion. Examples from Baron, Treiman, Wilf and Kellman (1980) include 'colonel' misspelled as 'colornel', 'colnel' and 'coloniel', all of which contain the unpredictable -ol- sequence, and 'rhythm' misspelled as 'rhythmn', 'rhythem' and 'rhythum', preserving the unpredictable rhy- beginning.

If you can spell a word then you can spell it in CAPITALS, in lower case print, or in *handwriting*; you can also spell it aloud or type it (albeit perhaps in a hesitant, one-fingered manner). The spelling that is retrieved from the graphemic output lexicon or assembled by phoneme-grapheme conversion has to be capable of being realised in any of these different ways. Ellis (1982, 1984a) has argued that the letter string is first retrieved as a *graphemic* description; something which is capable of being outputted in each of these ways but is itself more abstract than any of them. In Ellis's model, the next stage is to select the appropriate letter shape. As well as capital and lower-case letters, many writers have different forms of letters they use in different contexts, for example s and *s*, or f and *f*. Having selected the appropriate letter shape, the writing output system must then select the correct sequence of strokes, the appropriate size of the letters, which ones are going to be joined in connected writing, and so on. These are all part of the 'articulatory' processes of writing which make a person's hand-writing as distinctive and as individual as their speech.

Talking and writing

Writing is a comparatively new invention. Even among those societies which have it, only in the last hundred years or so has the ability to write become a widespread and necessary accomplishment. Writing calls for rather different language skills than most talking. The content is usually more organized and demands more advance planning, the production takes the form of a monologue rather than a dialogue, and the grammatical conventions are somewhat different. The style may have its counterpart in non-literate cultures when, as in storytelling, a speaker is called upon to produce a sustained monologue, but only in literate societies in recent years has its acquisition become a more or less mandatory prerequisite for success in certain spheres of life.

Not all writing requires use of the formal style, and once that style has been mastered it can also be used in speech (though people who 'talk like a book', using only well-formed, well-planned, literate sentences can be very disconcerting to try and hold a conversation with!). Cognitively we have argued that talking and writing use a common set of language production processes up to the moment when word forms are selected. At that point the requirement to produce phonemes in speech and letters in writing forces the two channels to diverge. This is not to deny that speech can still continue as you are writing, in the sense that most of us are aware of an 'inner voice' which accompanies our writing and speaks our words. That inner voice may play an important function in writing because, like all inner speech, it allows you to monitor and evaluate your own thoughts and expressions before you make them public (cf. Mead, 1934). By talking to ourselves as we write we can try out particular translations of our ideas into words and edit out those that do not come up to scratch before ever committing them to the page. Inner speech serves Hayes and Flower's (1980) reviewing function in advance of anything being written. Thus we see inner speech as an important source of high-level feedback, and at most playing only a minor role in lower level spelling and writing processes.

Finally, a_ we said at the start of this chapter, it is impossible to underestimate the importance of visible language to a modern society. It is everywhere – in books and newspapers, on billboards and cereal packets. Its permanence and reliability make business and commerce possible, create new art forms in novels, plays and poetry, sustain social continuity through written history, and document hypotheses about how the world works in a way that allows them to be subjected to the sort of critical analysis that is crucial to the growth and maintenance of science.

12 Language reception: recognizing spoken and written words

In the previous two chapters we considered how messages are translated into speech and writing. This and the next chapter are concerned with the reverse translation of speech and writing signals back into conceptual messages. For convenience we shall divide this decoding process into two stages. In this chapter we shall look at how words are identified in reading and listening, and in the next chapter at how messages are extracted from sequences of words (sentences, paragraphs, stories etc.).

The question at issue here, then, is how do we identify words in spoken and written signals? Put differently, how do we identify a particular sequence of sounds or letters as a word in our vocabulary whose meaning we know? Because word recognition in reading is a marginally easier topic to handle than word recognition in listening we shall begin with reading.

Word recognition in reading

To a skilled reader, recognizing written words is usually so easy and fluent that, as with so many skills, it is sometimes hard to appreciate or accept that complex mental processes *are* involved. To help us begin to realize the subtlety of those processes, consider the following eight strings of letters:

1)
2) YTCP
3) SATHE

4) PHLOOT
5) SHIP
6) *yacht*
7) SWORD
8) *pistol*

Some of these strings can be read with ease, some with difficulty, and some hardly at all (in what sense do we 'read' YTCP?). When we are able to progress right to the meaning of one of these strings, how is this done? Are there alternative 'routes' to meanings? Where do the strings we cannot read fail along the line? These are some of the issues we shall now address.

Let us propose, as most theories of reading do, that the first stage in visual word recognition is the *identification of the component letters of a word*. For most readers string 1 above will fall at this first hurdle. That is because it is written in shorthand, a writing-derived system widely used in business and commerce. If you do know how the letters of the alphabet are represented in shorthand, string 1 (actually the word 'house') would pass our first stage, but most of us do not know shorthand so string 1 remains just a jumble of meaningless squiggles. The example serves, however, to bring home the point that in order to be a successful reader you must know both the language of the text and the writing system used. Many languages can be written in several different scripts, each of which will have its own characteristics and properties. To read you must master both the language and the script – either alone is insufficient.

Whilst letter identification is possible for all of strings 2 to 8, it is certainly harder for the two handwritten words. The effort involved in reading untidy handwriting focusses our attention on the stage of letter identification.

After letter identification, the next process to examine is the *identification of familiar letter strings as known words*. Most theorists assume that as we learn to read we build up a set of *recognition units*, one for each word we are familiar with in written form. These recognition units collectively constitute a memory store for words which we shall call the *visual input lexicon* (an input counterpart of the speech and graphemic output lexicons we introduced in Chapters 7 and 11). A normal adult reader will have encountered the written words 'yacht', 'ship', 'sword' and 'pistol' numerous times before. Letter strings 5–8 will therefore pass successfully through our second processing stage by virtue of being strings which have their own recognition units uniquely activated by them.

The *purpose* of having recognition units is, of course, to allow words to make contact with the representations of their meanings which are stored in the reader's semantic system. This semantic system is commonly assumed to be the same one that initiates speech production. This provides us with a mechanism for reading words aloud via the semantic system and then the speech output lexicon.

Letter strings 2, 3 and 4 (YTCP, SATHE and PHLOOT) are all unfamiliar and so will have no recognition units. SATHE and PHLOOT differ from YTCP in that they are at least pronounceable while YTCP is not. An adequate theory of reading must include a set of procedures or rules for converting new and unfamiliar letter strings to pronunciations. These procedures are presumably used more by children and unskilled readers, who have yet to establish large quantities of visual recognition units, than by skilled readers (just as spelling from sound is more characteristic of young than old writers). It is no simple matter to convert new letter strings to pronunciations: in the case of SATHE, for example, the -TH- must be grouped together as two letters that map onto a single phoneme (sound), while the procedures must know that the effect of the final E is to lengthen the A from a short vowel to a long one. Similarly PHLOOT must be segmented into PH, L, OO and T before the letters can be successfully mapped onto sounds (phonemes).

Word recognition in speech perception

How can the principles we have just applied to modelling word recognition in reading be transferred to understanding word recognition in speech perception? One immediately transferable notion is the idea of an input lexicon containing word recognition units. The difference is that for speech perception we need not a visual input lexicon, but an *auditory input lexicon*. The idea is that each time a child (or an adult for that matter) hears a new word and learns its associated meaning, a new recognition unit is established in an auditory input lexicon. That recognition unit's job is to become activated every time its word is heard in future, and to activate in turn the representation of the meaning of the word in the semantic system.

A much more difficult problem is to specify the nature of the auditory processing prior to the auditory input lexicon and the nature of the information fed into the lexicon. A great deal of work has been done on what cues in the speech wave determine our perception of different sounds (see Foss and Hakes, 1978, Ch. 3, and Liberman, 1982), but we shall not venture far into this highly technical though interesting area. One problem is that, unlike letters in a printed word, phonemes in the speech wave are not discrete and separable. Rather than being spaced out like beads on a string, the acoustic cues for different speech sounds overlap and intermesh, so that a vowel sound might provide clues to the identity of both the preceding and the following consonants. Lisker (1978), for example, identified no fewer than sixteen different auditory cues available in the speech wave which might be used to distinguish between the middle consonants of the words 'rapid' and 'rabid'.

Another important difference between spoken and written words as signals is that whereas all the letters in a written word are simultaneously present and can be processed 'in parallel', the sounds of a spoken word are spread out in time. This forces a more 'serial' mode of processing on the listener, and also means that the listener must be capable of very fine temporal resolutions. For example, the sounds 'pa' and 'ba' differ only in the fact that 'pa' begins with a 40 or 50 millisecond burst of hissing noise which is absent from 'ba'. Forty milliseconds is less than one twentieth of a second, but a listener who cannot detect this ultrafine difference will be unable to distinguish between /p/ and /b/, and will be unable to distinguish many other speech sounds one from another. In fact, just this difficulty in fine discrimination has been found in some children with developmental language difficulties (Tallal and Piercy, 1975), and in some adults who, following injury to the brain such as a stroke, can no longer perceive speech properly (Albert and Bear, 1974).

Another implication of the spread-out nature of speech is that it may be possible to identify a word before the speaker has finished saying it. If, for example, you hear someone say, 'I went to the zoo and saw a giraffe, an elephant and a hippopotamus', it is unlikely that you wait for the final 's' of 'hippopotamus' before recognizing it. A series of experiments by Marslen-Wilson and his co-workers has shown that words are commonly identified as soon as enough auditory information has been heard to uniquely specify them (see Marslen-Wilson, 1980). For example, in one experiment subjects were asked to listen to a passage of speech and press a button each time they heard a particular target word. The average time for a button press, measured from the onset of the target word, was 275 msec, despite the fact that the average duration of the target word was 370 msec. If we subtract a reasonable 50–75 msec from the button push latency as the time necessary to actually execute the response, then we conclude that the listeners were identifying the target words around 200 msecs after onset. That is, they were identifying the words after hearing little more than half of each one.

Though there is known to be flexibility in the word recognition system, Marslen-Wilson (1980) concludes that, under normal listening conditions, 'a word is recognised at that point, starting from the beginning of the word, at which the word in question becomes *uniquely distinguishable* from all of the other words in the language *beginning with the same sound sequence*'. In our terms, recognition units in the auditory input lexicon are maximally active once enough information has been received to uniquely specify them.

Marslen-Wilson is careful not to specify the nature of the auditory information upon which word recognition is based. Some theorists (e.g. Rumelhart and McClelland, 1981) believe phonemes are extracted first like letters in visual word recognition, while others such as Klatt (1979) argue that auditory word recognition is performed upon a fairly raw acoustic description of the speech wave. Klatt has built a computer model to demonstrate the viability of this latter option. Klatt also notes that models of speech perception must include a route from input to output which does not go via word recognition to explain how we are able to repeat unfamiliar words we hear. This is similar in function to the nonlexical letter-phoneme conversion route used to read aloud unfamiliar words.

Listening is visual too

Much of the classical work on speech perception involves listeners hearing speech through headphones. Sometimes it is natural speech, sometimes it is artificial, computer-synthesized speech. Either way it is listened to by someone gazing into space or at a blank wall. Now we have tried in this book to emphasize that speech processing is normally carried out in the context of face-to-face conversational interaction. We are pleased, then, to relate the discovery (which sent tremors through many speech perception laboratories) that listening is visual too. It has been known for some time that visual cues from face and lip movements may aid speech perception. Cotton (1935) had a speaker sit in a sound-proof booth fitted with glass windows. The speaker's voice was transmitted via a microphone, amplifier and loudspeaker to an audience seated outside. The speech was distorted by removing high frequencies and adding a loud buzzing noise. When the lighting was adjusted so as to make the speaker invisible to the audience only an occasional word or two could be identified, yet when the speaker was visible the speech was correctly understood by the listeners. Cotton concluded that 'there is an important element of visual hearing in all normal individuals'. In similar vein Sumby and Pollack (1954) showed that if a listener is trying to identify words heard against a background of hissing noise, performance improves when the speaker's face and lip movements can also be seen.

More recently it has been shown that visual information does not merely *supplement* auditory information but rather *combines* with it in complex ways to determine what we hear. McGurk and MacDonald (1976) videotaped a speaker saying 'ga-ga' then replaced the soundtrack with the dubbed sound of someone saying 'ba-ba'. When listeners closed their eyes so they could not see the lip movements they indeed heard 'ba-ba', but when they opened their eyes the effect of the conflicting visual information was to make them *hear* neither 'ba-ba' nor 'ga-ga', but 'da-da'! Watching lip movements for 'ba-ba' while listening to the spoken 'ga-ga' resulted in the illusory perception of the speaker saying 'gab-ga' or 'bag-ba'. Visual and auditory speech information must combine *before* the stage of processing upon which conscious perception is based since they produce together a percept which may be neither what was seen, nor what was heard, but is some blending of the two aimed at reducing the discrepancy between them.

Top-down processes in word recognition

In our discussion of word recognition so far we may have given the impression that all recognition is entirely determined and controlled by incoming stimulus (signal) information. In the jargon of cognitive psychology we have talked about word recognition as if it were all 'bottom-up' or 'data-driven'. There are, however, experiments going back a long way showing that stored knowledge and experience can interact with external signal information to influence, and in part determine, what is actually perceived.

The experiments in question show that perception is affected by the *context* in which a letter, sound or word is encountered. For convenience we shall divide our discussion of these 'top-down' influences of context on perception into a) within-word context effects affecting letter or sound perception, and b) semantic and sentence context effects that influence perception at the level of word recognition.

Within-word context effects

The letters that surround a particular letter in a string can influence the way it is perceived. Experiments on the 'word superiority effect' have shown that a letter which is encountered as part of a familiar word is, under certain circumstances, actually perceived faster and better than the same letter occurring either on its own or as part of an unfamiliar string of letters.

In a typical experiment a word such as SHIP might be shown very briefly to a reader followed by a random jumble of bits of letters. The reader is then asked, 'Was the last letter P or D?' On a different trial the letter string might be YTCP and the question again, 'was the last letter P or D?' Numerous studies reviewed by Henderson (1982) have found that the question 'P or D?' is answered correctly more often when the target letter occurs as part of a real word like SHIP than as part of a random string like YTCP (or even a nonword like SHUP). The importance of this finding (known as the *word superiority effect*) lies in its demonstration that the perception of a letter is affected by whether or not it and the other letters round it feed into a recognition unit in the visual input lexicon.

In an influential computer simulation of human visual word recognition, McClelland and Rumelhart (1981) proposed that as soon as a string of letters on the page *begins* to activate letter recognition 'units' they, in turn, start to activate word recognition units. Those units then feed activation back down to the letter recognizers adding to their level of excitation. So, if SHIP is the word being read, as the letters S, H, I and P begin to be identified, they start to activate the recognition unit for the *word* SHIP. It replies by feeding activation back down to the letter detectors so that the final perception of each letter is a combination of contributions from below (the printed word out there) and above (the knowledge of words embodied in the visual input lexicon). A random letter string like YTCP, in contrast, will cause very little activity up in the visual input lexicon so that the perception of its letters will be largely a 'bottom-up' process driven by stimulus (signal) information.

The McClelland and Rumelhart model has a number of advantages, not the least of which is that it *is* a working computer system. It is additionally important in showing that each stage in a sequence of mental operations need not necessarily have been completed before the next stage begins. Instead, information can 'cascade' both ways through a succession of stages, so that work can have begun at stage 7 (say a semantic process) before work at stage 1 (say letter recognition) is finished. Additionally, because information (or activation) can cascade back down from higher to lower levels, this 'interactive' approach provides us with a way of conceptualizing how higher mental processes incorporating stored knowledge can contribute to the ongoing, moment-by-moment operations of lower processes. In other words, it provides us with a model (in the general sense) of how knowledge and experience can affect momentary perception.

As well as speeding up language reception processes, the combination of a strong context and weak signal may induce perceptions that are actually illusory in being top-down determined. Pillsbury (1897) omitted or changed letters in words which he then showed briefly to subjects. These alterations were often missed by the subjects who reported seeing the correctly spelled word, even when letters had been replaced by 'shapeless blurs'. Indeed, Pillsbury notes that, 'In many cases . . . the letters which were most certain and of whose presence the subject is most confident were not on the slide, but were added subjectively'.

Turning to speech perception, Bagley (1900–01) conducted auditory experiments similar in conception to Pillsbury's visual ones. In Bagley's experiments, 'words and sentences were recorded upon the cylinders of an Edison phonograph' but some words were mutilated by omitting consonants (e.g. saying 'scrilling' for 'scribbling', or 'diersity' for 'diversity'). Once again these mutilations were apt to be missed and the omitted sound restored perceptually by listeners. This phenomenon was rediscovered more recently by

Warren (1970) who removed speech sounds from tape-recorded sentences and replaced them with extraneous noises such as coughs, only to find that listeners perceptually restored the deleted sound which *should* have been there (see Cole and Rudnicky, 1983).

These restoration phenomena are understandable in terms of an interactive activation approach like that of the McClelland and Rumelhart (1981) model discussed earlier. As soon as the letters or sounds of a word begin to be perceived they start to activate that word's recognition unit in the visual or auditory input lexicon. That recognition unit then feeds activation back down to the appropriate sound or letter recognizers, *including those for sounds and letters not present in the signal*. Those sounds and letters may then be 'perceived' thanks to top-down rather than bottom-up activation. Viewed ecologically, this is clearly a good way of amplifying and enhancing weak or noisy signals, which speech signals in particular are apt to be.

Semantic and sentence context effects

'Context' in language reception can mean more than just the surrounding sounds or letters, it can also mean the surrounding words and sentences. Many experiments show that these wider contexts can also affect perception. For example, Pillsbury's (1897) letter restoration was more likely to occur if the mutilated word was presented in a plausible sentence context than if it was presented in isolation, and the same was true of Bagley's (1900–01) phoneme restoration effect. Siipola (1935) showed that if subjects were 'set' to perceive animal words they would often perceive the nonword 'sael' as 'seal', while if they were expecting boating words they would likely misperceive it as 'sail'. Likewise 'wharl' would be misread as either 'whale' or 'wharf'. O'Connor and Forster (1981) reported similar findings.

Priming by semantically related words assists veridical perception as well as inducing misperceptions. The boosting of word perception by prior presentation of related words is one of those phenomena which get rediscovered with monotonous regularity (e.g. Postman and Bruner, 1949; O'Neil, 1953; Russell and Storms, 1955; Engler and Freeman, 1956), but modern interest in the phenomenon stems from the work of Meyer and Schvaneveldt (1971). Using the 'lexical decision task' in which subjects must decide as quickly as possible whether successively presented strings of letters form words or not, Meyer and Schvaneveldt found that a string of letters like *nurse* is accepted as a word more rapidly when preceded by a related word such as *doctor* than when preceded by an unrelated word like *bread*. Subsequent research has found this phenomenon to be highly replicable and to apply also to a task in which each word shown must be named as quickly as possible (Henderson, 1982).

The two associated words do not need to be presented in the same modality for priming to occur. Pillsbury (1897) obtained priming from auditory primes to visual targets. This same result was obtained by Swinney, Onifer, Prather and Hirshkowitz (1979). Semantic priming between pictures and words has also been reported; for example between naming a picture of a fork and naming (or making a lexical decision about) the written word *knife* (Durso and Johnson, 1979; Sperber, McCauley, Ragain and Weil, 1979).

The interpretation commonly afforded these results is that pictures and words from different modalities converge upon a common semantic system. Within the semantic system there is 'spreading activation' such that activation of the semantics of *doctor* will spread to the semantic representations of related concepts such as *nurse* (e.g. Collins and Loftus, 1975; Anderson, 1976). Once the semantic node for *nurse* is activated it will feed activation back down to all the appropriate recognition units (visual word, auditory word and presumably object/picture units) so that less input from the outside world is necessary for those recognition units to be subsequently activated. To take another example, hearing the word 'bread' will activate the unit for that word in the auditory input lexicon which will, in turn, activate the semantic or conceptual representation of bread. That activation will spread to the related concept 'butter' whose auditory and visual recognition units will then gain activation by a top-down effect. The written word *butter* would then be perceived more easily than if it had not been preceded by 'bread'.

This sort of priming is readily obtainable and must be telling us something about how the language system works. As Foss (1982) remarks, 'While it is unlikely that the phenomenon exists to help us to do experiments on the structure of the lexicon, it is likely that priming has to do with the processing of natural language'. There are, however, problems in specifying just what that contribution might be, the major one having to do with the separation of semantically related words in natural language. Gough, Alford and Holley-Wilcox (1981) showed that if single words are presented in lists, then interposing just one or two unrelated words between a related pair dissipates any priming of the second member of the pair by the first. Now, even where related words occur close together in natural speech or writing they are likely to be separated by some intervening, unrelated words which, if the list experiments are to be believed, should eliminate any potential priming.

This apparent difficulty has, however, been countered by Foss (1982), who showed that what is true of the processing of lists of isolated words is not true of the processing of sentences. Using the 'phoneme monitoring' task, where listeners must press a button as quickly as possible after hearing a particular target sound, Foss examined the influence of two (priming) words on the identification of a target phoneme in a third, related word heard later. Substantial priming was found across sentence boundaries and across several intervening words when real sentences were used. Thus, hearing 'gills' and 'fins' primed the later identification of the /f/ in 'fish' when listeners heard: 'The entire group examined the *gills* and the *fins* with amazement. Everyone agreed that this was unlike any other *fish* caught in recent years.' In contrast, when the words were jumbled to make random, ungrammatical lists the priming disappeared as it had in Gough, Alford and Holley-Wilcox's earlier list experiments.

Foss's (1982) experiments bring us closer to what has been psychologists' second main line of attack on the influence of preceding context on present processing, namely to present an incomplete sentence followed by a target word which must be responded to in some way. Tulving and Gold (1963) showed readers all or part of a context sentence such as 'The skiers were buried alive by the sudden', followed by a target word to be identified. The target word was shown very briefly at first. If it was not identified, the context was shown again, followed by a longer exposure of the target word. This procedure was continued until the target word was identified correctly. Tulving and Gold found that if the target word was a plausible continuation of the preceding context (e.g. 'avalanche' in the present case), then it was identified at a briefer exposure than was necessary for it to be identified in isolation with no preceding context. If, however, the target word was an 'implausible' completion, then a longer exposure was required for identification than when the word was identified in isolation.

Context, then, appeared to have the capacity to either help or hinder identification of a briefly-shown word depending on whether the target word was likely or unlikely in that context. Similar results were obtained by Morton (1964).

Use of context in natural reading and listening

While the Tulving and Gold experiment just described certainly provides evidence of use of context by readers, there is undoubtedly something unnatural in their procedure. In natural reading incomplete sentences are not read over and over again with the final word being glimpsed repeatedly at progressively longer exposures. To use a much bandied term, the procedure lacks 'ecological validity'.

This criticism would not be too damning were it not for the fact that as reading tasks approximate more closely to fluent, skilled reading context effects become progressively harder to find. (Forster, 1981; Mitchell, 1982). For instance, Fischler and Bloom (1979) found that sentence contexts only primed lexical decision speed for words which were very highly predictable completions of sentences, not plausible but less predictable completions. Fischer and Bloom (1980) were unable to obtain even this limited priming when faster rates of presentation akin to normal reading speeds were used. Similarly, Stanovich (1981a) found priming of word naming speed by sentence contexts only when a 750 msec delay occurred between context and target word. When there was no delay there was also no significant degree of priming detectable.

The situation is very different in the realm of speech perception, though comparison between speech perception and reading is rendered more difficult by the fact that there has been little contact between research on context effects in the two modes of word recognition. It is, in Henderson's (1982) words, 'as if ears and eyes were connected to different psychologists'. Nevertheless, unlike the situation in skilled reading where context effects seem elusive, context effects in speech perception are readily obtainable in a variety of tasks including ones which approximate reasonably well to normal listening conditions. We have already made mention of Bagley's (1900–01) finding that presenting mispronounced words in sentence contexts led to fewer detections of the mispronunciations and more 'restoration effects'. Similar results have been obtained by Marslen-Wilson (1975) and Marslen-Wilson and Welch (1978).

Miller, Heise and Lichten (1951) had subjects try to identify words heard against a background of hissing noise. Words presented in isolation were found to be much less identifiable than words in sentence contexts. Marslen-Wilson and Tyler (1975, 1980) had their subjects listen to passages and press a button each time particular target words were heard. Reaction times were much shorter in normal passages of text where context could work its influence than in scrambled passages where raw stimulus information was all listeners had to go on. That is, in the normal passage conditions context information and stimulus information appeared to combine to lead to more efficient perception of the target word.

What determines the use of context?

Why should context effects be elusive for skilled reading and so pervasive for speech perception? Are we perhaps looking at some fundamental difference between the processing of writing and speech? We would prefer not to believe this and to argue instead, with Forster (1981), Henderson (1982), Stanovich and West (1983) and others, that the nature of speech and print *as communicative signals* determines the extent to which context is used in a top-down manner to assist on-going word identification.

As we have seen, the normal speech signal is not a high quality carrier of information; imprecise articulation, co-articulation effects, phonetic reduction, loss of quality in transmission and so on combine to make the reconstruction of the speaker's message a difficult task for the listener. This was demonstrated experimentally by Liberman (1963), and by Pollack and Pickett (1964), who showed that less than 50 per cent of words excised from perfectly intelligible conversational speech are identifiable when played to listeners without their surrounding context.

The impoverished quality of speech as signal contrasts sharply with the situation in reading where a printed word cut out of a newspaper or book remains perfectly readable. Now, as Forster (1981) points out, using context to aid recognition cannot be a simple, passive process but must instead require the complex, inferential enumeration of likely continuations of what is being heard or read, continuations which must be continuously updated as more language is processed. If the language processing system has any option in whether or not it indulges in these complex computations, then it may choose not to bother (or, at least, to bother less) when the signal is as readily decipherable as is the printed word.

This line of reasoning would lead us to predict that if the bottom-up processing of the written signal in reading were made more difficult, context effects would reappear. The traditional experiments such as those of Tulving and Gold (1963) and Morton (1964) which found evidence for the use of context in reading did, of course, make recognition of the primed words difficult by exposing them only briefly. Other experiments have shown that degrading the quality of the signal information in reading enhances context effects (e.g. Becker and Killion, 1977; Stanovich and West, 1983). Young children and poor readers have also been shown to make greater use of contextual information (e.g. Biemiller, 1970; Perfetti, Goldman and Hogaboam, 1979; Stanovich, West and Freeman, 1981), presumably to assist rather inefficient bottom-up recognition processes.

Interestingly this pattern of results with young readers completely contradicts a popular theory espoused by Goodman (1967) and Smith (1978) that extensive use of context is characteristic of skilled reading. The experiments we have just reviewed have shown instead that skilled readers faced with clear print make relatively little predictive use of context. As Stanovich and West (1983) put it, 'Adult readers normally do not use attentional capacity to predict upcoming words, but focus conscious attention on comprehending and integrating the text'.

Unconscious reception of language

There is quite a long tradition of work seeking to demonstrate that words a reader or listener has no conscious awareness of having seen or heard can still be shown to have been recognized and understood at some level (Dixon, 1981). This tradition is one which has tended to wax and wane: excitement mounts when a technique is reported which appears to demonstrate unconscious recognition, but subsides again as subsequent studies either fail to replicate the original findings or discover damaging methodological weaknesses. At the time of writing, unconscious word recognition is in the ascendent with some apparently replicable techniques for demonstrating the phenomenon having been reported (see Dixon, 1980; Fowler, Wolford, Slade and Tassinary, 1981; Henderson, 1982;

Marcel, 1983a,b). We would be reluctant, however, to stake our reputations on this situation not dissolving again over the next decade. We would note, though, that it is not sufficient for disbelievers to discredit one method and condemn the rest as guilty by association: if a single paradigm can be found which yields replicable results then the reality of unconscious recognition is established.

We shall concentrate on the reading sphere, and begin by considering a paper by Allport (1977). In Experiment II of that paper, subjects were asked to report a word (the target) displayed for a mere 20 msec (one fiftieth of a second) at the point on a screen they were fixating. On some trials a second word (the distractor) was presented above the target word, but its presentation was so brief (and was 'masked' by subsequent presentation of a jumble of letter fragments) that subjects were quite unaware of the distractor ever having been shown. Nevertheless, when the distractor was related in meaning to the target, report of the identity of the target word was higher than when the distractor was unrelated to the target (though both were lower than when there was no distractor at all).

It is not difficult to display a word so briefly that people are unaware that anything has been presented, particularly if the word is preceded and followed by a 'pattern mask' (a jumble of letter fragments). Although a word presented under such conditions may not be consciously perceived there is growing evidence that the word's meaning may nevertheless have been registered at some level. This evidence takes the form of showing that the meaning of the unconsciously perceived word can influence the simultaneous or subsequent perception of a related word. For example, the time to classify *butter* as a word may be speeded by the earlier unconscious presentation of *bread* (see for example Underwood, 1976, 1981; Evett and Humphreys, 1981; Fowler, Wolford, Slade and Tassinary, 1981; Balota, 1983; Marcel, 1983a,b).

How might the phenomenon of unconscious word recognition be explained in terms of the sorts of models of language perception we have proposed? Earlier in this chapter we followed McClelland and Rumelhart in proposing that the stages involved in word recognition are 'in cascade'. The stage of letter recognition does not need to be completed before activation of entries in the visual input lexicon can begin. Instead, as soon as letter recognition units begin to become active they begin to activate word recognition units which begin to activate semantic entries, and so on down the line. Most of the demonstrations of unconscious word recognition in reading depend on using very brief, masked presentations. Conscious awareness of a letter string may require a level of activation in the letter identification system greater than that generated by the fleeting presentations used in these experiments, but those fleeting presentations may still cause sufficient activity in the semantic system to spread and prime recognition of related words – and unconscious word recognition is, as we have seen, best demonstrated through its influence on the processing of other words. We would argue therefore that the phenomenon of unconscious word recognition, while of interest in its own right, is not incompatible with the sort of information-processing cognitive models we have advocated and used here. Finally, the issue of ecological validity does not go away just because we are dealing with an intriguing phenomenon like unconscious word recognition. If the unconscious apprehension of word meanings can be reliably and replicably demonstrated it may have much to teach us about the nature of consciousness and its role in mental processing. But do we do much unconscious recognizing in daily life? How often do we glimpse words so briefly or hear them so faintly that the conditions for unconscious recognition are met? We wonder.

Relations between reading and listening

There is one aspect of one of the eight letter strings we began this chapter with that we have refrained from commenting on up to now. The letter string in question is number 4, PHLOOT, which some readers may have spotted as an alternative possible spelling of 'flute'. Misspelled words like PHLOOT (or CHARE, or LEFE, or KATT) illustrate a mode of word recognition which arguably combines vision and hearing. This mode may be little used by skilled readers but is probably used a great deal by unskilled readers or young children learning to read.

   The point about PHLOOT, CHARE and the like is that they are unfamiliar letter strings which lack a recognition unit in the visual input lexicon but which can be understood by sounding them out and then somehow listening to the word internally to see if it *sounds* familiar even though it does not *look* familiar. 'Sounding out' we have already ascribed to letter-phoneme conversion which deposits the pronunciation of the word in the phonemic buffer.

'Listening to the word internally' must somehow involve cycling the phonemic form back and submitting it as input to the auditory input lexicon as if the word had been heard rather than read.

Is this identification of visually unfamiliar words the *only* function of silent, 'inner speech' in reading? Most people when they read are aware of an inner voice saying the words as they read them. It is important to note that the inner voice pronounces irregularly-spelled words like KNIGHT or TWO, and assigns the contextually appropriate pronunciation to words like TEAR and SOW whose pronunciation changes according to which of two meanings is implied (TEAR (when crying) *vs* TEAR (to rip), and SOW (some seed) *vs* SOW (a female pig)). Also the inner voice supplies suitable intonation and phrasing to what is being read. These three attributes of the inner voice mean that written words must be identified as wholes, understood and integrated with the meanings of the preceding words *before* they are articulated as inner speech.

Inner speech increases when people are reading passages they find difficult, and comprehension of such passages is disrupted more than the comprehension of conceptually straightforward passages by making people perform a task while they are reading which is designed to eliminate, or at least reduce, the incidence of inner speech. Other experiments using the technique of having people read whilst simultaneously repeating 'the, the, the' or 'one, two, three, four, five, six' have found that readers have no more difficulty detecting semantic anomalies in sentences like 'The chair jumped onto the cat', but find it hard to detect simple syntactic anomalies such as inappropriate word order, as in 'The cat jumped the onto chair' (Kleiman, 1975; Baddeley and Lewis, 1981; Levy, 1981). Syntactic processes in particular seem to perform best on auditory input or visual input plus inner speech. In a sense this is curious since syntactic operations are presumably needed to generate inner speech in the first place. Perhaps the detection of word order anomalies comes more naturally to a modality like reading where simultaneous identification and processing of more than one word at a time may be the norm.

13 Language comprehension and memory

We began this book by defining communication in Chapter 1 as the encoding of a message by one organism into a physical signal which passes to another organism who decodes the signal in order to recreate the original message. We have since noted how human beings employ not one but several channels of communication or 'signal systems', such as facial expressions, gestures, eye contact, speech etc. Chapter 7 was concerned with the encoding of a message into just one of those channels, namely speech. We saw then how speech planning involves linguistic units of different sizes, ranging from admittedly rather ill-defined 'idea units', through sentences, clauses, words and morphemes, to phonemes or letters. Evidence from slips of the tongue, pauses and other sources suggested that all of these units have 'psychological reality' as far as speech production is concerned.

In the previous chapter we looked at the parts played by phonemes, letters, morphemes and words in language reception (listening and reading). It should not surprise us that these units of planning also turned out to have a role in perception: that which is a unit of encoding is also likely to be a unit of decoding. In this chapter we turn to a consideration of the processes involved in comprehending clauses, sentences, and text.

Throughout this book we have tried to emphasize that the natural use of language, for which our cognitive processes are most likely to be adapted, is conversational give-and-take. Sadly, very little research has been done on either the production or comprehension of speech in conversational settings. In a typical language comprehension experiment a 'subject' (volunteer) sits in silence reading a passage of text, or listening to one through headphones. The subject's task might be to press a button when a specified target word occurs, or to recall parts of the text later (note our comment in Chapter 1 that communication only requires the decoder to have a *potential* response available). We can learn much from the results of such experiments, but we shall also argue that an over-concentration on isolated decoders processing text has caused psycholinguists to spend a lot of time and effort discovering things about language comprehension that a greater awareness of the cognitive requirements of conversational decoding would have made more obvious and less surprising.

High-level of units of language decoding

Clause and sentence

We shall begin our treatment of language comprehension by considering the higher-level *units of decoding*. Evidence that the clause plays an active role in comprehension comes from several sources. Fodor and Bever (1965) pioneered a technique for studying speech perception in which listeners hear a sentence into which an extraneous click has been dubbed. Immediately after hearing the sentence the listener has to write it down and indicate where in the sentence the click occurred. Several studies have found that clicks situated away from a clause boundary tend to migrate towards it; that is, listeners misreport clicks as having been closer to a boundary between two clauses than they actually were (see Fodor, Bever and Garrett, 1974). In a variation on this technique Abrams and Bever (1969) asked subjects to press a key as quickly as possible whenever they heard a click in a sentence. Time to press the key was found to be longer at the end of a clause than at the beginning.

Now there are known to be problems associated with the click location technique (see Clark and Clark, 1977, pp. 53–55), but the conclusion regarding clauses has received support from experiments using other procedures. For example, Caplan (1972) constructed pairs of two-clause sentences in which a 'target' word occurred the same number of words from the end of each sentence. In one sentence, however, the target word occurred in the first clause while in the other it occurred in the second clause. The positioning of the word OIL in the following two sentences (where a dash marks the clause boundary) illustrates Caplan's design:

1) 'Now that artists are working in OIL/prints are rare.'
2) 'Now that artists are working fewer hours/OIL prints are rare.'

Listeners heard many such sentences, and at the end of each sentence were presented with an additional, 'probe' word. Their task was to decide as quickly as possible whether or not the probe word occurred in the sentence they had just heard. Time to decide 'yes' for probe words positioned at the end of the first clause (like the word OIL in sentence 1) were longer than when the target had occurred in the second clause (OIL in sentence 2), though the actual distance of the target word from the end of the sentence was the same in both cases.

We noted in Chapter 7 how a surface clause often corresponds to an underlying proposition in the message. Slobin (1979) suggests that in perception the listener attempts to 'wrap up' that portion of the message at the end of each clause; that is, to arrive at a final interpretation from the various possibilities that may have been open as the clause was being decoded. But when two or more clauses are combined in a sentence, and especially if one is embedded in the other (e.g. 'The glass the girl dropped broke'), the sentence has a coherence of its own as a superordinate message unit.

There is evidence from speech comprehension experiments for an extra 'wrap up' at the ends of sentences. The subjects in experiments by Jarvella (1970, 1971) listened to long passages of text. At key points the text was interrupted and the listener told to 'write down as much of the end of the passage just immediately preceding the interruption' as they could. The interruption came after a sequence of three clauses. In one condition the first two clauses combined to form one sentence and the third clause another, for example:

'The document had also blamed him for *having failed to disprove the charges*. Taylor was later fired by the President.'

In the contrasting condition the first clause formed a sentence on its own, with the second and third clauses combining into another sentence, for example:

'The tone of the document was threatening. *Having failed to disprove the charges*, Taylor was later fired by the President.'

Now, the second clause, italicized in our examples, was identical in both conditions, as were the final clauses, yet recall of that second clause was more than twice as good in the condition where it was part of the most recent sentence heard (54% correct recall) as compared with the condition where a sentence boundary had intervened between it and the recall instruction (21% correct). It is worth noting, though, that recall *was* only 54% correct in the better of the two conditions, suggesting some wrapping up and loss of surface structure information at the clause boundary midway through the last sentence.

The experiments just described all use speech comprehension, but there is converging evidence from work on reading for the importance of clauses and sentences. When people are reading aloud, their eyes are usually looking ahead of the words they are saying (the so-called 'eye-voice span'). So if the text is suddenly removed, or the lights turned out, readers can continue saying the words up to and including those they were looking at when the text disappeared. Studies have shown that the eye-voice span usually stops at major grammatical boundaries (Levin, 1979). This implies that the eyes dwell at such boundary points while the reader finishes constructing a description of the encoded message, allowing the voice to catch up. Even in silent reading, eye fixations are extra long at clause and sentence boundaries (Aaronson and Scarborough, 1976; Mitchell and Green, 1978), again suggesting additional decoding effort at these points (Just and Carpenter, 1980; Mitchell, 1982).

Boundary clues in the signal

Writing marks the ends of sentences with full stops and capital letters, and clause boundaries may be indicated by commas, but does speech show any comparable marking of message boundaries? And if it does, do listeners utilize those cues to aid their decoding? There is growing evidence to suggest that the answer to both those questions is yes.

We saw in Chapter 7 how grammatical clauses often correspond to 'tone groups' – intonational units containing one prominent stressed syllable, held together by an overarching intonation contour, whose boundaries are often marked by a rapid fall in voice pitch and/or a pause. Separate evidence was presented in Chapter 7 to show that pauses tend to coincide with clause boundaries except where they signal obvious word-finding difficulties, and in Chapter 8 we noted the degree to which changes in eye-gaze, gesture and body posture may cue message boundaries. Other cues have been noted in the literature – Klatt (1975), for example, showed how syllables tend to lengthen as grammatical boundaries approach.

Cues to important message boundaries are clearly present in the auditory (and visual) signal and it would be foolish of listeners not to use them. A number of studies have presented listeners with speech that has been distorted in various ways, making the words totally unintelligible but leaving prosodic information (intonation, rhythm, pausing etc.) more or less intact. Under such conditions listeners are still able to indicate the locations of major syntactic boundaries (Kozhevnikov and Chistovich, 1965; Lehiste and Wang, 1977; Martin, 1970). Other studies using the click location technique that we discussed earlier have shown that syntactic and prosodic boundaries have independent powers to cause clicks to migrate towards themselves, though migration is greatest where the two coincide (Wingfield and Klein, 1971; Geers, 1978).

Cutler (1982a), Gee and Grosjean (1983) and Scott and Cutler (1984) analyse in greater detail the role of prosody in speech comprehension. Cutler (1982a) notes that monotone speech which lacks these cues is still comprehensible, so they can only facilitate decoding, not be necessary for it, but there is some evidence that *misleading* cues do positively hinder speech comprehension. Reich (1980) had subjects listen to long, complex sentences then write down as much as they could recall of the sentence's content. Performance was much better if the clauses were separated by standard pauses (330 msec) than if the pauses were distributed throughout the sentences in random, nongrammatical locations.

Lehiste (1979) extended the search for acoustic cues to message units above the sentence to what she calls 'paragraphs' in speech. These may well correspond to the 'idea units' that Butterworth (1975) identified as planning units in speech production (see Chapter 7, pp. 118–19). If so, then by Ellis and Beattie's Law ('That which is a unit of encoding will also be a unit of decoding') they should be utilized in sentence comprehension. Listeners proved capable of detecting paragraph boundaries in speech which had been distorted so as to render the words unintelligible, and could distinguish paragraph from sentence boundaries with reasonable success. Longer pauses between paragraphs, and slowing of speech as the end of a paragraph approaches, seem to be two cues used by listeners.

Kreiman (1982) had subjects press a key once for a sentence boundary and twice for a paragraph boundary as they listened to distorted speech. The times to detect paragraph boundaries were considerably longer than those for sentences, suggesting to Kreiman that paragraphs 'are cued both by characteristics of the end of one utterance and by the beginning of the next. Subjects are evidently comparing two blocks of speech; if the differences between them are great enough, a paragraph boundary is signalled.' A hint as to what that comparison might involve comes from an earlier study by Rees and Urquhart (1976). Their subjects read aloud two-paragraph passages after first reading them silently for understanding. When the subjects read them aloud Rees and Urquhart found that readers' voice pitch would generally start high at the beginning of a paragraph, gradually fall through it, then rise again at the start of the next. This change in key may have been one of the cues Kreiman's subjects were picking up on.

Finally, opponents of the view that prosodic information (stress, intonation, pausing etc.) influences grammatical aspects of sentence comprehension frequently cite the results of Lieberman (1963) and Martin (1967). Lieberman (1963) showed that the syntax of a sentence influences the stress pattern listeners perceive it as having, while Martin (1967) found that listeners tend to 'hear' pauses at grammatical boundaries even though there is no physical silence in the speech wave. The interpretation we should like to place on these results is influenced by our interpretation in the previous chapter of the 'phoneme restoration effect' discovered by Bagley (1900–01) and again by Warren (1970). If phonemes are experimentally deleted from spoken words listeners will perceptually restore them to their rightful place. No-one tries to argue from this that phonemes are not important in speech perception. Rather the effect is taken to indicate that the phoneme level and the word level (acoustic input lexicon) exert a mutual influence upon each other; that is, that they are in a state of 'interactive activation'. We believe that the results of Lieberman (1963) and Martin (1967) should be interpreted along similar lines. All the work we have just reviewed seems to leave little doubt that grammatical processing systems are influenced by systems which process prosodic information, but Lieberman's and Martin's results suggest that the influence works both ways. Where the grammatical and message structure of an utterance leads the listener strongly to expect a particular stress or pause pattern, that pattern may be perceptually restored by the listener. Prosodic systems affect grammatical systems and grammatical systems affect prosodic ones: the two are in interactive activation.

The processes of decoding

We have now demonstrated that the units of message encoding are also units of decoding, and that those units are additionally cued by nonverbal cues that listeners exploit in their comprehension. We have, however, said very little about the actual process of decoding – about how listeners recover the speaker's message from a string of identified words. In truth, and despite considerable experimental effort, we believe with Fodor (1983) that psychologists know very little about the process of decoding. Since the demise of Chomskyan transformational grammar as a literal model of how humans produce and comprehend speech (see Chapter 4, pp. 62–71), psycholinguists have largely been content to capture some general properties of the way language decoding works.

Continuous decoding

Models of language processing which incorporated transformational grammar in a very literal way had to assume that entire clauses or sentences are taken on board before decoding began. We now know – if it ever needed to be demonstrated – that the attempt to uncover the message encoded into a speech signal or line of print is a continuous, ongoing process, even though as we saw in the previous section 'wrapping up' may occur at important message boundaries. Three lines of evidence for moment-to-moment decoding to the message level will be considered.

1) The first line of evidence comes from studies by Marslen-Wilson (1973, 1975, 1976) in which subjects 'shadowed' speech they heard. The speech was played to the subjects through headphones and they had to repeat it continuously as they heard it. Some star 'fast shadowers' were able to repeat what they were hearing at a lag of only around 250 msec (a quarter of a second). Two observations showed that this was not mere mindless parrotting. Errors deliber-

ately introduced into the passages by mispronouncing words were often corrected by the shadowers without their noticing that a mispronunciation had occurred (a phenomenon reminiscent of the phoneme restoration effect). Thus, word recognition processes were actively (or interactively) involved in the shadowing. Also, the shadowers would sometimes misrepeat a word that was correctly pronounced in the passage. Their errors here were almost always other real words that were syntactically appropriate and, even more importantly, semantically plausible in the context. Thus even at a repetition lag of a quarter of a second (about the duration of a syllable), fast shadowers were decoding the signal to recover the conceptual message and utilizing message-level information to guide their ongoing speech perception.

2) Further evidence for moment-to-moment decoding comes from experiments looking at the comprehension of ambiguous sentences. We discussed ambiguous sentences in Chapter 4 as sentences permitting of more than one interpretation. One form of ambiguity arises when a word in a sentence has two possible meanings. For example, in the sentence 'He found a bug in the corner', the word 'bug' could refer either to an insect or to a concealed microphone. Usually the context will indicate which interpretation is meant. Thus what you are more likely to hear is something like, 'The secret agent carefully inspected the room. He found a bug in the corner', where the context indicates which meaning is likely. One might imagine that in such circumstances only the contextually relevant meaning of an ambiguous word is activated in the listener's mind, but an elegant experiment by Swinney (1979) shows that one would be wrong.

Subjects in Swinney's experiment listened to passages of text in which ambiguous words were embedded. The intended meaning of the word was, however, clearly indicated by the preceding context. At the same time as they were listening to the speech the subjects were watching a screen upon which letter strings were periodically displayed. The subjects were under instruction to indicate by pressing one of two buttons as quickly as possible whether the letter string on the screen formed a word or not (a 'lexical decision' judgement). On key trials the letter string was a real word that was related in meaning to one or other of the meanings of an ambiguous word the subject had just heard. In terms of our previous example the subject might see either 'microphone' or 'insect' after hearing 'bug'. Swinney found that hearing an ambiguous word speeded up the lexical decision time to targets related to both meanings of the ambiguous word if the letter string immediately followed the ambiguous word (a 'semantic priming' effect). However, if the string for visual lexical decision was displayed a mere three syllables after the ambiguous word, then only targets related to the contextually appropriate meaning were primed. What this result shows is that both meanings of an ambiguous word are momentarily activated, even if it is clear from the context which meaning is implied, but soon the most appropriate meaning is selected for incorporation into the growing message-level description and the unwanted, inappropriate meaning is suppressed.

Another form of ambiguity is the structural variety of the sort found in 'These days few people know how good bread tastes' (where 'good' could be referring either to 'bread' or 'tastes'). It is often possible in such cases to indicate by prosody (intonation and phrasing) which interpretation is meant. Lehiste (1973) found that when speakers were aware of the ambiguity of a sentence they could use prosody to communicate to listeners the desired interpretation. When the speakers were not aware of the ambiguity, however, listeners were much less successful at guessing the intended meaning. In addition, studies by Wales and Toner (1979) and van Lancker and Canter (1981) have shown that when one interpretation of an ambiguous sentence is much more likely than another, prosodic cues have very little success in combating the listeners' built-in biases (see Cutler, 1982, for more detail).

3) Our third and final line of evidence for moment-to-moment decoding comes from studies looking at the comprehension of so-called 'garden path sentences'. These are sentences whose early portion suggests an interpretation that their later portion proves to be incorrect. An example would be Bever's (1970) much-quoted sentence 'The horse raced past the barn fell'. What happens with this sentence is that listeners assume when they hear 'raced' that 'horse' is the subject of that verb. The verb 'fell' therefore comes as a surprise at the end, causing listeners to backtrack and eventually reinterpret the sentence as meaning 'The horse *that was* raced past the barn fell'.

We saw in Swinney's (1979) study of priming from ambiguous words like 'bug' that two interpretations may be momentarily entertained, but that the system rapidly selects one as the best bet and rejects the other. Garden path sentences are ambiguous in their early portions and show what happens when the wrong interpretation is selected at that stage. If whole sentences were taken on board before decoding began, the final portions could be used to prevent misinterpretation of the opening part of the sentence, but that is not the way language decoding works. Because language decoding *is* continuous listeners are sometimes led down the garden path only to have to backtrack later. This, incidentally, makes it important for listeners to keep a record of what they have just heard in some form of short-term memory which can be consulted if a first attempt at sentence decoding should prove incorrect (see below).

Crain and Steedman (1981) showed that listeners can use their knowledge of the real world to select between two possible interpretations of the initial portion of a sentence and so avoid being led down the garden path. They show how listeners are initially apt to misconstrue the sentence 'Teachers taught by the Berlitz method passed the test'. It takes a while to realize that the correct interpretation is 'Teachers *who were* taught by the Berlitz method . . .' Such a misconstrual rarely happens to the sentence 'Children taught by the Berlitz method passed the test.' The two sentences are identical grammatically, but listeners know that teachers usually teach while children get taught. Teachers do not often get taught, and listeners are misled by sentences in which they do. That is, where a sentence portion permits of more than one grammatical construal, listeners use their knowledge of the world to select the more likely one. We shall have more to say about the role of knowledge of the world in language comprehension later in this chapter.

Parsing

'Parsing' is the name linguists and psycholinguists give to the process of creating a structural, syntactic description of a sentence – one which assigns each word to a grammatical class (noun, verb, adjective, preposition etc.), indicates how the words group into phrases, clauses etc. and shows the relationship of words one to another. Once it became apparent that sentence decoding was an ongoing, left-to-right process, psycholinguists turned their attention to describing a set of operations, or *strategies*, which would create a structural description for a sequence of words arriving one at a time. An example of such a strategy (from Clark and Clark, 1977, p. 59) is: 'Whenever you find a relative pronoun (*that*, *which*, *who, whom*), begin a new clause.' Sentences which begin a new clause without signalling it with one of these pronouns create problems for the listener because (according to this view) they violate one of our parsing strategies. Thus 'The man the dog bit died' is harder to decode than 'The man *that* the dog bit died', even though the first sentence is shorter than the second.

This strategy approach to parsing is discussed at greater length by Clark and Clark (1977). Certain computer parsing systems called *augmented transition networks* have been built which effectively embody these sorts of strategies in programs which assign structural descriptions to sentences (see Kaplan, 1972), and psycholinguists are currently active in trying to assess the 'psychological reality' of these and other parsing systems (e.g. Bresnan, 1983; Johnson-Laird, 1983).

From the present authors' perspective a feature of the work on parsing has been its undue reliance on highly unnatural, hyper-complex sentences. We saw in Chapter 4 that a native speaker (i.e. a linguist) will accept as grammatical a sentence that no-one in their right mind would ever dream of saying. Unfortunately such sentences have too often found their way into psycholinguistic experiments. Thus the poor subjects in Fodor, Garrett and Bever's (1968) experiment found themselves being asked to paraphrase such monstrosities as 'The box the man the child liked carried was empty' (a 'doubly self-embedded' sentence). The same authors later admitted that, 'Experiments with double self-embedded sentences are always suspect because of the oddity of the stimulus materials' (Fodor, Bever and Garrett, 1974, p. 351), and Fodor (1983) has recently hypothesized that in trying to understand such freaks of language listeners bring to bear general cognitive problem-solving procedures quite different from those employed in normal language comprehension. As a general rule we believe that communication will be best understood by studying human beings engaged in tasks which bear at least a passing resemblance to normal communicative behaviour. The over-reliance on bizarre sentence forms must in part be responsible for explaining why, in Mitchell's (1982, p. 92) view, 'There are at present no adequate general theories of sentence parsing'.

Knowledge and inference in language comprehension

We mentioned earlier in this chapter the characteristically rapid loss of signal (surface structure) information in language comprehension. This phenomenon was further pursued in a series of experiments by Bransford and his colleagues. For example, Bransford, Barclay and Franks (1972) presented people with sentences like:

'Three turtles rested on a floating log and a fish swam beneath them.'

In a later recognition test the subjects were apt to claim that they had been presented with a different, gist-preserving sentence like:

'Three turtles rested on a floating log and a fish swam beneath *it*.'

Similarly, Johnson, Bransford and Solomon (1973) showed that people who had recently been presented with a short two-sentence passage like:

'John was trying to fix the bird house. He was pounding the nail when his father came out to watch him and to help him do the work.'

were likely to claim later that they had encountered the single sentence:

'John was using the hammer to fix the bird house when his father came out to watch him and to help him do the work.'

Now, there is no *mention* of a hammer in the original – its presence is *inferred* by the listener making use of his or her knowledge of the world to augment the information present in the signal (text).

Psychologists have only quite recently begun to appreciate the extent to which knowledge of the world is utilized in language understanding. As so often happens, it was the act of trying to build a machine (in this case, a computer) capable of performing the skill that brought home the complexity of the mental machinery we so take for granted in our everyday lives. Winograd (1972) has been in the forefront of those trying to program computers to understand language. To illustrate the sort of problems he and others ran into, consider the following sentence:

'The city council banned the protestors' meeting because they feared violence.'

To whom does the word 'they' in that sentence refer? Having made your mind up, try this sentence:

'The city council banned the protestors' meeting because they advocated violence.'

To whom does 'they' now refer? Most people, particularly if they have not encountered the alternative version, will say that 'they' refers to the city council in the first sentence, but to the protestors in the second sentence. The surface and deep structures of the sentences are exactly comparable; the only difference between them is the replacement of 'feared' by 'advocated'. People assume that 'they' refers to the city council in the first sentence and the protestors in the second sentence because their knowledge of the world leads them to believe (rightly or wrongly) that city councils are more likely to fear than advocate violence, while protestors are more likely to advocate than fear it. To get a computer to correctly assign a referent to 'they' in these two sentences you would need to equip it with that degree of knowledge about councils and protestors.

Another example now becoming something of a chestnut in the psycholinguistic literature is the contrast between these two sentences:

1) 'The Smiths saw the Rocky Mountains while they were flying to California.'
2) 'The Smiths saw the wild geese while they were flying to California.'

Listeners know that Rocky Mountains don't fly, so they assume in 1 that the Smiths were doing the flying and that 'they' refers to them. Wild geese do fly however, and listeners are likely to construe sentence 2 as meaning that the geese were flying and the Smiths were on the ground, so that 'they' now refers to the geese.

Inferences abound in language comprehension. If you read 'Mavis knocked the glass off the table. Andy went to the kitchen to fetch a broom,' you infer for yourself that the glass broke. Inferences, however, take time and effort. Smith and Collins (1981) showed that people take longer to read sentences of the form 'Dennis was having stomach pains. Sandra got out the telephone book', than sentences of the form 'Dennis needed a doctor fast. Sandra got out the telephone book.' The reason for the difference in reading speed is presumably that in the first pair of sentences the reader must infer that Dennis's pains were bad enough to require a doctor, and that that is why Sandra got out the telephone book.

In order that inferences may be applied, appropriate knowledge of the world must be activated. A sentence or passage may be quite baffling until the context in which it must be set is supplied. Take 'The notes were sour because the seams were split.' As Bransford and Johnson (1973) point out, most people are entirely bemused by that sentence until the context 'bagpipes' is supplied, whereupon it becomes reasonably comprehensible.

Ausubel (1960) demonstrated the advantages to be gained from the activation of an appropriate framework when detailed, unfamiliar material is being learned. His subjects were asked to read and then answer questions on a passage dealing with the metallurgical properties of plain carbon steel. He found that performance was greatly improved by providing the readers with a general introductory passage which discussed the differences between metals and alloys, their advantages and limitations, the reasons for making them and so on. Presumably this passage helped bring together snippets of information the readers had gleaned over the years, so providing them with a framework within which to integrate the detailed information of the experimental passage.

Several experimenters, beginning with Dooling and Lachman (1971), have shown that sentences or passages which are very difficult to comprehend and recall when presented on their own can become much easier once appropriate knowledge of the world is brought to play on them. Try making sense of the following:

'With hocked gems financing him our hero bravely defied all scornful laughter that tried to prevent his scheme. Your eyes deceive you, he had said, an egg not a table correctly typifies this unexplored planet. Now three sturdy sisters sought proof, forging along sometimes through calm vastness, yet more often over turbulent peaks and valleys. Days became weeks and many doubters spread fearful rumours about the edge. At last, from nowhere, welcome winged creatures appeared, signifying momentous success.'

You could probably make next to nothing of it. Dooling and Lachman's (1971) subjects had similar problems *unless* they were cued with the title, 'Christopher Columbus discovering America'. With the help of the background knowledge activated by that title the subjects' recall scores improved dramatically.

In similar vein, Bransford and McCarrell (1974) had subjects memorize easy sentences like 'The office was cool because the windows were closed', or harder ones like 'The haystack was important because the cloth ripped'. When recall was cued by a word from the sentence ('office' or 'haystack') recall of the easy sentences was, not surprisingly, better than recall of the difficult ones. A simple change in the experimental procedures, however, entirely did away with this difference. The change was to provide a context in the learning phase that made the 'difficult' sentence as intelligible as the 'easy' one. For the haystack sentence the context was the clue 'Parachutist.' If you re-read the sentence now we think you will agree that its difficulty has quite evaporated.

Using a passage recall task like the Christopher Columbus one mentioned above, Bransford and Johnson (1972) showed that, in order to improve recall, the title had to be presented *before* the passage. Presenting it after the passage was as bad as not presenting it at all. The point here is that relevant knowledge of the world must be activated *at the time when the message is being decoded* if it is to aid comprehension, and hence recall.

These and other experiments showing the extent to which knowledge of the world is brought to bear in text comprehension caused something of a stir when they were first published. We hope the reader of this book is a little stirred, but certainly not shaken. In Chapters 9 and 10 we analysed some of the properties of everyday conversational speech. We saw there that conversants *assume* that listeners will bring their knowledge of a topic to bear upon the conversation. They leave unsaid things that their partner will be able to supply, with the result that extracts of conversational speech removed from their context can be well-nigh incomprehensible. With written text the situation is different. Writer and reader may be miles and years apart. The writer can assume much less shared knowledge with the reader, so the text is more explicit and requires a lesser contribution from the reader. Psycholinguists, being highly literate members of a highly literate culture, took the comprehension of explicit text to be the norm, whereas from an evolutionary or sociolinguistic perspective it is the exception. It is only with an effort that psycholinguists are coming to understand the process of language comprehension as it must occur in all natural, conversational settings.

Finally, it is a truism in psychology that no two people perceive the same event in quite the same way. This is no less true of language comprehension: the knowledge and biases people bring to bear on a sentence or text may radically affect the interpretation they place upon it, and the things they remember from it. Anderson and Pichert (1978) provided a neat illustration of this phenomenon. They devised a passage about two boys who played truant from school, spending the day in one of their houses. The house was nice, but old, with a leaky roof and a damp basement. The parents who owned the house were well-to-do, and it harboured a rare coin collection, a colour television, ten-speed bikes and so on. Half the subjects who read the passage were asked to do so from the point of view of a prospective burglar, while the other half were asked to read it from the point of view of a prospective homebuyer.

After reading the story they were all asked to write down as much of it as they could remember. The 'burglars' at this point recalled more facts deemed by the experimenters to be relevant to a prospective burglar (e.g. information about portable valuables) while the 'homebuyers' recalled more facts deemed relevant to them (e.g. information about the general state of repair of the house). There then followed a short delay, after which the subjects were asked to have a second try at remembering what they could of the original passage. This time, however, half of each group maintained their original perspective, while the other half were asked to change perspectives ('homebuyers' became 'burglars', and vice versa). The subjects who maintained perspective actually recalled slightly less at the second attempt than at the first, but those who changed perspectives recalled more, and the extra facts they remembered were ones relevant to their new perspective.

At first glance this result may seem to be at odds with the study of Bransford and Johnson (1972) showing that an orienting title only helped recall of difficult passages if it was presented before the text. The discrepancy is, however, more apparent than real. Anderson and Pichert's passage about the boys playing truant was perfectly comprehensible from both of the perspectives their readers were asked to adopt. All of the facts in the passage should therefore have been understood and registered in memory. But some of the facts **were not** *relevant* to a particular perspective and were not recalled by people adopting that perspective. Under everyday circumstances this is an intelligent, well-adapted way for a memory system to behave. We normally only *want* to recall things that are relevant to the task we are engaged in – to our current perspective. But if we change tasks (or roles or perspectives) we now want to recall information stored in memory that is relevant to our new situation. And that is precisely what the subjects in Anderson and Pichert's experiment did.

Memory for language

Short-term memory

While a clause or sentence is being decoded its surface structure (wording) needs to be held in mind. But where in mind is it held? Psychologists have for a long time studied something called 'short-term memory'. The classic demonstration of short-term memory involves asking someone to repeat a series of random digits they have just heard. Normally they can manage something in the order of seven before accuracy begins to fall off (Miller, 1956). The classic illustration of short-term memory in action is remembering a telephone number in the interval between looking it up in a directory and dialling. But telephones have only been in common usage for the past sixty years or so, and we are unlikely to have evolved cognitive mechanisms specifically for dealing with them. The recent trend towards a greater regard for the everyday purposes of mental processes has brought with it long-overdue speculation about the role short-term memory might play in daily cognition.

The first point to be made is that there are probably several short-term memories rather than just one. Short-term memory for pictures, for example, has different properties from that for words (Pellegrino, Siegel and Dhawan, 1975), and certain forms of brain injury can impair verbal short-term memory without affecting the immediate recall of picture sequences (Shallice and Warrington, 1974). Hitch (1980) and Monsell (1984) make out a strong case for the existence of at least two short-term memories allied to language processing. One is an 'input register' holding speech while it is being decoded; the other is an output store involved in speech production which holds pre-planned stretches of speech in phonemic form while they await articulation (cf. Ellis, 1979, 1981). It is with the first of these two forms of short-term memory – the retention of recently-heard words – that we are concerned here.

The subjects in Sachs' (1967) experiment listened to passages describing some historical event, for example how Galileo first learned about the telescope. Contained within the passage was a test sentence such as:

'He sent a letter about it to Galileo, the great Italian scientist.'

Listeners were interrupted immediately at the end of the sentence, or after a further 80 or 160 syllables worth of intervening speech (assuming a normal speech rate of 3 syllables per second this means after around 25 or 50 seconds of intervening speech). The listeners were then presented with a 'probe' sentence and were asked to judge whether or not it was identical to the one recently heard in the passage. Sometimes it was identical; sometimes it differed systematically from the original. Specifically there could be a superficial change of word order which left the meaning quite unaffected (a *formal change*), for example:

'He sent Galileo, the great Italian scientist, a letter about it.'

(Can *you*, without looking back, say just how this differs from the original?). A third type of probe sentence involved a *syntactic change* of grammatical construction from an 'active' to a 'passive' sentence, as in:

'A letter about it was sent to Galileo, the great Italian scientist.'

The fourth type of probe sentence involved a *semantic change* in meaning from the original, for example:

'Galileo, the great Italian scientist, sent him a letter about it.'

When the interruption came immediately after the key sentence listeners were good at detecting all three types of change. After an interposed delay, however, listeners were very poor indeed at detecting formal changes of word order or syntactic changes from active to passive constructions, but were still good at detecting semantic changes in expressed meaning.

Further research by Sachs (1974) and Wanner (1974) suggested substantial loss of verbatim information when only 5 or 10 seconds of speech intervened between a test sentence and a surprise presentation of unexpected probes. This, of course, is what we would expect if verbatim information is usually discarded in the 'wrap up' operation which appears to occur at the ends of clauses and sentences. Indeed the experiments by Jarvella (1970, 1971) which we used to support that claim demonstrate the same rapid loss of verbatim information as the experiments of Sachs and Wanner.

Within the framework of short-term memory we might speculate with Hitch (1980) and Monsell (1984) that the job of the input register is to hold the words of an incoming clause or sentence while it is being decoded. Once the message has been extracted the contents of the register can be purged in readiness for the next unit of speech. Once the register has been emptied it can no longer contribute to the recall of what has just been heard – hence the poor performance of subjects in the experiments of Sachs and Wanner just mentioned, and in the experiments of Caplan (1972) and Jarvella (1970, 1971) that we discussed earlier.

Long-term memory

Until the early 1960s research on memory, particularly in the United States, had been dominated by a 'verbal learning' tradition which emphasized the verbatim memorization of word lists with little regard to their meaning. Yet the experiments just reviewed implied that under normal circumstances verbatim information is rapidly discarded. Additionally, the experiments of Bransford and others that we mentioned earlier showed that the residue left by language in memory is usually some highly abstract representation of the gist or meaning of the text.

These insights had, to an extent, been won and lost decades earlier. Binet and Henri (1894) showed that when children recall passages of text they will often substitute for words in the original others having a similar meaning. This, according to Binet and Henri 'indicates the disappearance of the verbal memory and the retention of the memory for ideas.' Bartlett (1932) studied the changes a story is likely to undergo in successive retellings. Some details may be 'sharpened' or brought into focus while others are 'levelled out'. Unexplained aspects in the original will be 'rational-ized' in the retelling, yet the general thread of the story – its gist –

will be retained. Zangwill (1939) showed how subjects are often unable to discriminate details belonging to the original text from details they themselves introduced in the retelling. Davis and Sinha (1950) had subjects listen to a story then view a picture which illustrated part of the story. When later asked to recall the story all the subjects incorporated details from the picture which had not been in the original story at all. They were also often unable to select accurately between the original story and a second version which included picture-only details. These authors followed Bartlett (1932) in claiming that listeners build up a mental 'schema' of the events in the story. That schema will incorporate information derived from an accompanying illustration, and may also include details added by the listener which will therefore become hard to discriminate from original text information.

The phenomenon of the inclusion into memory of information supplied by the listener (or reader) has been studied more recently by several experimenters. Sulin and Dooling (1974) devised a passage about a ruthless politician who become a dictator and ultimately brings about his country's downfall. In fact there were two versions of the passage. In one the dictator was called Gerald Martin (an invented name) while in the other version the dictator was called Adolf Hitler. Subjects were tested for their memory of the passage either 5 minutes or one week after reading it. The test consisted of 14 sentences. Half of these were 'old' sentences from the original passage, while half were 'new', and the subjects' task was to say which were which. The catch was that some of the 'new' sentences mentioned things most people know to be true about Adolf Hitler (e.g. 'He was obsessed with a desire to conquer the world', or 'He hated Jews particularly and so persecuted them'). At the 5-minute test few subjects were misled by the plausible 'new' sentences and categorized them correctly. At the one week test, however, false recognitions were high for the plausible 'new' sentences (i.e. people were apt to misclassify them as 'old'). This was particularly true of those subjects who had read the Adolf Hitler version of the passage.

In similar vein Bower, Black and Turner (1979) found that the most common error people make when recalling scripts about going to the doctor or to a restaurant is to import statements that were not in the script but were either implied in it or are part of people's general knowledge about things to do with doctors or restaurants. Now it would be easy to treat such experiments as demonstrations of the fallibility of memory, but we believe that is the wrong way to regard them. Human memory is the product of millions of years of evolution, and its properties will be those that have been found to be best adapted to the human situation. In our daily lives we gradually build up a body of knowledge about doctors, restaurants or dictators. That knowledge will have been distilled out of many separate experiences and occasions. We normally do not *want* to know when we learned this particular fact about Adolf Hitler, or that fact about what to do in restaurants. Instead we wish to be able to activate all the experience we have accumulated to help us cope effectively in whatever situation we find ourselves in. Subjects in psychology experiments add what they glean from a passage to the total pool of knowledge in their memories because that is what they (and psychologists when they are not being psychologists) do every day of their lives. It does not matter one jot from an evolutionary, biological, natural perspective that they cannot remember one week later which of the droplets in their knowledge pool were acquired from which source.

The myth of 'lengthy verbatim recall'

For our final insights into the relationship between language and memory we return to the work of Hunter (1985), which we discussed in Chapter 10 as indicating the powerful effect that literacy has on people's attitude to language and text. Hunter scoured anthropological records, historical accounts, folk archives, journals and pretty well everywhere else for examples of 'lengthy verbatim recall' which he defined as 'the recall with complete word-for-word fidelity of a sequence of fifty words or longer'. Reciting the Lord's Prayer (66 words) would count as an example of lengthy verbatim recall, as would Wordsworth's *Daffodils* or the American Oath of Allegiance. Reciting 6,666 verses of the *Koran* in six hours (*Guinness Book of Records*, 1984) is a more dramatic example. In popular (and some academic) mythology, dramatic feats of verbatim memorization and recall are characteristic of non-literate cultures. Were not Icelandic sagas, Homeric epics, African geneologies and the like transmitted word-for-word down through generation after generation before ever being written down? The answer, it would appear, is 'No, they were not'. On the contrary, lengthy verbatim recall appears only to occur among individuals in literate cultures possessed of writing.

How did this misapprehension come about? We can begin to understand if we consider with Hunter (1985) the case of Demo Zogic. Demo was a non-literate Yugoslavian tavern keeper and singer of folk songs who allowed his remarkable skills to be studied by Milman Parry and Albert Lord (see Lord, 1960). In addition to enjoying their food and wine, the regulars in Demo's taverna would be treated to a selection from his vast repertoire of narrative songs and chants. A typical song would comprise of a few hundred lines of ten syllables each, sung to a consistent rhythmic pattern, and accompanied by a one-stringed instrument (the gusle). Exceptional songs could be much longer: the longest recorded by Parry and Lord fills 97 12-inch records and lasts nearly 17 hours.

Demo learned new songs from other singers, and asserted most strongly that he only had to hear a song once to be able to reproduce it. Asked if his reproduction was 'the same song, word for word, and line for line' Demo was adamant: 'the same song, word for word, and line for line. I didn't add a single line, and I didn't make a single mistake.' The phonograph records, however, appear to contradict this claim. Demo, like all folk singers and story tellers of non-literate cultures, never repeated a performance in exactly the same way twice. Rather, when he learned a new song he learned its narrative – its gist. When performing he would employ great artistry to relate the tale within the strict metrical confines of the traditional format. In other words, he recomposed a song each time he sang it. What made him an acknowledged master of the genre was first of all the number of narratives whose essential details he had memorized, and secondly the effortless ease with which he seemed able to reformulate them as songs.

Yet why did Demo claim that his songs were word for word, line for line the same from one performance to the next? According to Hunter (1985):

It is almost certain that Demo does not know what a literate person means by a 'word' or a 'line'. When singers are asked to say what a 'word' is, and to give examples, they make a poor showing. They either reply that they do not know, or they give a sound group which may vary in length from what we call a word, to a line of poetry, or even an entire song. For them, a 'word' means nothing more than an 'utterance'. So, when Demo reports that he sang the song 'word for word', he cannot be saying that he sung the song verbatim. He is saying that he repeated the song faithfully in terms of its essential story and the traditional way of singing songs.

This message is repeated time and again across all the supposed cases of marvellous recall in non-literate cultures. Western investigators, steeped in literacy, often entirely misinterpret what the native narrator is doing, and the teller, for whom a story is a plot not a text, in turn misinterprets the investigators' questions. It took a long time for anthropologists, historians and psychologists to piece together what was going on and to appreciate just how much conceptions of language and memory are affected when a country is invaded by literacy. Modern folk singers in Yugoslavia, only 50 years on from Demo Zogic, pay close allegiance to the text and aim for word-perfect recitations. Demo's art of analysis and resynthesis is now all but lost.

So lengthy word-for-word memorization is probably absent from non-literate cultures, and is not particularly prevalent within literate ones, yet it is precisely the type of memorization which has been the focus of so much traditional psychological research on learning and memory. A whole 'verbal learning' tradition, stemming from the seminal work of Ebbinghaus (1885), studied the verbatim memorization of lists of words or even meaningless nonsense syllables. To men and women who were among the most literate members of a highly literate culture, list learning seemed the natural, prototypical example of memorization – the ideal task upon which to study the effects of practice, repetition, rehearsal and the other variables that interested them. We must view language, thought and the world through their eyes to appreciate why the rediscovery of gist and creative recall by Sachs, Bransford and others caused so much excitement. After all, the gist experiments only served to bring into focus once more memory in its natural form; memory as it evolved to work and always did work until some 5,000 years ago when writing was invented and began to spread.

From a total emphasis on verbatim memory, the pendulum swung perhaps a little too far towards memory for gist to the exclusion of any original wording. Hopefully the pendulum is now settling in a reasonable middle position. People *can* memorize the Koran – they can also forget all the original wording of a text and remember only its gist. But often they do a bit of both: they will remember the content of what was written or said, but also remember the occasional phrase or sentence that 'sticks in the memory'. Keenan, MacWhinney and Mayhew (1977) recorded and transcribed seminar discussions involving tutors and students. They were able to demonstrate that the participants retained a day later some verbatim information, particularly for statements with personal significance for the participants, such as sarcasm, personal criticism and witty remarks. Bates, Kintsch, Fletcher and Giulani (1980) similarly demonstrated some verbatim recall of the details of such 'natural discourse' as lectures or TV soap operas.

Human language comprehension and memory are the products of complex, but subtle and flexible, cognitive processes which we all possess, but which we are only beginning to understand.

14 The cognitive neuropsychology of language and communication

In the book so far we have tried to draw various conclusions about the nature of human communication and language. To support our claims we have made reference to observations and data. Sometimes these were simple assertions about the way language works or the way people communicate; sometimes the observations arose out of more carefully controlled studies or experiments. Recently an increasing number of psychologists are being attracted by another source of pertinent observations and constraints on how we conceptualize communication and language. This other source is the effects of brain injury on the communicative and linguistic abilities of previously normal people.

The first and perhaps most important point to note is that brain injury (such as a stroke or missile wound) can disrupt communicative and linguistic skills in a great many different ways. Following a stroke one rarely loses all language abilities and perhaps never loses all capacity for communication. Usually a subset of language skills is impaired. One patient may, for example, develop severe word-finding problems and have difficulty putting words to concepts, while a second can still produce single words but can no longer string them together to form grammatical sentences. A third patient may have problems specific to understanding speech and complain that everything sounds like a foreign language, while a fourth may have a discrete and not too disabling problem in 'sounding out' new and unfamiliar written words.

Whereas language and other disorders have traditionally been studied for what they can teach us about the way the brain works, they are now also being studied for what they can teach us about how communication and language work. If, for instance, a patient has a word finding problem for speech but not writing, then this constrains our models and theories of how *normal* word finding in speech and writing is organized. Specifically, we must conceive of them as being the responsibilities of processes which are at least partially separate psychologically, so that one set of processes can be impaired while the other remains intact.

This approach to brain injury which emphasizes the relevance of disorders for understanding how the normal, intact system works is coming to be known as *cognitive neuropsychology* (Ellis and Young, 1986). In reality it is not an entirely new enterprise: from at least the time of the Greeks and Romans, scholars have been trying to discern what patterns of disorder had to tell us about normal mental processes. In particular much of the work on language disorders (*aphasia*) in the late 19th and early 20th centuries stands comparison with the best modern work (e.g., Wernicke, 1874; Lichtheim, 1885, Bramwell, 1897).

This band of 19th-century neuropsychologists counted among its number a certain Sigmund Freud who is, of course, best remembered today as the founder of psychoanalysis. In fact, Freud was over 40 before he began to develop his psychoanalytic theories. He was trained initially as a neurologist and published in 1891 a short monograph called *On aphasia* (English translation, 1953). Apart from its intrinsic value this book is of interest because the germs of many psychoanalytic ideas can be found within it. We have discussed in Chapter 7 the theory the older Freud proposed in *The psychopathology of everyday life* (1901) to explain slips of the tongue. In *On aphasia* (1891) he treated tongue slips from a different angle, being concerned with whether the speech errors made by brain injured aphasic patients could be regarded as exaggerations of the lapses to which we are all prone. He decided that they could, arguing that, 'the paraphasia (i.e. speech error) in aphasic patients does not differ from the incorrect use and the distortion of words which the healthy person can observe in himself'. Similarly, Freud discusses in *On aphasia* the idea proposed by the English neurologist John Hughlings Jackson that some forms of aphasia may represent a regression to a level of language skill characteristic of young children (an idea which, incidentally, has now largely been discarded). Freud resurrected this idea in psychoanalytic theory when he proposed that neurotic adults regress to levels of personality development typical of young children.

A major difference between today's cognitive neuropsychologists and their predecessors (including Freud) is that many, if not all, cognitive neuropsychologists now believe that it is both legitimate and feasible to analyse and interpret the cognitive problems of patients *entirely* in cognitive psychological terms, without needing to consider the site of injury to the patient's brain. The theoretical rationale for this belief is discussed by Marshall (1982) and Mehler, Morton and Jusczyk (1984). The argument in simple form is that psychology (the science of the structure and function of the mind) and physiology (the science of the structure and function of the nervous system) are logically independent 'levels of explanation'. While a scientist may legitimately be interested in how the two levels interrelate – being interested, for example, in what brain injury can tell us about which regions of the brain are responsible for which language skills – it is also legitimate to treat cognitive disorders as 'natural experiments', albeit distressing, unfortunate ones, which speak directly to theories at the *psychological* level of explanation.

This point of view will perhaps become more persuasive if, instead of arguing it from abstract philosophical principles, we demonstrate cognitive neuropsychology in action. Initially we shall stay within the language system and look at disorders of the production and perception of speech and writing; later we shall look briefly at what little work has been done on disorders of other aspects of communication such as gesture and facial expressions.

Speaking

Speech production is a complex skill which, not surprisingly perhaps, is subject to a whole host of different aphasic disorders, only a few of which will be considered here.

Conceptual jargon

Imagine walking up to a patient who is sitting in a hospital bed recovering from a stroke. 'Well Mr X', you say, 'How are you feeling today'?. 'Well,' he replies, 'it has been suggested that there were certain oddities and restrictions, technically the activities of the student body, so to speak.' You try again. 'This is a nice day', you comment. 'This is a terrific beautiful day', he says, 'The only reason I say it is a nice day I see all the girls working behind the floor and believe me when I worked for people on Broadway they were glad to work because it is nice to do it in the afternoon.'

Such strange, rambling, incoherent, confabulatory speech is a form of 'jargon aphasia' produced by patients sometimes referred to as 'fluent' or 'Wernicke's' aphasics (after the 19th-century German neuropsychologist Carl Wernicke). The above extracts were taken from Weinstein (1981): other reports can be found in Kinsbourne and Warrington (1963) and Brown (1981). The patients who produce this sort of jargon understand little of what is said to them. They are often disoriented and confused. They will relate long, rambling tales containing bits of their past life plus apparent inventions hopelessly mixed together. Not uncommonly they will deny having a language problem or claim that their difficulties in speaking are trivial – due perhaps to having mislaid their false teeth (Weinstein, 1981).

At the outset of this book, back in Chapter 1, we defined communication as the transmission of a message from one organism to another as a signal. Most of the communication disorders we shall discuss in this chapter compromise the patient's ability to convert a message into an effective, decodable signal. These jargon aphasics seem different. They seem to suffer from a central conceptual disorder which prevents them from ever formulating a coherent, intelligible message in the first place. They can formulate sentences and populate them with words, but with no sensible message to communicate they can utter only rambling jargon. Their speech is still grammatical because there is no syntactic deficit, and contains real words well articulated because there is no lexical or phonemic deficit. We saw back in Chapter 4 how a Chomskyan generative grammar left to its own devices will mostly generate grammatical nonsense ('Colourless green ideas sleep furiously' – that sort of thing). Conceptual jargon aphasics vividly demonstrate what happens if an intact grammar is robbed of sensible input.

Syntactic problems in speaking

Contrast the conceptual jargon above with the following attempt of a different type of aphasic patient to describe a picture of a girl giving flowers to her teacher:

> 'Girl . . . wants to . . . flowers . . . flowers and wants to . . . The
> woman . . . wants to . . . The girl wants . . . the flowers and the
> woman.'

Here is the same patient trying to describe a picture of a woman
kissing a man:

> 'The kiss . . . the lady kissed . . . the lady is . . . the lady and the
> man and the lady . . . kissing'

This patient, reported by Saffran, Schwartz and Marin (1980a)
knows what she wants to say. She also seems able to remember and
say the individual words she needs – 'girl', 'flowers', 'lady', 'man',
'kissing' and so on. What she cannot do is arrange those elements
into a grammatical sentence under the control of the message she
wishes to communicate.

This *syntactic deficit* often occurs with a cluster of other difficulties including problems with inflections and effortful articulation
in patients known as 'Broca's' or 'agrammatic' aphasics. We now
know that these problems are *dissociable* – you can have one
without the others, though they commonly co-occur (Berndt and
Caramazza, 1985). The likely explanation of this co-occurrence is
that these processes are mediated by adjacent areas of cortex in the
left hemisphere so that injury which damages one will also tend to
damage the others.

Saffran, Schwartz and Marin (1980b) showed that this syntactic
difficulty extended to a task in which the patient simply had to
arrange written words to form a sentence. In fact, they perform
reasonably well when a sentence contains one animate and one
inanimate noun. In such sentences the animate noun is usually the
subject and the inanimate noun the object (e.g. 'The *boy* is kicking
the *ball*, not vice-versa). This pragmatic strategy falls apart,
however, when subject and object are either both animate ('The
dog is chasing the *cat*) or both inanimate ('The *book* is under the
table). When asked to construct such sentences from the words in
response to a picture, the patients have great difficulty knowing
which noun to put before the verb and which after. The Subject-
Verb-Object order is one of those features of the syntax of English
that speakers must acquire as they learn to talk. Other languages

use different orders (see Chapter 5). The evidence of these Broca's aphasics suggests that use of syntax is a skill that can be selectively impaired by brain injury, implying that at least some aspects of what linguists identify as the syntax of language are mediated by cognitive processes which are separate from those responsible for other requirements of successful linguistic communication.

Anomia

Next consider the following extract of speech from an *anomic aphasic* discussed by Allport and Funnell (1981). The patient is describing a hazardous kitchen scene which includes an overflowing sink and a boy about to fall off a stool.

> 'Well it's a . . . it's a place, and it's a . . . girl and a boy, and they've got some . . . made . . . Well . . . it's just beginning to . . . go and be rather unpleasant . . . And . . . this is the . . . the woman, and she is . . . putting some . . . stuff, and the . . . it's . . . it's . . .'

The patient clearly has tremendous difficulty remembering the names of things. He manages one or two very common names ('girl', 'boy', 'woman') but resorts to very general terms like 'place', or 'stuff' for everything else. The speech appears as grammatically correct as one could hope for given such a profound word-finding problem, and is fluently articulated. Furthermore, the anomic patient recognizes perfectly well the objects he or she cannot name, being able to use them properly, and can repeat their names when spoken by someone else. We would seem able, then, to rule out object recognition, syntax and articulation as causes of the anomic deficit.

The speech output lexicon – the component which mediates between meanings and spoken forms – is one plausible candidate as the locus of the anomic disorder, but there would seem to be at least three reasons for ruling this out. First, anomics can sometimes successfully read aloud a number of irregularly-spelled object names ('sword', 'yacht', 'castle' etc.), though the pronunciations of such words are widely thought of as emanating from the speech output lexicon (see Chapter 7). Secondly, anomics will sometimes manage, after a prolonged struggle, to name an object, showing that the words are present but inaccessible. Thirdly, some anomics recover very rapidly in a way which also suggests re-accessing stored words rather than relearning.

Allport (1983; Allport and Funnell, 1981) believes that the anomic deficit may lie in the activation of precise word meanings. His anomic patient A.L. was shown line drawings of objects, one at a time. Each time a picture was shown to A.L. the examiner spoke two words, one of which was the picture's name. A.L.'s task was to indicate which of the two words was the correct name. Sometimes the second, distractor word was quite unrelated in meaning to the picture name – for example a picture of nail with the words 'nail' and 'bird'. On these occasions A.L. had no difficulty choosing the correct word. On other trials, however, the distractor word had a similar meaning to the target, for example, a picture of a nail with the words 'nail' and 'screw'. Under these conditions A.L. became hesitant and made many incorrect choices.

Allport (1983) argues from these results that A.L. 'can assign words to a broad semantic field, but . . . has difficulty making more precise *differentia* of word-meanings'. If A.L. heard 'nail', he might know it was long, metallic, and used to join things together. This would often be sufficient to allow him to select the nail from a range of profferred objects. It would also permit him to reject 'nail' if it was offered as a candidate name for a chair or brick. But 'screw' might elicit the same semantic information, making it hard for A.L. to reject 'screw' as the appropriate name for a nail. Now A.L. would never attempt to hammer a screw into wood, or screw in a nail. He knew what the objects were *and* what to do with them. His difficulty lay in translating between that conceptual knowledge and the appropriate English words.

Saffran (1982) believes we should distinguish conceptual knowledge of the world and the things in it from semantic knowledge of the meanings of individual words. She argues that separate cognitive systems handle these two sorts of knowledge, and that in anomics the semantic system, but not the conceptual system, is impaired. Anomics cannot activate precise, detailed word meanings either in comprehension or production (because the same semantic system is employed in both decoding and encoding). In speaking, the semantic deficit means that the patient is limited to words like 'thing' or 'stuff' with very general meanings because the entries in the speech output lexicon for more detailed words, though present, are inaccessible.

Is anomia one of those defects Freud talked about which may be regarded as exaggerations of normal difficulties? Ogle (1867) thought so. He likened anomia to the commonplace experience of momentarily being able to remember the name of a person, place, or thing. 'Most of us,' he wrote,

> . . . know what it is to have the pictorial image of some familiar object in our mind, and yet be perfectly unable to call up its name. The idea is there, but the idea does not suggest the proper symbol. The moment, however, some other person uses the word in our presence it is at once perfectly recognised. Now a similar forgetfulness of words, but more extensive – a similar inability, that is, to translate ideas into symbols – constitutes one form of aphasia. (Ogle, 1867, p. 94).

Neologistic jargonaphasia

A different type of word-finding difficulty occurs in another type of aphasia which labours under the name of *neologistic jargonaphasia* (Buckingham and Kertesz, 1976; Butterworth, 1979; Ellis, Miller and Sin, 1983). When these patients (who, remember, were perfectly normal before their brain injury) try to say words they often produce distorted approximations known as 'neologisms'. Listen to the speech of patient R.D. reported by Ellis, Miller and Sin (1983) trying to describe the goings-on in a picture of activities around a scout camp (R.D.'s neologisms are printed in italics with the authors' best guess at what he was trying to say following in capitals within brackets):

> A *bun, bun* (BULL) . . . a *buk* (BULL) is *cherching* (CHASING) a boy or *skert* (SCOUT). A *sk* . . . boy *skut* (SCOUT) is by a *bowne powe* (POST) of pine. A . . . post . . . *powne* (POST) with a, er, *towne tow* (LINE?) with *woshingt* (WASHING) hanging on including his socks *saize*(?). A . . . a *nek* (TENT) is by the washing. A b-boy is *swi'ing* (SWINGING) on the bank with his hand (FEET) in the *stringt* (STREAM). A table with *orstrum* (SAUCEPAN?) and . . . I don't know . . . and a three-legged *strowe* (STOOL) and a *strane* (PAIL) – table, table . . . near the water. A er *trowlvot* (TRIVOT), three-legged er er means for hanging a *tong, tong* (PAN?) on the *fiyest* (FIRE) which is blowed by a boy-boy. A boy *skrut* (SCOUT) is up a tree and looking at . . . through . . . *howne*(?) glasses. A man is

knocking a paper . . . paper with a *notist* (NOTICE) by the er t-
tent, tent er *tet* (TENT) er tent.

'Buk' for *bull*, 'skut' for *scout*, and 'trowlvot' for *trivot* are all typical
'target-related neologisms'. The reader may have noticed that these
neologisms only affect 'content words' in the passage (nouns and
verbs), with 'function words' like 'the', 'and', 'to', 'through' etc.
emerging unscathed. Ellis et al. (1983) were able to show for patient
R.D. that it was the greater frequency of usage of the function
words which rendered them less error-prone. R.D. was more likely
to name correctly everyday objects with commonly used names
(e.g. chair, table) than ones whose names figure less often in
conversation (e.g. lamppost, cloud). Further, he produced exactly
the same neologistic errors when trying to read words aloud – a fact
which enabled Ellis et al. to assess his pronunciation of less common
function words like 'except' or 'beneath'. R.D. was as likely to
neologize such words as equally common content words.

Following a proposal by Butterworth (1979), Ellis et al. (1983)
argue that neologisms are not caused by a defect within syntax, but
by a defect in or around the speech output lexicon (see also Ellis,
1985a; Miller and Ellis, 1985). By this account the job of the speech
output lexicon is to transmit activation from semantics down to
phoneme units at the phoneme level. In neologistic jargonaphasics
either too little activation reaches the lexicon or too little is passed
on. When, as with commonly-used words, the resting level of
activation for that word in the lexicon is already high, the small
amount of additional activation is enough to trigger the full set of
phoneme units, enabling the word to be pronounced correctly.
However, the units in the lexicon for less commonly used words
('scout', for example) have lower resting levels of activation and are
not boosted enough to be able to pass adequate activation on down
to the phoneme level. Only some of the required phonemes are
activated, so the patient must try to construct an attempt at the word
based on the partial phonemic information available (producing
'skrut', 'skert' and 'skut' as attempts at 'scout').

Do normal people ever produce neologisms? One would have
thought not, but Ellis, Miller and Sin (1983) quote a neologistic type
of response given by normal speakers struggling to say a word which
is 'on the tip of their tongue'. One speaker trying to recall the word
'pedestal' said 'past . . . pestul . . . peda . . . pedestal'. Another
searching for 'dyslexia' said 'flexi . . . plexi . . . plexia . . . dyslexia'.

Arguably these are 'normal neologisms' produced by speakers trying hard to activate the lexical units for words they have used very seldom before and which, as a consequence, have extremely low resting levels of activation. In the course of boosting that activation level up high enough to eventually say the word correctly they pass through an intermediate stage at which they have activated partial phonemic information and so can, if requested, generate a neologistic type of approximation. Where the neologistic jargonaphasics differ is that for many words they once had no difficulty in saying they can now no longer progress beyond that level of incomplete, partial activation.

Morphology in aphasia

An interesting observation that has been made about neologisms is that they are usually inflected properly. If a target word is meant to be plural, it may be neologized but it will still receive an appropriate plural ending. 'Scout' may become 'skrut', but 'two scouts' will still be 'two skruts', and if the final /t/ of 'scout' was corrupted to /d/, the plural would change accordingly from an /s/ to a /z/ sound – 'skrudz'.

In Chapter 7 we discussed evidence from normal slips of the tongue pointing to the conclusion that what is stored in the speech output lexicon are 'free' or 'root' morphemes, and that inflections like the plural -s and past tense -ed are added later. The above observations regarding neologisms point to the same conclusion – an impairment at the level of the speech output lexicon prevents these patients from retrieving many 'free' morphemes correctly, but the intact inflectional system ensures that the neologisms are at least inflected correctly.

The converse pattern of intact retrieval of root morphemes with impairment to the inflectional system may also be seen in aphasia as a component of the disorder (or rather the combination of disorders) known as 'agrammatism'. Inflection is a dominant feature of the Italian language. Miceli, Mazzucchi, Menn and Goodglass (1983) described an Italian agrammatic aphasic who misapplied inflections when speaking. He seemed to know when and where an inflection was due, but often supplied the wrong one. Apart from that feature, sentences were reasonably well constructed and words properly pronounced. Here, then, we would appear to be seeing a fairly pure 'morphonogical deficit'.

The phoneme level

Normal speakers make slips of the tongue involving the substitution of misordering of phonemes, for example saying 'all these *b*agnificent sights' instead of 'all these *m*agnificent sights' (substitution of /b/ for /m/), or '*b*lake f*r*uid' instead of '*b*rake f*l*uid' (reversal of /l/ and /r/ – examples from Appendix to Fromkin, 1973).

Phoneme substitutions and reversals also occur in aphasic speech. Examples from Blumstein (1973) include aphasics saying '*k*eams' instead of '*t*eams' (substitution of /k/ for /t/) or '*ge*drees' for '*de*grees' (reversal of /g/ and /d/). Apart from their superficial similarity there are several fine-grain points of comparison between these aphasic errors and the normal tongue slips. Both, for example, tend to involve pairs of phonemes that are similar in their articulation. In both cases the misordering errors tend to involve phonemes from content words rather than function words, phonemes from comparable positions in their respective syllables, and so on (see Ellis, 1985a). Aphasic phoneme errors appear, then, to comply with Freud's requirement that aphasic errors be exaggerations of normal tendencies.

Automatic speech in aphasia

Most normal speech is conceptually driven – it is speech for the purpose of expressing ideas and communicating messages, and is assembled under the direction of a conceptual (propositional) message representation. But we have in earlier chapters discussed some exceptions to this generalization. First there are the over-learned phrases like 'Good morning', 'I don't know' or 'Have a nice day' which, though they may have some communicative function, are certainly not assembled afresh each time they are spoken, but are retrieved as ready-made wholes for use in certain situations. The second exception is the rote memorization of lengthy passages of text – the lyrics of a song, for example, or a poem or the Lord's Prayer (N.B. we noted in Chapter 11 that such feats are probably only found in literate cultures where writing focuses attention on the signal (text) as an object in itself, rather than just as the vehicle for a message).

Back in 1878 Hughlings Jackson observed that patients who are so severely aphasic that they can hardly assemble any propositional speech may still retain control of 'automatic' speech such as overlearned phrases and memorized texts. For example, a patient described by Smith (1966) suffered a malignant tumour in the left (language dominant) hemisphere of his brain which necessitated complete removal of the left hemisphere. Post-operatively his expressive speech was severely limited. Smith observes that his 'attempts to reply to questions immediately after operation were totally unsuccessful. He would open his mouth and utter isolated words, and after apparently struggling to organize words for meaningful speech, recognized his inability and would utter expletives or short emotional phrases (e.g. "Goddamit!"). Expletives and curses were well articulated'. Five months after the operation he suddenly showed recall of entire songs, being able to sing *Home on the Range*, *My Country 'Tis of Thee*, and church hymns.

From expletives to hymns these modes of speech have in common the fact that they do not require the controlled translation of conceptual representations into language (van Lancker, 1975). Hughlings Jackson believed that such speech emanates from the right hemisphere of the brain. This would be compatible with Smith's (1966) report, though if Hughlings Jackson was right, then damage to the right hemisphere should abolish automatic speech and this, to our knowledge, has never been reported.

Writing

Writing is a complex and, in many people, little-used skill requiring intact linguistic and motor processes. Of all the language processes it is the one most likely to be impaired by brain injury. Patients who suffer from high-level conceptual or semantic disorders show the same problems in writing as in speech, supporting the contention that the language formulation processes are shared in common by the two output modalities.

The point at which speech and writing appear to diverge is when the choice must be made between activating a phoneme string (for speech) or a letter string (for writing). A patient reported by Bub and Kertesz (1982) was severely 'anomic'. Presented with pictures of objects she could say very few of their names. She could, however, write many of them. This suggests first that there are two separate output lexicons, one for speech and the other for writing.

The former is inaccessible to Bub and Kertesz's patient while the latter can still be accessed. Secondly, it suggests that one does not need to have available the phonemic form of a word in order to be able to spell it. This last conclusion is supported by the observation that R.D., the 'neologistic jargonaphasic' patient of Ellis, Miller and Sin (1983) discussed above, could write correctly many words which, when he attempted to say them, came out as distorted neologisms. For example, he called an elephant an 'enelust . . . kenelton' but went on to write it correctly, and did the same for penguin which he called a 'senstenz'.

Further confirmation of the claim that skilled writers of English retrieve the spellings of familiar words as wholes from a lexicon rather than assembling them piecemeal from their sound comes from a 'phonological dysgraphic' patient reported by Shallice (1981). This man could still spell correctly many familiar, real words but was, as a consequence of his brain injury, no longer able to assemble a plausible spelling for even the simplest invented nonword. Thus he would be able to spell 'table' correctly but have no idea how to begin to spell 'chable'. He could still spell from his graphemic output lexicon but had lost the use of those rules or procedures normal spellers have which allow them to create plausible candidate spellings using low-level phoneme-grapheme (letter) conversion. Such conversion cannot therefore be essential, or even important, when fluent writers spell familiar words.

Almost exactly the opposite pattern occurred in a patient reported by Hatfield and Patterson (1983). This lady was no longer able to remember/retrieve the spellings of words she once knew perfectly well. She could, however, still assemble spellings from sound, but given the vagaries of English spelling this meant that she now misspelled 'flood' as FLUD, 'biscuit' as BISKIT, 'nephew' as NEFFUE and so on. Set against Shallice's patient this pattern of deficits illustrates the independence of the two spelling routes available to writers of English.

Finally some patients acquire disorders which affect the motor execution aspects of writing rather than spelling as such. The key observation is that these patients can still spell aloud orally, or can rearrange plastic letters so as to spell a word, but experience great difficulty in actually writing. Several different patterns of peripheral disorder like this have been reported (Ellis, 1985c). The patient of Margolin and Binder (1984) showed no disorder of speech pro-duction, speech comprehension or reading. He could spell words aloud or by using letter blocks, but his attempts to write letters resulted in distorted and mostly unintelligible squiggles. His difficulties could not be ascribed to any simple loss of motor control or co-ordination since he performed manual gestures well and could imitate sequences of hand or finger movements. It appears that Margolin and Binder's patient could no longer remember the shapes of letters or execute them as sequences of pen strokes. More detailed accounts of writing disorders can be found in Ellis (1982) and Margolin (1984).

Recognizing written words

In Chapter 12 we argued for the existence of two routes by which a letter string may access its meaning in reading. The 'direct' or 'visual' route involves activating the stored representation of the word's written form in a visual input lexicon through which the semantic representations of familiar words can be accessed. The alternative 'phonic' route involves sounding out an unfamiliar letter string then recognizing it on the basis of its internally generated acoustic form.

Cognitive neuropsychological evidence supports such a dual-route model in that patients have been reported who, as a consequence of their brain injury, have largely lost the use of one or other of these two routes and must rely predominantly on the remaining one. Impairment to the visual route with consequent reliance on the phonic route is the more disabling for a reader of English because the irregularity of English spelling makes phonic reading inefficient and error-prone. This pattern of symptoms has been called 'surface dyslexia' (Marshall and Newcombe, 1973; Patterson, Coltheart and Marshall, 1985). Patients with surface dyslexia can no longer recognize as wholes many words which were formerly familiar. Their attempts to sound words out often produce the correct pronunciation for regular words which they can therefore identify, but when faced with irregular words they are apt to pronounce them as if they were regular. Thus *colonel* might be pronounced as 'kollonell', or *island* as 'izland'. If the pronunciation incorrectly assigned to a word happens to be a word in its own right, then the patient will misidentify the word. This phenomenon is well illustrated in the much-quoted example from Marshall and Newcombe (1973) of the patient who, when presented with *listen* to read, mispronounced it in the way the phonic route would, as 'liston', then added '. . . the boxer' (this being the era of the heavyweight boxer Sonny Liston).

The opposite syndrome – disorder of the phonic route with a preserved visual route – has been called 'phonological dyslexia', and is much less disabling to the already skilled reader. The phonological dyslexic patients described by Beauvois and Dérousné (1979), Patterson (1982), and Funnell (1983) could understand and pronounce the majority of written words they were familiar with before their strokes, but were extremely poor at pronouncing new and unfamiliar letter strings. They could repeat nonwords they heard, so the problem did not lie in articulating new sound sequences; rather it appears that these patients are no longer able to apply the rules or procedures which will convert an unfamiliar letter string such as SATHE or PHLOOT into spoken form. The fact that they can still understand and pronounce familiar words shows that low-level, letter-sound conversion processes are not involved in extracting the meaning of well-known words. Other patients can understand familiar written words despite having little or no knowledge of the sounds of those words (e.g. Levine, Calvanio and Popovics, 1982; Caramazza, Berndt and Basili, 1983; Ellis, Miller and Sin, 1983). These patients also suggest that, though English writing may be partially alphabetic and derived from the spoken language, psychologically it is decoded (and encoded) as an independent language channel by at least partially independent processes.

Finally there is cognitive neuropsychological evidence for the possible existence of a *third* route from print to pronunciation. Schwartz, Saffran and Marin (1980a) studied a 62-year-old woman suffering from a progressive presenile dementia which severely impaired her ability either to produce or comprehend spoken or written language. In one task she was asked to sort written words into three piles according to whether they were animals, colours, or body parts. She managed fairly well with common words like 'horse', 'red', or 'finger', but very poorly with less common words like 'giraffe', 'magenta' or 'chin'. However she could still read aloud the words she was unable to classify, including ones with irregular spellings (e.g. 'leopard', 'beige' and 'thumb'). Now the pronunciations of such words cannot be assembled piecemeal – they must be recognized as wholes and their pronunciations retrieved as wholes. In other words Schwartz et al.'s patient must have been recognizing these words via her visual input lexicon and pronouncing them via her speech output lexicon. Yet this apparently happened without the semantic representations of the words being activated ('hyena . . . hyena . . .' she said on one occasion, 'what in the heck is that?'). Schwartz, Saffran and Marin conclude that there must exist a *third route* from print to pronunciation, mediated by direct, one-to-one connections between units in the visual input lexicon and corresponding units for the same words in the speech output lexicon. The exciting thing about this proposal for the cognitive neuropsychologist is that it is a claim about the way the normal, intact language processing system works that stems from the study of a brain-injured patient. There is now evidence from experiments on normal readers to support the existence of a third route (Ellis, 1984a), but the original motivation came from a neuropsychological investigation.

Recognizing spoken words

There exists yet another collection of aphasic disorders having to do with the recognition of spoken words. Patients with *pure word deafness* have reasonably intact speech production, reading and writing, but have great difficulty understanding speech addressed to them. The patient of Hemphill and Stengel (1940) complained, 'I can hear you dead plain, but I cannot get what you say. The noises are not quite natural. I hear your voice, but not the words. I can hear, but not understand.' A common complaint is that speech sounds 'foreign'; that is, the patient can *hear* the words but can extract no meaning from them (Goldstein, 1974).

Detailed analysis of these patients shows that they can perceive vowel sounds quite well, but are poor at identifying consonant sounds in natural speech. If speech is reduced to one-half or less of its normal rate, performance improves dramatically. It seems likely that these patients have suffered damage to a left hemisphere system capable of very fine temporal analysis of an acoustic signal. Under normal circumstances this system performs the acoustic analysis necessary for successful speech perception. Without this system the pure word-deaf patient must rely on a coarser right hemisphere acoustic analysis system which can identify steady-state vowels but cannot discriminate consonants one from another unless the speech signal is slowed down considerably.

We saw in Chapter 12 how the visual analysis of lip movement information plays an integral role in normal, everyday speech perception. Patients with pure word deafness have been observed to utilize lip information to compensate for their acoustic problem. One patient commented, 'If I go blind, I won't hear anything!' (Auerbach, Allard, Naeser, Alexander and Albert, 1982). These patients also rely on context to aid word identification. They may show reasonably good comprehension while the talk remains on one topic, but will be at sea when the topic changes. Saffran, Marin and Yeni-Komshian (1976) showed how their patient identified words better when presented in a useful sentence context than when presented in isolation. This use of context mirrors that made by normal listeners, especially when signal quality is poor as it is permanently for the pure word-deaf patient (see Chapter 13).

Patients with *word meaning deafness* are like the cases of pure word deafness in that they also have an isolated speech comprehension deficit with reasonably intact speech production, reading and writing (Bramwell, 1897; Ellis, 1984). Bramwell's patient 'could read aloud anything which was placed before her', 'seemed able to say almost everything she wished to say', and also wrote tolerably well. She found the greatest difficulty understanding speech addressed to her. 'Is it not a strange thing,' she remarked, 'that I can hear the clock ticking and cannot hear you speak?' The difference between these patients and those with pure word deafness is that the word meaning deaf patients can repeat and write to dictation the words they do not comprehend. Thus, when Bramwell's patient was asked, 'Do you like to come to Edinburgh?', she failed to understand the question, but repeated it correctly and wrote it down. Having written it down her intact reading processes allowed her to understand what she had just written.

It is not entirely clear how this extraordinary and rare syndrome is to be explained, but it seems likely that patients with word meaning deafness have suffered at least a partial disconnection of their auditory input lexicons from their semantic systems. Auditory word recognition units are still activated, but they can no longer activate the representations of the corresponding word meanings. By some roundabout route, however, activation is able to pass to the corresponding units in the graphemic output lexicon allowing words which are not understood to be written to dictation (Allport, 1983, and Ellis, 1984b, discuss possible routes).

In Chapter 12 we mentioned the need for a by-pass route from early speech analysis to articulation, a route which enables normal people to repeat aloud words they have never heard before. Arguably this route is most important for young children still building up their vocabulary. Beauvois, Dérousné and Bastard (1980) described a patient with a syndrome they termed *auditory phonological agnosia* who could still understand and repeat words he was familiar with before his stroke, but could no longer repeat or write to dictation unfamiliar words or invented nonwords. In everyday life this meant that his only problems were with things like new technical terms, or the names of new places or people. It appears that this patient had a very discrete deficit affecting only the auditory-articulatory by-pass route.

The same by-pass route is also apparently impaired in patients with *deep dysphasia*, because these patients are similarly unable to repeat aloud new words or invented nonwords. Their attempts to repeat familiar words, however, result in semantic errors where the patient produces a word different to the one he or she was asked to repeat, but related in meaning to it. Thus, Michel and Andreewsky's (1983) patient repeated (in French) 'balloon' as 'kite', 'beggar' as 'tramp' and 'kernel' as 'shell'. Although this disorder has only recently been identified, and it is too early to make confident pronouncements, it appears from the current evidence that the problem for the deep dysphasic patient is rather like that of the patient with word meaning deafness, namely a problem in accessing word meanings. The difference is that the deep dysphasic *almost* gets there. He or she seems able to activate the approximate semantics of a heard word, and so knows roughly what it means, but cannot access the details of its meaning. Thus, when Michel and Andreewsky's patient was asked to write the word 'brain', he wrote 'heart, liver, lungs . . .', making it clear by the dots and his gestures that he knew it was an internal body part, but he did not know exactly which one. Presumably the loss of the nonlexical by-pass route means that if an examiner insists that a deep dysphasic patient should try to repeat a word, the patient is obliged to run the gauntlet of rather defective semantic access processes.

Language comprehension

In addition to the disorders of word recognition and production we have just discussed there exists a variety of other disorders of language comprehension. We mentioned earlier patients who had lost the productive use of syntax and were no longer able to order words in grammatical sequence. Such patients may also have problems utilizing syntactic features of language in their comprehension. If we say in English that 'The dog is chasing the cat', only the syntactic structure of the sentence tells us who is doing the chasing and who is being chased. The 'agrammatic' patients studied by Schwartz, Saffran and Marin (1980b) could no longer utilize word order information in this way. If presented with the sentence 'The dog is chasing the cat', they would know it was about a dog and a cat, and that some chasing was going on, but they would not know who was chasing whom.

In fact it is only in reversible sentences like this that their deficit becomes strikingly apparent. With many everyday sentences (e.g. 'The dog is chasing the ball') one's general knowledge of the things referred to is sufficient to make it obvious what the relationship between them is. Having a syntactic deficit creates substantially less of a problem for language comprehension than for language production, which is undoubtedly why the nature of the comprehension deficit in these patients has only recently begun to be appreciated.

If your auditory processes are intact, if you can recognize words and utilize the syntax of word order, surely you have all it takes to be an entirely successful language comprehender. Well almost – but not quite. Winner and Gardner (1977) presented metaphorical sentences such as 'A heavy heart can really make a difference' to normal adults and to patients with injury to either left or right hemisphere of their brains. After each sentence a choice of four pictures was offered. One of these pictures depicted the metaphorical interpretation of the sentence (a person crying) while another depicted a literal interpretation (a person staggering under the weight of a large, red heart). The normal and left-hemisphere injured (aphasic) patients both selected the metaphorical interpretation significantly more often than the literal one. The right-hemisphere patients, however, were as apt to choose the literal interpretation as the metaphorical one and, unlike the normal or aphasic patients, found nothing amusing or absurd about the literal pictures. Hier and Kaplan (1980) similarly found that right-hemisphere injured patients tend to give literal interpretations of proverbs, claiming that 'Don't judge a book by its cover' means 'The story may be more interesting than the cover picture'. They also found the right hemisphere patients to be deficient at answering logical questions, particularly ones requiring an understanding of spatial relationships (e.g., 'The elephant sat on the mouse. Was the mouse on top?').

It is not obvious what metaphorical interpretation and spatial reasoning might have in common, nor what they might share with other deficits reported in right-hemisphere patients such as inability to do creative literary work (Critchley, 1962), or to select an appropriate punchline for a joke (Brownell, Michel, Powelson and Gardner, 1983). Sometimes we may relate the deficit to other known right-hemisphere competencies – for example by comparing the difficulty solving spatial problems with the general right-hemisphere spatial and imaginal skills (Caramazza, Gordon, Zurif and DeLuca, 1976). Most of the time, however, we can simply note how 'high-level' these deficits are, and question whether they are in any genuine sense 'linguistic' as opposed to general cognitive skills required for the successful interpretation (and creation) of messages. Most of all these deficits teach us the virtual impossibility of saying at the highest level where language stops and nonlinguistic thought begins. There are, however, some things that neuropsychological evidence enables us to say about the relationship between language and thought, and it is to these that we now turn.

Language and thought

If a patient suffers a stroke which results in serious language problems how, if at all, does this affect the patient's other thought processes? Consider the case of the Russian composer V. S. Shebalin reported by Luria, Tsvetkova and Futer (1965). Shebalin was born in Russia in 1902. He showed early signs of outstanding musical ability, writing his first symphony whilst still at school. By the age of 40 he was established as a successful composer and was elected Professor at the Moscow Conservatoire. During the next decade he composed a series of symphonies and an opera which was performed by the Bolshoi Theatre. He suffered a minor stroke at the age of 51, but the disturbance of speech which followed this lasted only a few weeks. Six years later, however, he suffered a second and more serious stroke, the results of which were a severe difficulty understanding speech addressed to him (though he could read with understanding), and hesitant speech containing many incorrect and distorted words. What is remarkable, however, is that despite his language difficulties Shebalin continued his work as a composer and produced a number of pieces which critics and other musicians considered to be as good as any of his previous work. For example, of his Fifth Symphony, written in 1962, Shostakovitch wrote, 'Shebalin's Fifth Symphony is a brilliant creative work, filled with highest emotions, optimistic and full of life. This symphony composed during his illness is a creation of a great master.' Gardner (1982) provides further examples of the independence of linguistic and artistic skills (both musical and visual).

Allport (1983) discusses the case of a severely aphasic man, H.K., who 'was unable to understand or respond in any appropriate and consistent way to even the simplest words or phrases, either written or spoken to him', and whose speech was 'a fluent but uninterpretable babble' devoid of all recognizable content. Despite all this, H.K. could make his way safely and surely across central London, could play various board-games and learn new ones with complex rules, and 'was still capable of forming and maintaining vigorous and courteous social relations'. Allport notes that several studies of groups of aphasic patients have reported unimpaired levels of nonverbal reasoning and intelligence (e.g. Basso, De Renzi, Faglioni, Scotti and Spinnler, 1973; Corkin, 1979). Even when differences between groups of aphasics and groups of normals are found, the possibility still exists that *some* of the aphasic patients are performing entirely normally. As Allport observes, 'The crucial question is therefore whether major impairment of language competence is *invariably* accompanied by loss or reduction of other intellectual functions. Even a single contrary instance could, in principle, upset the hypothesis that intellectual function is dependent on intact linguistic function'. Several such contrary instances can be found in the literature.

Thought is not, as some Behaviourists once believed, merely a sort of suppressed speech. A person can be virtually robbed of language yet still perform intelligently in other domains. Thought and intelligence are the products of many cognitive abilities or 'modules', each independent from the rest, but all working in an organized and orchestrated manner to make our daily lives possible.

Nonverbal communication

Finally we turn to some aspects of the neuropsychology of

nonverbal communication. This is not an area in which a great deal of work has been done, and we shall limit ourselves to briefly discussing three aspects of nonverbal communication – vocal-nonverbal, gestural, and facial.

Vocal-nonverbal

There is more information to be extracted from a speech wave than just the propositional content expressed in the words and sentences. From a speaker's voice one can often judge with reasonable accuracy the speaker's sex, approximate age, geographical region of origin, emotional state and so on. Patients with 'pure word deafness' (see above) can hear speech but are poor at recognizing the phonemes and words (we argued earlier that this was due to their inability to do the analysis of rapidly changing acoustic signals necessary to discriminate consonants one from another). Though very poor at extracting the propositional message from speech, these patients are reported to be still able to judge such things as speaker sex and accent, and to be able to identify familiar individuals from their voices.

The patients reported by Heilman, Scholes and Watson (1975) and Tucker, Watson and Heilman (1977) had a different problem. They could understand the content of a spoken message but could not tell from the sound of a voice whether the speaker was happy, sad, angry or indifferent. Two patients reported by Ross and Mesulam (1977) had a similar difficulty affecting the *production* of speech. They could inject no emotion or 'feeling' into their voices. One patient, a teacher, spoke in an 'unmodulated, monotonous voice' and found it hard to control either her own children or those in her classroom because they 'could not detect when she was angry, upset, or really "meant business".' Even when she prefaced a statement with 'God damn it, I mean it' her words came out in a flat monotone. She claimed that she still felt emotions internally and that she could tell how other people felt from their voices. Fortunately this lady had recovered when she was retested eight months after her stroke, and had regained control in her home and classroom.

Gesture has been but little studied by neuropsychologists (Feyereisen and Seron, 1982 a,b). Such work as has been done has usually focused on the class of gestures called 'illustrators' (see

Chapter 3), and has too often lumped together different sorts of expressive hand and body movement which really need to be kept separate. One line of research has been concerned with the question of whether and how patients with aphasic language disorders manage to communicate gesturally. It would appear that if one excludes the very severest global aphasics there is not much relationship between the overall severity of aphasia and the capacity to utilize and comprehend gestures (Goodglass and Kaplan, 1963; De Renzi, Motti and Nichelli, 1980). There may, however, be an association with the *type* of aphasia and the way the patient is able to use the gestural channel.

Cicone, Wapner, Foldi, Zurif and Gardner (1979) compared the spontaneous gesturing of two 'Wernicke's' aphasics and two 'Broca's' aphasics. The Wernicke's aphasics had fluent but vacuous and rather incoherent speech production (semantic jargon), with poor speech comprehension, suggestive of a high-level conceptual or semantic deficit. These patients produced gestures which were profuse but, like their speech, hard to interpret and often unclear in their reference. The Broca's aphasics, on the other hand, had hesitant, agrammatic speech suggestive of grammatical and morphological deficits. Their gestures, though simpler and fewer in number than those of the Wernicke's aphasics, were clear and informative. A normal pattern of gesturing was also found for the gesturing of a neologistic jargonaphasic studied by Butterworth, Swallow and Grimstone (1981). This patient had a severe word-finding difficulty and produced large numbers of neologisms (see Butterworth, 1979). The neologisms were often preceded by hesitant pauses during which the patient would be gesturing in an attempt to communicate by that channel what he was unable to say. Sometimes he would abandon a gesture and drop his hands. This behaviour tended to accompany neologisms which bore no resemblence to any contextually plausible target word, and which seem to have been more or less randomly generated to maintain the speech flow following a prolonged but unsuccessful word search.

The different patterns of gesture in different types of aphasic are readily interpretable, at least in general terms. Gestures are an alternative channel to speech for the communication of messages or intentions. If you can formulate a coherent message then a defect in the language channel will not prevent you from at least trying to communicate your thoughts gesturally. Cicone et al.'s 'Broca's' aphasics with their grammatical deficits and Butterworth et al.'s neologistic jargonaphasic with his word-finding problem were in this position. But as we saw earlier, some fluent, 'Wernicke's' aphasics seem to suffer from a high-level conceptual deficit which impairs their ability to formulate messages and results in vacuous, confabulatory speech. Without a coherent message no coherent gestural communication will be possible, which is just what Cicone et al. found for their 'Wernicke's' aphasics.

Sign languages may be regarded as a very highly developed form of gestural communication. Brain injury may cause loss of the ability to use a sign language the patient acquired in earlier life (Marshall, 1980). Like aphasia, this tends to occur after left-hemisphere injury. There is a complicating factor in that left-hemisphere injury also tends to cause 'apraxia' (loss of control of sequenced movements), but at least some cases of 'sign language aphasia' have been reported sufficiently well that one can rule out apraxia as the cause of the deficit.

The Japanese patient reported by Hamanaka and Ohashi (1974) had married a woman who had been deaf-mute from the age of 8 years. As a girl 'she learned a kind of sign language practiced by Geisha girls to maintain professional secrecy in the guest room'. The sign language worked by having a different gesture for each syllable in the spoken language. Some of these gestures modelled the shape of the Japanese letter for that syllable, others mimed a concept whose name began with that syllable (e.g. a gesture of thrusting a spear represented the syllable ya because the Japanese word for spear is 'yari'). After their marriage her (hearing) husband learned this sign language and had used it in their daily conversation ever since. When the husband suffered a stroke at the age of 56 he escaped with only very slight aphasia (principally some word finding difficulty) and slight apraxia, but a considerable loss of facility in the Geisha sign language. The degree of difficulty fluctuated from day to day: some days he could remember and interpret a particular sign, other days he could not. The class of signs he had greatest difficulty with were those derived from the sounds of objects. It would be interesting to know if one can suffer apparently selective loss of other late-acquired sign systems. Do Cistercian monks ever experience a selective loss of the gestural language they employ as a result of their vow of silence? Do referees ever lose the range of gestures they employ in matches? The neuropsychology of gesture is a topic about which we know tantalizingly little at present.

Facial expression

Another area where research is only just taking off is the neuro-psychology of communication by the facial channel (see Hay and Young, 1982; Campbell, 1982; Rinn, 1984). Patients with disorders of face processing are called 'prosopagnosic'. According to Hécaen and Angelergues (1962), some of these patients can no longer recognize faces that were once perfectly familiar: they can still *see* the faces clearly enough; they just fail to recognize them. They are, however, still able to 'read' facial expressions accurately (see Bruyer et al., 1983). This suggests a degree of independence between cognitive systems for recognizing faces as belonging to particular people, and systems for interpreting expressions. This conclusion is strengthened by the work of Kurucz, Feldmar and Werner (1979; Kurucz and Feldmar, 1979). They reported that elderly patients with dementia or other disorders may still be able to recognize faces but be unable to interpret emotions from expressions (the opposite of the pattern shown by the 'prosopagnosics').

Turning to the production of facial expression, a common finding is that if people are asked deliberately to adopt a particular expression (say smiling) the left side of the face displays the expression in more exaggerated form than does the right half. Given that the right half of the brain controls the movement of the left half of the body, and conversely, we could be seeing in this asymmetry a right hemisphere superiority for emotional expression. However, non-emotional expressions like winking and pulling faces are also more pronounced on the left side of the face, so it seems more likely that we are dealing with a right hemisphere superiority for the control of *any* voluntary facial expression. We say 'voluntary' because if people are laughing, smiling, frowning etc. for natural, spontaneous reasons then their expressions are not asymmetrical but are equally displayed on both sides of the face (Campbell, 1982).

If you suffer damage to part of the motor area of one or other hemisphere of your brain you may be unable to move the opposite half of your face voluntarily. A posed expression will therefore be confined to the non-paralysed half. If, however, you are genuinely happy, sad, puzzled or afraid, the 'paralysed' half of your face will come to life and your emotional state will be signalled by both halves of your face. This is because voluntary movements are controlled by the cortex of the brain, divided between the two hemispheres, one of which is damaged in the type of case under discussion. But 'involuntary' or, better, spontaneous and genuine emotional expressions emanate from intact lower and evolutionarily older brain centres. If *these* centres are paralysed, as sometimes happens for example in Parkinson's Disease, your face becomes a mask which can be contorted under voluntary control, but upon which no natural emotions play (Rinn, 1984).

For a practical application, it may be worth remembering all this next time you go to see your bank manager. If he is smiling a nice, symmetrical smile he is genuinely pleased to see you. But if it is a slightly lopsided smile that greets you, then the chances are you're in for a hard time.

General implications of cognitive neuropsychology for understanding communication and language

As we hope we have shown, cognitive neuropsychological analysis of disorders of language and communication carries many implications for how we model the underlying cognitive processes responsible. Thus we have argued for the existence of two, or possibly four, separate internal lexicons; for separate acoustic analysis systems mediating phonetic perception and the extraction of emotional/attitudinal information from tone of voice; for distinct conceptual, syntactic, lexical-semantic and morphological systems; for the existence of several distinct reading and spelling routes; for a separation of linguistic from various nonlinguistic thought processes; for a distinction between person recognition and expression recognition in face processing, and so on. These are all specific, detailed conclusions about the psychology of language and communication that emerge from neuropsychological work.

But what of general conclusions? Are there any broader morals to be drawn from this sort of investigation? One moral surely has to be that *language and communication are the products of many discrete and separable, but interacting, cognitive sub-systems.* This follows inescapably from the bewildering array of selective deficits to which language and communication are liable – deficits in which one or two of these many sub-systems are impaired while the others continue to function normally.

Analysis of these different patterns of disorder has once more reinforced a point we have made repeatedly throughout this book, namely that from the psychological perspective, it is virtually impossible to draw any clear dividing line between linguistic and non-linguistic cognitive processes. Some of our cognitive sub-systems – the lexicons, for example, and the syntactic and morpho-logical components – seem clearly, and exclusively, linguistic. Others, such as those mediating musical performance or geographic awareness, seem equally clearly non-linguistic (they can survive a severe, global aphasia). But there are a third group of components which are involved in both language processing *and* other cognitive skills. The message formulation system is necessary for effective gestural as well as linguistic communication. Spatial knowledge is required for answering various logical questions. And so on. It thus makes little sense to us to talk of discrete 'language organ' (Chomsky, 1980), or 'language module' (Fodor, 1983). Instead we would regard language as the *product* of a large set of sub-systems, some of which are uniquely dedicated to its production and comprehension, while others partake in other domains of cognitive life too.

David Marr worked on the psychology of vision at the Massa-chusetts Institute of Technology from 1973 until his death in 1980 from leukemia at the age of 35. Marr campaigned strongly for a view of the mind (and the brain) as being made up of many interacting cognitive sub-systems, or 'modules' as he called them (cf. Fodor, 1983). What is more, Marr had a hypothesis as to *why* the mind might be modular. People trying to program computers to perform complex tasks had learned through experience that the best way to achieve this goal was to break the task down into as many independent parts as possible, write a sub-program to deal with each part, and then re-assemble the sub-programs to perform the total task. A major advantage of this way of proceeding is that if you think of a better way of implementing one component part of the overall task, then you can rewrite that sub-program without needing to tinker with all the others. The same reasoning can be applied to your home hi-fi. If you have a 'modular' sytem made up of separate record deck, cassette deck, radio tuner, amplifier, speakers, headphones etc., then if a new, improved cassette deck comes on the market it is a relatively simple matter to unplug your old one and replace it with the new, without needing to change all the other parts of your total system.

Marr argued that what goes for computers and hi-fi's, also goes for minds and brains, except that in the latter instances the improvements are achieved by evolution rather than by a human designer (Marr, 1976, 1982). If you have a mind constructed from a host of separate modules, each with its own specialized responsibility (a syntax module, a speech output lexicon module, a voice recognition module, a facial expression recognition module, etc., etc), then evolution can modify one component without needing to alter all the others. A non-modular architecture would be far harder to improve. Additionally, with a modular architecture it is easier to slot in new components (like adding a tape deck if you didn't already have one). In the course of language evolution this is what must have happened. Also, given the fact that writing and reading are subject to their own *selective* neuropsychological impairments, it would seem that the process of education can cause new modules to be developed and interfaced with others which are presumably part of our genetic endowment (Ellis, 1985c). It is to issues of endowment, education and development that we now turn.

15 The development of language and communication

The linguist Leonard Bloomfield once described learning to talk as 'doubtless the greatest intellectual feat any one of us is ever required to perform' (1933, p. 29). In one chapter we cannot hope, and shall not attempt, to summarize and encapsulate the vast body of research into language acquisition that has accumulated, particularly over the past 20 years or so. Instead we shall attempt to provide a selective overview. In keeping with our general orientation we shall set language acquisition in the broader context of learning to communicate, and take in such things as development of the facial and gestural channels.

As with adult psycholinguistics, language acquisition research received a great boost from the ideas of Noam Chomsky in the 1960s. Some authors, for example, sought to demonstrate the 'psychological reality' of Chomsky's transformational grammar through an investigation of the order of acquisition of different sentence types (e.g. Brown and Hanlon, 1970). One senses in the literature of the 1960s a feeling that language acquisition may be easier to understand than mature language use, as if the study of embryology were easier than studying the anatomy and physiology of the mature organism. In retrospect that was perhaps a slightly naïve expectation. It is no easier to understand how an acorn grows into an oak, or a caterpillar into a butterfly, than it is to understand how the grown oak or butterfly functions. Indeed the former is probably harder than the latter, for whereas the mature organism exists in a more or less steady state, the developing organism is constantly changing. A theory of development carries the additional burden of having to explain how and why change occurs.

Another complicating factor is that development occurs on several fronts at once. At any one moment a child may be expanding his or her vocabulary, acquiring new concepts, mastering a wider range of sentence structures, learning to use facial expression, tone of voice and gesture in more sophisticated ways, and so on. Unravelling how these simultaneous developments interact one with another is going to prove a mammoth task that will keep developmental psychologists busy for many decades yet.

Early studies

Read a selection of books on language acquisition written over the past 15 years or so and you could be forgiven for thinking that serious investigation in this area only began with the work of Roger Brown and other Chomskyan psycholinguistics in Harvard in the 1960s. Campbell and Wales (1970) complained of 'a tendency to forget that the scientific study of child language has an important and thoroughly respectable heritage of observation and theoretical discussion'. They point to the 18th-century German biologist Dietrich Tiedemann as the initiator of a long line of observational 'diary studies' of individual children growing up and learning to talk (Tiedemann, 1787). The child that Tiedemann observed was born on 23 August 1781. By the following March he began 'to articulate consciously and to repeat sounds. His mother said to him the syllable "Ma"; he gazed attentively at her mouth, and attempted to imitate the syllable.' By late April he would point to familiar objects named by adults; that is, he had formed 'the most difficult of all the associations of the ideas . . . the connection of an idea with its verbal symbol.' On 9 September, aged 12 months, 'he gave distinct signs of increased conceptions. Beholding a glass of water, he pointed to it, as also to his cradle, when he was weary'. On 14 September he was observed to make appropriate movements in response to 'Make a bow' and 'Swat the fly'. On 27 November he was heard to utter 'Mama' and 'Papa'. His expressive vocabulary expanded rapidly thereafter, so that by the end of March, aged 18 months, he could name 'almost all the external parts of his body' and also several familiar objects which he would ask for by name when he wanted them, thus demonstrating for the first time the 'purposive use of speech'.

On 3 June he 'succeeded in saying short sentences, consisting of a noun and a verb, though without correct grammatical form'. By 30 July he could produce complete, though still short, sentences like 'There he stands', or 'There he lies'. Come the following April when the boy was 2½ years old he was observed to look out at the evening sky and say, 'The sun has gone to bed; tomorrow he will get up again, drink his tea and eat his bread and butter'.

Tiedemann's account, translated by Murchison and Langer (1927), from whom these extracts are taken, ends prophetically:

This is as far as my observations go. Other business prevented me from their continuation. I greatly desire that others may make similar ones; it will then be possible to determine various things by comparison, and that important branch of psychology, too little exploited as yet, which studies the development of human faculties . . . will make appreciable progress thereby.

Charles Darwin, better remembered today as the man who formulated the theory of evolution by natural selection, contributed his own diary study of language development in 1877. This was followed by a succession of observational studies from Preyer (1882) to the monumental work of Leopold (1939–1949). What the 1960s witnessed was the *re-emergence* of the study of language acquisition following the stultifying period of Behaviourist domination in the United States (Europe having largely escaped the ravages of that doctrine). Although the emphasis at the beginning of the renaissance was primarily upon syntactic development, research expanded to include semantic and phonological development, the precursors of language in the preverbal child, the mastery of conversational skill and so on, making the modern scene harder to summarize in a few pages but at the same time truer to the complex reality of learning to communicate.

Speech is the last of the communication channels to appear in childhood. Before it appears infants are especially reliant on facial expressions, gestures and the like to express their wants and generally to interact with others around them (cf. Tiedemann above). We shall look now at the development of the facial and gestural channels, both before the onset of speech and in later childhood.

Faces

Even very young infants find faces fascinating things to look at. From at least two weeks of age they will fixate a face in preference to other visual stimuli, particularly if the face is moving (Carpenter, 1974; Sherrod, 1979). This fascination could reflect some innate schema for faces which is captured and captivated by them, but it could also be a simple consequence of the fact that a moving, talking face is a captivating *son et lumière* of flickering shapes, colours and textures to a young infant. Goren, Sarty and Wu (1975) claimed that newborn infants a mere nine minutes old attended more to a moving schematic (cartoon) face than to moving rearranged faces containing the same features in a different orientation, though Barrera and Maurer (1981a, b) were unable to obtain evidence for selective attention to the configuration of a face as a whole in children less than two months old.

Meltzoff and Moore (1977; 1983a, b) have made even more dramatic claims about the responsiveness of very young infants to faces. They report that infants as young as 2 or 3 days old will attempt to *imitate* facial gestures made by an adult (for example lip protrusion, tongue protrusion or mouth opening). Hayes and Watson (1981) had some difficulty replicating these findings, though Jacobson (1979) was reasonably successful. Meltzoff and Moore (1983b) discuss the conditions under which they believe imitation can most readily be elicited. If future research substantiates the claim that infants are born able to imitate a range of facial gestures or expressions, then it is another weapon in the armoury of those nativists who believe in a major contribution of innate 'knowledge' to infant abilities (cf. Bower, 1979). If true, the Meltzoff and Moore findings imply a complex, inborn hardwiring between perceptual systems for describing a seen facial configuration and motor systems for recreating that configuration on the infant's own face.

Infants seem able to recognize their mother's face and distinguish it from other faces by at least age 3 months (Roe, 1978; Barrera and Maurer, 1981a; Melhuish, 1982). Three-month-olds recognize and discriminate facial expressions better when produced by the mother than when produced by strangers (Barrera and Maurer, 1981b). By at least the age of 5 months children reserve their smiles for familiar adults whom they must therefore be able to recognize and discriminate from unfamiliars (Schaffer, 1971).

In addition to possibly being able to imitate adult expressions from a very early age, young preverbal infants also display a wide range of spontaneous expressions. Happiness, sadness, surprise, disgust etc. are all mirrored distinctively on the infant's face. At least some of these expressions appear to be innate: smiling, for example, is displayed by congenitally blind infants who have had no opportunity to observe and learn expressions from others (e.g. Darwin, 1872; Goodenough, 1932; Freedman, 1964). But these are spontaneous expressions: posed expressions are a very different kettle of fish. Everyone possesses gruesome, embarrassing photographs of themselves aged 5 or 7 years trying to smile at the camera. Photographers soon learn that the only way to elicit a natural-looking smile from a young child is to make the child amused so that the smile is a genuine one.

The explanation for this difference between children's natural and posed smiles is almost certainly to be found in the previous chapter. Natural, spontaneous facial expressions emanate from midbrain structures while posed expressions are controlled by the right cerebral hemisphere. The natural expressions are probably innately hardwired into the midbrain, but the right hemisphere must *learn* how to reproduce them volitionally. In support of these claims we may cite the results of Ekman, Hager and Friesen (1981), who found the posed expressions of 5-, 9-, and 13-year-olds to be stronger on the left side of the face than on the right (indicating right hemisphere dominance) while natural, spontaneous expressions were symmetrical (see Young, in press, for a more detailed coverage of the developmental neuropsychology of face recognition).

Many, perhaps most, people never gain full volitional (right hemisphere) control over facial expressions. Few of us can produce a posed smile that would be mistaken for the real thing. But at least we can manage an approximation. Ladavas (1982) found 4- and 5-year-old children to be incapable of producing posed expressions that others could reliably discriminate as portraying happiness, surprise or sadness.

Gestures

According to Meltzoff and Moore (1977; 1983a, b), newborn infants will not only imitate facial expressions but will also make rudimentary attempts to imitate manual gestures. The truly communicative use of hand and arm movements comes later, but by the age of 12 months an infant will raise its arms as a gestural request to be lifted up, will hold out an open palm to be given an object, will point to objects it wants or finds interesting, wave goodbye and so on (Escalona, 1973; Greenfield and Smith, 1976; Clark and Clark, 1977; Lock, 1978; 1980). Bates (1976) regards such gestures as primitive 'speech acts' performing the same social functions that utterances later satisfy.

A point is commonly an *assertion* of something (cf. 'Look, there's a . . .') while an outstretched open hand is usually a *request* (cf. 'Can I have the . . .'). For Greenfield and Smith (1976), Bates (1976), Lock (1980) and others, the child at the gestural stage is learning what can be achieved by communicative acts, how intentions can be conveyed as signals, and so on. Lock argues that in combining gestures, or gestures and nonverbal vocalizations, the child is learning to transmit messages with more than one element (e.g. Whimper + point at apple = '[I] want that apple').

We shall return in a little while to the tie-in between gestures and early words, but we shall first digress a little to look at the spontaneous development of gestural communication in children who, for one reason or another, are speechless.

Gestures without speech

1) Royal investigations of language acquisition: Philosophers often derive a perverse pleasure from asking 'What if' questions – for example, 'What would happen if a group of preverbal children were reared on a desert island by mute caretakers? Would they learn to talk? If not, how (if at all) would they communicate?' It comes as something of a surprise to learn that conditions somewhat like these have actually been created at least once, and possibly three or four times, in the past (Campbell and Grieve, 1982). In all cases the experiments are said to have been performed at the behest of rulers with the power to ordain such things and none of the ethical qualms that might inhibit lesser souls. The Egyptian Pharoah Psamtik I (663–610 BC), Frederick II of Sicily, Holy Roman Emperor (1194–1250), King James IV of Scotland (1473–1513), and Akbar the Great, Moghul Emperor of India (1542–1605) are all credited with having interned children with silent caretakers to see what language, if any, they would develop of their own accord. Doubts linger over the veracity of the accounts relating to Psamtik, Frederick and James, but Akbar's experiment is well documented. From accounts provided in Campbell and Grieve (1982) it would appear that Akbar virtually imprisoned 20 or 30 infants in a house in Faizabad, attended by silent caretakers, up to the age of 14. On 10 August, 1582 he went to inspect the results of his experiment, and found the children to be speechless. The moral drawn at the time (that 'The world is a miserable abode of sceptics. To shut the lips is really to indulge in garrulity. They have hamstrung the camel of the Why and Wherefore') is a trifle opaque to us nowadays, but the account of Catrou (1705) is intriguing. He writes:

> When these children appeared before the emperor, to the surprise of everyone, they were found incapable of expressing themselves in any language, or even of uttering any articulate sounds. *They had learnt, from the example of their nurses, to substitute signs for articulate sounds. They used only certain gestures to express their thoughts, and these were all the means they possessed of conveying their ideas, or a sense of their wants.* [our italics].

2) Spontaneous development of gestural communication by deaf children: A more recent case bearing some similarities to these royal investigations has been carefully documented by Susan Goldin-Meadow, Heidi Feldman and their collaborators (see Feldman, Goldin-Meadow and Gleitman, 1978; Goldin-Meadow, 1983). They studied in depth a group of six congenitally deaf children growing up in Philadelphia where their parents were instructed by the school authorities 'not to gesture to them formally or informally, lest this interfere with the motivation for acquiring spoken English'. (In fact this advice is probably ill founded. Such evidence as exists suggests that early exposure to manual sign language *facilitates* the later acquisition of speech by deaf children – see Montgomery, 1976). Deprived of speech through their deafness, and sign language through the advice their parents received, these children developed their own gestural communication systems with which to transmit messages to those around them.

Pointing at people, places or things figured large in the communication of these deaf children. Other signs were pantomimic 'emblems'. Actions were most commonly pantomimed (e.g. hands jiggling on an imaginary wheel for 'drive', or hammering motions for 'hit'), though attributes and objects could also be denoted this way (e.g. arms spread, open palm down for 'big', or arms held out parallel, hands flat, palms downward, then arms gradually lowered with fingers fluttering for 'snow'). The gestures could be combined in sequences which the investigators claim were grammatical and similar to the early two-word utterances of speaking children. As evidence for grammaticality Feldman et al. (1978) cite restrictions on sign order. Signs for actions, for example, always preceded signs for the recipient of the action and followed signs denoting the thing being acted upon. Thus, if David (one of the children) wanted to be given a book he would sign book – give – David, not give – book – David or David – book – give. David was, in fact, the star signer of the group. He had the largest vocabulary and produced the longest sequences, developing procedures for combining more than one proposition into a single 'utterance' (Goldin-Meadow, 1983). Table 15.1 shows the string of gestural utterances elicited from four-year-old David on being shown a picture of a snow-shovel.

Table 15.1: Six gestural 'sentences' produced by David (a deaf 4-year-old) on being shown a picture of a snow-shovel (from Feldman, Goldin-Meadow and Gleitman, 1978)

1) Shovel – dig
2) Shovel – put-on-boots – outside – downstairs – shovel – dig – put-on-boots
3) David
4) dig – outside – snow – shovel – snow
5) dig – yes
6) shovel – downstairs – dig – downstairs.

Signs

Shovel – points to picture of snow-shovel.
Dig – digging motion with hands holding an imaginary shovel.
Put-on-boots – hands pulling upwards from toe to middle of leg.
Outside – points towards door of room.
Downstairs – jabbing points toward the floor – toward the basement where the shovel is stored.
David – points to own chest.
Snow – arms held parallel, flat hands, palm downward; fingers flutter as arms are gradually lowered to the sides.
Yes – nod.

3) Martin: The creation of quite complex gestural communication systems is not the prerogative of the deaf children of non-signing parents, nor the hapless participants in royal 'experiments'. One of us (A.E.) had the opportunity to observe at close quarters the sophisticated gestural communication of a young boy, Martin, whose only abnormality was that he was a 'late talker'.

Table 15.2: Martin's repertoire of gestures at age 2.1

Gesture	Meaning/context of use
1) Pointing (generally)	To denote objects and locations
2) Nod	Yes
3) Head shake	No. (Refusal).
4) Wave	i) Goodbye *or* ii) Task finished
5) Clap hands	Finished eating
6) Patting stomach	Full
7) Finger on tongue	[I want] food or a drink
8) Finger on lips	Sleep
9) Arms raised	Pick me up
10) Points to head	i) rain or wind ii) he's fallen on his head (made when he hears someone crying).
11) Points to cheek	Kiss
12) Points to foot	Poorly or broken
13) Points to open palm	[I want] keys or money
14) Holds back of pants	I want to use my potty
15) Slaps own bottom	Bad
16) Arms bent, moving to and fro in front of body	[I want a] dance or a record on.

Martin's first recognizable word ('more') appeared at the age of 2 years 1 month (much to the relief of his parents), but from the age of about one year he had been communicating through the use of an expanding repertoire of gestures. The set in use by the time his first word came is shown in Table 15.2. Pointing was widely employed, but three particular points had special meanings. Pointing to the top of his head could mean one of two things. First it could mean 'rain' or 'wind', in which case it was often accompanied by a wind-like 'woo' sound. Because he got his hair wet when out in the rain, this gesture generalized to mean 'wet hair'. So at the age of 2.3 Martin was watching a swimming programme on television when he pointed first to the top of his head then to himself. His parents took this to mean 'wet hair – Martin' (i.e. 'Martin gets his hair wet when he goes swimming'). Martin also pointed to the top of his head when he heard someone crying. This originated from having fallen on his head and was used to comment on the possible cause of someone's cry. Pointing to his cheek meant 'kiss', while pointing to his foot meant 'ill' or 'broken'. This last gesture derived from an occasion when the house cat hurt its foot, but was generalized by Martin to mean 'ill' or 'broken'. (For example, pointing to his foot when a record stuck to remark that the record was 'ill').

The origins of most of the rest of Martin's gestures are fairly obvious. It is not, for example, hard to interpret holding the back of his pants as 'I need my potty', particularly when, as usually happened, the gesture was accompanied by a graphic straining

Table 15.3: 'Conversation' at age 2.1 between Martin and his father

Martin is lying down having his nappy changed. He is looking at a picture of trains in a station stuck on the wall next to him.

Martin:	points to a train
Father:	'That's a train . . . in the station'
Martin:	points to window
Father:	'Yes, the railway station's down in town . . . you can hear the trains through the window.'
Martin:	points to cheek
Father:	'You want a kiss?'
Martin:	1. points out of the door, finger pointing downstairs to where his grandmother is.
	2. points to cheek.
Father:	'Oh! we met your grandma at the station. She came on a train didn't she, and gave you a kiss?'
Martin:	smiles and nods. Points to train picture, points downstairs, points to his cheek.
Father:	'Yes, your grandma came on a train and gave you a big kiss.'
Martin:	points to Father.
Father:	'Yes, she gave Daddy a kiss too, didn't she?'
Martin:	smiles and nods.

noise. The exchange between Martin and his father shown in Table 15.3 gives an impression of the richness of the 'conversations' which Martin could sustain through his gestures. Routine hearing tests between 6 months and 2 years all proved normal. Martin's *understanding* of speech was normal for his age, so it was not necessary to gesture back at him. We do not have enough data to look for syntactic regularities in his gesture sequences, but any regularities would have had to be very different from the regularities of spoken English before we would have been able to conclude that his syntax was not borrowed from the speech he understood. Also, though his parents became increasingly worried by his speechlessness, and were delighted when his first words appeared, they were also receptive to his gestures (which presumably is a necessary condition for the development of such a system).

Although his first word appeared at 2.1, Martin did not immediately cease to develop his gestures. By age 2.4 he had added two new ones. The first was a thumbs up sign meaning 'Daddy's off to get a lift to work'(!). The second involved looking at his wrist as one would look at a watch. This meant 'It's time for . . .'. So when he was playing upstairs with his mother and she said, 'It's time to go downstairs' Martin looked at his wrist then placed his finger on his tongue – i.e. time – food ('It's time for food'). Of Martin's first 20 words, achieved by age 2.4, four were verbal equivalents of his gestures – 'yeh', 'no', 'upah' (meaning 'lift me up'), and 'bad'; the rest represented concepts for which he had not had a specific gesture (e.g., 'more', 'Mum', 'Dad', 'car', 'cup' and 'stop'). Gradually his idiosyncratic gestures disappeared as his speech developed, though cultural 'emblems' like nodding and waving naturally persist. At age 7 he still has a tendency to clap his hands when he has finished a meal, but otherwise talks (and reads) perfectly normally for his age. His younger brother, incidentally, began to talk earlier than average and only shuts up when he is asleep or fishing.

Gestures during language acquisition

Returning to the development of the typical, average child, we mentioned earlier Lock's (1980) hypothesis that combining gestures, or gestures and nonverbal vocalizations, somehow prefigures the combining of message elements in simple two-word 'sentences'. A child's first words often accompany manual gestures

(Leopold, 1949; Von Raffler Engel, 1975) and may combine with them in a complementary manner. Halliday (1975) produced a fascinating analysis of his son Nigel's early language development within a British tradition of 'systemic linguistics' very different from the Chomskyan linguistics which has shaped most work on language acquisition, paying closer attention to the social functions of language. Many of Nigel's first combinations were of a gesture and a word, but unlike saying 'bye-bye' while waving, the word and gesture expressed different elements. For example, Nigel said his version of 'star' while shaking his head, meaning 'I can't see the star'. On another occasion he said 'dabi' (his version of Dvořak) while beating time with his hand, a combination which was glossed as meaning 'I want the Dvořak record on'. Only later did words combine in the same way to express different elements of an underlying message (e.g. 'more meat', 'two book' or 'play rao Bartok', meaning 'Let's play at being lions with the Bartok record on')!

Little research has been done on gestural communication in older children. It is clear, however, that even school-age children can involve gestures extensively in their communication. Evans and Rubin (1979) taught 5- to 10-year-old children a new boardgame, then observed the children explaining the rules of the game to adults. Sixty-five percent of rule explanations given by 5-year-olds required their accompanying gestures to be seen before the rule could be understood. Jancovic, Devoe and Wiener (1975) recorded the gestures made by children from 4 to 18 years when talking about a Woody Woodpecker cartoon they had just seen. As the children grew older there was a change in the proportions of different types of gestures made. Iconic pantomime-like gestures expressing concepts which could equally well be expressed in words (or which were simultaneously expressed in words) declined in frequency with age, but gestures which modify, amend or emphasize the verbal content increased. Examples of this latter category include a flip-flop of the palm to indicate that there are more sides to an argument than the position just outlined in the verbal channel, or a palm-up gesture indicating that the speaker is open to alternative points of view. But this sort of subtle interplay between verbal and gestures channels shown by the teenagers in Jancovic et al.'s study is effectively the adult gestural competence. It is time now to switch to the verbal channel and study the development of sounds, words and sentences.

The sound system

Mastering the sound system (phonology) of the language of the community into which a child has been born is clearly an important aspect of learning to talk. The child must be able both to perceive and produce all the contrasts between different phonemes (speech sounds) that its language employs. It used to be assumed that the human infant was born a 'blank slate' upon which experience wrote, and that mastering the sound system would be one aspect of that general learning process. We now know differently, for research has shown that infants come into the world selectively pre-tuned to perceive many of the contrasts between sounds that languages employ.

For example, there is a set of pairs of sounds in English that are distinguished one from another by the feature of 'voicing'. The phonemes /p/ and /b/ are one such pair. To produce a /b/ sound you open your lips whilst simultaneously vibrating your vocal cords. To produce a /p/ sound the only difference is that you delay the onset of vocal cord vibration for 30 msec or more after the lips have parted. Linguists say that the phoneme /b/ is 'voiced' while /p/ is 'unvoiced'. Similarly, /g/, /d/, and /v/ are voiced while their partners /k/, /t/ and /f/ are unvoiced.

Eimas, Siqueland, Jusczyk and Vigorito (1971) showed that infants as young as one month old could discriminate between synthetic speech sounds which differed only on the feature of voicing. To demonstrate this they used what is called the 'high amplitude sucking' technique. The infant sucks on a soother within which is a tiny electronic sensor. Sucking on the soother controls the presentation of a sound (for example the phoneme /p/) through loudspeakers. Initially the infant finds the sound interesting and sucks at a high rate, but after a while the novelty wears off and the rate declines. If, however, the sound is changed from /p/ to /b/ the sucking rate increases again. This shows that the infant can hear the difference between /p/ and /b/ when a mere one month old. Using the same technique Morse (1979) showed that six-week-old infants could perceive the difference between pairs of phonemes like /b/ and /g/ which differ on the feature of 'place of articulation'.

Returning to the voicing distinction, there is a further interesting point to be made about the way adults and infants perceive the difference between pairs like /b/ and /p/. Using a speech synthesizer it is possible to create a succession of stimuli in which the onset of voicing is delayed by degrees from 0 msec to 50 msec or more. Voice onset times of 0–20 msec are all perceived as /p/ by English speaking adults, who are actually incapable of hearing any difference between them. As soon, however, as voice onset time is delayed over the critical 30 msec boundary perception slips from /p/ to /b/. Two stimuli which differ by 15 msec but which stay within either the /p/ range (e.g. +5 versus +20 msec) or the /b/ range (e.g. +35 versus +50 msec) will sound identical to adults, whereas two which differ by the same physical amount but which cross the /p/ – /b/ boundary (e.g. +25 vs. +40 msec) will sound totally different. Psycholinguists say that adult auditory system *categorizes* voice onset times as voiced or voiceless. Experiments with infants have shown that they too perceive speech sounds categorically. They will not, for example, increase sucking rate for a change of stimuli within the /p/ or /b/ range, but will increase when the charge takes the new stimulus across the boundary.

Work on these and other contrasts is reviewed by Mehler and Bertoncini (1979), Morse (1979) and Miller and Eimas (1983). Infants show an impressive range of perceptual abilities as soon as they are capable of being tested, prompting Gleitman and Wanner (1982) to comment that 'no learning apparatus is required for an initial segmentation of the acoustic wave into discrete phones (i.e. speech sounds). The segmentation has been provided in the nervous system'. This may be largely true, but we may also need to enter one or two qualifications. First, not all speech contrasts are easy for infants to perceive – for example, the English /f/ – /θ/ ('th') distinction can cause difficulty even in 4- and 5-year-olds. Spanish has a different voicing boundary to English: theirs is placed between −20 and +20 msec. Lasky, Syrdal-Lasky and Klein (1975) found Spanish infants unable to discriminate this boundary. They could, however, discriminate between stimuli which crossed the English +30 msec boundary, though that boundary is not exploited in Spanish.

This brings us to our second qualification, which is another issue of cause and effect. Is the human auditory system selectively tuned to certain contrasts that many human languages exploit, or do many human languages exploit contrasts to which the human auditory system is selectively tuned? Clues hinting at the latter possibility come from work on speech perception in animals (recall the perceptual skills of 'Fellow' discussed in Chapter 1). The cuddly chinchilla can be taught to discriminate speech sounds one from another and turns out to be particularly sensitive to contrasts in the +30 msec voice onset time region (Kuhl and Miller, 1975). The same is true of the rhesus monkey (Morse and Snowdon, 1975; see Kuhl, 1979, for a review). The issue is by no means settled yet, but it is at least possible that the reason many languages employ certain contrasts in their sound systems is that those are contrasts to which the general mammalian auditory system is particularly sensitive.

We saw in Chapter 12 how lip movement cues interact with auditory information in normal adult speech perception. Dodd (1979) reports evidence showing that young infants are also sensitive to congruence between these auditory and visual channels. Infants aged 10 to 16 weeks watched their mother's face reciting a nursery rhyme. The sound was either in synchrony with the lip movements, or artificially delayed by 400 milliseconds so that the two were out of synchrony. Dodd found that the infants looked at their mother's face more when lips and voice were synchronized than when they were asynchronous. This shows that very young infants are aware of match or mismatch between auditory and lip movement channels. Whether this is innate or develops in the first few weeks of life, and whether incongruous lip information changes the sound perceived as it does for adults, is not yet known.

Being capable of discriminating speech sounds is not the same as being able to produce speech. Stark (1979) has summarized the development of vocalization in the preverbal infant as follows:

> *Stage 1:* (0 to 8 weeks): Reflexive crying and 'vegetative' sounds such as burping, swallowing or sneezing.
> *Stage 2:* (8 to 20 weeks): Cooing and laughing.
> *Stage 3:* (16 to 30 weeks): Vocal play.
> *Stage 4:* (25 to 50 weeks): 'Reduplicative' babbling – i.e. repeating one 'syllable' over and over again (e.g. 'ba. . . ba. . .ba').
> *Stage 5:* (9 to 18 months): 'Nonreduplicative babbling – i.e. mixed syllable sequences (e.g. 'abigabudibi') upon which stress and intonation are superimposed to produce 'expressive jargon'.

The relationship between babbling and later speech development has engendered some debate. Jakobson (1968) argued for a discontinuity between the two. He noted, for example, how one can hear in an infant's babbling sounds that the same child may be unable to produce voluntarily a few years later. Menyuk (1977) made a case for a closer relationship. She argues that changes during the babbling phase in the frequency with which certain phonemes featured are produced are mirrored in order of acquisition of these features when speech begins.

Children who can make the voiced/voiceless discrimination at 6 weeks of age, and who produce voiced and voiceless sounds in their babbling at age 12 months, must still master the contrast voluntarily when they learn to talk. A one-year-old's attempts at 'big' and 'pig' may be indistinguishable to the adult ear. That does not mean, however, that the two attempts are physically identical. The children studied by Macken and Barton (1980) went through a phase when their voice onset times for words beginning with voiceless sounds ('pig', 'cap', 'tip', 'fan' . . .) were measurably shorter than for words beginning with voiced sounds ('big', 'gap', 'dip', 'van' . . .). All the voice onset times were, however, over +30 msec, so all the sounds were perceived as voiced by the adult categorical auditory system (and presumably by the children's own). One assumes that with practice these children get the voice onset time for voiceless consonants below the 30 msec boundary whereupon they will be perceived by those around them as having begun to make that distinction in their speech.

If a young child says /g/ for /d/, is it always because the child is simply unable to say the /d/ sound? Smith (1973) showed that at least on some occasions something more complicated is going on. When his son tried to say 'puddle' it came out as 'puggle'. But the boy *could* say 'puddle' because that is what came out when he tried to say 'puzzle'. That is;

puddle → 'puggle', but
puzzle → 'puddle'.

The explanation Smith proposed for the 'puddle-puggle puzzle' was that certain phonological simplification rules operate upon an underlying phoneme form which is the adult version of the word. Those rules operate on puzzle to produce 'puddle', but change puddle into 'puggle'. We should admit, however, that this theory is not yet universally accepted. Waterson (1983), for example, questions Smith's assumption that the correct adult form always underlies the child's mispronunciation. We do know, however, that children do not respond to their own mispronunciations as they do to the correct adult form (Smith, 1973; Dodd, 1975). Thus Smith's son would always take 'puddle' to mean a patch of water not a puzzle, and he would not easily understand what a 'puggle' was meant to be.

Acquiring a vocabulary

At what age do children typically produce their first words? A simple enough question, but the reader will know by now not to expect too simple an answer. As Grieve and Hoogenraad (1979) note, there is a systematic discrepancy between different accounts as to when this milestone is achieved. Some put it around 9 months; others between one and one-and-a-half years. The source of this discrepancy according to Grieve and Hoogenraad probably lies in different criteria as to what shall count as a 'word'. The later age is the one at which children usually begin to produce recognizable approximations to words in the adult language, but children may use sounds earlier in a word-like manner to regulate social interactions. For example, Halliday's (1975) son Nigel aged 9–10½ months used 'ey' to mean 'that's nice' and 'na' to mean 'give me that'.

Nigel acquired a few adult-type words between 12 and 18 months, whereafter his vocabulary expanded rapidly. This pattern, according to Nelson (1973), is typical. The average child will have a vocabulary of 10 words by 15 months and 50 words by 19½ months (though there is much individual variation). The first 20 or 30 words are acquired fairly slowly over 4–5 months, but then vocabulary growth takes off exponentially in the explosion that many researchers and countless numbers of parents have borne witness to.

What *sort* of words make up the child's early vocabulary? Sixty-five per cent of the first 50 words produced by children in Nelson's (1973) study were what she calls 'nominals' – words referring to things. Common among these are words referring to food, drink, animals, clothes, toys and familiar people. Working with mother–infant pairs, Ninio and Bruner (1978) saw how mothers typically begin by drawing the infant's attention to an object whose name is to be learned. This drawing of attention often takes the form of pointing to the object. A question philosophers are prone to ask on such occasions is how, when a mother points to a cow and says 'cow', does the child know that 'cow' refers to the whole object rather than to some part of it, some attribute of it, something it is doing, or some combination of the object and the context in which it is set? In a study of 40 mother–infant pairs Ninio (1980) found that in 95% of the cases when a mother pointed to something then named it, the name referred to the whole object divorced from its setting. When the mother wished to refer to part of an object, some attribute of it, or what it was doing, she would first name the whole object then add the additional information. ('Here's a kettle, and there's its spout', or 'Here's a bus. It's a red bus and it's driving along'). Thus while children may not come into the world innately equipped with the answer to the philosopher's question, if they early on form the hypothesis that new names refer to whole objects then they will only occasionally be misled. That this does sometimes happen, though, is shown in the example related by Macnamara (1972) of the child who referred to an oven as a 'hot' after an adult had pointed to the oven and said 'hot!'

Brown (1958) noted in his classic paper 'How shall a thing be called?' that many common objects have more than one possible name and that the names vary in their level of specificity. One and the same dog may, for example, be called 'animal', 'pet', 'dog', 'mongrel' or 'Muffin'. Which name should a child be taught? Brown argued that adults supply the name the child will find most useful in interacting with the object and most useful in conversation with others. The point about interaction with the object is that the child is provided with the name at the level of detail at which the child should treat it and others like it in a similar manner. If it is any old dog it will be called 'dog' (but not 'animal' or 'pet' since appropriate behaviours with any old dog are different from those with any old bull or any old goldfish). If the dog is a particular dog to be afforded special treatment – a bad-tempered one to be given a wide berth or a docile creature that can safely be leapt upon – then the dog's own unique name will be supplied by the adult; the name which singles it out from others of its kind.

Although adults clearly do what they can to make the child's acquisition of a vocabulary straightforward and useful, the child still has work to do in learning precisely when and where a word can appropriately be used. A young girl whose language development was observed by Eve Clark (1973; 1974; Clark and Clark, 1976) made a type of naming error that is characteristic of children learning to talk. She first used the word 'gumene' to refer to a coat button, but then applied it to a collar stud, a door handle, a light switch, in fact anything small and round. 'Ticktock' first referred to a particular watch, but was then applied to all watches and clocks, a gas meter, a firehose wound on a spool, and a set of bathroom scales with a round dial. This phenomenon of overextending the domain of application of a word is known as 'overgeneralization'. Young vervet monkeys do it when learning their alarm calls (see Ch. 1, pp. 2–3). All children seem to do it, though only about a third or less of the words children learn show the phenomenon (Nelson, Rescorla, Gruendel, and Benedict, 1977). Overgeneralizations are based on similarities the child perceives between objects. In the above examples the similarity is of size and shape; in other cases similarity of movement, texture, taste or sound may be involved.

Quite a high proportion of overgeneralizations seem to occur because the child fails to apply (or to appreciate) the rule that adults' first names typically refer to the thing itself rather than to some attribute. Eve Clark's subject first said 'mooi' when looking at the moon. But rather than taking 'mooi' to be the moon's name she seems to have assumed that it referred to the attribute of roundness, for she went on to use 'mooi' when talking about cakes, round marks on windows, round postmarks, the letter O, and so on. Objects do not come ready-named. Dogs, for example, come in all shapes and sizes, as do toys, clothes, fruit etc., and a child must presumably learn by trial and error what the appropriate domains are for words like 'dog', 'toy', 'clothes' and 'fruit'. The child tests out hypotheses as to what range of things a word can be used to denote. Sometimes the hypothesis is too wide, in which case an overgeneralization results. Sometimes it is too narrow and the child 'undergeneralizes' (that is, fails to apply a word in its vocabulary to an object for which the word would, in fact, be appropriate). To be efficient, hypothesis testing needs feedback concerning the effectiveness of a trial. Presumably overgeneralizations, at least on some occasions, are either overtly corrected by an adult or fail because the attempt at communication is unsuccessful. When this happens the child must change its hypothesis as to what a new word means. This process, combined with the acquisition of new words for things the child might previously have overgeneralized an old word to cover, allows the child gradually to approximate its use of words to that of the language community it is joining.

Back in Chapter 4 we noted the existence of units of meaning smaller than the word. Those units are *morphemes*. The word 'jumped', for example, is made up of the 'free' or 'root' morpheme *jump*, plus the past tense marking 'bound' morpheme *-ed*. The past tense forms of many English verbs are constructed in this way ('kicked', 'touched', 'cuddled', 'walked' etc.), but other past tenses are formed differently. 'Drink', for example, becomes 'drank', 'light' becomes 'lit', 'go' becomes 'went', and 'bring' becomes 'brought'. Studies of the development of the use of past tense forms show four basic stages (Clark and Clark, 1976, pp. 342–4).

Children begin with little or no use of past forms. Next they learn a small set of particular past tense forms which may include irregular ones like 'went' or 'brought' as well as regular versions. At this second stage both regular and irregular forms are used correctly. At the third stage children seem to realize that there are certain principles or rules governing the formation of many past tense forms of verbs. They now begin to use the bound morpheme suffix *-ed* to form all past tenses of verbs, so that the child who a few months earlier was using 'went' and 'brought' correctly now starts to say 'goed' and 'bringed' as well as 'drinked', 'lighted', 'breaked', 'eated' and so on. In the fourth and final stage they relearn which verbs are exceptional and take peculiar past forms rather than the *-ed* rule. 'Went', 'brought', 'drank', 'lit', and 'broke' now reappear.

Developmental psycholinguists leaped upon errors like 'goed' and 'bringed' as evidence for the creativity and rule-governed nature of child language. They pointed out that children never hear adults say 'goed' or 'bringed', so simple imitation cannot account for all the facts about language acquisition. Instead children must be credited with rules which they use to generate sentences, even if those rules are sometimes misapplied. The concept of generative rules – central, of course, to Chomsky's conception of language (see Chapter 4, pp. 62–71) – was also applied to the next domain of language development we shall consider, the acquisition of syntax.

The development of sentences

Once children begin to talk they do not dwell for long at the single-word stage, but soon begin to combine words into simple two-word 'sentences'. From the outset it is clear that these combinations are not random but are governed by rules or regularities which determine the order in which the two words involved occur. The developmental psycholinguist, of course, wants to write a grammar for the two-word stage which will capture and explain the observed regularities. Several such grammars have been proposed. All have been criticized for one reason or another, but that is only to be expected. It is largely through exploring the shortcomings of existing theories that we are able to develop better ones.

Braine (1963) pioneered the writing of grammars for two-word 'sentences' when he proposed that at this stage children's words could be divided into just two classes. A small class of 'Pivot' words (e.g. 'want', 'see', 'all', 'it', 'off', 'come',) combined in Braine's grammar with a larger class of 'Open' words (e.g. 'car', 'get', 'broke', 'sock, 'boot', 'daddy', 'mummy') to produce sentences in either Pivot-Open combination, e.g.

'want car'
'all broke'
'see daddy'

or in Open-Pivot combination, e.g.

'boot it'
'sock off'
'daddy come'

but not in Pivot-Pivot or Open-Open combinations.

McNeil (1970) reported apparent Open-Open sentences in contradiction of Braine's grammar, but a more telling criticism voiced by Bloom (1970) and others was that the grammar failed to capture important properties of words relating to their functions in the utterances. Bloom's much-quoted illustration of this point was that her subject, Kathryn, uttered the sentence 'Mommy sock' on two separate occasions for two different purposes. On one occasion the context in which Kathryn said 'Mommy sock' led Bloom to infer that it meant 'Mommy (is putting on my) sock' whereas in the second context it meant '(Here is) Mommy('s) sock'.

It was to capture such distinctions between and among two-word sentences that a variety of semantically-based grammars were proposed by Bloom (1970), Brown (1973), Braine himself (1976) and Schlesinger (1974) among others. Brown, for example, classified utterances in terms of relations like Nominative ('That doggie'), Locative ('Sock there'), Agent-Action ('Daddy hit') or Action-Object ('Hit ball'). In order to write this sort of grammar it is essential first to observe the context in which the utterances occurred and then to form a hypothesis as to the fuller message the child was trying to communicate (as in Bloom's two 'Mommy sock' examples). This method is known as 'rich interpretation' and has not gone uncriticized. We saw back in Chapter 1 the problems rich interpretation caused in the area of animal communication, and there must be a danger that researchers project into children's utterances meanings and relations that exist in the adult's head but not in the child's.

Another criticism has recently been levelled against semantically-based grammars. At some time or other the child is going to have to master syntactic categories such as Subject and Object which we know to be only complexly related to semantic categories like Agent or Recipient. Is it adaptive, then, for the child to develop an early grammar whose principles of organization are quite different from those of the adult grammar? Gleitman and Wanner (1983, p. 30) pose this question from the point of view of the grammar-writing research strategy most likely to succeed, asking 'Is it valuable to postulate a system that describes the earliest stages of learning . . . even if this simple system fails to describe the learner who manages to survive to age 3 or 4? If learning is taken to be continuous . . . then semantics-based syntax is a false step'. Halliday (1975) argued for discontinuity in the case of the language acquisition of his son Nigel. Halliday proposed that from age 9 months to 2 years, Nigel employed a two-tier system with semantic concepts and relations being directly expressed by words (or gestures). Only from around age 2 onwards did Halliday think it necessary to credit Nigel with a three-tier system in which a syntactic level came to mediate between semantics and words. At present it is not possible to predict what approach to very early grammar will prove most successful.

But children do not dwell for long at the two-word stage. By age 2½ Tiedemann's (1787) subject was saying, 'The sun has gone to bed; tomorrow he will get up again, drink his tea and eat his bread and butter'. In the 1960s, the study of the acquisition of progressively more complex sentence structures was one attempt to validate the Derivational Theory of Complexity (see Chapter 4, pp. 69–71). The idea was that children's early sentences were closest to the straight expression of deep structures, with transformations and the different surface structures they generate being gradually acquired. Brown and Hanlon (1970) studied the development of eight different sentence structures. They found the earliest of their types to be produced was the transformationally simple declarative sentence (e.g. 'We had a ball'). The next to appear were questions ('Did we have a ball?'), negatives ('We didn't have a ball') and so-called 'truncated active' sentences ('We did'). Later the children learned to combine, for example, negative + question ('Didn't we have a ball?') or truncation + negative ('We didn't'). Last to appear was the triple combination – the truncated negative question, 'Didn't we?' Brown and Hanlon (1970) interpreted this order of acquisition in terms of the children learning different transfor-mation rules. With the decline in adherence to transformational grammar as a literal model of sentence production, this interpret-ation is not now favoured. That fact does not, however, alter Brown and Hanlon's findings. They must be accounted for by any alternative theory of syntax acquisition. A point to note in passing is that the truncated form of a particular sentence type always appeared after the fuller version ('We did' after 'We had a ball'; 'We didn't' after 'We didn't have a ball'), despite the fact that the truncated forms are always shorter sentences.

One might get the mistaken impression from our account of Brown and Hanlon's study that negative sentences, for example, suddenly pop out, correct and ready formed. They don't, as Klima and Bellugi (1966) showed in their work on the development of negation. The first negatives a child produces simply place 'no' or 'not' either before or after the utterance the child might have employed to make the corresponding positive sentence (e.g., 'no singing song', 'no play that', or 'wear mitten no'). Bloom (1970) found that this type of negative is first used to remark upon the absence or non-existence of any object, then to reject an object or suggestion offered by an adult, and finally to deny the truth of a proposition made by another. Bloom's point once again is that purely grammatical analysis is not enough, and developmental psycholinguists must look at the functions utterances are serving as well as the forms they take. Wode (1977) notes examples from several languages of the still earlier use of 'no' on its own, making the point that concepts like refusal, denial and rejection exist before their incorporation into the language system as grammatical devices (head shaking and turning away are further illustrations).

Returning to Klima and Bellugi's analysis, the next stage arrives when the child begins to incorporate the negative into the body of the utterance, saying things like 'He no bite you' or 'You can't dance'. From the outset the negative element is slotted correctly between Subject and Verb: children never say 'He bite no you' or 'I know don't his name'. These negative utterances include 'can't' and 'don't', but there is no evidence that children understand that 'can't' is composed of *can* + *not* or that 'don't' is composed of *do* + *not*. Later, however, they begin to use 'can' and 'do' in a positive sense contrasted with 'can't' and 'don't'. They have now reached Klima and Bellugi's third and final stage. They still make occasional mistakes, for example saying 'I not crying' instead of 'I'm not crying', or 'No-one didn't come in' instead of 'No-one came in', but their grasp of negation is by now very close to the adult usage.

Language acquisition as decipherment, and the case of 'motherese'

Macnamara (1970) likened language acquisition to a process of code-breaking or decipherment. The child, he argued, is trying to crack the language code – to work out how it encodes entities and the relations between them. But there is a paradox here, because in order to understand how a code works you must already know what messages are being sent in it. An archaeologist must, for example, know what language a newly uncovered script is being used to write before decipherment can begin. So, Macnamara argued, the child must possess independent knowledge of the message encoded in an adult's utterance. Only if the child already knows what is being talked about can he or she begin to develop hypotheses as to just how that information can be encoded into a verbal signal. That is why, when children are beginning to acquire language, adults talk to them about things that are immediately present and blindingly obvious. 'Look', you say as Muffin chews his ball, 'Muffin's chewing his ball'. Now the information in that sentence is redundant – the child can see perfectly well what Muffin is doing – but that, perversely, is why you say it. You say it so that the child can hear how to put into words the event it has just witnessed. The child may know what 'Muffin' and 'ball' mean and so be well placed to form a hypothesis as to what 'chews' refers to (encodes). That initial hypothesis may not be correct, in which case the child will over- or under-extend in the ways we discussed earlier. Also the very fact that you say 'Muffin's chewing his ball' rather than, say 'His ball is chewing Muffin' or even 'Chewing his is Muffin ball' allows the child to begin to construct a set of hypothesized grammatical rules regarding the determinants of word order in English. (This is, of course, a sloppy shorthand way of talking. What constructs the rules is some form of language processing device within the child's head into whose operations the child has no more conscious access than we have conscious access to the processes that intervene between having an idea and giving it verbal expression).

For Chomsky and the developmental psycholinguists who followed him, the language processing device we have just referred to was an innate Language Acquisition Device. It came equipped with a knowledge of Universal Grammar; that is, of those general, abstract properties thought to be true of all human languages (see Chapter 5). The Language Acquisition Device's job was to work out how those universals were realized or expressed in the language of the community into which the child was born and to compute from input the particular grammar of that language. It was generally assumed that the quality of the input the child received was poor – replete with ungrammatical sentences, false starts, errors and so on. Indeed, the degeneracy of the speech around the child was one of the reasons put forward for why the child would need to be endowed with an innate Language Acquisition Device.

It took a surprisingly long time for developmental psycholinguists to realize that the speech children typically hear is far from degenerate. The decision to study the properties of adult speech to children can be seen as part of the general emancipation of psycholinguistics from an over-reliance on Chomskyan formulations that occurred in the 1970s. Child language researchers went out into homes to record the speech of parents to their children. The language they heard turned out to be systematically different from speech between adults in a number of ways (Snow and Ferguson, 1977). This list of differences includes:

1) Higher pitch and exaggerated intonation.
2) Shorter utterances.
3) A higher proportion of 'content' to 'function' words.
4) Simpler syntax.
5) More interrogatives (questions) and imperatives (commands).
6) More repetitions.

Developmental psycholinguists, like most people, work a 9 to 5 day. The world being what it is, the parents they found in the homes to record were mostly mothers. So it was that the term 'motherese' was coined to label this type of speech to children. We shall have no truck with such a blatantly sexist term. 'Parentese' might be better, though some might prefer 'caretakerese'. None of these terms would be true, however, to when and where this speech style is used. For a start, children are capable of modifying their speech to other children in this way. Gleason (1973) showed that 4- to 8-year-old children will simplify their speech when talking to children younger than themselves. Shatz and Gelman (1973) made similar observations, showing in Elliot's (1981) phrase that 'motherese is not the prerogative of mothers'. Indeed speech of this sort may not only be addressed to children: Ferguson (1975; 1977) observes that speech to foreigners who have only a limited knowledge of English is simplified in much the same way as speech to children. He argues from a sociolinguistic perspective that this speech style should be regarded as one of a number of 'registers' that the native speaker can command, and which is employed in a range of circumstances, of which speech to children is just one.

That said it is the role of what we might call 'simplespeak' in language acquisition that concerns us here. *Why* do adults talk to children in this way? An obvious answer is, 'In order to be understood'. Simplespeak is adapted to the child's limited comprehension skills and you are thus more likely to be understood if you address a child in that register than if you use the style of language you would use in addressing a fellow adult. Simplespeak will promote understanding and facilitate conversational interaction – surely an ample motive for using it. But the developmental psycholinguists wanted more. They wanted to tell the Chomskyans that learning *could* play a major role in language acquisition because the speech the child heard was not after all riotously fragmentary and ungrammatical, but was beautifully adapted to the needs of a learner. The mother was now a biologically engineered language tutor, innately endowed with a Language Simplification Device which, when triggered by the appropriate stimulus (a child), generated precisely the sort of linguistic data the child needed at that moment to promote his or her language development.

This last view of the role of simplespeak has not, however, fared well at the hands of subsequent empirical and theoretical work. It transpired that mothers vary quite considerably in the extent to which they simplify their speech to their children, and that there is little in the way of a correlation between the syntactic complexity of the maternal speech and the child's linguistic level (Newport, 1977; Newport, Gleitman and Gleitman, 1978; Cross, 1978). That is, being fluent in simplespeak does not seem to significantly advance your child's linguistic development. The little girl observed by Leiven (1978) learned to talk despite the fact that her mother responded to only a small proportion of the girl's utterances, and that the few responses were typically noncommital, unrelated replies such as 'Oh, really?' The young girl's speech was repetitive and uninteresting because she hadn't learned how to converse or introduce new topics to chat about, but it was grammatical, and it was English.

If parents really are intent on tutoring their children in the intricacies of syntax, starting with the simplest sentence structures and progressively (if unconsciously) introducing more complex ones, then surely their speech would abound with simple, active, declarative sentences like 'Muffin is on the bed'. As Gleitman and Wanner (1982, p. 39) observe, 'It would seem that *any* syntactic theory would have to regard the active, declarative sentences as simplest, but they are not the forms favoured by caretakers in their speech to the youngest learners'. As we noted earlier, parents favour questions ('Is Muffin on the bed?') or imperatives ('Shoo Muffin off the bed'), not the active declaratives that the Omniscient Mother hypothesis would predict.

But Gleitman and Wanner (1982) mount a much more fundamental attack on the Omniscient Mother hypothesis based on the work of Gold (1967) and Wexler (1982; Wexler and Cullicover, 1980). Gold (1967) demonstrated that no device could induce with certainty the grammar of a language if only positive information and instances are provided. Negative information about which strings are *ungrammatical* is also needed to eliminate rival candidate grammars, yet as Gleitman and Wanner (p. 6) note, 'caretakers do not seem to provide the negative information said to be required. Mothers do not respond to their children's rudimentary attempts (say, "Me wuvs yer, Mom") with negative feedback ("String not in the language, Johnnie")'. Wexler and his colleagues developed learnability theory still further. They point out that the narrower the range of sentence types a learner hears, the greater the number of different grammars that are capable of describing them. A rich and varied input *simplifies* the task of the learner.

The simple claims for simplespeak seem not to have withstood critical scrutiny. There appear to be a number of conflicting requirements at work here. The child-as-formal-linguist needs a varied range of sentence types to learn the grammar of the particular language community into which he or she is born. But the *reason* adults talk to children is to communicate – to get a message across – and *that* requires the adult to use simple sentences of whatever type the child is *currently* able to decode. As with all paradoxes, the solution to this one has to involve realizing that the problem has been incorrectly formulated.

Literacy and language awareness

It is surprising (to us) how few books on the psychology of language make any mention of the psychology of literacy. In part this neglect of literacy is probably a carry-over from the low status afforded written language by linguists from Leonard Bloomfield onwards. They typically treated writing as a mere code for language and claimed that their concern was with the spoken word and sentence (this despite the fact that they woefully neglected all those aspects of language such as intonation, rhythm and stress, which writing captures badly or not at all). In part the present neglect also stems from the curious division of cognitive psychologists and psycho-linguists into those working on reading and writing. In Henderson's (1982) memorable phrase, it is 'as if eyes and ears were connected to different psychologists'. Finally, much of the research on reading and learning to read has been directed at practical concerns, comparing this or that method of teaching, investigating the effects of home background, school environment and so on (e.g. Chall, 1967; Downing and Leong, 1982). One has to dig around a little for information of relevance to the cognitive psychologist or psycho-linguist, but it is there – increasingly so in recent years – and warrants space in any book purporting to cover the psychology of language and language development.

Learning to read

The young child coming to written language for the first time has much to learn – that individual words are represented by different and distinctive letter sequences and so can be recognized visually as wholes; that there is some correspondence (albeit a rather un-reliable one) between letters, or letter groups, and sounds so that an unfamiliar written word can be 'sounded out' with at least some hope of success; that punctuation signals message units with degrees of internal coherence ranging from phrases, through clauses, sentences and paragraphs to chapters and volumes; and so on. But the first thing a child must appreciate is that writing represents language. To a skilled reader the fact that writing is a medium for the expression of language is one of those things that is so obvious it comes as a shock to realize that not everyone knows it (though, after all, inscriptions on stone in 'runic' (Anglo-Saxon) or 'Ogham' (Celtic) script passed unrecognized as forms of writing for centuries).

When Reid (1966), Downing (1970) and Francis (1973) quizzed young pre-readers about what writing is and does they obtained a variety of strange answers from many of the children. Some thought numbers were writing; many did not appreciate the difference between letters and words ('You say one word at a time . . . m-u-s-t. *m* is a word, *u* is a word'). These pre-readers not uncommonly failed to realize that when their parents read to them from picture books they do not just make the words up as they go along, improvising the story in response to the pictures. Gough and Hillinger (1980) argue that the child's first task in learning to read is to realize that the job is one of 'cryptanalysis' – breaking the strange code that freezes language onto a page.

Once this realization has dawned, what course does the acqui-sition of literacy then take? Back in Chapter 12 we noted that skilled readers have two strategies at their disposal for recognizing written words. If the word in front of them is already familiar it is recognized visually as a letter string with a known meaning and a known pronunciation. If the word in front of them is an unfamiliar one skilled readers can adopt the strategy of 'phonic mediation' – breaking it down into its component letters and letter groups, converting it into a phoneme string which can then be pronounced either aloud or internally to see if it sounds familiar even though it does not look familiar. We might dub these two strategies 'reading by eye' and 'reading by ear' respectively (Ellis, 1984a). How do these two strategies develop in readers of English? Which comes first?

Reading is an artificial culturally transmitted skill, so it is probably unwise to look for universal sequences in acquisition.

Nevertheless, Marsh, Friedman, Welch and Desberg (1981) have described a developmental sequence which seems to capture how a great many children learn to read. The child begins by acquiring a small sight vocabulary of words recognized 'by eye'. Lacking any phonic skills, the only thing the child can do with an unfamiliar word is to use the context in which it occurs to make an educated guess. As the child's sight vocabulary grows, an unfamiliar word may sufficiently resemble one previously encountered in print to cause that word to be generated as a best guess. Errors now typically show a degree of resemblance to the target word and are drawn from the set of words the child has encountered in print before (Biemiller, 1970).

Fairly soon after starting to read the child begins to learn the sound values of letters and letter groups. Familiar words continue to be read visually as wholes, but the child can now attempt to decode unfamiliar words by applying letter-sound correspondences. If an unfamiliar word is spelled in a regular manner the child has a fair chance of pronouncing it correctly, and if the word is one the child has heard before, then it will be recognized. The phonic strategy may even succeed on some 'irregular words': the silent *b* on the end of *thumb* may not prevent a child from recognizing the word by phonic mediation particularly if, as is normally the case, the word is embedded in a helpful context ('The needle pricked Snow White's . . .').

The possession of phonic skills makes a child a more independent reader. It is now no longer always necessary to ask a grown-up what a new word is. As the child grows older, phonic skills become more sophisticated. According to Baron (1977) and Marsh et al. (1981), the older reader will use a strategy of analogy to pronounce a new word if it resembles a familiar one. Thus 'node' might be read by analogy with 'rode', or 'gaunt' by analogy with 'haunt'. Other words – 'syntax', for example, or 'lexicon' – are fairly distinctive and do not suggest analogies, so may cause a reversion to low-level letter-sound correspondences. It is important to remember, however, that phonic mediation will only be applied on the first one or two occasions that a word is met. A 'recognition unit' will soon be established for it in the 'visual input lexicon' (cf. Chapter 12), and thereafter the word will be recognized 'by eye.'

The developmental sequence proposed by Marsh and his colleagues progresses from an initially purely visual strategy of word recognition to a flexible combination of visual and phonic strategies. Seymour and MacGregor (1984) and Frith (1985) propose similar developmental schemes and, in addition, attempt to use those schemes to explain different forms of developmental reading difficulty (dyslexia). Developmental dyslexics are not all alike in the way they read and the problems they have. Some – probably the majority – have very poor phonic skills and rely for their limited reading on visual recognition. Others, however, acquire a reasonable facility with phonics, and can 'sound out' and recognize regular words, but do not easily make the transition from recognizing a word phonically to recognizing it visually. The two-route model of reading accounts reasonably well for these different patterns (see Ellis, 1984a; 1985d).

The visual to visual-plus-phonic sequence is only a broad generalization, not a rigid necessity. You could, in principle, begin by teaching a child the sound values of single letters, then introduce letter groups, then practice blending on nonsense syllables like 'hon', or 'deg', before finally inducing a child to read his or her very first real word entirely by phonic mediation – 'hen', say, or 'dog'. Of course you could not prevent 'hen' and 'dog' being recognized visually on second and subsequent occasions. What we have just described would be an extreme 'phonic' regime. Phonic methods tutor phonic mediation, and in the history of teaching reading they have vied for supremacy with 'whole-word' or 'look-and-say' methods which tutor reading by eye (Chall, 1967). If the sequence described by Marsh et al. (1981) of visual to visual-plus-phonic reading is one conducive to the successful acquisition of literacy, then an early concentration on whole-word methods followed by a gradual, supplementary introduction of phonics seems called for. (This in fact is the sequence many reading schemes seem to have opted for without need of prompting by cognitive developmental psychologists).

Finally, we have already mentioned the use children make of context to constrain their guesses at unfamiliar words (and remember that a young child encounters a far higher proportion of words unfamiliar in appearance in normal daily reading than does a typical adult). When children make errors reading passages of text their errors are usually both grammatically and semantically plausible in that context (Clay, 1968; Weber, 1968; 1970). Goodman (1967) and F. Smith (1978) urged teachers to be more receptive to such contextually plausible errors and less critical of the child who makes them. They argued that skilled readers play a 'psycholinguistic guessing game' with print, making heavy use of context and taking in only as much visual information as is necessary to confirm or disconfirm their hypothesis as to what is coming up next. Though this theory is well-meant and possibly harmless, more recent research suggests that Goodman's and Smith's advice is based on an incorrect theory of the nature of skilled reading. Stanovich (1980; 1981) summarizes a substantial body of evidence showing that skilled adult readers make *less* use of context than do younger and/or less skilled readers (see also Mitchell, 1982). Using context to predict upcoming words must be a complex process requiring considerable cognitive resources. It may be worthwhile for the unskilled reader, in whom stimulus-driven recognition (both visual and phonic) may be slow and error-prone, to compensate by making extensive, predictive use of context. The skilled reader, however, has a large sight vocabulary and rapid, automatic access to meaning from print. At this point it ceases to be worth investing expensive cognitive resources for the return of just a few milli-seconds' saving in recognition time per word. As we saw in Chapter 12, skilled readers may make use of context if print quality is poor (such that stimulus-driven reading becomes slow, as it is for the unskilled reader), but in normal reading situations the trend as reading skill increases appears to be a progressive *reduction* in the use of context and increasing reliance on the signal itself to communicate its message.

Learning to write

Literacy is a two-sided coin. A fully literate person should be able to write as well as read. That said, we noted in Chapter 11 that writing is for most people a much less practised skill than reading, and psychologists tend to have reflected this inequality by devoting less research effort to understanding the psychology of writing. Such work as has been done has tended to focus on learning how to spell – a not inconsiderable problem for writers of English (Frith, 1980a; Ellis, 1984a).

Bauer (1937) reports an alphabet invented by a school child for the purpose of secret communication. What fascinated Bauer as an archaeologist was the similarity between the child's invented shapes and the letters of early Semitic writing systems. De Groot (1931) asked a 9-year-old girl to compose a new alphabet and noted resemblances between her shapes and Phoenecian, Sinaitic, Cretan and Cypriote writing systems. A mind of a fanciful disposition might detect the collective unconscious at work here, or the recapitulation in childhood of evolutionarily earlier stages, but Gelb (1963) is probably closer to the mark in noting that if lines and curves in various arrangements are the raw materials for one's letters, then quite independent attempts at devising sets of simple but maximally distinctive characters are likely to come up with the same ones time and again.

Children's invented writing systems also formed the basis of studies by C. Chomsky (1970), Read (1971; 1975) and Bissex (1980). The children in these studies were pre-schoolers who had invented their own spellings of words, but with obvious knowledge of English letter-sound correspondences. The spellings generated by the children were consistent and very phonetic. They also adhered closely to the actual pronunciation of the words in casual everyday speech. 'Troubles', for example, was spelled as CHRIBLS by one child, and 'dragon' as JRAGIN. We cannot do justice here to the insights these spellings can yield into the child's conception of the sound system of the language, but one observation is worth noting in the light of the claims made in Chapters 11 and 12 that inflectional bound morphemes like the plural -s or past tense -ed (a) are spelled consistently despite variations in their pronunciation, and (b) have their own visual recognition processes in reading. Read's (1975) young spellers began by changing their spelling of the past tense -ed to reflect changes in its phonetic form (e.g., MARED for 'married' but HALPT for helped), but later stuck to -D (WALKD for 'walked', PEKD for 'peeked', STARTID for 'started', and ARIVD for 'arrived'). They always spelled the plural as either -S or -IS, never -Z or IZ, so 'tigers' might be TIGRS but never TIGRZ, though that is closer to its pronunciation.

Young children involve the sound forms of words much more in their spelling than in their reading. This is clearly shown in a study by Bryant and Bradley (1980). Six- and seven-year-olds were given a list of 30 words to read on one occasion and write on another. It was found that there was one set of words the children could often read correctly but not spell. These included 'school', 'light', 'train' and 'egg' – words which are visually distinctive, and therefore easy to read 'by eye', but not guaranteed to be spelled correctly by low-level sound-to-spelling correspondences. The words most likely to be spelled correctly but misread were 'bun', 'pat', 'leg' and 'mat' –

visually nondescript but highly regular. In fact, although the children frequently misread these words when presented in lists of other words, Bryant and Bradley found that the children read them correctly if they were presented in a list of non-words which pushed them towards using the phonic reading strategy that they seem to find less easy or natural.

Some people never become good spellers. We all have friends, relatives or colleagues who are good readers but poor spellers. Frith (1978a, b; 1980b) studied this phenomenon among teenage schoolchildren. Her studies show that intelligent good readers/poor spellers who score at their expected level on standard reading tests are, in fact, highly visual readers and very poor at phonic reading. Their spelling, in contrast, is highly phonic: they can generate spellings which sound right but have difficulty memorizing each word's conventional correct spelling. This pattern of visual reading with phonic spelling is, of course, exactly the same as that shown by Bryant and Bradley's 6- and 7-year-olds.

What these studies show is that it is possible to become a good reader of English with only limited phonic skills as far as spelling-sound translation is concerned, and that even very good phonic skills in the sound-spelling direction will not help you become an accomplished speller. The reason for this is the inconsistencies and irregularities which have crept into English over the centuries (see Chapter 11 and which mean that skilled reading and spelling must nowadays be done on a whole-word basis.

Language awareness

Young children may experience difficulty segmenting a spoken phrase or sentence into its constituent words. They find it harder still to divide words into syllables, and have great difficulty segmenting words into phonemes (Fox and Routh, 1975). Calfee, Chapman and Venezky (1972) found pre-school children quite unable to judge whether or not two words start ('dog'/'dip') or end ('dog'/'leg') with the same sound. The young children studied by Liberman, Shankweiler, Fischer and Carter (1974) were reasonably capable of tapping out the number of syllables in a multisyllabic word (tap 5 for 'hippopotamus'), but again very poor at tapping out the number of phonemes in a one-syllable word (tap 5 for 'blast').

It is not that children do not talk in words, syllables and phonemes – descriptions of their acquisition of morphology and phonology show that these units have psychological reality in their speech production. Their problem lies in gaining sufficient conscious control over the units of language – sufficient 'language awareness' – to allow them to consciously manipulate those units in segmentation, comparison, counting and similar tasks.

Several studies have shown that children who are good readers show better 'language awareness' than poor readers (Golinkoff, 1978; Ehri, 1979). The relationship is clear enough, but deciding upon the correct interpretation is more difficult. Following Ehri (1979), we can distinguish four possible reasons why the two skills might be associated (or 'correlated') in this way. First, skill A might be a *prerequisite* for the acquisition of skill B. In the present context this might work two ways: it could be that language awareness is a prerequisite for learning to read, *or* it could be that learning to read is a prerequisite for language awareness. Both would generate the observed association. Second, skill A might be a *facilitator* of skill B – something which improves it without being absolutely essential. Again there are two variants compatible with a simple association: language awareness might facilitate reading ability, or reading ability might facilitate language awareness. Third, skill A might be a *consequence* of skill B. Reading proficiency could be a consequence of language awareness, or language awareness could quite conceivably be a consequence of becoming literate. Fourth and finally, skills A and B could be *incidental correlates* of one another, fortuitously associated because of their mutual association with some third factor. Thus it could be that some parents put effort into helping their children learn to read and also develop their children's language awareness by poems, puns, jokes, language games, etc. Or, from the biological end of the explanatory spectrum, it could be that a clear division of labour between the two hemispheres of the brain (left hemisphere linguistic; right hemisphere visuo-spatial) is somehow conducive to both language awareness and becoming literate. Variants of the incidental correlate hypothesis are virtually limitless.

Can we begin to tease apart these alternative causes of the undeniable association between reading ability and language awareness as revealed in segmentation and similar tasks? For our first piece of evidence we must travel to Panama where dwell the Kuna Indians. These Indians possess no fewer than five different 'play languages' – coded versions of their language constructed by reordering the syllables of words, inserting meaningless phoneme sequences at systematic points, and so on (Sherzer, 1982). They are used mostly by children as a form of play. For example, one Kuna play language inserts /r/ after the vowel of every syllable plus the previous syllable itself. This turns 'merki' (North American) into 'mererkiri', 'tanikki' (he's coming) into 'taranirikkiri', and so on. The relevance of all this to our present concerns is that these play languages require considerable 'language awareness' (phoneme segmentation, insertion, reordering, etc.) yet they may be spoken fluently by children who are totally illiterate. The same applies to several of the other play languages discussed by Sherzer (1982).

The Kuna show that literacy cannot be the only source of language awareness. Literacy cannot be a *prerequisite* of language awareness, nor can awareness be solely a *consequence* of literacy. There is evidence, however, that literacy may be a *facilitator* of language awareness, and for that evidence we must travel to the more remote regions of Portugal. Morais, Cary, Alegria and Bertelson (1979) contrasted the segmentation skills of literate Portugese adults with those of adults who were illiterate through simple lack of educational opportunity. The illiterate adults turned out to possess some segmentation ability but were considerably less skilled than their literate counterparts. Further evidence for a facilitating effect of literacy on language awareness is provided by Barton (1985) in a comparison of literate and illiterate adults in California.

But if literacy can facilitate language awareness there is substantial evidence showing that the reverse may also apply: language awareness may facilitate the acquisition of literacy. Studies by Helfgott (1976), Fox and Routh (1980) and Bradley and Bryant (1983) have shown early segmentation ability to be a good predictor of later reading ability. This finding is compatible with an *incidental correlate* relationship between the two, but a more causal relationship is indicated by the work of Bradley and Bryant (1983). They first assessed phoneme awareness in 403 4- and 5-year-old pre-readers. Performance at this stage was found to be a good predictor of reading level three or four years later. In addition they selected groups of children with poor awareness and gave them different forms of training in 40 sessions over two years. Training children to classify pictures according to whether or not their names shared phonemes in common promoted reading development, particularly if the children were simultaneously taught which letters represent the sounds that were forming the basis of their categorization. The training had no effect on the growth of arithmetic skill, so the benefits of language awareness training are specific to the acquisition of literacy.

It would seem then that literacy can facilitate the growth of language awareness and that language awareness can facilitate the growth of literacy. So far so good, but we sought in Chapters 11 and 12 to show that literacy – reading and writing – is sustained by several independent but co-ordinated cognitive processes. Is the acquisition of all of these processes facilitated by language awareness or just some of them? We earlier identified two routes or strategies for recognizing written words and two for producing them. In both cases there was a whole-word strategy (visual recognition of whole familiar words in reading, and retrieval of the spellings of whole familiar words in writing) and a phonic strategy ('sounding out' unfamiliar words in reading, and assembling spellings from sound in writing). It is fairly easy to see why an ability to segment words into syllables or phonemes would aid the phonic processes of sounding out unfamiliar written words or generating plausible spellings for words whose conventional spelling you have not yet memorized, but it is considerably more difficult to see how language awareness could facilitate direct visual word recognition or the retrieval of learned spellings as wholes from memory.

There are a few indicators that language awareness might be more closely allied to phonic than whole-word skills. Perin (1983) found language awareness in teenage children to be more closely related to spelling ability than reading ability, and we have seen that phonics is habitually more involved in spelling than reading. Alegria, Pignot and Morais (1982) found that children taught in schools which employed phonic teaching methods showed better language awareness than children taught by whole-word ('look-and-say') methods. If we ask why language awareness correlates so highly with reading ability when we have argued that phonic word recognition is only ever supplementary to whole-word visual recognition, then we must seek the answer in the greater independence that phonic skills bestow upon a child. We made the point earlier that the child with phonics who encounters a new word in a book can sound it out and, with the aid of context, often identify it as a word he or she has heard but not seen before. The child can then inspect the word, establish a 'recognition unit' for it, and thereafter recognize it by sight. Thus phonic skills, for which language awareness is necessary, facilitate the *growth* of a sight vocabulary.

And that, we would contend, is how language awareness and reading ability come to be so highly correlated.

Coda

We noted at the outset of this chapter the apparent belief of developmental psycholinguists that language acquisition would be easier to understand than mature language use. We also noted at the outset our doubts concerning this belief. Progress in child language study since the 1960s has certainly given researchers a humbler perspective towards the complexity of the subject matter. The acquisition of syntax is a case in point. We can poke holes in Pivot-Open grammars, suggest why semantic grammars may conceivably be misguided, and so on, but we can say very little about precisely how mastery of sentence structure develops. Developmental psycholinguistics does not exist in isolation. New theories of adult grammar are being put forward every year, and developments in theories of adult syntax are bound to cause changes in theories of development. Our own suspicion is that language acquisition will turn out to be the most difficult of all areas of psycholinguistics and the last to be cracked.

Finally we would like to endorse a point made by Ervin-Tripp (1971) when she wrote that, 'Children's language development involves far more than grammar and phonology . . . children's developing skills include coming to say the right thing in the right way at the right time and place as defined by their social group' (p. 37). We have endeavoured throughout this book to place language in its natural setting, emphasizing the need of a psychology of language to take cognizance of such things as the regulation of conversational give-and-take and the many social influences on forms of linguistic expression. The study of the development of these last aspects of language, like the study of nonverbal communication, has hardly begun.

References

Aaronson, D. and Scarborough, H. S. (1976). Performance theories for sentence coding: some quantitative evidence. *Journal of Experimental Psychology: Human Perception and Performance*, *2*, 56–70.

Abrams, K. and Bever, T. G. (1969). Syntactic structure modifies attention during speech perception and recognition. *Quarterly Journal of Experimental Psychology*, *21*, 280–290.

Aitchison, J. (1981). *Language change: progress or decay?* Bungay: Fontana.

Aitchison, J. (1983). *The articulate mammal: an introduction to psycholinguistics (2nd ed.)*. London: Hutchinson.

Akinasso, F. N. (1982). On the differences between spoken and written language. *Language and Speech*, *25*, 97–125.

Albert, M. L. and Bear, D. (1974). Time to understand: a case study of word deafness with reference to the role of time in auditory comprehension. *Brain*, *97*, 373–384.

Alegria, J., Pignot, E. and Morais, J. (1982). Phonetic analysis of speech and memory codes in beginning readers. *Memory and Cognition*, *10*, 451–456.

Allport, D. A. (1977). On knowing the meaning of words we are unable to report: the effects of visual masking. In S. Dornic (Ed.), *Attention and performance VI*. Hillsdale, N.J.: Lawrence Erlbaum Associates.

Allport, D. A. (1983). Language and cognition. In R. Harris (Ed.), *Approaches to language*. Oxford: Pergamon.

Allport, D. A. and Funnell, E. (1981). Components of the mental lexicon. *Philosophical Transactions of the Royal Society* (London), *B295*, 397–410.

Anderson, J. R. (1976). *Language, memory and thought*. Hillsdale, N.J.: Lawrence Erlbaum.

Anderson, R. C. and Pichert, J. W. (1978). Recall of previously unrecallable information following a shift in perspective. *Journal of Verbal Learning and Verbal Behaviour*, *17*, 1–12.

Argyle, M. (1972). *The psychology of interpersonal behaviour* (2nd ed). London: Penguin.

Argyle, M. (1974). *Social interaction*. London: Methuen.

Argyle, M., Alkema, F. and Gilmour, R. (1971). The communication of friendly and hostile attitudes by verbal and nonverbal signals. *European Journal of Social Psychology*, *1*, 385–402.

Argyle, M. and Cook, M. (1976). *Gaze and mutual gaze*. Cambridge: Cambridge University Press.

Argyle, M. and Dean, J. (1965). Eye-contact, distance and affiliation. *Sociometry*, *28*, 289–304.

Argyle, M. and Kendon, A. (1967). The experimental analysis of social performance. In L. Berkowitz (Ed.), *Advances in experimental social psychology, Vol 3*. New York: Academic Press.

Argyle, M., Salter, V., Nicholson, H., Williams, M. and Burgess, P. (1970). The communication of inferior and superior attitudes by verbal and nonverbal signals. *British Journal of Social and Clinical Psychology*, *9*, 222–231.

Argyle, M. and Trower, P. (1979). *Person to person: ways of communicating*. London: Harper and Row.

Auerbach, S. H., Allard, T., Naeser, M., Alexander, M. P. and Albert, M. L. (1982). Pure word deafness: An analysis of a case with bilateral lesions and a defect at the prephonemic level. *Brain*, *105*, 271–300.

Ausubel, D. P. (1960). The use of advance organizers in the learning and retention of meaningful verbal material. *Journal of Educational Psychology*, *51*, 267–272.

Baars, B. J. (1980). The competing plans hypothesis: a heuristic viewpoint on the problem of speech errors. In H. W. Dechert & R. M. Raupach (Eds), *Temporal variables in speech*. The Hague: Mouton.

Baddeley, A. D. and Lewis, V. (1981). Inner active processes in reading: The inner voice, the inner ear, and the inner eye. In A. M. Lesgold and C. A. Perfetti (Eds), *Interactive processes in reading*. Hillsdale, N.J.: Lawrence Erlbaum Associates.

Bagley, W. C. (1900–01). The apperception of the spoken sentence: a study in the psychology of language. *American Journal of Psychology*, *12*, 80–130.

Ball, P. (1975). Listener responses to filled pauses in relation to floor apportionment. *British Journal of Social and Clinical Psychology*, *14*, 423–424.

Balota, D. A. (1983). Automatic semantic activation and episodic memory encoding. *Journal of Verbal Learning and Verbal Behaviour*, *22*, 88–104.

Barik, H. C. (1968). On defining juncture pauses: a note on Boomer's 'Hesitation and grammatical encoding'. *Language and Speech*, *11*, 156–159.

Baron, J. (1977). What we might know about orthographic rules. In S. Dornic (Ed.), *Attention and performance VI*. Hillsdale, N.J.: Lawrence Erlbaum.

Baron, J., Treiman, R., Wilf, J. F. and Kellman, P. (1980). Spelling and reading by rules. In U. Frith (Ed.), *Cognitive processes in spelling*.

London: Academic Press.

Barrera, M. E. and Maurer, D. (1981a). Recognition of mother's photographed face by the three-month-old infant. *Child Development*, *52*, 714–716.

Barrera, M. E. and Maurer, D. (1981b). The perception of facial expressions by the three-month-old. *Child Development*, *52*, 203–206.

Bartlett, F. C. (1932). *Remembering: A study in experimental and social psychology*. Cambridge: Cambridge University Press.

Barton, D. (1985). Awareness of language units in adults and children. In A. W. Ellis (Ed.), *Progress in the psychology of language*, *Vol. 1*. London: Lawrence Erlbaum.

Basso, A., De Renzi, E., Faglioni, P., Scotti, G. and Spinnler, H. (1973). Neuropsychological evidence for the existence of cerebral areas critical to the performance of intelligence tests. *Brain*, *96*, 715–728.

Bates, E. (1976). *Language and context: the acquisition of pragmatics*. New York: Academic Press.

Bates, E., Kintsch, W., Fletcher, C. R. and Giulani, V. (1980). The role of pronominalization and ellipsis in texts: some memory experiments. *Journal of Experimental Psychology: Human Learning and Memory*, *6*, 676–691.

Bauer, H. (1937). In *Der Alte Orient*, *36*, 36 (cited in Gelb, 1963).

Bawden, H. H. (1900). A study of lapses. *Psychological Review Monograph Supplements*, *3*, 1–121.

Baxter, J. C., Winters, E. P. and Hammer, R. E. (1968). Gestural behaviour during a brief interview as a function of cognitive variables. *Journal of Personality and Social Psychology*, *8*, 303–307.

Beattie, G. W. (1977). The dynamics of interruption and the filled pause. *British Journal of Social and Clinical Psychology*, *16*, 283–284.

Beattie, G. W. (1978a). Sequential temporal patterns of speech and gaze in dialogue. *Semiotica*, *23*, 29–52.

Beattie, G. W. (1978b). Floor apportionment and gaze in conversational dyads. *British Journal of Social and Clinical Psychology*, *17*, 7–16.

Beattie, G. W. (1979a). Planning units in spontaneous speech: some evidence from hesitation in speech and speaker gaze direction in conversation. *Linguistics*, *17*, 61–78.

Beattie, G. W. (1979b). Reflections on *Reflections on language*, by Noam Chomsky. *Linguistics*, *17*, 907–923.

Beattie, G. W. (1981a). A further investigation of the cognitive interference hypothesis of gaze patterns during conversation. *British Journal of Social Psychology*, *20*, 243–248.

Beattie, G. W. (1981b). Language and nonverbal communication – the essential synthesis. *Linguistics*, *19*, 1165–1183.

Beattie, G. W. (1981c). Interruption in conversational interaction and its relation to the sex and status of the interactants. *Linguistics*, *19*, 15–35.

Beattie, G. W. (1982). Turn-taking and interruption in political interviews

– Margaret Thatcher and Jim Callaghan compared and contrasted. *Semiotica*, *39*, 93–114.

Beattie, G. W. (1983). *Talk: an analysis of speech and nonverbal behaviour in conversation*. Milton Keynes: Open University Press.

Beattie, G. W. (1984). "Are there cognitive rhythms in speech?" – a reply to Power (1983). *Language and Speech*, *27*, 193–195.

Beattie, G. W. and Barnard, P. J. (1979). The temporal structure of natural telephone conversations (directory enquiry calls). *Linguistics*, *17*, 213–230.

Beattie, G. W. and Beattie, C. A. (1981). Postural congruence in a ‹ naturalistic setting. *Semiotica*, *35*, 41–55.

Beattie, G. W. and Bogle, G. (1982). The reliability and validity of different video-recording techniques used for analysing gaze in dyadic interaction. *British Journal of Social Psychology*, *21*, 31–34.

Beattie, G. W. and Bradbury, R. J. (1979). An experimental investigation of the modifiability of the temporal structure of spontaneous speech. *Journal of Psycholinguistic Research*, *8*, 225–248.

Beattie, G. W. and Butterworth, B. (1979). Contextual probability and word frequency as determinants of pauses and errors in spontaneous speech. *Language and Speech*, *22*, 201–211.

Beattie, G. W., Cutler, A. and Pearson, M. (1982). Why is Mrs. Thatcher interrupted so often? *Nature*, *300*, 744–747.

Beattie, J. (1788). *Theory of language*. London.

Beauvois, M-F. and Dérousné, J. (1979). Phonological alexia: three dissociations. *Journal of Neurology, Neurosurgery and Psychiatry*, *42*, 1115–1124.

Beauvois, M-F., Dérousné, J. and Bastard, V. (1980). Auditory parallel to phonological alexia. Paper presented at the Third European Conference of the International Neuropsychological Society, Chianciano, Italy, June, 1980.

Becker, C. A. and Killion, T. H. (1977). Interaction of visual and cognitive effects in word recognition. *Journal of Experimental Psychology: Human Perception and Performance*, *3*, 389–401.

Bereiter, C. and Engelmann, S. (1966). *Teaching disadvantaged children in the pre-school*. New York: Prentice-Hall.

Berndt, R. S. and Caramazza, A. (1985). A multi-component deficit view of agrammatic Broca's aphasia. In M. L. Kean (Ed.), *Agrammatism*. New York: Academic Press.

Bernstein, B. (1974). *Class, codes and control, Vol 1*. London: Routledge and Kegan Paul.

Bever, T. G. (1970). The cognitive basis for linguistic structures. In J. R. Hayes (Ed.), *Cognition and the development of language*. New York: Wiley.

Biemiller, A. (1970). The development of the use of graphic and contextual information as children learn to read. *Reading Research Quarterly*, *6*,

75–96.

Binet, A. and Henri, V. (1894). La mémoire des phrases (mémoire des idées). *L'Année Psychologique*, *1*, 24–59.

Birdwhistell, R. L. (1970). *Kinesics and context: essays in body-motion communication*. Harmondsworth: Penguin.

Bissex, G. L. (1980). *GYNS AT WRK: A child learns to read and write*. Cambridge, Mass.: Harvard University Press.

Blackwood, B. (1935). *Both sides of the Buka Passage*. Oxford: Oxford University Press.

Blood, D. (1962). Women's speech characteristics in Cham. *Asian Culture*, *3*, 139–143.

Bloom, A. H. (1981). *The linguistic shaping of thought: a study in the impact of language on thinking in China and the West*. Hillsdale, N.J.: Lawrence Erlbaum.

Bloom, L. (1970). *Language development: form and function in emerging grammars*. Cambridge, Mass.: MIT Press.

Bloomfield, L. (1933). *Language*. New York: Henry Holt.

Blumenthal, A. L. (1970). *Language and psychology: historical aspects of psycholinguistics*. New York: John Wiley.

Blumstein, S. (1973). *A phonological investigation of aphasic speech*. The Hague: Mouton.

Boas, F. (1911). *Handbook of American Indian languages*. Bureau of American Ethology Bulletin No. 40.

Bock. J. K. (1982). Toward a cognitive psychology of syntax: information processing contributions to sentence formulation. *Psychological Review*, *89*, 1–47.

Boomer, D. S. (1965). Hesitation and grammatical encoding. *Language and Speech*, *8*, 148–158.

Boomer, D. S. and Laver, J. D. M. H. (1968). Slips of the tongue. *British Journal of Disorders of Communication*, *3*, 2–12. Reprinted in Fromkin (1973).

Bower, G. H., Black, J. B. and Turner, T. J. (1979). Scripts in memory for text. *Cognitive Psychology*, *11*, 177–220.

Bower, T. G. R. (1979). *Human development*. San Francisco: W. H. Freeman.

Boyle, C. M. (1975). Differences between patients' and doctors' interpretations of some common medical terms. In C. Cox and A. Mead (Eds.), *A sociology of medical practice*. London: Collier-Macmillan.

Bradley, L. and Bryant, P. E. (1983). Categorizing sounds and learning to read: a causal connection. *Nature*, *301*, 419–421.

Braine, M. (1963). On learning the grammatical order of words. *Psychological Review*, *70*, 423–448.

Braine, M. (1976). Children's first word combinations. *Monographs of the Society for Research in Child Development*, *41* (Serial No. 164).

Bramwell, B. (1897). Illustrative cases of aphasia. *The Lancet*, *1*, 1256–

1259. (Reprinted in *Cognitive Neuropsychology*, 1984, *1*, 245–258).

Bransford, J. D., Barclay, J. R. and Franks, J. J. (1972). Sentence memory: a constructive versus interpretative approach. *Cognitive Psychology*, *3*, 193–209.

Bransford, J. D. and Johnson, M. K. (1972). Contextual prerequisites for understanding: some investigations of comprehension and recall. *Journal of Verbal Learning and Verbal Behaviour*, *11*, 717–726.

Bransford, J. D. and Johnson, M. K. (1973). Consideration of some problems in comprehension. In W. Chase (Ed.), *Visual information processing*. New York: Academic Press.

Bransford, J. D. and McCarrell, N. S. (1974). A sketch of a cognitive approach to comprehension: some thoughts about understanding what it means to comprehend. In W. B. Weimer and D. S. Palermo (Eds), *Cognition and the symbolic processes*. Hillsdale, N.J.: Lawrence Erlbaum.

Bresnan, J. W. (1983) (Ed.). *The mental representation of grammatical relations*. Cambridge, Mass.: MIT Press.

Brown, G. (1977). *Listening to spoken English*. London: Longman.

Brown, J. W. (1981). Semantic jargon. In J. W. Brown (Ed.), *Jargonaphasia*. New York: Academic Press.

Brown, R. (1958). How shall a thing be called? *Psychological Review*, *65*, 14–21.

Brown, R. (1973). *A first language: the early stages*. London: George Allen and Unwin.

Brown, R. (1979). Reference: in memorial tribute to Eric Lenneberg. *Cognition*, *4*, 125–153.

Brown, R. and Ford, M (1961). Address in American English. *Journal of Abnormal and Social Psychology*, *62*, 375–385.

Brown, R. and Hanlon, C. (1970). Derivational complexity and order of acquisition in child speech. In J. R. Hayes (Ed.), *Cognition and the development of language*. New York: John Wiley & Sons.

Brownell, H. H., Michel, D., Powelson, J. and Gardner, H. (1983). Surprise but not coherence: sensitivity to verbal humour in right-hemisphere patients. *Brain and Language*, *18*, 20–27.

Bruyer, R., Laterre, C., Seron, X., Feyereisen, P., Strypstein, E., Pierrard, E. and Rectem, D. (1983). A case of prosopagnosia with some preserved covert remembrance of familiar faces. *Brain and Cognition*, *2*, 257–284.

Bryant, P. E. and Bradley, L. (1980). Why children sometimes write words which they do not read. In U. Frith (Ed.), *Cognitive processes in spelling*. London: Academic Press.

Bub, D. and Kertesz, A. (1982). Evidence for lexicographic processing in a patient with preserved written over oral single word naming. *Brain*, *105*, 697–717.

Buck, R. W., Savin, V. J., Miller, R. E. and Caul, W. F. (1972).

Communication of affect through facial expressions in humans. *Journal of Personality and Social Psychology*, *23*, 362–371.

Buck. R., Miller, R. E. and Caul, W. F. (1974). Sex, personality and physiological variables in the communication of affect via facial expression. *Journal of Personality and Social Psychology*, *30*, 587–596.

Buckingham, H. W. and Kertesz, A. (1976). *Neologistic jargonaphasia*. Amsterdam: Swets and Zeitlinger, B. V.

Bull, P. E. (1978a). The interpretation of posture through an alternative methodology to role play. *British Journal of Social and Clinical Psychology*, *17*, 1–6.

Bull, P. E. (1978b). The psychological significance of posture. Unpublished Ph.D. thesis, University of Exeter.

Butterworth, B. (1975). Hesitation and semantic planning in speech. *Journal of Psycholinguistic Research*, *4*, 75–87.

Butterworth, B. (1979). Hesitation and the production of verbal paraphasias and neologisms in jargon aphasia. *Brain and Language*, *8*, 133–161.

Butterworth, B. (1980a). Constraints on models of language production. In B. Butterworth (Ed.) *Language production, Vol 1*. London: Academic Press.

Butterworth, B. (1980b). Evidence from pauses. In B. Butterworth (Ed.), *Language production, Vol 1*. London: Academic Press.

Butterworth, B. (1980c). *Language production, Vol 1*. London: Academic Press.

Butterworth, B. and Beattie, G. W. (1978). Gesture and silence as indicators of planning in speech. In R. N. Campbell and P. T. Smith (Eds), *Recent advances in the psychology of language: formal and experimental approaches*. New York: Plenum.

Butterworth, B., Hine, R. R. and Brady, K. D. (1977). Speech and interaction in sound-only communication channels. *Semiotica*, *20*, 81–99.

Butterworth, B., Swallow, J. and Grimston, M. (1981). Gestures and lexical processes in jargonaphasia. In J. W. Brown (Ed.), *Jargonaphasia*. New York: Academic Press.

Calfee, R. C., Chapman, R. and Venezky, R. (1972). How a child needs to think to learn to read. In L. W. Gregory (Ed.), *Cognition in learning and memory*. New York: Wiley.

Campbell, R. (1982). The lateralisation of emotion: A critical review. *International Journal of Psychology*, *17*, 211–229.

Campbell, R. N. and Grieve, R. (1982). Royal investigations of the origins of language. *Historiographia Linguistica*, *9*, 43–74.

Campbell, R. and Wales, R. (1970). The study of language acquisition. In J. Lyons (Ed.), *New horizons in linguistics*. Harmondsworth: Penguin.

Caplan, D. (1972). Clause boundaries and recognition latencies for words in sentences. *Perception and Psychophysics*, *12*, 73–76.

Caramazza, A., Berndt, R. S. and Basili, A. G. (1983). The selective impairment of phonological processing: a case study. *Brain and Language*, *18*, 128–174.

Caramazza, A., Gordon, J., Zurif, E. B. and DeLuca, D. (1976). Right-hemisphere damage and verbal problem solving behaviour. *Brain and Language*, *3*, 41–46.

Carpenter, G. (1974). Visual regard of moving and stationary faces in early infancy. *Merrill-Palmer Quarterly*, *20*, 181–194.

Catrou, F. F. (1705). *Histoire générale de l'Empire du Mogol. Sur les mémoires portugais de M. Manonchi*. (English translation, 1709). Paris.

Chall, J. (1967). *Learning to read: the great debate*. New York: McGraw-Hill.

Charny, E. J. (1966). Psychosomatic manifestations of rapport in psychotherapy. *Psychosomatic Medicine*, *28*, 305–315.

Chatterji, S. K. (1921). Bengali phonetics. *Bulletin of the School of Oriental Studies*, *2*, 6.

Cheshire, J. (1982). *Variation in an English dialect*. Cambridge: Cambridge University Press.

Chomsky, C. (1970). Reading, writing and phonology. *Harvard Educational Review*, *40*, 287–309.

Chomsky, N. (1957). *Syntactic structures*. The Hague: Mouton.

Chomsky, N. (1959). Review of B. F. Skinner's 'Verbal Behaviour'. *Language*, *35*, 26–58.

Chomsky, N. (1965). *Aspects of the theory of syntax*. Cambridge, Mass.: MIT Press.

Chomsky, N. (1966). *Cartesian linguistics*. New York: Harper and Row.

Chomsky, N. (1969). *American power and the new Mandarins*. New York: Pantheon Books.

Chomsky, N. (1972a). *Language and mind*. (Extended edition). New York: Harcourt Brace Jovanovich.

Chomsky, N. (1972b). *Problems of knowledge and freedom*. London: Fontana.

Chomsky, N. (1973). *For reasons of state*. New York: Pantheon Books.

Chomsky, N. (1976). *Reflections on language*. Glasgow: Fontana.

Chomsky, N. (1979). *Language and responsibility*. Sussex: Harvester Press.

Chomsky, N. (1980). *Rules and representations*. New York: Columbia University Press.

Cicone, M., Wapner, W., Foldi, N., Zurif, E. B. and Gardner, H. (1979). The relation between gesture and language in aphasic communication. *Brain and Language*, *8*, 324–349.

Clark, H. H. (1973). The language-as-fixed effect fallacy: a critique of language statistics in psychological research. *Journal of Verbal Learning and Verbal Behaviour*, *12*, 335–359.

Clark, H. H. and Clark, E. V. (1977). *Psychology and language*. New

York: Harcourt Brace Jovanovich.

Clay, M. M. (1968). A syntactic analysis of reading errors. *Journal of Verbal Learning and Verbal Behaviour*, 7, 434–438.

Clay, M. M. (1969). Reading errors and self-correction behaviour. *British Journal of Educational Psychology*, 39, 47–56.

Cohen, A. A. (1980). The use of hand illustrators in direction-giving situations. In W. Von Raffler-Engel (Ed.), *Aspects of nonverbal communication*. Lisse: Swets and Zeitlinger.

Cole, R. A. and Rudnicky, A. I. (1983). What's new in speech perception? The research and ideas of William Chandler Bagley, 1874–1946. *Psychological Review*, 90, 94–101.

Collins, A. M. and Loftus, E. F. (1975). A spreading-activation theory of semantic processing. *Psychological Review*, 82, 407–428.

Condon, W. S. and Ogston, W. D. (1966). Sound film analysis of normal and pathological behaviour patterns. *Journal of Nervous and Mental Disease*, 143, 338–347.

Condon, W. S. and Ogston, W. D. (1967). A segmentation of behaviour. *Journal of Psychiatric Research*, 5, 221–235.

Cook, M. and Lalljee, M. G. (1972). Verbal substitutes for visual signals in interaction. *Semiotica*, 6, 212–221.

Comrie, B. (1983). Form and function in explaining language universals. *Linguistics*, 21, 87–103.

Corkin, S. (1979). Hidden-figures test performance: lasting effects of unilateral penetrating head injury and transient effects of bilateral cingulotomy. *Neuropsychologia*, 17, 585–605.

Cotton, J. (1935). Normal "visual hearing". *Science*, 82, 592–593.

Coulthard, M. (1969). A discussion of restricted and elaborated codes. *Educational Review*, 22, 38–50.

Crain, S. and Steedman, M. J. (1981). On not being led up the garden path: the use of context by the psychological parser. Paper presented to the Sloan Conference on Modelling Human Parsing, University of Texas at Austin.

Critchley, M. (1962). Speech and speech-loss in relation to the duality of the brain. In V. B. Mountcastle (Ed.), *Interhemispheric relations and cerebral dominance*. Baltimore: Johns Hopkins University Press.

Cross, T. G. (1978). Mothers' speech and its association with rate of linguistic development in young children. In N. Waterson and C. E. Snow (Eds), *The development of communication*. Chichester: John Wiley.

Crystal, D. (1975). *The English tone of voice*. Bristol: Edward Arnold.

Cutler, A. (1982a). Prosody and sentence perception in English. In J. Mehler, E. C. T. Walker and M. Garrett (Eds), *Perspectives on mental representation*. Hillsdale, N.J.: Lawrence Erlbaum.

Cutler, A. (1982b). (Ed.), *Slips of the tongue*. The Hague: Mouton.

Cutler, A. and Isard, S. (1980). The production of prosody. In B.

Butterworth (Ed.), *Language production, Vol 1*. London: Academic Press.

Cutler, A. and Pearson, M. (in press). On the analysis of prosodic turn-taking cues. In C. Johns-Lewis (Ed.), *Intonation in discourse*. London: Croom Helm.

Daiute, C. A. (1981). Psycholinguistic foundations of the writing process. *Research in the Teaching of English, 15*, 5–22.

Darwin, C. (1872). *The expression of the emotions in man and animals*. London: Murray.

Darwin, C. (1877). A biographical sketch of an infant. *Mind, 2*, 285–294.

Davis, D. R. and Sinha, D. (1950). The influence of an interpolated experience upon recognition. *Quarterly Journal of Experimental Psychology, 2*, 132–137.

Davis, J. D. (1976). Self-disclosure in an acquaintance exercise: responsibility for levels of intimacy. *Journal of Personality and Social Psychology, 33*, 787–792.

Deese, J. (1978). Thought into speech. *American Scientist, 66*, 314–321.

Deese, J. (1980). Pauses, prosody and the demands of production in language. In H. W. Dechert and M. Raupach (Eds), *Temporal variables in speech*. The Hague: Mouton.

de Groot, J. (1931). In *Nieuwe Theologische Studien, 14*, 137ff. (cited in Gelb, 1963).

De Long, A. J. (1974). Kinesic signals at utterance boundaries in preschool children. *Semiotica, 11*, 43–73.

De Long, A. J. (1975). Yielding the floor: the kinesic signals. *Communication in Infancy and Early Childhood, 1*, 98–103.

De Renzi, M., Motti, F. and Nichelli, P. (1980). Imitating gestures: a quantitative approach to ideomotor apraxia. *Archives of Neurology, 37*, 6–10.

Deutsch, F. (1947). Analysis of postural behaviour. *Psychoanalytic Quarterly, 16*, 195–213.

Deutsch, A. F. (1952). Analytic posturology. *Psychoanalytic Quarterly, 21* 196–214.

Dittmann, A. T. (1972). The body-movement/speech rhythm relationship as a cue to speech encoding. In A. W. Siegman and B. Pope (Eds), *Studies in dyadic communication*. New York: Pergamon.

Dixon, N. F. (1981). *Preconscious processing*. London: Wiley.

Dodd, B. (1975). Children's understanding of their own phonological forms. *Quarterly Journal of Experimental Psychology, 27*, 165–172.

Dodd, B. (1979). Lip reading in infants: attention to speech presented in and out of synchrony. *Cognitive Psychology, 11*, 478–484.

Dooling, D. J. and Lachman, R. (1971). Effects of comprehension on retention of prose. *Journal of Experimental Psychology, 88*, 216–222.

Douglas, M. (1966). *Purity and danger*. London: Routledge and Kegan Paul.

Downing, J. (1970). Children's concepts of language in learning to read. *Educational Research*, *12*, 106–112.

Downing, J. and Leong, C. K. (1982). *Psychology of reading*. New York: Macmillan.

Duncan, S. (1972). Some signals and rules for taking speaking turns in conversation. *Journal of Personality and Social Psychology*, *23*, 283–292.

Duncan, S. (1973). Toward a grammar for dyadic conversation. *Semiotica*, *9*, 29–47.

Duncan, S. (1974). On the structure of speaker-auditor interaction during speaking turns. *Language in Society*, *2*, 161–180.

Duncan, S. (1975). Interaction units during speaking turns in dyadic face-to-face conversations. In A. Kendon, R. M. Harris and M. R. Key (Eds), *The organization of behaviour in face-to-face interaction*. The Hague: Mouton.

Duncan, S. and Fiske, D. W. (1977). *Face-to-face interaction: Research, methods and theory*. Hillsdale, N.J.: Lawrence Erlbaum.

Durso, F. T. and Johnson, M. K. (1979). Facilitation in naming and categorizing repeated pictures and words. *Journal of Experimental Psychology: Human Learning and Memory*. *5*, 449–459.

Ebbinghaus, H. (1885). *Memory: a contribution to experimental psychology* (Translated by H. A. Ruger and C. E. Bussenius). New York: Dover Publications, 1964.

Efron, D. (1941). *Gesture and environment*. New York: King's Crown Press.

Ehri, L. C. (1979). Linguistic insight: threshold of reading acquisition. In T. G. Waller and G. E. MacKinnon (Eds), *Reading research: advances in theory and practice, Vol. 1*. New York: Academic Press.

Eimas, P., Siqueland, E. R., Jusczyk, P. and Vigorito, J. (1971). Speech perception in infants. *Science*, *171*, 303–306.

Ekman, P. (1978). Facial expression. In A. W. Siegman and S. Feldstein (Eds), *Nonverbal behaviour and communication*. Hillsdale, N.J.: Lawrence Erlbaum.

Ekman, P. and Friesen, W. V. (1969a). Nonverbal leakage and cues to deception. *Psychiatry*, *32*, 88–106.

Ekman, P. and Friesen, W. V. (1969b). The repertoire of nonverbal behaviour: categories, origins, usage and coding. *Semiotica*, *1*, 49–98.

Ekman, P., Friesen, W. V. and Ellsworth, P. C. (1972). *Emotion in the human face: guidelines for research and an integration of findings*. New York: Pergamon.

Ekman, P., Hager, J. C. and Friesen, W. V. (1981). The symmetry of emotional and deliberate facial expressions. *Psychophysiology*, *18*, 101–106.

Elliot, A. J. (1981). *Child language*. Cambridge: Cambridge University Press.

Ellis, A. W. (1979). Speech production and short-term memory. In J.

Morton and J. C. Marshall (Eds.), *Psycholinguistics series, Vol 2*. London: Elek and Cambridge, Mass.: MIT Press.

Ellis, A. W. (1980a). On the Freudian theory of speech errors. In V. A. Fromkin (Ed.), *Errors in linguistic performance: slips of the tongue, ear, pen and hands*. New York: Academic Press.

Ellis, A. W. (1980b). Errors in speech and short-term memory: the effects of phonemic similarity and syllable position. *Journal of Verbal Learning and Verbal Behaviour*, *19*, 624–634.

Ellis, A. W. (1982). Spelling and writing (and reading and speaking). In A. W. Ellis (Ed.), *Normality and pathology in cognitive functions*. London: Academic Press.

Ellis, A. W. (1984a). *Reading, writing and dyslexia: a cognitive analysis*. London: Lawrence Erlbaum.

Ellis, A. W. (1984b). Introduction to Bramwell's (1897) case of word meaning deafness. *Cognitive Neuropsychology*, *1*, 245–258.

Ellis, A. W. (1985a). The production of spoken words: a cognitive neuropsychological perspective. In A. W. Ellis (Ed.), *Progress in the psychology of language, Vol 2*. London: Lawrence Erlbaum.

Ellis, A. W. (1985b). Intimations of modularity, or, the modelarity of mind. In M. Coltheart, R. Job and G. Sartori (Eds), *The cognitive neuropsychology of language*. London: Lawrence Erlbaum.

Ellis, A. W. (1985c). Modelling the writing process. In G. Denes, C. Semenza, P. Bisiacchi and E. Andreewsky (Eds), *Perspectives in cognitive neuropsychology*. London: Lawrence Erlbaum.

Ellis, A. W. (1985d). The cognitive neuropsychology of developmental (and acquired) dyslexia: a critical survey. *Cognitive Neuropsychology*, *2*.

Ellis, A. W. and Marshall, J. C. (1978). Semantic errors or statistical flukes? A note on Allport's 'On knowing the meaning of words we are unable to report'. *Quarterly Journal of Experimental Psychology*, *30*, 569–575.

Ellis, A. W., Miller, D. and Sin, G. (1983). Wernicke's aphasia and normal language processing: a case study in cognitive neuropsychology. *Cognition*, *15*, 111–144.

Ellis, A. W. and Young, A. W. (1986). *Human cognitive neuropsychology*. London: Lawrence Erlbaum.

Elzinger, R. H. (1978). Temporal organization of conversation. *Socio-linguistics Newsletter*, *9* (2), 29–31.

Engler, J. and Freeman, J. T. (1956). Perceptual behaviour as related to factors of associative and drive strength. *Journal of Experimental Psychology*, *51*, 399–404.

Ervin-Tripp, S. (1971). An overview of theories of grammatical development. In D. I. Slobin (Ed.), *The ontogenesis of grammar: some facts and theories*. New York: Academic Press.

Escalona, S. K. (1973). Basic modes of social interaction: their emergence and patterning during the first two years of life. *Merrill-Palmer*

Quarterly, *19*, 205–232.

Esposito, A. (1979). Sex differences in children's conversation. *Language and Speech*, *22*, 213–221.

Evans, M. A. and Rubin, K. H. (1979). Hand gestures as a communicative mode in school-aged children. *The Journal of Genetic Psychology*, *135*, 189–196.

Evett, L. J. and Humphreys, G. W. (1981). The use of abstract graphemic information in lexical access. *Quarterly Journal of Experimental Psychology*, *33A*, 325–350.

Exline, R. V. (1971). Visual interaction: the glances of power and preference. *Nebraska Symposium on Motivation*, 163–206.

Exline, R. V. and Winters, L. C. (1965). Effects of cognitive difficulty and cognitive style upon eye contact in interviews. Paper read to the Eastern Psychological Association.

Fay, D. and Cutler, A. (1977). Malapropisms and the structure of the mental lexicon. *Linguistic Inquiry*, *8*, 505–520.

Feldman, H., Goldin-Meadow, S. and Gleitman, L. (1978). Beyond Herodotus: the creation of language by linguistically deprived deaf children. In A. Lock (Ed.), *Action, gesture and symbol: the emergence of language*. London: Academic Press.

Feldman, S. S. (1959). *Mannerisms of speech and gestures in everyday life*. New York: International Universities Press.

Ferguson, C. A. (1975). Towards a characterisation of English foreigner talk. *Anthropological Linguistics*, *17*, 1–14.

Ferguson, C. A. (1977). Baby talk as a simplified register. In C. E. Snow and C. A. Ferguson (Eds), *Talking to children*. Cambridge: Cambridge University Press.

Ferguson, N. (1977). Simultaneous speech, interruptions and dominance. *British Journal of Social and Clinical Psychology*, *16*, 295–302.

Feyereisen, P. and Seron, X. (1982a). Nonverbal communication and aphasia: a review. I. Comprehension. *Brain and Language*, *16*, 191–212.

Feyereisen, P. and Seron, X. (1982b). Nonverbal communication and aphasia: a review. II. Expression. *Brain and Language*, *16*, 213–236.

Firth, R. (1970). Postures and gestures of respect. Reprinted in T. Polhemus (Ed.), *Social aspects of the human body*. Harmondsworth: Penguin (1978).

Fischler, I. and Bloom, P. A. (1979). Automatic and attentional processes in the effects of sentence contexts on word recognition. *Journal of Verbal Learning and Verbal Behaviour*, *18*, 1–20.

Fischler, I. and Bloom, P. A. (1980). Rapid processing of the meaning of sentences. *Memory and Cognition*, *8*, 216–225.

Fodor, J. A. (1983). *The modularity of mind*. Cambridge, Mass.: MIT Press.

Fodor, J. A. and Bever, T. G. (1965). The psychological reality of linguistic segments. *Journal of Verbal Learning and Verbal Behaviour*, *4*, 414–420.

Fodor, J. A., Bever, T. G. and Garrett, M. F. (1974). *The psychology of*

language: an introduction to psycholinguistics and generative grammar.
New York: McGraw-Hill.

Fodor, J. A. and Garrett, M. F. (1966). Some reflections on competence and performance. In J. Lyons and R. J. Wales (Eds), *Psycholinguistic papers.* Edinburgh: Edinburgh University Press.

Fodor, J. A., Garrett, M. F. and Bever, T. G. (1968). Some syntactic determinants of sentential complexity, II: verb structure. *Perception and Psychophysics, 3*, 453–461.

Forster, K. I. (1981). Priming and the effects of sentence and lexical contexts on naming time: evidence for autonomous lexical processing. *Quarterly Journal of Experimental Psychology, 33A*, 465–495.

Forston, R. F. and Larson, C. V. (1968). The dynamics of space: an experimental study in proxemic behaviour among Latin Americans and North Americans. *Journal of Communication, 18*, 109–116.

Foss, D. J. (1982). A discourse on semantic priming. *Cognitive Psychology, 14*, 590–607.

Foss, D. J. and Hakes, D. T. (1978). *Psycholinguistics.* Englewood Cliffs: Prentice-Hall.

Fouts, R. S. and Rigby, R. L. (1977). Man-chimpanzee communication. In T. A. Sebeok (Ed.), *How animals communicate.* Bloomington: Indiana University Press.

Fowler, C. A, Wolford, G., Slade, R. and Tassinary, L. (1981). Lexical access with and without awareness. *Journal of Experimental Psychology: General, 110*, 341–362.

Fox, B. and Routh, D. K. (1975). Analyzing spoken language into words, syllables and phonemes: a developmental study. *Journal of Psycholinguistic Research, 4*, 331–342.

Fox, B. and Routh, D. K. (1980). Phonemic analysis and severe reading disability. *Journal of Psycholinguistic Research, 9*, 115–119.

Francis, H. (1973). Children's experience of reading and notions of units in language. *British Journal of Educational Psychology, 43*, 17–23.

Freedman, D. G. (1964). Smiling in blind infants and the issue of innate vs. acquired. *Journal of Child Psychology and Psychiatry, 5*, 171–184.

Freedman, N. and Hoffman, S. P. (1967). Kinetic behaviour in altered clinical states: approach to objective analysis of motor behaviour during clinical interviews. *Perceptual and Motor Skills, 24*, 527–539.

Freud, S. (1891). *On aphasia.* (Translated by E. Stengel). London: Imago, 1935.

Freud, S. (1901) *The pyschopathology of everyday life.* Harmondsworth: Penguin, 1975.

Freud, S. (1905). Fragments of an analysis of a case of hysteria. In *Standard edition of the complete psychological works of Sigmund Freud, Vol 7.* London: Hogarth Press.

Freud, S. (1916/17). *Introductory lectures on psychoanalysis.* Harmondsworth: Penguin, 1974.

Frith, U. (1978a). Spelling difficulties. *Journal of Child Psychology and*

Psychiatry, *19*, 279–285.

Frith, U. (1978b). From print to meaning and from print to sound, or how to read without knowing how to spell. *Visible Language*, *12*, 43–54.

Frith, U. (1980a). *Cognitive processes in spelling*. London: Academic Press.

Frith, U. (1980b). Unexpected spelling problems. In U. Frith (Ed.), *Cognitive processes in spelling*. London: Academic Press.

Frith, U. (1985). Beneath the surface of developmental dyslexia. In K. E. Patterson, J. C. Marshall and M. Coltheart (Eds), *Surface dyslexia*. London: Lawrence Erlbaum Associates.

Fromkin, V. A. (1971). The non-anomalous nature of anomalous utterances. *Language*, *47*, 27–52.

Fromkin, V. A. (1973) (Ed.), *Speech errors as linguistic evidence*. The Hague: Mouton.

Fromkin, V. A. (1980) (Ed.), *Errors in linguistic performance: slips of the tongue, ear, pen and hand*. New York: Academic Press.

Fromkin, V. and Rodman, R. (1978). *An introduction to language* (2nd ed.). New York: Holt, Rinehart & Winston.

Fromm-Reichmann, F. (1950). *Psychoanalysis and psychotherapy*. Chicago: University of Chicago Press.

Funnell, E. (1983). Phonological processes in reading: new evidence from acquired dyslexia. *British Journal of Psychology*, *74*, 159–180.

Gallois, C. and Markel, N. N. (1975). Turn taking: social personality and conversational style. *Journal of Personality and Social Psychology*, *31*, 1134–1140.

Gardner, A. and Gardner, B. T. (1978). Comparative psychology and language acquisition. In K. Saltzinger and F. L. Denmark (Eds), *Psychology: the state of the art. (Annals of the New York Academy of Sciences, Vol 309)*. New York: New York Academy of Sciences.

Gardner, H. (1982). Artistry following damage to the human brain. In A. W. Ellis (Ed.), *Normality and pathology in cognitive functions*. London: Academic Press.

Garfinkel, H. (1967). *Studies in ethno-methodology*. New Jersey: Prentice-Hall.

Garrett, M. F. (1975). The analysis of sentence production. In G. H. Bower (Ed.), *The psychology of learning and motivation, Vol. 9*. New York: Academic Press.

Garrett, M. F. (1976). Syntactic processes in sentence production. In R. Wales and E. Walker (Eds), *New approaches to language and mechanisms*. Amsterdam: North-Holland.

Garrett, M. F. (1982). Production of speech: observations from normal and pathological language use. In A. W. Ellis (Ed.), *Normality and pathology in cognitive functions*. London: Academic Press.

Gazdar, G. (1979). Class, 'codes' and conversation. *Linguistics*, *17*, 199–211.

Gazdar, G. (1980). Pragmatics and language production. In B. Butterworth (Ed.), *Language production, Vol 1*. London: Academic Press.

Gee, J. P. and Grosjean, F. (1983). Performance structures: a psycholinguistic and linguistic appraisal. *Cognitive Psychology*, *15*, 411–458.

Geers, A. E. (1978). Intonation contour and syntactic structure as predictors of apparent segmentation. *Journal of Experimental Psychology: Human Perception and Performance*, *4*, 273–283.

Gelb, I. J. (1963). *A study of writing* (2nd ed.). Chicago: University of Chicago Press.

Gleason, J. Berko. (1973). Code switching in children's language. In T. E. Moore (Ed.), *Cognitive development and the acquisition of language*. New York: Academic Press.

Gleitman, L. R. and Wanner, E. (1982). Language acquisition: the state of the art. In E. Wanner and L. R. Gleitman (Eds), *Language acquisition: The state of the art*. Cambridge: Cambridge University Press.

Goffman, E. (1963). *Behaviour in public places*. New York: The Free Press.

Goffman, E. (1967). *Interaction ritual*. New York: Anchor Press.

Goffman, E. (1979). *Gender advertisements*. London: Macmillan.

Gold, E. M. (1967). Language identification in the limit. *Information and Control*, *10*, 447-474.

Goldin-Meadow, S. (1983). The resilience of recursion: a study of a communication system developed without a conventional language model. In E. Wanner and L. Gleitman. (Eds), *Language acquisition: the state of the art*. Cambridge: Cambridge University Press.

Goldman-Eisler, F. (1961). The significance of changes in the rate of articulation. *Language and Speech*, *4*, 171–174.

Goldman-Eisler, F. (1967). Sequential temporal patterns and cognitive processes in speech. *Language and Speech*, *10*, 122–132.

Goldman-Eisler, F. (1968). *Psycholinguistics: experiments in spontaneous speech*. London: Academic Press.

Goldstein, M. N. (1974). Auditory agnosia for speech ('pure word deafness'): an historical review with current implications. *Brain and Language*, *1*, 195–204.

Golinkoff, R. M. (1978). Phonemic awareness skills and reading achievement. In F. Murray and J. J. Pikulski (Eds), *The acquisition of reading*. Baltimore, MD: University Park Press.

Gollmer, C. A. (1885). On African symbolic messages. *Journal of the Royal Anthropological Institute of Great Britain and Ireland*, *14*, 169–181.

Goodenough, F. L. (1932). Expression of the emotions in a blind–deaf child. *Journal of Abnormal and Social Psychology*, *27*, 328–333.

Goodglass, H. and Kaplan, E. (1963). Disturbance of gesture and pantomime in aphasia. *Brain*, *86*, 703–720.

Goodman, K. S. (1967). Reading: a psycholinguistic guessing-game.

Journal of the Reading Specialist, 6, 126–135.

Goren, C. G., Sarty, M. and Wu, P. Y. K. (1975). Visual following and pattern discrimination of face-like stimuli by newborn infants. *Pediatrics*, 56, 544–549.

Gough, P. B. (1965). Grammatical transformations and speed of understanding. *Journal of Verbal Learning and Verbal Behaviour*, 4, 107–111.

Gough, P. B. (1966). The verification of sentences: the effects of delays of evidence and sentence length. *Journal of Verbal Learning and Verbal Behaviour*, 5, 492–496.

Gough, P. B., Alford, J. A. Jr., and Holley-Wilcox, P. (1981). Words and contexts. In O. L. Tzeng and H. Singer (Eds), *Perception of print: reading research in experimental psychology*. Hillsdale, N.J.: Lawrence Erlbaum.

Gough, P. B. and Hillinger, M. L. (1980). Learning to read: an unnatural act. *Bulletin of the Orton Society*, 30, 179–196.

Graham, J. A. and Argyle, M. (1975). A cross-cultural study of the communication of extra-verbal meaning of gestures. *Journal of Human Movement Studies*, 1, 33–39.

Graham, J. A. and Heywood, S. (1975). The effects of elimination of hand gestures and of verbal codability on speech performance. *European Journal of Social Psychology*, 5, 189–195.

Greene, J. (1972). *Psycholinguistics: Chomsky and psychology*. Harmondsworth: Penguin Books.

Greenfield, P. and Smith, J. (1976). *The structure of communication in early language development*. New York: Academic Press.

Gregg, L. W. and Steinberg, E. R. (Eds), (1980). *Cognitive processes in writing*. Hillsdale, N.J.: Lawrence Erlbaum.

Grice, H. P. (1975). Logic and conversation. In P. Cole and J. L. Morgan (Eds), *Syntax and semantics, Vol 3*. New York: Academic Press.

Grieve, R. and Hoogenraad, R. (1979). First words. In P. Fletcher and M. Garman (Eds), *Language acquisition*. Cambridge: Cambridge University Press.

Gumperz, J. J. (1982). *Discourse strategies*. Cambridge: Cambridge University Press.

Hall, E. T. (1959). *The silent language*. New York: Doubleday.

Hall, E. T. (1963). A system for the notation of proxemic behaviour. *American Anthropologist*, 65, 1003–1026.

Hall, E. T. (1966). *The hidden dimension*. London: Bodley Head.

Hall, J. A. (1978). Gender effects in decoding nonverbal cues. *Psychological Bulletin*, 85, 845–857.

Hall, J. A. (1979). Gender, gender roles, and nonverbal communication skills. In R. Rosenthal (Ed.), *Skill in nonverbal communication: individual differences*. Cambridge, Mass.: Oelgeschlager, Gunn and Hain.

Halliday, M. A. K. (1975). *Learning how to mean: explorations in the development of language.* London: Edward Arnold.

Hallpike, C. R. (1969). Social hair. *Man, 4,* 256–264.

Hamanaka, T. and Ohashi, H. (1974). 'Aphasia' in pantomime sign language. *Studia Phonologica, 8,* 23–35.

Hartley, J. (1980). *The psychology of written communication.* London: Kogan Page.

Hatfield, F. M. and Patterson, K. E. (1983). Phonological spelling. *Quarterly Journal of Experimental Psychology, 35A,* 451–468.

Hawkins, P. R. (1969). Social class, the nominal group and reference. *Language and Speech, 12,* 125–135.

Hawkins, P. R. (1973). The influence of sex, social class and pause location in the hesitation phenomena of seven-year-old children. In B. Bernstein (Ed.), *Class, codes and control, Vol 2.* London: Routledge and Kegan Paul.

Hay, D. C. and Young, A. W. (1982). The human face. In A. W. Ellis (Ed.), *Normality and pathology in cognitive functions.* London: Academic Press.

Hayakawa, S. I. (1964). *Language in thought and action.* (2nd ed.). New York: Harcourt, Brace.

Hayduk, L. A. (1983). Personal space: where we now stand. *Psychological Bulletin, 94,* 293–335.

Hayes, K. J. and Haynes, C. H. (1952). Imitation in a home-raised chimpanzee. *Journal of Comparative and Physiological Psychology, 45,* 450–459.

Hayes, L. A. and Watson, J. S. (1981). Neonatal imitation: fact or artefact? *Developmental psychology, 17,* 655–660.

Hayes, J. R. (1970). *Cognition and the development of language.* New York: Wiley.

Hayes, J. R. and Flower, L. S. (1980). Identifying the organization of writing processes. In L. W. Gregg and E. R. Steinberg (Eds), *Cognitive processes in writing.* Hillsdale, N.J.: Lawrence Erlbaum.

Hearn, L. (1894). *Glimpses of unfamiliar Japan.* New York.

Hécaen, J. and Angelergues, R. (1962). Agnosia for faces (prosopagnosia). *Archives of Neurology, 7,* 92–100.

Heider, E. R. (1972). Universals in colour naming and memory. *Journal of Experimental Psychology, 93,* 10–20.

Heilman, K. M., Scholes, R. and Watson, R. T. (1975). Auditory affective agnosia. *Journal of Neurology, Neurosurgery and Psychiatry, 38,* 69–72.

Helfgott, J. (1976). Phonemic segmentation and blending skills of kindergarten children: implications for beginning reading acquisition. *Contemporary Educational Psychology, 1,* 157–169.

Hemphill, R. E. and Stengel, E. (1940). A study of pure word-deafness. *Journal of Neurology, Neurosurgery and Psychiatry, 3,* 251–262.

Henderson, A., Goldman-Eisler, F. and Skarbek, A. (1966). Sequential temporal patterns in spontaneous speech. *Language and Speech, 9,* 207–

216.

Henderson, L. (1982). *Orthography and word recognition in reading.* London: Academic Press.

Henderson, L. (1985). The psychology of morphemes. In A. W. Ellis (Ed.), *Progress in the psychology of language, Vol 1.* London: Lawrence Erlbaum.

Heslin, R. (1974). Steps toward a taxonomy of touching. Paper presented to the Midwestern Psychological Association, Chicago, May 1974.

Heslin, R. and Alper, T. (1983). Touch: a bonding gesture. In J. M. Wiemann and R. P. Harrison (Eds), *Nonverbal interaction.* Beverley Hills: Sage.

Heslin, R. and Boss, D. (1980). Nonverbal intimacy in airport arrival and departure. *Personality and Social Psychology Bulletin*, 6, 248–252.

Hewes, G. (1955). World distribution of certain postural habits. *American Anthropologist*, 57, 231–244.

Hewes, G. A. (1973a). Primate communication and the gestural origin of language. *Current Anthropology*, 14, 5–12.

Hewes, G. A. (1973b). Reply to critics. *Current Anthropology*, 14, 19–21.

Hier, D. B. and Kaplan, J. (1980). Verbal comprehension deficits after right hemisphere damage. *Applied Psycholinguistics*, 1, 279–294.

Hill, C. A. and Varenne, H. (1981). Family language and education: the sociolinguistic model of restricted and elaborated codes. *Social Science Information*, 20, 187–228.

Hitch, G. J. (1980). Developing the concept of working memory. In G. Claxton (Ed.), *Cognitive psychology: new directions.* London: Routledge and Kegan Paul.

Hockett, C. (1967). Where the tongue slips, there slip I. In *To honour Roman Jakobson, Vol. 2.* The Hague: Mouton. (Reprinted in V. A. Fromkin (Ed.), *Speech errors as linguistic evidence.* The Hague: Mouton.)

Holldobler, B. (1977). Communication in social hymenoptera. In T. A. Sebeok (Ed.), *How animals communicate.* Bloomington: Indiana University Press.

Hunter, I. (1985). Lengthy verbatim recall. In A. W. Ellis (Ed.), *Progress in the psychology of language, Vol 1.* London: Lawrence Erlbaum.

Jackson, J. H. (1878). On affectations of speech from diseases of the brain. *Brain*, 1, 304–330.

Jaffe, J. and Feldstein, S. (1970). *Rhythms of dialogue.* New York: Academic Press.

Jakobson, R. (1968). *Child language, aphasia and phonological universals* (trans. A. R. Keiler). The Hague: Mouton.

James, W. (1890). *The principles of psychology.* New York: Holt.

James, W. R. (1932). A study of the expression of bodily posture. *Journal of General Psychology*, 7, 405–437.

Jancovic, M., Devoe, S. and Wiener, M. (1975). Age-related changes in hand and arm movements as nonverbal communication: some conceptualizations and an empirical exploration. *Child Development*, *46*, 922–928.

Jarvella, R. J. (1970). Effects of syntax on running memory span for connected discourse. *Psychonomic Science*, *19*, 235–236.

Jarvella, R. J. (1971). Syntactic processing of connected speech. *Journal of Verbal Learning and Verbal Behaviour*, *10*, 409–416.

Jastrow, J. (1906). The lapses of consciousness. *Popular Science Monthly*, *67*, 481–502.

Jenni, D. A. and Jenni, M. A. (1976). Carrying behaviour in humans: analysis of sex differences. *Science*, *194*, 859–860.

Jesperson, O. (1949). *Language*. New York: Macmillan.

Johnson, M. K., Bransford, J. D. and Solomon, S. K. (1973). Memory for tacit implications of sentences. *Journal of Experimental Psychology*, *98*, 203–205.

Johnson-Laird, P. B. (1983). *Mental models*. Cambridge: Cambridge University Press.

Johnson-Laird, P. N. and Stevenson, R. (1970). Memory for syntax. *Nature*, *227*, 412.

Jourard, S. M. (1966). An exploratory study of body-accessibility. *British Journal of Social and Clinical Psychology*, *5*, 221–231.

Just, M. A. and Carpenter, P. A. (1980). A theory of reading: from eye fixations to comprehension. *Psychological Review*, *87*, 329–354.

Kaplan, R. (1972). Augmented transition networks as psychological models of sentence comprehension. *Artificial Intelligence*, *3*, 77–100.

Katz, J. J. (1981). *Language and other abstract objects*. Totowa, N. J.: Rowman and Littlefield.

Keenan, J. M., MacWhinney, B. and Mayhew, D. (1977). Pragmatics in memory: a study of natural conversation. *Journal of Verbal Learning and Verbal Behaviour*, *16*, 549–560.

Kendon, A. (1967). Some functions of gaze direction in social interaction. *Acta Psychologica*, *26*, 22–63.

Kendon, A. (1972). Some relationships between body motion and speech: an analysis of an example. In A. W. Siegman and B. Pope (Eds), *Studies in dyadic communication*. New York: Pergamon.

Kendon, A. (1978). Looking in conversation and the regulation of turns at talk: a comment on the papers of G. Beattie and D. R. Rutter *et al.* *British Journal of Social and Clinical Psychology*, *17*, 23–24.

Key, M. R. (1975). *Male/female language*. New Jersey: Scarecrow Press.

Kasl, S. V. and Mahl, G. E. (1965). The relationship of disturbances and hesitations in spontaneous speech to anxiety. *Journal of Personality and Social Psychology*, *1*, 425–433.

Kinsbourne, M. and Warrington, E. (1963). Jargon aphasia. *Neuropsychologia*, *1*, 27–37.

Klatt, D. H. (1975). Vowel lengthening is syntactically determined in connected discourse. *Journal of Phonetics*, *3*, 129–140.

Klatt, D. H. (1979). Speech perception: a model of acoustic-phonetic analysis and lexical access. *Journal of Phonetics*, *7*, 279–312.

Kleck, R. E. and Nuessle, W. (1968). Congruence between the indicative and communicative functions of eye-contact in interpersonal relations. *British Journal of Social and Clinical Psychology*, *7*, 241–246.

Kleiman, G. M. (1975). Speech recording in reading. *Journal of Verbal Learning and Verbal Behaviour*, *14*, 323–339.

Klima, E. S. and Bellugi, U. (1966). Syntactic regulation in the speech of children. In J. Lyons and R. J. Wales (Eds), *Psycholinguistic papers*. Edinburgh: Edinburgh University Press.

Klineberg, O. (1935). *Race differences*. New York: Henry Holt.

Kortlandt, A. (1973). Comment on Hewes. *Current Anthropology*, *14*, 13–14.

Korzybski, A. (1933). *Science and sanity: an introduction to non-Aristotelian systems and general semantics*. Lancaster, Pa.: International Non-Aristotelian Library (4th ed., 1958).

Kozhevnikov, V. A. and Chistovich, L. A. (1965). *Speech: articulation and perception*. Washington, D.C.: U.S. Department of Commerce Translation, Joint Publications Research Service, No. 30.

Kreiman, J. (1982). Perception of sentence and paragraph boundaries in natural conversation. *Journal of Phonetics*, *10*, 163–175.

Kuhl, P. K. (1979). Models and mechanisms in speech perception. *Brain, Behaviour and Evolution*, *16*, 374–408.

Kuhl, P. K. and Miller, J. D. (1975). Speech perception by the chinchilla: voiced-voiceless distinction in alveolar plosive consonants. *Science*, *190*, 69–72.

Kurucz, J. and Feldmar, M. A. (1979). Prosopo-affective agnosia as a symptom of cerebral organic disease. *Journal of the American Geriatrics Society*, *27*, 225–230.

Kurucz, J., Feldmar, M. A. and Werner, W. (1979). Prosopo-affective agnosia associated with chronic brain syndrome. *Journal of the American Geriatrics Society*, *27*, 91–95.

La Barre, W. (1947). The cultural basis of emotions and gestures. *Journal of Personality*, *16*, 49–68.

Labov, W. (1966). *The social stratification of English in New York City*. Washington, D.C.: Center for Applied Linguistics.

Labov, W. (1969). The logic of nonstandard English. *Georgetown Monographs on Language and Linguistics*, *22*, 1–31.

Labov, W. (1972). *Sociolinguistic patterns*. Oxford: Basil Blackwell.

La France, M. (1979). Nonverbal synchrony and rapport: analysis by the cross-lag panel technique. *Social Psychology Quarterly*, *42*, 66–70.

La France, M. and Broadbent, M. (1976). Group rapport: postural sharing as a nonverbal indicator. *Group and Organization Studies*, *1*, 328–333.

La France, M. and Mayo, C. (1978). *Moving bodies: nonverbal com-*

munication in social relationships. Monterey: Brooks/Cole.

Lakoff, G. and Johnson, M. (1980). *Metaphors we live by.* Chicago: University of Chicago Press.

Lakoff, R. (1975). *Language and woman's place.* New York: Harper and Row.

Landis, C. (1927). National differences in conversations. *Journal of Abnormal and Social Psychology, 21*, 354–357.

Landis, M. H. and Burtt, H. E. (1924). A study of conversations. *Journal of Comparative Psychology, 4*, 81–89.

Ladavas, E. (1982). The development of facedness. *Cortex, 18*, 535–545.

Lashley, K. S. (1951). The problem of serial order in behaviour. In L. A. Jeffress (Ed.), *Cerebral mechanisms in behaviour.* New York: Wiley.

Lashley, K. S. (1958). Cerebral organization and behaviour. In 'The brain and human behaviour', *Proceedings of the Association for Research in Nervous and Mental Diseases, 36*, 1–18.

Lasky, R. E., Syrdal-Lasky, A. and Klein, R. E. (1975). VOT discrimination by four- to six-and-a-half-month old infants from Spanish environments. *Journal of Experimental Child Psychology, 20*, 215–225.

Leech, G., Deuchar, M. and Hoogenraad, R. (1982). *English grammar for today.* London: The Macmillan Press.

Lehiste, I. (1973). Phonetic disambiguation of syntactic ambiguity. *Glossa, 7*, 107–122.

Lehiste, I. (1979). Perception of sentence and paragraph boundaries. In B. Lindblom and S. Öhman (Eds), *Frontiers of speech communication research.* New York: Academic Press.

Lehiste, I. and Wang, W. (1977). Perception of sentence and paragraph boundaries with and without semantic information. In W. Dressler and R. Pfeiffer (Eds), *Phonologica, 1976.* Innsbruck: Institut fur Sprachwissenschaft der Universität Innsbruck.

Lehmann, W. P. (1973). *Historical linguistics.* (2nd ed). New York: Holt.

Leopold, W. (1939–1949). *Speech development of a bilingual child. Vols 1* (1939), *2* (1947), *3* (1949), and *4* (1949). Northwestern Universities Studies in the Humanities.

Levin, H. and Addis, A. B. (1979). *The eye-voice span.* Cambridge, Mass.: MIT Press.

Levine, D. N., Calvanio, R. and Popovics, A. (1982). Language in the absence of inner speech. *Neuropsychologia, 20*, 391–409.

Levy, B. A. (1981). Interactive processing during reading. In A. M. Lesgold and C. A. Perfetti (Eds), *Interactive processes in reading.* Hillsdale, NJ.: Lawrence Erlbaum Associates.

Libby, W. L. (1970). Eye contact and direction of looking as stable individual differences. *Journal of Experimental Research in Personality, 4*, 303–312.

Liberman, A. M. (1982). On finding that speech is special. *American Psychologist, 37*, 301–323.

Liberman, I. Y., Shankweiler, D., Fischer, F. W. and Carter, B. (1974). Explicit syllable and phoneme segmentation in the young child. *Journal of Experimental Child Psychology*, *18*, 201–212.

Lichteim, L. (1885). On aphasia. *Brain*, *7*, 433–484.

Lieberman, P. (1963). Some effects of semantic and grammatical context on the production and perception of speech. *Language and Speech*, *6*, 172–187.

Lieberman, P. (1965). On the acoustic basis of the perception of intonation by linguists. *Word*, *21*, 40–54.

Lieberman, P. (1979). Hominid evolution, supralaryngeal vocal tract physiology and the fossil evidence for reconstructions. *Brain and Language*, *7*, 101–126.

Lieberman, P. (1981). On the evolution of human speech. In T. Myers, J. Laver and J. Anderson (Eds), *The cognitive representation of speech*. Amsterdam: North-Holland.

Lieven, E. V. M. (1978). Conversations between mothers and young children: individual differences and their possible implication for the study of language learning. In N. Waterson and C. E. Snow (Eds), *The development of communication*. Chichester: John Wiley.

Lisker, L. (1978). Rapid vs. rabid: a catalogue of acoustic features that may cue the distinction. *Haskins Laboratories Status Report on Speech Research*, 1978, *SR–54*, 127–132.

Lock, A. (1978). (Ed.), *Action, gesture and symbol: the emergence of language*. London: Academic Press.

Lock, A. (1980). *The guided reinvention of language*. London: Academic Press.

Lord, A. B. (1960). *The singer of tales*. Harvard: Harvard University Press.

Love, K. D. and Aiello, J. R. (1980). Using projective techniques to measure interaction distance: a methodological note. *Personality and Social Psychology Bulletin*, *6*, 102–104.

Luria, A. R., Tsvetkova, L. S. and Futer, D. S. (1965). Aphasia in a composer. *Journal of Neurological Science*, *2*, 288–292.

Lyons, D. (1972). Human language. In R. A. Hine (Ed.), *Nonverbal communication*. Cambridge: Cambridge University Press.

McNeill, D. (1970). *The acquisition of language: the study of developmental psycholinguistics*. New York: Harper and Row.

Machotka, P. (1965). Body movement as communication. In *Dialogue: behaviour science research*. Boulder, Colorado: Western Interstate Commission for Higher Education.

Macken, M. A. and Barton, D. (1980). The acquisition of the voicing contrast in English: the study of voice onset time in word-initial stop consonants. *Journal of Child Language*, *7*, 41–74.

Macnamara, J. (1972). Cognitive basis of language learning in infants. *Psychological Review*, *79*, 1–13.

Mahl, G. F., Danet, B. and Norton, N. (1959). Reflection of major personality characteristics in gestures and body movement. Paper presented to the Annual Meeting of the American Psychological Association. Cincinatti, September, 1959.

Malinowski, B. (1923). The problem of meaning in primitive languages. In C. K. Ogden and I. A. Richards, *The meaning of meaning*. London: Routledge and Kegan Paul.

Manes, J. and Wolfson, N. (1981). The compliment formula. In F. Coulmas (Ed.). *Conversational routine: explorations in standardized communication situations and prepatterned speech*. The Hague: Mouton.

Marcel, A. J. (1983a). Conscious and unconscious perception: experiments on visual masking and word recognition. *Cognitive Psychology*, *15*, 197–237.

Marcel, A. J. (1983b). Conscious and unconscious perception: an approach to the relations between phenomenal experience and perceptual processes. *Cognitive Psychology*, *15*, 238–300.

Margolin, D. I. (1984). The neuropsychology of writing and spelling: semantic, phonological, motor and perceptual processes. *Quarterly Journal of Experimental Psychology*, *36A*, 459–489.

Margolin, D. I. and Binder, L. (1984). Multiple component agraphia in a patient with atypical cerebral dominance: an error analysis. *Brain and Language*, *22*, 26–40.

Marler, P. and Tenaza, R. (1977). Signalling behaviour of apes with special reference to vocalization. In T. A. Sebeok (Ed.), *How animals communicate*. Bloomington: Indiana University Press.

Marr, D. (1982). *Vision*. San Francisco: W. H. Freeman.

Marr, D. (1976). Early processing of visual information. *Philosophical Transactions of the Royal Society of London*, *B275*, 483–524.

Marsh, G., Friedman, M., Welch, V. and Desberg, P. (1981). A cognitive-developmental theory of reading acquisition. In G. E. Mackinnon and T. G. Waller (Eds), *Reading research: advances in theory and practice, Vol. 2*. New York: Academic Press.

Marshall, J. C. (1980). Clues from neurological deficits. In U. Bellugi and M. Studdert-Kennedy (Eds), *Signed and spoken language: biological constraints on linguistic form*. Weinheim: Verlag Chemie GmbH.

Marshall, J. C. (1982). Models of the mind in health and disease. In A. W. Ellis (Ed.), *Normality and pathology in cognitive functions*. London: Academic Press.

Marshall, J. C. and Newcombe, F. (1973). Patterns of paralexia: a psycholinguistic approach. *Journal of Psycholinguistic Research*, *2*, 175–199.

Marslen-Wilson, W. D. (1973). Linguistic structure and speech shadowing at very short latencies. *Nature*, *244*, 522–523.

Marslen-Wilson, W. D. (1975). Sentence perception as an interactive parallel process. *Science*, *189*, 226–268.

Marslen-Wilson, W. D. (1976). Linguistic descriptions and psychological assumptions in the study of sentence perception. In R. J. Wales and E. C. T. Walker (Eds), *New approaches to language mechanisms*. Dortrecht: D. Reidel.

Marslen-Wilson, W. D. (1980). Speech understanding as a psychological process. In J. C. Simon (Ed.), *Spoken language generation and understanding*. Dortrecht: D. Reidel.

Marslen-Wilson, W. D. and Tyler, L. K. (1975). Processing structure of sentence perception. *Nature, 257*, 784–786.

Marslen-Wilson, W. D. and Tyler, L. K. (1980). The temporal structure of spoken language understanding. *Cognition, 8*, 1–71.

Marslen-Wilson, W. D. and Welsh, A. (1978). Processing interactions and lexical access during word recognition in continuous speech. *Cognitive Psychology, 10*, 29–63.

Martin, J. G. (1967). Hesitations in the speaker's production and listener's reproduction of utterances. *Journal of Verbal Learning and Verbal Behaviour, 6*, 903–909.

Martin, J. G. (1970). Some acoustic and grammatical features of spontaneous speech. In D. L. Horton and J. J. Jenkins (Eds), *The perception of language*. Columbus, Ohio: Merrill.

Martin, J. G. (1972). Rhythmic (hierarchical) versus serial structure in speech and other behaviour. *Psychological Review, 79*, 487–509.

Martlew, M. (1983). (Ed.), *The psychology of written language: developmental and educational perspectives*. Chichester: John Wiley.

McClelland, J. L. and Rumelhart, D. E. (1981). An interactive activation model of context effects in letter perception: Part 1. An account of basic findings. *Psychological Review, 88*, 375–407.

McDowall, J. J. (1978). Interactional synchrony: a reappraisal. *Journal of Personality and Social Psychology, 36*, 963–975.

McGurk, H. and MacDonald, J. (1976). Hearing lips and seeing voices. *Nature, 264*, 746–748.

McMillan, J. R., Clifton, A. K., McGrath, D. and Gale, W. S. (1977). Women's language: uncertainty or interpersonal sensitivity and emotionality. *Sex Roles, 3*, 545–555.

McNeill, D. (1970). *The acquisition of language: the study of developmental psycholinguistics*. New York: Harper and Row.

McNeill, D. (1975). Semiotic extension. In R. L. Solso (Ed.), *Information processing and cognition: the Loyola symposium*. Hillsdale, N.J.: Lawrence Erlbaum.

Mead, G. H. (1934). *Mind, self and society*. Chicago: Chicago University Press.

Mead, M. (1928). *Coming of age in Samoa*. New York: Morrow.

Mehler, J. (1963). Some effects of grammatical transformations on the recall of English sentences. *Journal of Verbal Learning and Verbal Behaviour, 2*, 346–351.

Mehler, J. and Bertoncini, J. (1979). Infants' perception of speech and other acoustic stimuli. In J. Morton and J. Marshall (Eds), *Psycholinguistics series, Vol. 2*. London: Elek and Cambridge, Mass.: MIT Press.

Mehler, J., Morton, J. and Jusczyk, P. W. (1984). On reducing language to biology. *Cognitive Neuropsychology*, *1*, 83–116.

Mehrabian, A. (1968). Relationship of attitude to seated posture, orientation and distance. *Journal of Personality and Social Psychology*, *10*, 26–30.

Mehrabian, A. (1969). Significance of posture and position in the communication of attitude and status relationships. *Psychological Bulletin*, *71*, 359–372.

Mehrabian, A. (1972). *Nonverbal communication*. Chicago: Aldine.

Melhuish, E. C. (1982). Visual attention to mothers' and strangers' faces and facial contrast in 1-month-old infants. *Developmental Psychology*, *18*, 229–231.

Meltzoff, A. N. and Moore, M. K. (1977). Imitation of facial and manual gestures by human neonates. *Science*, *198*, 75–78.

Meltzoff, A. N. and Moore, M. K. (1983a). Newborn infants imitate adult facial gestures. *Child Development*, *54*, 702–709.

Meltzoff, A. N. and Moore, M. K. (1983b). The origins of imitation in infancy: paradigm, phenomena and theories. In L. P. Lipsitt and C. K. Rovee-Collier (Eds), *Advances in infancy research, Vol 2*. New Jersey: Ablex.

Menyuk, P. (1977). *Language and maturation*. Cambridge, Mass.: MIT Press.

Meringer, R. (1908). *Aus dem Leben der Sprache*. Berlin: B. Behr.

Meringer, R. and Mayer, C. (1895). *Versprechen und Verlesen: eine psychologisch-linguistische Studie*. Stuttgart: G. J. Goschen. (Reprinted with an introduction by A. Cutler and D. Fay, Amsterdam: J. Benjamins, 1978).

Meyer, D. E. and Schvaneveldt, R. W. (1971). Facilitation in recognizing pairs of words: evidence of a dependence between retrieval operations. *Journal of Experimental Psychology*, *90*, 227–234.

Miceli, G., Mazzucchi, A., Menn, L. and Goodglass, H. (1983). Contrasting cases of Italian agrammatic aphasia without comprehension disorder. *Brain and Language*, *19*, 65–97.

Michel, F. and Andreewsky, E. (1983). Deep dysphasia: an analogue of deep dyslexia in the auditory modality. *Brain and Language*, *18*, 212–223.

Miller, D. and Ellis, A. W. (1985). Speech and writing errors in 'neologistic jargonaphasia': a lexical activation hypothesis. In M. Coltheart, R. Job and G. Sartori (Eds), *The cognitive neuropsychology of language*. London: Lawrence Erlbaum.

Miller, G. A. (1956). The magic number seven, plus or minus two: some limits on our capacity for processing information. *Psychological Review*,

63, 81–93.

Miller, G. A. (1981). *Language and speech.* San Francisco: W. H. Freeman.

Miller, G. A., Heise, G. A. and Lichten, W. (1951). The intelligibility of speech as a function of the context of the test materials. *Journal of Experimental Psychology, 41*, 329–335.

Miller, G. A. and McKean, K. (1964). A chronometric study of some relations between sentences. *Quarterly Journal of Experimental Psychology, 16*, 297–308.

Miller, J. L. and Eimas, P. D. (1983). Studies on the categorization of speech by infants. *Cognition, 13*, 135–165.

Mishler, E. G. (1975). Studies in dialogue and discourse II: types of discourse initiated by, and sustained through, questioning. *Journal of Psycholinguistic Research, 4*, 99–121.

Mitchell, D. C. (1982). *The process of reading.* Chichester: John Wiley.

Mitchell, D. C. and Green, D. W. (1978). The effects of context and content on immediate processing in reading. *Quarterly Journal of Experimental Psychology, 30*, 609–636.

Modigliani, A. (1971). Embarrassment, facework and eye-contact: testing a theory of embarrassment. *Journal of Personality and Social Psychology, 17*, 15–24.

Monsell, S. (1984). Components of working memory underlying verbal skills: a 'distributed capacities' view. In H. Bouma and D. G. Bouwhuis (Eds), *Attention and performance, X.* London: Lawrence Erlbaum.

Montgomery, G. (1976). Changing attitudes to communication. Supplement to *The British Deaf News*, June 1976.

Moore, H. T. (1922). Further data concerning sex differences. *Journal of Abnormal and Social Psychology, 4*, 81–89.

Morais, J., Cary, L., Alegria, J. and Bertelson, P. (1967). Does awareness of speech as a sequence of phones arise spontaneously? *Cognition, 7*, 323–331.

Morris, D. (1967). *The naked ape.* London: Jonathan Cape.

Morris, D. (1977). *Manwatching.* London: Jonathan Cape.

Morris, D., Collett, P., Marsh, P. and O'Shaughnessy, M. (1979). *Gestures: their origins and distribution.* London: Jonathan Cape.

Morsbach, H. (1973). Nonverbal communication in Japan. Unpublished paper, Department of Psychology, University of Glasgow.

Morse, P. A. (1979). The infancy of speech perceptions: the first decade of research. *Brain, Behaviour and Evolution, 16*, 351–373.

Morse, P. A. and Snowdon, C. T. (1975). An investigation of categorical speech discrimination by rhesus monkeys. *Perception and Psychophysics, 17*, 9–16.

Morton, J. (1964). The effect of context on the visual duration threshold for words. *British Journal of Psychology, 55*, 165–180.

Morton, J. (1979). Word recognition. In J. Morton and J. C. Marshall

(Eds), *Psycholinguistics series, Vol 2*. London: Elek Science and Cambridge, Mass.: MIT Press.

Morton, J. (1980). The logogen model and orthographic structure. In U. Frith (Ed.), *Cognitive processes in spelling*. London: Academic Press.

Motley, M. T. (1980). Verification of 'Freudian slips' and semantic prearticulatory editing via laboratory-induced spoonerisms. In V. A. Fromkin (Ed.), *Errors in linguistic performance: slips of the tongue, ear, pen and hand*. New York: Academic Press.

Motley, M. T., Camden, C. T. and Baars, B. J. (1983). Polysemantic lexical access: evidence from laboratory-induced double entendres. *Communication Monographs*, *50*, 193–305.

Moulton, J. and Robinson, G. (1981). *The organization of language*. Cambridge: Cambridge University Press.

Mowrer, O. H. (1950). *Learning theory and personality dynamics*. New York: Ronald.

Mowrer, O. H. (1954). The psychologist looks at language. *American Psychologist*, *9*, 660–694.

Murchison, C. and Langer, S. (1927). Tiedemann's observations on the development of the mental faculties of children. *Pedagogical Seminary*, *34*, 205–230.

Natale, M., Entin, E. and Jaffé, J. (1979). Vocal interruptions in dyadic communication as a function of speech and social anxiety. *Journal of Personality and Social Psychology*, *37*, 865–878.

Nelson, K. (1973). Structure and strategy in learning to talk. *Monographs of the Society for Research in Child Development*, *38*, (1–2, serial no. 149).

Nelson, K., Rescorla, L., Gruendel, J. and Benedict, H. (1977). Early lexicons: what do they mean? Paper presented at the Biennial Meeting of the Society for Research in Child Development, New Orleans, March 1977.

Newport, E. L. (1977). Motherese: the speech of mothers to young children. In N. Castellan, D. Pisoni and G. Potts (Eds), *Cognitive theory, Vol. 2*. Hillsdale, N. J.: Lawrence Erlbaum Associates.

Newport, E. L., Gleitman, H. and Gleitman, L. R. (1977). Mother, I'd rather do it myself: some effects and non-effects of maternal speech style. In C. E. Snow and C. A. Ferguson (Eds), *Talking to children*. Cambridge: Cambridge University Press.

Nielsen, G. (1962). *Studies in self confrontation*. Copenhagen: Monksgaard.

Ninio, A. (1980). Ostensive definition in vocabulary teaching. *Journal of Child Language*, *7*, 565–573.

Ninio, A. and Bruner, J. S. (1978). The achievement and antecedents of labelling. *Journal of Child Language*, *5*, 1–15.

Nystrand, M. (1982). (Ed.), *What writers know: the language, process and structure of written discourse*. New York: Academic Press.

O'Connor, R. E. and Forster, K. I. (1981). Criterion bias and search sequence in word recognition. *Memory and Cognition*, *9*, 78–92.

Ogle, W. (1867). Aphasia and agraphia. *St George's Hospital Reports*, *2*, 83–122.

Oller, D. K. (1973). The effect of position in utterance on speech segment duration in English. *Journal of the Acoustical Society of America*, *54*, 1235–1247.

O'Neil, W. M. (1953). The effect of verbal association on tachistoscopic recognition. *Australian Journal of Psychology*, *5*, 42–45.

Orwell, G. (1933). *Down and out in Paris and London*. Harmondsworth: Penguin (reprinted 1982).

Osthoff, H. and Brugman, K. (1878). *Morphologische Untersuchungen . . ., 1*. Leipzig: S. Hirzel.

Pascal, B. (1670). *Pensées*. Paris: Librairie Larousse.

Patterson, K. E. (1982). The relation between reading and phonological coding: further neuropsychological observations. In A. W. Ellis (Ed.), *Normality and pathology in cognitive functions*. London: Academic Press.

Patterson, K. E., Coltheart, M. and Marshall, J. C. (1985). *Surface dyslexia*. London: Lawrence Erlbaum.

Patterson, M. L. (1975). Personal space – time to burst the bubble. *Man-Environment Systems*, *5*, 67.

Paul, H. (1880). *Prinzipien der Sprachgeschichte*. (8th ed.) Tubingen: Max Niemeyer, 1968.

Pellegrino, J. W., Siegel, A. W. and Dhawan, M. (1975). Short-term retention of pictures and words: evidence for dual coding systems. *Journal of Experimental Psychology: Human Learning and Memory*, *104*, 95–101.

Pepperberg, I. M. (1981). Functional vocalizations by an African Grey parrot (*Psittacus erithacus*). *Zeitschrift fur Tierpsychologie*, *55*, 139–160.

Pepperberg, I. M. (1983). Cognition in the African Grey parrot: preliminary evidence for auditory/vocal comprehension of the class concept. *Animal Learning and Behaviour*, *11*, 179–185.

Perfetti, C. A., Goldman, S. R. and Hogaboam, T. W. (1979). Reading skill and the identification of words in discourse context. *Memory and Cognition*, *4*, 273–282.

Perin, D. (1983). Phonemic segmentation and spelling. *British Journal of Psychology*, *74*, 129–144.

Pick, A. (1931). *Aphasia* (English translation by J. W. Brown). Springfield, Ill.: C. C. Thomas, 1973.

Pillsbury, W. B. (1897). A study in apperception. *American Journal of Psychology*, *8*, 315–393.

Pillsbury, W. B. and Meader, C. L. (1928). *The psychology of language*. New York: D. Appleton.

Pollack, I. and Pickett, J. M. (1946). The intelligibility of excerpts from fluent speech: auditory versus structural context. *Language and Speech*, 6, 151–165.

Popper, K. (1972). *Unended quest: an intellectual autobiography*. Glasgow: Collins.

Postman, L. and Bruner, J. S. (1949). Multiplicity of set as a determinant of perceptual behaviour. *Journal of Experimental Psychology*, 39, 369–377.

Power, M. J. (1983). Are there cognitive rhythms in speech? *Language and Speech*, 26, 253–261.

Power, M. J. (1984). 'Are there cognitive rhythms in speech?' – a reply to Beattie (1984). *Language and Speech*, 27, 197–200.

Preyer, W. (1882). *Die Seele des Kindes*. Leipzig. (English translation in H. W. Brown, *The mind of the child*, 2 vols. New York: Appleton, 1888–90).

Priebsch, R. and Collinson, W. E. (1934). *The German language* (revised 5th ed.). New York: Barnes and Noble, 1962.

Quain, B. (1948). *Fijian village*. Chicago: University of Chicago Press.

Read, C. (1971). Pre-school children's knowledge of English phonology. *Harvard Educational Review*, 41, 1–34.

Read, C. (1975). Lessons to be learned from the pre-school orthographer. In E. H. Lenneberg and E. Lenneberg (Eds). *Foundations of language development, Vol 2*. New York: Academic Press.

Rees, M. and Urquhart, S. (1976). Intonation as a guide to the reader's structuring of prose text. University of Edinburgh, Department of Linguistics, *Work in Progress No. 9*, 19–26.

Reich, S. S. (1980). Significance of pauses for speech perception. *Journal of Psycholinguistic Research*, 9, 379–389.

Reid, J. F. (1966). Learning to think about reading. *Educational Research*, 9, 56–62.

Rid, S. (1612). *The art of juggling*. Cited in T. A. Sebeok (1979), op. cit.

Rinn, W. E. (1984). The neuropsychology of facial expression: a review of the neurological and psychological mechanisms for producing facial expressions. *Psychological Bulletin*, 95, 52–77.

Roe, K. V. (1978). Mother-stranger discrimination in three-month-old infants and subsequent Gesell performance. *Journal of Genetic Psychology*, 133, 111–118.

Roger, D. B. and Schumacher, A. (1983). Effects of individual differences in dyadic conversational strategies. *Journal of Personality and Social Psychology*, 45, 700–705.

Rolfe, J. M. (1972). Ergonomics and air safety. *Applied Ergonomics*, 3, 75–81.

Rosch, E. (1975). Cognitive representations of semantic categories. *Journal of Experimental Psychology: General*, 104, 192–233.

Rosch, E. (1977). Human categorization. In N. Warren (Ed.), *Advances in cross-cultural psychology, vol 1*. London: Academic Press.

Rosenfeld, L. B., Kartus, S. and Ray, S. (1976). Body accessibility revisited. *Journal of Communication*, *26*, 27–30.

Ross, E. D. and Mesulam, M-M. (1979). Dominant language functions of the right hemisphere? Prosody and emotional gesturing. *Archives of Neurology*, *36*, 144–148.

Rubin, A. (1970). Measurement of romantic love. *Journal of Personality and Social Psychology*, *16*, 265–273.

Rumelhart, D. E. and McClelland, J. L. (1981). Interactive processing through spreading activation. In A. M. Lesgold and C. A. Perfetti (Eds), *Interactive processes in reading*. Hillsdale, N.J.: Lawrence Erlbaum Associates.

Russell, W. A. and Storms, L. H. (1955). Implicit verbal chaining in paired-associate learning. *Journal of Experimental Psychology*, *49*, 287–293.

Rutter, D. R. and Stephenson, G. M. (1977). The role of visual communication in synchronising conversation. *European Journal of Social Psychology*, *7*, 29–37.

Rutter, D. R., Stephenson, G. M., Ayling, K. and White, P. A. (1978). The timing of looks in dyadic conversation. *British Journal of Social and Clinical Psychology*, *17*, 17–21.

Sachs, J. S. (1967). Recognition memory for syntactic and semantic aspects of connected discourse. *Perception and Psychophysics*, *2*, 437–442.

Sachs, J. S. (1974). Memory in reading and listening to discourse. *Memory and Cognition*, *2*, 95–100.

Sacks, H., Schegloff, E. A. and Jefferson, G. A. (1974). A simplest systematics for the organization of turn-taking for conversation. *Language*, *50*, 697–735.

Saffran, E. M. (1982). Neuropsychological approaches to the study of language. *British Journal of Psychology*, *73*, 317–337.

Saffran, E. M., Schwartz, M. F. and Marin, O. S. M. (1980a). Evidence from aphasia: isolating the components of a production model. In B. Butterworth (Ed.), *Language production, Vol 1*. London: Academic Press.

Saffran, E. M., Schwartz, M. F. and Marin, O. S. M. (1980b). The word order problem in agrammatism. II. Production. *Brain and Language*, *10*, 263–280.

Saffran, E. M., Marin, O. S. M. and Yeni-Komshian, G. (1976). An analysis of speech perception in word deafness. *Brain and Language*, *3*, 209–228.

Sampson, G. (1980). *Schools of linguistics: competition and evolution*. London: Hutchinson.

Sapir, E. (1929). The status of linguistics as a science. *Language*, *5*, 207–214.

Sapir, E. (1970). *Culture, language and personality: selected essays* (Ed. D. G. Mandelbaum). Berkeley: University of California Press.

Saussure, F. de (1915). *Cours de linguistique générale*. Paris: Payot

(English translation by W. Baskin, *Course in general linguistics*. Glasgow: Fontana, 1974).

Savin, H. and Perchonock, E. (1965). Grammatical structure and the immediate recall of English sentences. *Journal of Verbal Learning and Verbal Behaviour*, *4*, 348–358.

Schaffer, H. R. (1971). *The growth of sociability*. Harmondsworth: Penguin.

Scheflen, A. E. (1964). The significance of posture in communication systems. *Psychiatry*, *27*, 316–331.

Scheflen, A. E. (1965). Quasi-courtship behaviour in psychotherapy. *Psychiatry*, *28*, 245–257.

Schegloff, E. A. and Sacks, H. (1973). Opening up closings. *Semiotica*, *8*, 289–327.

Scherwitz, L. and Helmreich, R. (1973). Interactive effects of eye contact and verbal content on interpersonal attraction in dyads. *Journal of Personality and Social Psychology*, *26*, 6–14.

Schlauch, M. (1936). Recent studies in linguistics. *Science in Society*, *1*, 157.

Schlesinger, I. M. (1974). Relational concepts underlying language. In R. L. Schiefelbusch and L. Lloyd (Eds), *Language perspectives: acquisition, retardation and intervention*. Baltimore: University Park Press.

Schwartz, M. F., Saffran, E. M. and Marin, O. S. M. (1980a). Fractionating the reading process in dementia: Evidence for word-specific print-to-sound associations. In M. Coltheart, K. E. Patterson and J. C. Marshall (Eds), *Deep dyslexia*. London: Routledge and Kegan Paul.

Schwartz, M. F., Saffran, E. M. and Marin, O. S. M. (1980b). The word order problem in agrammatism. I. Comprehension. *Brain and Language*, *10*, 249–262.

Scott, D. R. and Cutler, A. (1984). Segmental phonology and the perception of syntactic structure. *Journal of Verbal Learning and Verbal Behaviour*, *23*, 450–466.

Sebeok, T. A. (1977). *How animals communicate*. Bloomington: Indiana University Press.

Sebeok, T. A. (1979). Looking in the destination for what should have been sought in the source. In T. A. Sebeok, *The sign and its masters*. Austin: University of Texas Press.

Sebeok, T. A. and Umiker-Sebeok, J. (1980) (Eds), *Speaking of apes: a critical anthology of two-way communication with man*. New York: Plenum Press.

Seidenberg, M. S. and Petito, L. A. (1979). Signing behaviour in apes: a critical review. *Cognition*, *7*, 177–215.

Seyfarth, R., Cheney, D. L. and Marler, P. (1980). Monkey responses to three different alarm calls: evidence of predator classification and semantic communication. *Science*, *210*, 801–803.

Seymour, P. H. K. (1979). *Human visual cognition*. West Drayton: Collier

Macmillan.

Seymour, P. H. K. and MacGregor, J. (1984). Developmental dyslexia: a cognitive experimental analysis of phonological, morphemic and visual impairments. *Cognitive Neuropsychology*, *1*, 43–82.

Shallice, T. (1981). Phonological agraphia and the lexical route in writing. *Brain*, *104*, 413–429.

Shallice, T. and Warrington, E. K. (1974). The dissociation between short-term retention of meaningful sounds and verbal material. *Neuropsychologia*, *12*, 553–555.

Shatz, M. and Gelman, R. (1973). The development of communication skills: modifications in the speech of young children as a function of listener. *Monographs of the Society for Research in Child Development*, *38* (Serial No. 152).

Shaughnessy, M. P. (1977). *Errors and expectations: a guide for the teacher of basic writing*. New York: Oxford University Press.

Sherrod, L. R. (1979). Social cognition in infants: attention to the human face. *Infant Behavior and Development*, *2*, 279–294.

Sherzer, J. (1982). Play languages: with a note on ritual languages. In L. K. Obler and L. Menn (Eds), *Exceptional language and linguistics*. New York: Academic Press.

Shuter, R. (1976). Proxemics and tactility in Latin America. *Journal of Communication*, *26*, 46–52.

Siipola, E. M. (1935). A group study of some effects of preparatory set. *Psychological Monographs*, *46*, No. 6, 27–38.

Simonini, R. C. (1956). Phonemic and analogic lapses in radio and television speech. *American Speech*, *31*, 252–263.

Skinner, B. F. (1957). *Verbal behaviour*. New York: Appleton-Century-Crofts.

Slobin, D. I. (1966). Grammatical transformations and sentence comprehension in childhood and adulthood. *Journal of Verbal Learning and Verbal Behaviour*, *5*, 219–227.

Slobin, D. I. (1979). *Psycholinguistics* (2nd ed.). Glenview, Ill.: Scott, Foresman & Co.

Slugoski, B. R. (1984). A pragmatics approach to conversational turn-taking. Paper presented to the Conference on Interdisciplinary Approaches to Interpersonal Communication. University of York, April 1984.

Smith, A. (1966). Speech and other functions after left (dominant) hemispherectomy. *Journal of Neurology, Neurosurgery and Psychiatry*, *29*, 467–471.

Smith, E. E. and Collins, A. M. (1981). Use of goal-plan knowledge in understanding stories. *Proceedings of the Third Annual Conference of the Cognitive Science Society*. Berkeley, CA, 115–116.

Smith, F. (1978). *Understanding reading: a psycholinguistic analysis of reading and learning to read* (2nd ed.). New York: Holt, Rinehart and

Winston.

Smith, N. V. (1973). *The acquisition of phonology: a case study.* Cambridge: Cambridge University Press.

Smith, N. V. (1979). Syntax for psychologists. In J. Morton and J. C. Marshall (Eds), *Psycholinguistics Series, Vol 2.* London: Elek.

Smith, N. V. and Wilson, D. (1979). *Modern linguistics.* Harmondsworth: Penguin.

Snow, C. E. and Ferguson, C. A. (1977) (Eds), *Talking to children: language input and acquisition.* Cambridge: Cambridge University Press.

Spender, D. (1982a). *Man made language.* London: Routledge and Kegan Paul.

Spender, D. (1982b). Don't keep your trap shut. *The Guardian,* Monday 23 August.

Sperber, R. D., McCauley, C., Ragain, R. and Weil, C. M. (1979). Semantic priming effects on picture and word processing. *Memory and Cognition, 7,* 339–345.

Stanovich, K. E. (1980). Toward an interactive-compensatory model of individual differences in the development of reading fluency. *Reading Research Quarterly, 16,* 32–71.

Stanovich, K. E. (1981a). Attentional and automatic context effects in reading. In A. M. Lesgold and C. Perfetti (Eds), *Interactive processes in reading.* Hillsdale, N.J.: Lawrence Erlbaum.

Stanovich, K. E. (1981b). Word recognition skill and reading ability. In M. H. Singer, (Ed.), *Competent reader, disabled reader: research and application.* Hillsdale, N.J.: Lawrence Erlbaum.

Stanovich, K. E. and West, R. F. (1983). On priming by a sentence context. *Journal of Experimental Psychology: General, 112,* 1-36.

Stanovich, K. E., West, R. F. and Freeman, D. J. (1981). A longitudinal study of sentence context effects in second-grade children: tests of an interactive-compensatory model. *Journal of Experimental Child Psychology, 32,* 185–199.

Stark, R. E. (1979). Pre-speech segmental feature development. In P. Fletcher and M. Garman (Eds), *Language acquisition.* Cambridge: Cambridge University Press.

Stemberger, J. P. (1985). An interactive activation model of language production. In A. W. Ellis (Ed.), *Progress in the psychology of language, Vol 1.* London: Lawrence Erlbaum.

Stephens, J. (1983). The regulation of speaker turns in natural telephone and face-to-face conversation. Unpublished dissertation, University of Sheffield.

Stratton, G. M. (1921). The control of another person by obscure signs. *Psychological Review, 28,* 301–314.

Stubbs, M. (1980). *Language and literacy: the sociolinguistics of reading and writing.* London: Routledge and Kegan Paul.

Sulin, R. A. and Dooling, D. J. (1974). Intrusion of a thematic idea in retention of prose. *Journal of Experimental Psychology*, 103, 255–262.

Sumby, W. H. and Pollack, I. (1954). Visual contribution to speech intelligibility in noise. *Journal of the Acoustical Society of America*, 26, 212–215.

Sutcliffe, D. (1982). *British Black English*. Oxford: Blackwell.

Swinney, D. (1979). Lexical access during sentence comprehension: (re)consideration of context effects. *Journal of Verbal Learning and Verbal Behaviour*, 18, 645–659.

Swinney, D. A., Onifer, W., Prather, P. and Hirshkowitz, M. (1979). Semantic facilitation across sensory modalities in the processing of individual words and sentences. *Memory and Cognition*, 7, 159–165.

Tallal, P. and Piercy, M. (1975). Developmental aphasia: the perception of brief vowels and extended stop consonants. *Neuropsychologia*, 13, 69–74.

Terrace, H. S. (1979). *Nim*. New York: Knopf.

Tiedemann, D. (1787). *Beobachtungen uber die Entwicklung der Seelenfahigkeiten bei Kindern*. Altenburg. (For English translation see Murchison and Langer, 1927).

Tinbergen, N. (1951). *The study of instinct*. London: Oxford University Press.

Trager, G. L. and Smith, H. L. (1957). *An outline of English structure*. Washington, D.C.: American Council of Learned Societies.

Trower, P., Bryant, B. and Argyle, M. (1978). *Social skills and mental health*. London: Methuen.

Trudgill, P. (1974). *The social differentiation of English in Norwich*. Cambridge: Cambridge University Press.

Trudgill, P. (1975). *Accent, dialect and the school*. London: Edward Arnold.

Tucker, D. M., Watson, R. T. and Heilman, K. M. (1977). Discrimination and evocation of affectively intoned speech in patients with right parietal disease. *Neurology*, 27, 947–950.

Tulving, E. and Gold, C. (1963). Stimulus information and contextual information as determinants of tachistoscopic recognition of words. *Journal of Experimental Psychology*, 66, 319–327.

Tyack, P. (1981). Why do whales sing? *The Sciences*, 21, 22–25.

Underwood, G. (1976). Semantic interference from unattended printed words. *British Journal of Psychology*, 67, 327–338.

Underwood, G. (1981). Lexical recognition of embedded unattended words: some implications for reading processes. *Acta Psychologica*, 47, 267–283.

van Lancker, D. (1975). Heterogeneity in language and speech: neurolinguistic studies. *UCLA Working Papers in Phonetics No. 29*.

van Lancker, D. and Canter, G. J. (1981). Idiomatic versus literal interpretations of ditropically ambiguous sentences. *Journal of Speech and Hearing Research*, *24*, 64–69.

van Lawick-Goodall, J. (1971). *In the shadow of man*. London: Collins.

Von Frisch, K. (1967). *The dance and orientation of bees*. (trans. L. E. Chadwick). Cambridge, Mass.: Harvard University Press.

Von Raffler Engel, W. (1975). The correlation of gesture and verbalisation in first language acquisition. In A. Kendon, R. M. Harris and M. Ritchie Key (Eds), *Organization of behaviour in face to face interaction*. The Hague: Mouton.

Vuchinich, S. (1977). Elements of cohesion between turns in ordinary conversation. *Semiotica*, *20*, 229–257.

Vygotsky, L. S. (1965). *Thought and language*. Cambridge, Mass.: MIT Press.

Wales, R. J. and Toner, H. (1979). Intonation and ambiguity. In W. E. Cooper and E. C. T. Walker (Eds), *Sentence processing: psycholinguistic studies presented to Merrill Garrett*. Hillsdale, N.J.: Lawrence Erlbaum.

Wanner, E. (1974). *On remembering, forgetting, and understanding sentences*. The Hague: Mouton.

Warden, C. J. and Warner, L. H. (1928). The sensory capacities and intelligence of dogs, with a report on the ability of the noted dog 'Fellow' to respond to verbal stimuli. *Quarterly Review of Biology*, *3*, 1–28.

Warren, R. M. (1970). Perceptual restoration of missing speech sounds. *Science*, *167*, 392–393.

Wason, P. C. (1965). The contexts of plausible denial. *Journal of Verbal Learning and Verbal Behaviour*, *4*, 7–11.

Wason, P. C. (1980). Specific thoughts on the writing process. In L. W. Gregg and E. R. Steinberg (Eds), *Cognitive processes in writing*. Hillsdale, N.J.: Lawrence Erlbaum.

Waterson, N. (1983). A tentative developmental model of phonological representations. In T. Myers, J. Laver and J. Anderson (Eds), *The cognitive representation of speech*. Amerstam: North-Holland.

Watson, O. M. (1970). *Proxemic behaviour: a cross-cultural study*. The Hague: Mouton.

Watson, O. M. and Graves, T. D. (1966). Quantitative research in proxemic behaviour. *American Anthropologist*, *68*, 971–985.

Watson, W. H. (1975). The meaning of touch: geriatric nursing. *Journal of Communication*, *25*, 104–112.

Watzlawick, P., Beavin, J. and Jackson, D. (1968). *Pragmatics of human communication*. London: Faber.

Weber, R. M. (1968). The study of oral reading errors: a survey of the literature. *Reading Research Quarterly*, *4*, 96–119.

Weber, R. M. (1970). A linguistic analysis of first-grade reading errors. *Reading Research Quarterly*, *5*, 427–451.

Weimann, J. M. and Knapp, M. L. (1975). Turn-taking in conversation. *Journal of Communication*, *25*, 75–92.

Weinstein, E. A. (1981). Behavioural aspects of jargonaphasia. In J. W.

Brown (Ed.), *Jargonaphasia*. New York: Academic Press.

Weitz, S. (1974). *Nonverbal communication*. London: Oxford University Press.

Wells, F. L. (1906). Linguistic lapses. In J. McK. Cattell and F. J. E. Woodbridge (Eds), *Archives of Philosophy, Psychology and Scientific Methods, No. 6*. New York: Science Press.

Wernicke, C. (1874). *Der aphasische symptomencomplex*. Breslau: Cohn and Weigart. (Translated in G. H. Eggert, *Wernicke's works on aphasia*. The Hague: Mouton, 1977.)

West, C. and Zimmerman, D. H. (1977). Women's place in everyday talk: reflections on parent–child interaction. *Social Problems*, 24, 521–529.

Wexler, K. (1982). A principle theory for language acquisition. In E. Wanner. and L. R. Gleitman (Eds), *Language acquisition: the state of the art*. Cambridge: Cambridge University Press.

Wexler, K. and Cullicover, P. (1980). *Formal principles of language acquisition*. Cambridge, Mass.: MIT Press.

Whitney, D. (1870). On the present state of the question as to the origin of language. In *Oriental and linguistic studies*. New York: Scribner (1873).

Whorf, B. L. (1941). Languages and logic. In Whorf (1956), op. cit.

Whorf, B. L. (1956). *Language, thought and reality: selected writings* (Ed. J. B. Carroll). Cambridge, Mass.: MIT Press.

Williams, P. C. and Parkin, A. J. (1980). On knowing the meaning of words we are unable to report: confirmation of a guessing explanation. *Quarterly Journal of Experimental Psychology*, 32, 101–107.

Wilson, E. O. (1975). *Sociobiology*. Cambridge, Mass.: Harvard University Press.

Wingfield, A. and Klein, S. J. (1971). Syntactic structure and acoustic pattern in speech perception. *Perception and Psychophysics*, 9, 23–25.

Winner, E. and Gardner, H. (1977). The comprehension of metaphor in brain-damaged patients. *Brain*, 100, 717–729.

Winograd, T. (1972). *Understanding natural language*. New York: Academic Press.

Wode, H. (1977). Four early stages in the development of Ll negation. *Journal of Child Language*, 4, 87–102.

Wolfram, W. (1969). Linguistic correlates of social stratification in the speech of Detroit Negroes. Unpublished thesis, Hartford Seminary Foundation.

Wright, P. (1974). *The language of British industry*. London: Macmillan.

Wundt, W. (1900). *Die Sprache*. Leipzig: Engelmann.

Wundt, W. (1973). *The language of gestures*. The Hague: Mouton.

Yngve, V. H. (1970). On getting a word in edgewise. *Papers from the sixth regional meeting of the Chicago Linguistics Society*. Chicago: Chicago Linguistic Society.

Young. A. W. (in press). Subject characteristics in lateral differences for face processing by normals: age. In R. Bruyer (Ed.), *The neuro-*

psychology of face perception and facial expression. Hillsdale, N.J.: Lawrence Erlbaum.

Young, A. W., Gifted, B. X. and Black, C. Y. (1984). Lateral asymmetries in the bearded sandpiper, *R. S. P. B. Monthly*, *123*, 2–31.

Zangwill, O. L. (1939). Some relations between reproducing and recognizing prose material. *British Journal of Psychology*, *29*, 371–382.

Zimmermann, D. H. and West, C. (1975). Sex roles, interruptions and silences in conversation. In B. Thorne and N. Henley (Eds), *Language and sex: difference and dominance*. Rowley, Mass.: Newbury House.

Zuckerman, M., Larrance, D. T., Hall, J. A., De Frank, R. S. and Rosenthal, R. (1979). Posed and spontaneous communication of emotion via facial and vocal cues. *Journal of Personality*, *47*, 712–733.

Subject Index

Author Index